DA/2

Armand
Cleggar

21/-

Literature and Locality

By the same author

THE ENGLISHMAN AT WAR
(An Anthology edited with Introduction and Notes)

THOMAS FULLER'S *WORTHIES OF ENGLAND*
(Edited with Introduction and Notes)

LONDON FOR EVERYMAN
(Revised by J. F. after William Kent)

JOHN FREEMAN

Literature
and Locality

The Literary Topography of Britain and Ireland

 CASSELL · LONDON

CASSELL & COMPANY LTD

35 Red Lion Square . London WC1

and at

MELBOURNE · SYDNEY · TORONTO · CAPETOWN

JOHANNESBURG · AUCKLAND

———

Printed in Great Britain by
T. & A. Constable Ltd
Hopetoun Street, Edinburgh

F. 1262

To the Memory of

JEAN LOUISA MARY HOBBS
1927-1959

and

ADOLPH JOHN EDELSTEN
1900-1960

Preface

This book, which I believe is the first attempt at a comprehensive and systematic guide to the literary topography of the whole of Britain and Ireland needs, I hope, no apology, but does require some explanation. It has been planned so as to make it easy for the literary pilgrim, whether he be motorist, cyclist or hiker, to follow up the associations of writers that particularly interest him, or to search out the associations of a particular area. The broad basis of the work is a text linked with maps, plans and a full index. The roads are indicated both in the text and on the maps, but in order not to overload the text and overcrowd the maps, routes mentioned are confined mainly to localities where there are visible reminders of the past. Many places are mentioned where, unhappily, there are no such reminders, so as to complete the record, at any rate for the more important writers. Moreover, there are interesting associations that have been forgotten even locally. The place-names in the text are given references to the maps in the following form: 'Lichfield (IV, A3)', i.e., the map number followed by the grid reference.

The index is an integral part of the book. Under a writer's name are grouped all the localities with which he is associated. The arrangement of localities is not alphabetical, but follows the chronology of the

vii

writer's life, so that the reader who wishes to browse may follow a connected story. Under each locality entered in the index are given the writers connected with it. I have tried to say something about the topography of more important works, and these are entered in the index under their authors.

In a book designed as a handy guide to the associations of about three hundred and fifty writers, I have not been as expansive as I desired, and have obtruded my own opinions sparingly, aiming above all at helpfulness and comprehensiveness. I do not claim, however, that this book is a complete record, for that were an impossible realization within the limits of a modest volume; but I do claim, first, that never before have the topographical associations of so many English, Scottish, Welsh and Irish writers been brought together in a single volume, and secondly, that the plan of the work is systematic and makes for easy reference. I particularly regret that I could not devote more space to the numerous London associations, but some sacrifice was inevitable to keep the book to a reasonable length. But I hope that sufficient information has been provided to make the pursuit of literary associations both interesting and rewarding.

The hours when literary houses, libraries, museums with literary records and other institutions are open will be found in footnotes, and the first-mentioned group are repeated under writers (alphabetically arranged) in the Appendix. All other extant houses mentioned are in private hands (or in a few instances used as public offices) and privacy must be respected. Some information is given on a few living writers, but for obvious reasons their residences (except in one or two cases) are not mentioned.

My grateful thanks are due to my friend Carolyn Wells for kindly criticism and encouragement, and to many friends and kindly strangers who have answered my inquiries with courteous helpfulness and aided in other ways. My thanks are due, too, to the publishers for their encouragement and patient endurance for a book long overdue. None of these is responsible for my errors of fact and of omission, and over such the co-operation of readers is invited and will be gratefully welcomed.

Contents

CONTENTS

South-West England

Eastern England

Cambridge

The Midlands

CONTENTS

CONTENTS

Appendix

Index

Maps

London

LONDON

We are concerned in this opening section with the literary associations of the County of London, that is, the City of London and the twenty-eight metropolitan boroughs; but the London of Chaucer, with whom we begin, was just the square mile of the City, which more than a hundred years before his birth had already reached out beyond the Roman wall to its modern boundaries.

Geoffrey Chaucer was born about 1343-4, probably in Thames Street, where his father was a vintner. We know nothing of his earliest days, but we do know that as a youth he served in a princely household and a little later in the army of Edward III, when he was taken prisoner. After being ransomed, he saw further royal service and went on several diplomatic missions abroad. In 1374 he was granted the lucrative post of Comptroller of Customs in the Port of London, and took a house in Aldgate, just by this City gate. The site of his house is marked by a tablet over the post office in Aldgate High Street (I, F3,62). It was probably towards the end of his tenure of this house that Chaucer began writing his *Canterbury Tales*. He left Aldgate about 1386, and three years later was appointed Clerk of the King's Works at St

3

George's Chapel, Windsor, at Woolwich, Smithfield and other royal properties. Among these was Eltham Palace, but the buildings that have survived there were built after Chaucer's time. He lost his position in 1391, received royal pensions but no further appointments. In 1399 he rented a house in the grounds of St Mary's Chapel, Westminster (later replaced by Henry VII's Chapel), and died there on October 25, 1400. Having been a royal servant, a poet and a tenant of Westminster Abbey, (I, E4,64) he was buried in its south transept, the first writer to be buried in what has for so long been known as Poets' Corner. In 1555 Nicholas Brigham, an antiquary, poet and admirer of Chaucer, erected close to his grave the tomb that we now see.

The 'nyne and twenty in a compaignye' whom Chaucer met at the Tabard in Southwark has made it the most famous of all the old London inns. There were many hostelries in Southwark catering for those 'redy to wenden' on pilgrimage, but all have vanished, the Tabard itself perishing in a great fire in 1676. A modern tavern of the same name stands on its site. It was not only at the Tabard that Chaucer was able to observe the pilgrims, for he lived at one time in Greenwich, which lay by the pilgrim route.

William Langland, an almost exact contemporary of Chaucer and the author of *Piers Plowman*, has told us in that poem that he lived in Cornhill with his wife and daughter and tried to make a living as a scrivener, by singing requiems for the dead, and was reduced at times to begging. One of Chaucer's disciples, John Gower, has a connexion with Southwark. Born somewhere in Kent, late in life he resided in the priory of St Mary Overies, to which he had been a generous benefactor, and died there in 1408. He was buried in the priory church, now Southwark Cathedral (I, E4,12), in the chapel of St John. The head of his effigy rests on three volumes of his works. Referred to as 'moral Gower' by Chaucer, whom he knew, he was used as prologue by Shakespeare in *Pericles*.

Another disciple and contemporary of Chaucer was Thomas Hoccleve (or Occleve), who held a post in the Privy Seal office. What little we know of him is derived from an autobiographical poem, in which he confesses that he had been overeating and overdrinking for twenty years. He was a frequenter of the taverns and cook-shops of

Westminster, and at one time lived at the Chester Inn in the Strand. He lived to a very ripe age and died about 1450. Like Gower and Hoccleve, John Lydgate once stood in high esteem, and like them is little regarded now except in the historical development of literature. He made frequent visits to London, and wrote an amusing poem called *London Lickpenny*, which depicts the troubles besetting those without money in London.

Caxton was not only the first man to introduce printing into England, but a writer in his own right. Apprenticed to a London mercer, he later set up business in Bruges. It was not until he was fifty or older that he began to learn the craft of printing. In 1476 he decided to set up a press in Westminster, and the first book printed in England, *The Dictes and Sayings of the Philosophers*, appeared in November 1477. It has been discovered only recently that the actual site of Caxton's press was near or adjoining the Chapter House of Westminster Abbey, beside a path that led from the south door of the Abbey to the king's palace opposite. It must have been very near the house in which Chaucer died, and was possibly chosen so as to be under the notice of rich potential customers—the king and his court. Later Caxton rented more spacious quarters in the Almonry, which was situated at the junction now made by Victoria Street and Great Smith Street, but continued to use his other premises. Caxton's industry is scarcely credible, for besides printing over eighty books, he translated at least twenty others. He died in 1491, aged about seventy, and was buried in the church of St Margaret, Westminster (I, E4,65). The site of his grave is unknown, but a tablet to his memory was placed in the church by the Roxburghe Club in 1820.

The man who carried on Caxton's business, Wynkyn de Worde, had been one of his assistants, and deserves mention here because he was the first to introduce printing into Fleet Street, thus beginning its long association with the printed word. Incidentally, the few acres comprising Fleet Street and its tributaries have more literary associations than any other area of this size in Britain or Ireland. Wynkyn de Worde died in 1534 or 1535, and was buried in the old church of St Bride's, Fleet Street (I, E3,15). His remains were found when the church was undergoing restoration.

Among the productions of the presses of Wynkyn de Worde and his contemporary Richard Pynson were the works of John Skelton, who began writing at an early age in honour of the aristocracy and the royal family, which led eventually to appointment as tutor to Henry VII's second son, later Henry VIII. He lived at Westminster or wherever the court happened to be. No mere sycophant, he castigated the follies of court life in his poems. When Wolsey became powerful, Skelton was at first deferential towards him, but later let loose his satiric arrows against the pride and pomp of the great cardinal. Wolsey sent him to prison on more than one occasion, but on the last occasion that he tried to apprehend the saucy poet, the latter took sanctuary in Westminster Abbey. Much as he regretted his loss of freedom, Skelton remained there until his death on June 21, 1529. He was buried in the chancel of St Margaret's Church, but his grave is unmarked.

The chief claim of a contemporary of Skelton's, Sir Thomas More, for a place in English literary annals is a charming Tudor translation of his *Utopia*. He was born in Milk Street, Cheapside, on February 7, 1478. His connexion with Lincoln's Inn, where he studied law, is commemorated by a statuette in Carey Street, Chancery Lane; and a window in the church of St Lawrence Jewry commemorates the fact that he lectured there when a lay brother at the Charterhouse. For many years he had a fine house at Chelsea, and on what is probably the site of its garden there now stands Crosby Hall, part of what was once a large merchant's house in Bishopsgate Street which More rented for a short time, but it is not known if he actually lived in it. More was executed on Tower Hill on July 6, 1535. In Chelsea Old Church (I, D4,6) is a tomb (in the More Chapel) More designed for himself, but there is no record of his being buried in it.

Sir Thomas Wyatt, who shares with the Earl of Surrey the honour of introducing the sonnet into England, has little connexion with London, and the only distinct knowledge we have of his whereabouts here is that he was twice imprisoned in the Tower of London (I, F3,11) for short terms. Henry Howard, Earl of Surrey, was the first poet to use blank verse in England. Born about 1517, he became a soldier and courtier, getting more and more involved in the political factions of Henry VIII's time. His enemies managed to bring trumped-up charges against him, and after trial and conviction at the Guildhall he was executed on Tower Hill on January 21, 1547. He was at first buried in the church of All Hallows-by-the-Tower and later reinterred at Framlingham in Suffolk.

Sir Philip Sidney, one of the most brilliant figures at the court of Elizabeth, was a great deal in London, though none of the buildings in which he lived has survived. He was often at Whitehall Palace, where on one occasion he quarrelled with the seventeenth Earl of Oxford (one of the candidates for the authorship of Shakespeare's work), and as a result was in disgrace for a time. At times he sickened of court life and preferred the company of men of learning, especially writers. At his uncle the Earl of Leicester's house in the Strand he saw a good deal of Spenser, who dedicated to 'the president of noblesse and chivalry' his *Shepherd's Calendar*. Sidney and his friends were persuaded by the critic Gabriel Harvey to form a literary society to help naturalize classical metres in English verse. Called the Areopagus, the society met frequently during the years 1578-9, probably in Leicester's house.

Sidney was a frequent guest at Durham House in the Strand, the residence of the first Earl of Essex, whose dying wish was that Sidney should marry his daughter Penelope. Sidney was Astrophel and Penelope Stella of the famous *Astrophel and Stella* sonnet sequence. Desiring a more active life (he had secretly tried to join Drake) he was appointed Governor of Flushing; he volunteered for the attack to relieve Zutphen, where he received the wound that resulted in his death on October 17, 1586. He was buried behind the high altar of Old St Paul's, but his tomb was destroyed in the Great Fire of 1666.

Little is known of Shakespeare's greatest predecessor in drama, Christopher Marlowe. He came to live in London in 1586; became one of the circle known as University Wits, knew Ralegh, and was suspected of atheism. A warrant was issued for his arrest shortly before he was killed in a tavern brawl at Deptford on June 1, 1593, by a certain Ingram Frizer. He was buried in the churchyard of St Nicholas, Deptford (I, G4,18), but nothing marks his grave. The old church was rebuilt, except for the tower, in 1697, and was seriously damaged in the last war. There is a memorial brass to Marlowe inside the church.

Edmund Spenser was born probably in East Smithfield about 1552, and educated at Merchant Taylors School, founded at about the time he entered, just off Upper Thames Street. He became a member of the Earl of Leicester's household in 1577 or 1578 and was, like Sidney, a member of the Areopagus. Probably through Leicester's and Sidney's influence he obtained a post in Ireland. We catch only fleeting glimpses of him in London until he left Ireland finally, after the outbreak of rebellion there in 1598. A sick man now, he took a lodging in King Street, Westminster (now covered over by Whitehall and Parliament Street), and died there on January 13, 1599. Ben Jonson's story that Spenser died 'for lack of bread' is an improbable one, as he was in receipt of a pension from the Crown. He was buried in Westminster Abbey, near Chaucer, whom he acknowledged as his master. William Camden says that his hearse was 'attended by poets, and mournful elegies and poems, with the pens that wrote them, were thrown into the tomb', and tradition asserts that Shakespeare was of the company. A marble monument executed by Nicholas Stone pays tribute to 'the Prince of Poets in his time'.

When Ralegh first came to London in 1576 he lodged in the Middle Temple, but apparently not as a student of law. Tradition connects him with a house in Islington at this period, and another some years later, but both have long since disappeared. The story of Ralegh laying his cloak in a 'plashy place' at Greenwich to save the queen from wetting her feet is probably true, and he certainly became one of the most brilliant and most rewarded of Elizabeth's courtiers. His chief residence in London was Durham House, granted to him in 1584, and it remained in his possession until James I deprived him of it. Many years later John Aubrey visited the house. 'I well remember his study,' he says, 'which was a little turret that looked into and over the Thames.' Ralegh belonged to a coterie of writers (Marlowe among them) suspected of being atheistic, and it is thought that Shakespeare refers to it as 'the school of night'.

On James I's accession Ralegh's days as a courtier were over, and his enemies helped the king to bring about his downfall. After trial and condemnation at Winchester he was imprisoned in the Tower of London, to which he was no stranger, having been there for a short spell when he offended Elizabeth by courting one of her maids of honour. Except for the interval of the disastrous venture to Guiana, he was in the Tower for the rest of his life. He lived in the Bloody Tower, and there conducted scientific experiments and wrote his *History of the World*. The ramparts he used to pace outside the Bloody Tower have since then become known as Ralegh's Walk. On the night before his execution he was taken to the Gate House, a prison which stood near the west end of Westminster Abbey, and there he wrote his greatest poem, 'Even such is time . . .'.

On the morning of October 29, 1618, he was taken to Old Palace Yard, Westminster. When he laid his head on the block the Dean of Westminster said that it ought to be toward the east. 'What matter,' Ralegh replied, 'how the head lie, so the heart be right?' He was buried in St Margaret's Church, below the altar, and a tablet marks the approximate site. A memorial window, with an inscription by James Russell Lowell, was placed in the church through American subscription in 1882. Ralegh's head was embalmed and kept by Lady Ralegh until her death. It is thought that it may be buried with his son Carew in the church of St Mary at West Horsley in Surrey. Three hundred and fifty years after his death, a public statue was at last erected in his honour, in Whitehall.

Of George Chapman, one of the greatest and most neglected of Shakespeare's contemporaries, we have very little knowledge, though he spent many years in London. Nothing is known of his whereabouts in London but that he died in the parish of St Giles, May 12, 1634, and was buried in the churchyard of St Giles-in-the-Fields (I, E3,68). His friend Inigo Jones designed the tombstone, which is now inside the church (rebuilt in 1734), but owing to the decay of the original inscription the lettering was recut, partly from memory.

Of Michael Drayton, who probably knew Shakespeare, John Aubrey said that he lived in a house beside the east end of St Dunstan's Church, Fleet Street (I, E3,14). It apparently survived till the end of the nineteenth century. He died in 1631 and was buried in Poets' Corner, 'near to Chaucer's grave and Spenser's', said Thomas Fuller, but his grave is unmarked. The inscription on his monument has been ascribed to Ben Jonson, among others, but it is unlikely as Jonson did not esteem

Drayton. Thomas Campion, one of the greatest of Elizabethan lyric poets, eludes us as to his whereabouts in London, but died there in 1620, and was buried on March 1 in the church or churchyard of St Dunstan, Fleet Street.

There are several untrustworthy stories about Shakespeare's early years in London, and we have no certain knowledge of his presence here until he was attacked by the dying and jealous Robert Greene in *A Groatsworth of Wit* in 1592. He was living in 1596 in Southwark, near the Bear-Garden on Bankside; next year he was in a house somewhere in St Helen's, Bishopsgate, and may have remained there until he returned to Southwark in 1599. This time he went to a dwelling in the Clink, the name given to the Bishop of Winchester's manor in Southwark, and all the Southwark playhouses were situated within the Clink. He lived there until 1608, but with an interval or intervals as lodger with a Huguenot tiremaker called Christopher Mountjoy at the corner of Silver Street off Cheapside.

In 1599 Richard Burbage, the leading actor of the day, together with his brother, Shakespeare and a few leading actors of their company (the Lord Chamberlain's), erected the Globe Theatre on Bankside. The site is covered by Barclay Perkins's brewery, and there is a commemorative tablet. The Globe opened with Shakespeare's *Henry V*. They also took over the Blackfriars Theatre in the City, leased it to the Children of the Queen's Revels, and when that company was suppressed in 1608 took it over for winter performances—it was a roofed-in playhouse, unlike the Globe. The Globe was burned down on June 29, 1613, during the first performance of *Henry VIII*, after Shakespeare had retired to Stratford.

In the churchyard of St Mary the Virgin, Aldermanbury, there is a bust of Shakespeare, who is supposed to have worshipped in the former church on this site. Below the bust there is a marble representation of the title-page of the First Folio, and an inscription commemorates its editors, John Heminge and Henry Condell, who were buried in the old church. Middle Temple Hall,* off Fleet Street, has an association with Shakespeare, for *Twelfth Night* was performed there at a feast on

* Open during law terms 10 a.m. to 12.30 p.m., 3 to 5 p.m.; during vacations 10 a.m. to 5 p.m.

February 2, 1602; and *The Comedy of Errors* was performed at Gray's Inn (I, E3,36) during the Christmas festivities of 1594.

Ben Jonson, the greatest Elizabethan and Jacobean dramatist after Shakespeare, was born possibly in Westminster in June 1572. Educated first at a school in St Martin's Church, he then went to Westminster School (I, E4,66), and was taught by and at the expense of William Camden the great antiquary. He became bricklayer's apprentice, soldier, actor and finally dramatist. His first play, *Every Man in his Humour*, was produced at the Globe Theatre with Shakespeare in the cast. Jonson lived at one period in Blackfriars, and it is supposed that he lived latterly in Westminster, where he died on August 6, 1637, and was buried in the north nave aisle of Westminster Abbey. According to one traditional story he was buried in an upright position to signify his readiness for the Resurrection; to another, because he asked Charles I for the favour of eighteen inches of square ground in the Abbey.

Some of his old tavern haunts have become famous: the Dog Tavern somewhere in Westminster, the Mermaid in Bread Street off Cheapside, and the Devil Tavern in Fleet Street (a tablet on the wall of No. 1 Fleet Street marks the site of the last). At the Devil Jonson founded a club called the Apollo, for which he drew up twenty-four rules in Latin, and there he dominated company more completely than any other literary figure has done except Dr Johnson. The wit combats between Jonson and Shakespeare made famous by Fuller may have taken place at the Mermaid, and certainly not at the Devil, which was founded after Shakespeare's death.

Jonson placed Bacon at the head of all the writers of his own age. Francis Bacon was born at York House, Strand, on January 22, 1561, the son of Lord Keeper Bacon. He lived in York House during most of the time that he was in London. He was admitted to Gray's Inn in 1576, and after being called to the Bar had chambers there which he retained to the end of his life. He had some hand in the laying out of the gardens at Gray's Inn, and tradition says that he planted the catalpa tree there, but the species was unknown in England in his time, though it looks hoary enough to lend some colour to the tradition. Gray's Inn has a statue of him in South Square. He was married in 1606 in Marylebone Parish Church, replaced in 1740 by the present church on the same site. Bacon died from bronchitis after trying to prove to himself that meat might be preserved by chilling. He bought a chicken and stuffed it with snow at Highgate, became very ill and was taken to the Earl of Arundel's house, where he died on April 9, 1626. The site of Arundel House, demolished in 1825, is partly covered by St Michael's Church on Highgate Hill.

'The first poet in the world in some things,' said Jonson of John Donne, who was born in the parish of St Olave, Bread Street, in 1571 or 1572. His father was a prosperous ironmonger and his mother the daughter of John Heywood the dramatist and granddaughter of Sir Thomas More's sister. Donne lived for a time in Drury Lane, but his chief connexion with London is as the dean of St Paul's, which he was appointed in 1621, and some of the sermons he preached are among the greatest masterpieces of English prose. From 1624 he was also rector of St Dunstan's, Fleet Street. The deanery he occupied has been rebuilt since his time. Donne has also a connexion with Lincoln's Inn, where he studied after leaving the university, and for a time was divinity reader there and during term time preached twice every Sunday. He died at the deanery of St Paul's on March 31, 1631, and was buried in the cathedral, but his tomb perished in the Great Fire. However, Nicholas Stone's effigy of Donne in a funeral shroud (copied from a painting Donne ordered during his last illness) survived the fire and is to be seen in the south choir aisle of the cathedral (I, E3,8). St Dunstan's commemorates him with a carved stone head inside the porch.

So meagre is our knowledge of many of Shakespeare's fellow-dramatists that it is difficult, and sometimes impossible, to assign them to earthly habitations and homes. Thomas Dekker was born and died in London; John Webster was born probably in London, and lived for a time in Holywell Street off the north side of the Strand, but of another powerful tragedian, Cyril Tourneur, we know next to nothing. John Ford can be traced only at the Middle Temple; Philip Massinger was buried in the churchyard of St Saviour (Southwark Cathedral) and John Marston in the Temple Church, but there is no trace of either grave; and Thomas Heywood is very deep in the shades.

John Fletcher apparently lived with his collaborator Francis Beaumont near the Globe Theatre, died of the plague in 1625 and was buried in Southwark Cathedral. His name is cut on a stone in the choir, but it does not necessarily mark the site of his remains. Beaumont, we know from his celebrated poem, was a companion of Ben Jonson at the Mermaid Tavern. He died in 1616, aged only thirty-one or thirty-two, and was buried in Poets' Corner, but where exactly is unknown, though his name is recorded with several others on a slab in front of the bust of Dryden. Thomas Middleton, the son of a bricklayer, was born somewhere in London in April 1580. He apparently spent his last years in Newington Butts, and was buried in the parish church there (demolished in 1720) on July 4, 1627.

Izaak Walton came to London to take up the trade of ironmongery, and had a shop (demolished in 1799) between Chancery Lane and St Dunstan's, Fleet Street, came to know John Donne whose biographer he became, and successfully combined literature with his trade. The initials *I.W.* can be seen scratched on the monument of Isaac Casaubon in Westminster Abbey, and since Walton was a great admirer of Casaubon, the initials are probably his. Another of Walton's biographies was that of George Herbert, who has a slight connexion with London through his education at Westminster School from about 1604 to 1609.

Herrick, who celebrated the 'lyric feasts' with Ben Jonson at 'the Sun, the Dog, the Triple Tun', was born off Cheapside, probably in Wood Street, on August 24, 1591. His father died when he was an infant, and he was eventually apprenticed to his uncle, one of the richest goldsmiths of his day, but did not serve his time. Herrick spent many years in Devonshire, but when ejected in 1647 came to live in St Anne's Lane (now St Ann's Street) off Great Peter Street, Westminster. His connexion is commemorated by Herrick Street, named after him in 1897. He returned to Devonshire in 1662.

James Shirley, often described as the last of the Elizabethans, was born near the Mansion House on September 18, 1596. For a time he lived at Gray's Inn, but disappeared from London during the Civil War. Latterly he lived in Whitefriars off Fleet Street, but he and his wife were driven from their home by the Great Fire and fled to what was then the village of St Giles, and died from shock and exposure within a few hours of each other. They were buried in the churchyard of St Giles-in-the-Fields, but there is nothing to indicate the where-abouts of their graves.

A tablet at the corner of Cheapside and St Martin's-le-Grand records the approximate site of the birthplace of Sir Thomas Browne, but in no other sense was he a Londoner. A very short distance away John Milton, the son of a scrivener, was born in Bread Street, Cheapside, on December 9, 1608. His birthplace was destroyed in the Great Fire. He was sent to St Paul's School, then near by beyond the east end of the cathedral. After his university career and some years in Buckinghamshire and abroad, he lodged by St Bride's churchyard. Thereafter there were a number of London residences: Aldersgate Street, the Barbican, High Holborn (where his garden overlooked Lincoln's Inn Fields), Whitehall, Petty France (Westminster), Holborn (near Red Lion Fields), Jewin Street off Aldersgate Street (where the greater part of *Paradise Lost* was composed), and finally in 1663, Artillery Row (now called Bunhill Row) in Bunhill Fields. All his London residences have disappeared; the site of the Artillery Row house is marked by a tablet. There he completed *Paradise Lost* and composed *Paradise Regained* and *Samson Agonistes*.

He died in Artillery Row on November 8, 1674, and was buried in the church of St Giles, Cripplegate (I, E3,13), beside his father. A bust was placed inside the church in 1793, and a statue in the churchyard in 1904, but the latter was displaced by bombs in 1940 and has not yet been re-erected. Poets' Corner commemorates him with a tablet, and in the church of St Margaret, Westminster (in which Milton's second marriage took place), there is a memorial window that was given by G. W. Childs of Philadelphia. It was unveiled by Matthew Arnold, and Browning was present. Outside Bow Church in Cheapside there is a commemorative tablet transferred from the demolished Allhallows Church which was the successor of that in which Milton was christened.

Andrew Marvell, friend and colleague of Milton, appears to have settled in London about 1653. Much of his London residence was in Maiden Lane, Covent Garden, though he had a cottage at Highgate, and a tablet on the wall of Waterlow Park commemorates his residence there. He died on August 18, 1678, either at Highgate or in Maiden

Lane, and was buried in the church of St Giles-in-the-Fields. The church was rebuilt about fifty years after his death, and a marble slab was placed on the north wall by his grandson in 1764 stating that *near to this place lyeth the body of Andrew Marvell Esquire.*

We are now very much in the midst of Roundheads and Cavaliers. Thomas Fuller, a Royalist supporter, came to London on the eve of the Civil War, preached at the Inns of Court and was appointed lecturer at the Savoy Chapel. A sermon that offended the Parliamentarians resulted in Fuller's flight to Oxford. After the Restoration he returned to his post at the Savoy. He died of typhus at his lodgings in Covent Garden on August 16, 1661, working on his *Worthies of England* to the last. A tablet inside the church of St Clement, Eastcheap, commemorates the fact that he preached at the former church on this site.

Edmund Waller, at first a Royalist and then a Parliamentarian, spent a good deal of his earlier life in London. He was married to his first wife in St Margaret's Church, Westminster. For his part in the plot to seize London for Charles I (he abjectly informed on his fellow-conspirators to save his own life) he was sent first to the Tower of London and then into banishment abroad. After being pardoned he returned to his country home, but lodged sometime during 1654-6 in Bow Street, Covent Garden.

Samuel Butler, the Royalist satirist, spent much of his later life in London. His *Hudibras* made him famous, and though Charles II was much taken with it, Butler never received the preferment he expected. He died of consumption and in poverty at his lodging in Rose Street (now Garrick Street), Covent Garden, on September 25, 1680, and was buried in the churchyard of St Paul's, Covent Garden, but there is nothing to mark his grave. There is a monument to him in Poets' Corner. A poet of very different temperament, Richard Crashaw, was born somewhere in London probably in 1613, and educated at Charterhouse School (I, E3,20), after which he had little or no connexion with London.

Also educated at Charterhouse was that tragic figure Richard Lovelace, born in Woolwich in 1618. He was chosen in 1642 to present the petition of Kentish Royalists on behalf of Charles I to the House of Commons. The House questioned him, and not satisfied with his answers, committed him to the Gate House prison in Westminster where Ralegh had spent his last night. In prison he wrote that great lyric 'To Althea from Prison'. Released after about seven weeks, he resumed Royalist activities, went soldiering abroad and was captured on his return in 1648. He was confined in Lord Petre's house (used as a prison for Royalists) in Aldersgate, and there prepared his poems for publication. Released in 1649, he was now a poor man, having given his all in a lost cause, and his last years were spent in miserable destitution. He died in 1658 in a mean lodging in Gunpowder Alley, Shoe Lane, and was buried in the old church of St Bride, Fleet Street.

Amidst Cavaliers and Puritans, satirists and dramatists, we must take note of a man out of sympathy with them all. John Bunyan often visited London, even while he was serving a long sentence in prison, and preached to large enthusiastic congregations. On his last visit he had been riding through heavy rain, and became ill with fever. He died at the house of his friend John Strudwick on Snow Hill, Holborn Bridge, August 31, 1688. He was buried in Bunhill Fields (I, F3,21). At the suggestion of an American visitor, a stained-glass window was placed, in 1912, in the north transept of Westminster Abbey in honour of Bunyan. It represents him and four episodes from *The Pilgrim's Progress*.

Our final notice of a Royalist is that of Abraham Cowley, born somewhere in London in 1618, the posthumous son of a stationer. In early childhood he imbibed a love of poetry, and was in print when only fourteen or fifteen. He was educated at Westminster School. He lived at various times in Fleet Street, Battersea and Barn Elms, and spent retirement in Chertsey in Surrey, where he died. He was buried with great splendour in Poets' Corner, near Chaucer and Spenser.

Dryden, who lavished fulsome praise on Cowley, was also educated at Westminster School, and thereafter does not reappear in London until 1657. He commemorated Cromwell in verse, and when Charles II was restored did the like for him. He was married in the church of St Swithin, London Stone, destroyed in the Great Fire, and Wren's church that succeeded it has been demolished after damage in the last war. He lived on the south side of Fleet Street during 1673-82, and until 1686 in Long Acre. His last home, 43 Gerrard Street (I, D3,74), has survived and is marked with a tablet. He died there on May 1, 1700, and was buried near Chaucer in Poets' Corner. His great haunt was the famous Will's Coffee-house in Bow Street, Covent Garden, where he reigned as a literary dictator. Pepys, going there for the first time in 1664, saw 'Dryden the poet (I knew at Cambridge) and all the wits of the town'. There was a special chair reserved for Dryden at Will's, in the warmest nook by the fire in winter and on the balcony in summer.

Dryden, whose hatreds were somewhat intense, hated the dramatist Shadwell more than he did any other man, and savagely satirized him in *MacFlecknoe*. Shadwell entered the Middle Temple, lived for a time in Salisbury Court (now Salisbury Square) and later in Church Lane (now Old Church Street), Chelsea, where he died on November 19, 1692. He was buried in Chelsea Old Church, but the site of his grave is unknown. One of his best plays, *The Squire of Alsatia*, provided Scott with some of the finest scenes in *The Fortunes of Nigel*.

Three early members of the Royal Society call for mention together. John Aubrey was a student at the Middle Temple, but never called to the Bar. He was frequently in London and in 1662 was elected a Fellow of the Royal Society. He was a member of the Rota Club at Miles's Coffee-house in Westminster, of which Wren, Dryden and Pepys were also members. Only one of his London lodgings can be traced, and that was in Gray's Inn Lane (now Gray's Inn Road). John Evelyn was also at the Middle Temple, but for less than a year. He settled in London in 1652 at a large house called Sayes Court in Deptford, and its site is now marked by Sayes Court Park. His friend Pepys visited him there. It was at Evelyn's suggestion that the Royal Society was founded, and he became a founder member. He left Sayes Court in 1694 and let it to an admiral who sublet it to Peter the Great.

Samuel Pepys, the son of a tailor, was born above his father's shop in Salisbury Court off Fleet Street on February 23, 1633, and the site of his birthplace is marked by a tablet. Educated first in Huntingdon, he went later to St Paul's School and then to Cambridge. His great administrative career began when he became Clerk of the Acts to the Navy Board in 1660. His office was in Seething Lane in the City, and his house beside it. Not far away is the brick tower of the church of All Hallows-by-the-Tower, which he climbed to watch the Great Fire.

Pepys's office and house were burned down in 1673, the year that he became Secretary of the Admiralty. In 1679 he was falsely accused of being a papist, deprived of office and imprisoned for a short time in the Tower of London. Afterwards he went to live at 12 Buckingham Street (I, E3,77) with his former chief clerk, Will Hewer. This fine house survives and is marked with a tablet. On being reappointed Secretary to the Admiralty he moved his office to this house and took over the lease. He moved house and office again in 1688 to 14 Buckingham Street (marked by a tablet, but the house is of later date than Pepys's time). On William III's accession he lost office again and was never reappointed. A ridiculous charge of giving information to the French resulted in a short imprisonment in the Gate House in Westminster, where Ralegh and Richard Lovelace had been imprisoned. His last years were spent in Clapham, where he died on May 26, 1703, and is buried beside his wife in St Olave's, Hart Street (I, F3,9), where he had so often worshipped. Pepys was elected a Fellow of the Royal Society in 1665 and was twice its president.

The only known London abode of the misanthropic William Wycherley, one of the most brilliant of the Restoration dramatists, was in Bow Street. Admitted to the Middle Temple, he soon took to literature and a gayer life. He married a jealous shrew who died about a year later and left him all her money, but his title to her estate was disputed; the resulting litigation completely impoverished him and he had to go to the Fleet Prison. He married again only eleven days before his death on December 31, 1715, and was buried in the church of St Paul, Covent Garden, but his grave is unmarked.

William Congreve, the most brilliant of the Restoration dramatists, also studied law at the Middle Temple only to give it up for literature. He lived successively in Southampton Street, Howard Street and Surrey Street, all off the Strand, and thought more of being a gentleman than a dramatist. When Voltaire (who lived in Maiden Lane, Covent Garden) called on him, Congreve hinted that he should be visited upon no other footing than that of a gentleman. Voltaire replied that if he, Congreve, had been merely a gentleman, he would not have bothered to call. He died in Surrey Street on January 19, 1729, and was buried in Poets' Corner. His monument was erected at the expense of his friend the Duchess of Marlborough, to whom he left most of his fortune.

Congreve's collaborator in a translation from Molière, Sir John Vanbrugh, was an unique case of a man attaining unusual eminence in both drama and architecture. He was born in the parish of St Nicholas Acon in the City of London on January 24, 1664. Trained as an architect, he attained success in drama before securing any important commission as an architect. He built for himself that extraordinary essay in Gothic on Maze Hill, Greenwich (I, G4), now a girls' school and called Vanbrugh Castle. He also had a hand in the building of Greenwich Hospital. He died at a house of his own design in Whitehall on March 26, 1726, and was buried in the family vault in St Stephen's, Walbrook (I, E3,10).

Joseph Addison was educated at Charterhouse School. In his earlier and less prosperous days he lived in a garret in Haymarket, and later in St James's Place and Chelsea. He was married to the Dowager Countess of Warwick in the church of St Edmund King and Martyr in Lombard Street, and thereafter lived in Holland House, Kensington (I, C4,37). This great mansion was largely destroyed in the last war, but a portion survived and is incorporated in a hostel. He died there on June 17, 1719, and was buried in the north aisle of Henry VII's Chapel, Westminster Abbey. There is a monument to him in Poets' Corner.

Sir Richard Steele was a contemporary of Addison at Charterhouse School, and their friendship continued until they quarrelled towards the end of Addison's life. Steele began the *Tatler* newspaper, in which he introduced an intimate form of essay new to English letters. Addison contributed to this and to the later venture, the *Spectator*. Steele lived at several places in London: Great Smith Street in Westminster, Bury Street in St James's, Bloomsbury Square, and Villiers Street in the Strand. For a time he had a cottage on Haverstock Hill at Chalk Farm, and Steele's Road there commemorates the connexion.

'The greatest genius of the age,' said Addison of Jonathan Swift, who first came to live in London in 1699 and lodged in many places, though with one long break of ten years, until his final retirement to Ireland in 1727. He was with Pope at Twickenham when he heard of his beloved

Stella's illness, and brooded in Bond Street for three weeks before setting out, for the last time, to Ireland.

Swift called Defoe a stupid, illiterate scribbler. He may have been an unsavoury character, but was certainly neither stupid nor illiterate. He was born about 1660 in the parish of St Giles, Cripplegate, the son of a butcher and a dissenter. He was educated at a dissenting academy in Newington Green, after which he took to business and soldiering, and then to political pamphleteering. His *Shortest Way with the Dissenters* resulted in fine and imprisonment, and when made to stand in the pillory many people gathered round and roared sympathetic applause. He had a shop in Cornhill at one time, and in later and more prosperous days built a house in Stoke Newington. Its site is indicated by a tablet at 95 Church Street. He died in Ropemakers' Alley (which has disappeared) in Moorfields on April 26, 1731, and was buried in Bunhill Fields. His grave remained for long unmarked, and in 1870 a monument was erected on the approximate site from money raised by an appeal, as the inscription states, *to the boys and girls of England*. Defoe Road in Tooting commemorates him, but his connexion with that district is based only on conjecture.

In an age of violent political and literary antagonisms, Defoe and Pope stand out as the most malicious personalities. Alexander Pope was born on May 21, 1688, in Lombard Street, probably in Plough Court, where he is commemorated with a tablet. He learned little at the various schools he attended and much from the priests employed as tutors by his father, a Catholic linen-draper. The dramatist Wycherley introduced him to town life when he was sixteen. He came into literary notice when his *Pastorals* appeared in 1709, and soon became acquainted with Addison, Steele and their circle. Pope had a powerful friend and patron in Lord Bolingbroke, one wing of whose great house in Church Road, Battersea, survived until recent years. In this particular wing Pope is supposed to have written the *Essay on Man*.

Pope was no friend to Matthew Prior, and said of the latter that the 'Chloe' of his poems was the wife of a common soldier. Prior, educated at Westminster School, had a London home in Duke Street (which has disappeared) in Westminster. At his own wish he was buried at the feet of Spenser in Poets' Corner. He left £500 for a monument, which was

duly erected, surmounted by a bust presented to him by Louis XIV.
John Gay, a close friend of Pope and Swift, first came to London when
apprenticed to a mercer, disliked being in a shop, and after a short
sojourn in his native Barnstaple sought a literary career in London. After
attaining some success, he used the money to amass a large fortune in
the South Sea Bubble craze, but lost all by disregarding advice to sell in
time. Help came from the Duke and Duchess of Queensberry and other
friends, including Pope who employed him as secretary. An idea from
Swift was taken up and developed into *The Beggar's Opera*. When his
health failed the Queensberrys looked after him in Queensberry House
(long since demolished) in Burlington Gardens, where he died on
December 4, 1732. His patrons saw to it that he was buried with
tremendous pomp in Poets' Corner. On his monument (which has
been removed to the triforium gallery) is his own epitaph:

> *Life is a jest, and all things shew it.*
> *I thought so once, and now I know it.*

One of Gay's friends was James Thomson, who wrote one part
('Summer') of his *Seasons* in Little Tower Street, and at the Doves Inn
(which survives) in Upper Mall, Hammersmith (I, B4,24), he is supposed to have written 'Winter' in an upper room.

Thomas Gray was born on December 26, 1716, in Cornhill, where a
tablet with a medallion portrait at No. 35 marks the site of his birthplace. He was little in London in later life, and on his visits stayed in
Jermyn Street. In 1759, when he wished to make use of the newly
opened British Museum, he stayed in Southampton Row.

The 'Father of the English Novel' is the title accorded by some to
Richardson, by others to Fielding. Samuel Richardson was a very
successful printer of Fleet Street (moving later to Salisbury Square)
before he took to writing novels. He had a residence at 40 North End
Crescent, Fulham (it has most unfortunately been demolished recently),
where he wrote his novels in a little summer-house in the garden. He
left this house for one in New King's Road (now King's Road) by
Parsons Green in Fulham in 1754, and died there on July 4, 1761.
He was buried in St Bride's Church, Fleet Street. When the foundations of the church were being excavated during restoration,

Richardson's coffin was found, and it is now preserved in the crypt.

Fielding, who made fun of Richardson's *Pamela* in *Joseph Andrews*, came to London in 1727 and indulged recklessly in the pleasures of the town, but necessity soon forced him to seek a living. He took to writing plays, but that came to an end when a law was brought in requiring all stage performances to be licensed by the Lord Chamberlain. He decided to study law at the Middle Temple, was called to the Bar and had chambers in Pump Court. Then he began to parody Richardson's *Pamela*, but soon forgot parody and produced the great novel of *Joseph Andrews*. In 1748 Fielding became a Justice of the Peace for Westminster, and was provided with a house in Bow Street, probably the same one in which Edmund Waller had lived. During his magistracy the Bow Street Runners were instituted. He threw himself with great ardour into his work as magistrate, and this was also the period of his greatest literary activity. His health was undermined; he sought health in Lisbon, but survived only two months, dying on October 8, 1754. He was buried in the English cemetery there. There is no public memorial to one of the very greatest of English novelists, memorable too as a great reforming magistrate; only a reminder on a tablet in Bow Street that he lived there.

The eighteenth-century novelists are colourful personalities, and not the least colourful was Laurence Sterne, who came to London for the first time after the publication of the early volumes of *Tristram Shandy* to enjoy his enormous fame and to arrange publication of further volumes. Politicians, nobility and wits fêted him, and Dr Johnson, who disliked his pruriency, said that 'the man Sterne' had engagements for three months. He visited London several times, and lived latterly at 41 Old Bond Street. The building probably survives, but owing to renumbering is impossible to identify. He died there on March 18, 1768, and was buried behind the Chapel of the Ascension in Bayswater Road (I, D3,39). There are two very long inscriptions, and that on the headstone begins: *Alas, Poor Yorick*. There is a tradition that Sterne's body was removed by body-snatchers two days after burial and sold by them to the professor of anatomy at Cambridge.

There was no love lost between Sterne and Smollett. The latter attacked *Tristram Shandy* with his usual ferocity; subsequently they met in Rome, and Sterne later pilloried Smollett as 'Smelfungus' in *A Sentimental Journey*. Smollett had arrived in London at the age of eighteen to secure patronage for a play; disappointed, he sailed as ship's surgeon on a ship bound for the West Indies. On his return he set up as a surgeon in Downing Street. Later he moved to Curzon Street, Mayfair, and in 1750 to a fine Elizabethan house at Chelsea. This last house was demolished in 1835 and its site at 16 Lawrence Street is marked by a tablet. In his last and greatest novel, *Humphry Clinker*, one of the characters describes a visit to the Chelsea house, which was 'open to all unfortunate brothers of the quill'. Severe application to literary activity undermined his health, and he sought relief in journeys to Bath and the Continent. In 1769 he left for Italy, and wrote most of *Humphry Clinker* in a villa near Leghorn. He died there on September 17, 1771, and was buried in the English cemetery at Leghorn.

The first acquaintance with London of that unfortunate poet Christopher Smart appears to have been through confinement for madness in the Bethlehem (Bedlam) Hospital, the site of which is now occupied by the Imperial War Museum. About twelve years later he was again in a madhouse, probably Bethlehem Hospital, and is supposed to have written his great 'Song to David' during this confinement. Dr Johnson visited him, and said that he was harmless and should not have been confined. The final act of his miserable drama opened with committal for debt to the King's Bench Prison in Southwark, and there he died on May 20, 1771. A contemporary poet of a very different character, Mark Akenside, after early success with his *Pleasures of Imagination*, became a most successful doctor but his poetic imagination became atrophied. The last ten years of his life were spent in Old Burlington Street, where he died (in the same bed in which Milton had died, so it was alleged) on June 23, 1770, and is buried in an unmarked grave in St James's Church, Piccadilly.

The fourth Earl of Chesterfield, famous for his *Letters* to his natural son, was born in St James's Square on September 22, 1694. He is more often recalled to mind, perhaps somewhat unfairly, as the victim of Dr Johnson's superbly dignified rebuff. The house where Johnson first called on him used to stand in Grosvenor Square, and the house where he received Johnson's letter, a magnificent mansion in South Audley

Street, was unfortunately demolished in 1934. One house of his, Chesterfield House on Blackheath (I, G4,19), has survived. There is a house on the south side of Bloomsbury Square, and although the tablet states that Chesterfield lived there, it is uncertain if he did so. He died in South Audley Street on March 24, 1773.

Johnson himself arrived in London in 1737 to seek his fortune through literature, and a hard struggle he had of it for many years. Boswell gives a list of sixteen houses in which he lived, and the only one which has survived is that known as Dr Johnson's House* at 17 Gough Square off Fleet Street (I, E3,7). He lived there from 1749 until 1759, and there in the long room at the top of the house he toiled, with the help of six amanuenses, on his great *Dictionary*. In this house he wrote *Rasselas* and the essays for the *Idler* and the *Rambler*, and here it was that his wife died in 1752. After Gough Square he was for a short period at Staple Inn and Gray's Inn, and then for five years at Inner Temple Lane, where Johnson's Buildings covers the site of the house. Then he moved to Johnson's Court (not named after him) off Fleet Street, and the site of his house is marked by a tablet. His final move was to Bolt Court near by, where he wrote the *Lives of the Poets*, and where he died on December 13, 1784. He was buried in Poets' Corner near his friend Garrick, and Nollekens's bust of him was placed there in 1939. The sculptor Bacon's full-length figure of Johnson is in St Paul's Cathedral. Johnson used to worship in St Clement Danes Church (I, E3,67), and his pew used to be marked, but the interior of the church was gutted in the last war. At its east end is a statue of him.

A great frequenter of taverns, his favourite appears to have been the Mitre, the site of which is marked at 37 Fleet Street, and he was also at the Devil (site marked at 1 Fleet Street) where Ben Jonson had ruled his literary kingdom. There is a tradition that he and Goldsmith frequented the Cheshire Cheese in Wine Office Court, and 'Dr Johnson's Corner' is preserved there. Johnson has connexions with Southwark and Streatham. He used to stay with his friends the Thrales in Southwark, and when Henry Thrale died he was one of the executors

---

* Open weekdays 10.30 a.m. to 5 p.m.; October to April 10.30 a.m. to 4.30 p.m. Contains first editions, portraits and personal relics of Johnson and his circle.

who helped to dispose of Thrale's brewery. Barclay Perkins's office is on the site. The Thrales had a fine house, Streatham Park (demolished in 1863) on the south side of Streatham Common, where Johnson was a visitor for about twenty years.

Johnson's 'faithful chronicler' James Boswell first arrived in London in 1760, and the famous first meeting with Johnson took place at a bookshop in Russell Street, Covent Garden, in 1763. Boswell was frequently in London and stayed in several places, but all his residences have disappeared, two of them within this century. In Queen Anne Street, Marylebone, he worked on his *Life of Johnson*. His last home was in Great Portland Street, and a tablet at No. 122 marks the site. He died there on May 19, 1795.

In Johnson's brilliant circle, none was more endearing, and none possessed more varied gifts than Oliver Goldsmith, who arrived in London in 1756 destitute after about two years of wandering on the Continent. His first recorded job was that of assistant to a chemist, and then became an unsuccessful physician on Bankside, Southwark. After some schoolmastering in Peckham he secured some hackwork which eventually led to better things, and was able to move to lodgings in Wine Office Court, opposite the Cheshire Cheese. At these lodgings he first met Johnson, and it may have been here that Johnson read *The Vicar of Wakefield*, secured sixty guineas for it and rescued Goldsmith from embarrassing circumstances.

Goldsmith's last residence was at 2 Brick Court in the Middle Temple, most unfortunately destroyed in the last war. He died there on April 4, 1774, and was buried in the north-east corner of the Temple churchyard (I, E3,16). His tombstone was removed some years later and for long the exact site of his grave was unknown. In 1860 a memorial stone was placed on the approximate site, and at present this site is bricked over. There is a memorial tablet in Poets' Corner for which Johnson wrote the Latin inscription.

If Johnson could be said to have stood in awe of any man, it was another Irish member of his circle, Edmund Burke, who came to study at the Middle Temple in 1750. One residence of his has survived, 37 Gerrard Street, Soho (I, D3,74), where he lived from 1787 until about 1793, and it is marked with a tablet.

Another member of the circle was Edward Gibbon, referred to in Boswell's letters as an 'ugly, affected, disgusting fellow'. He was born on April 27, 1737, in a house long since demolished, at the bottom of Putney Hill. Gibbon Walk in Putney commemorates him. He was educated locally, at Kingston-upon-Thames and at Westminster School. He lived in Bond Street in 1760, but did not settle in London until he took 7 Bentinck Street, Manchester Square, in 1772, and called it 'the best house in the world', but it has disappeared. There he lived for over ten years, and much of the *Decline and Fall* was written in that house. Thereafter he lived abroad, returned in 1793 when he heard of the death of his friend Lady Sheffield, and took lodgings in the house of a publisher in St James's Street. After a round of visits he became ill, probably with dropsy, and returned to St James's Street, where he died on the following day, January 16, 1794. The site of the house in which he died is now covered over by the Conservative Club.

One member of the Johnson circle, Fanny Burney, survived into the early Victorian period. A house she lived in for several years in St Martin's Street, Leicester Square, had been Sir Isaac Newton's home, and in her time Newton's observatory was still there. Many distinguished visitors called here, including Dr Johnson, and here Fanny Burney worked in secret on her *Evelina*. The house ultimately became Bertloni's Restaurant, which was frequented by Thomas Hardy, and after many alterations was demolished in 1925. One of Fanny Burney's residences, 11 Bolton Street, Piccadilly (I, D3,83), has survived and is marked with a tablet. She lived there for ten years and was twice visited by Scott. She died in Grosvenor Street on January 6, 1840.

The youngest male member of the Johnson circle of any eminence was Richard Brinsley Sheridan. He occupied a large number of houses, and two that survive, 10 Hertford Street, Westminster (I, D3,86), and 14 Savile Row (I, D3,81), are marked with tablets. He died at the latter on July 7, 1816, though it has been asserted that he died at No. 17, which for long was supposed to have been haunted by his ghost. He was buried in Poets' Corner, next to Garrick, after a funeral of great splendour. Sheridan is connected with Drury Lane Theatre, though more intimately with the two previous buildings on the site, and he was a member of Brooks's Club.

A man who did not belong to the Johnson circle, who in fact disliked Johnson and gave Boswell short shrift when he wanted information, was Horace Walpole. The youngest son of Sir Robert Walpole, he was born at 17 Arlington Street, Piccadilly (the house is not extant), on September 24, 1717. When his father was granted 10 Downing Street (I, E4,88) Horace Walpole also lived there, and when the former resigned office they went to live at 5 Arlington Street (I, D4,84), which survives and is marked with a tablet. Horace Walpole inherited the house and used it until he moved to Berkeley Square, where he died on March 2, 1797. Berkeley Square House covers the site of his last town residence.

'I do not believe there ever existed so masterly a genius', said Walpole of Thomas Chatterton, who came to seek his fortune in London. One disappointment after another dogged his efforts, and on the morning of August 25, 1770, he was found dead in his room with a nearly empty phial of arsenic in his hand. He was given a pauper's funeral in the burial ground of the Shoe Lane workhouse, very near the spot where another poet, Richard Lovelace, had died in 1658. The site of the house where Chatterton died, 39 Brooke Street, Holborn, is marked with a tablet.

The quiet, sad figure of William Cowper seems out of place in London, but he was educated at Westminster School, where he was a contemporary of Warren Hastings and Charles Churchill, and referred in later years to the latter as 'the great Churchill'. He entered the Middle Temple in 1748, and was called to the Bar. The madness that was to recur throughout his life began during his period of study; anxiety about securing a particular post deepened his depression, and in 1763 he entered a madhouse in St Albans. There is a memorial to him in the Warriors' Chapel (sometimes referred to as 'Little Poets' Corner') in Westminster Abbey.

One of the greatest writers born in London is William Blake. The son of a hosier, he was born on November 28, 1757, at 28 Broad Street, Golden Square, now 74 Broadwick Street (I, D3,73). The house survives and is marked with a tablet. He was christened in St James's church, Piccadilly. He lived in Broad Street until 1782, returning two years later to set up as a print-seller at the adjoining house. From 1788 until 1793 Blake lived in Poland Street, where he wrote *Songs of Innocence* and *The Marriage of Heaven and Hell* and designed the illustrations for the Book of Job. Then he moved to Hercules Buildings, Lambeth, where he lived for seven years; his house there was demolished in 1920, and a memorial tablet is affixed to Blake House which occupies the site. For three years Blake lived out of London, and then in 1803 settled at 17 South Molton Street (I, D3,80, marked by a tablet), where he lived for seventeen years. His last years were spent at Fountain Court in the Strand, which stood beyond the east side of the Savoy Hotel, but it has been entirely built over and the name has disappeared. 'Nothing could exceed the squalid air both of the apartment and his dress,' said Crabb Robinson the diarist. Blake died there on August 12, 1827, and is buried in Bunhill Fields Burial Ground. There is a medallion of him in the crypt of St Paul's Cathedral, and a bust by Epstein in Poets' Corner.

That pugnacious character William Cobbett, who called London 'a hellish and all-devouring wen', as a youth spent a few months as copying clerk to an attorney in Gray's Inn. In 1800 he ran a bookshop in Pall Mall, and three years later when living in Fleet Street began *Cobbett's Weekly Political Register*. In 1820 he started a seed farm in Kensington and farmed also at Barn Elms on the east side of Putney. He had a house whose site is covered by the railway station in Kensington High Street.

Wordsworth, not a Londoner in any usual sense, often visited the capital. The seventh book of *The Prelude* is headed 'Residence in London' and records the impressions of the young Wordsworth. A later visit resulted in 'The Reverie of Poor Susan', in which a country girl is depicted in St Peter's churchyard, Cheapside, dreaming of her country home. It seems to be generally assumed that the singing thrush of the poem was in the old tree (which may date from Wordsworth's time) in the churchyard, but the thrush Poor Susan heard was a caged bird. Wordsworth's visits of 1802–3 are especially memorable because they inspired some great sonnets, including that 'Composed upon Westminster Bridge'. He is commemorated in Poets' Corner with a statue.

His friend Coleridge was educated at Christ's Hospital (the Bluecoat

School, then in Newgate Street). Two of Coleridge's London residences have survived and are marked with tablets: 7 Addison Bridge Place, Hammersmith (I, C4,25, 7 Portland Place in his time), and 3 The Grove, Highgate (I, D1,29), where he lived the last eighteen years of his life. The site of another residence, 71 Berners Street, is marked with a tablet. Many famous people went to hear Coleridge talk at Highgate; Hazlitt said that he 'talked on for ever; and you wished him to talk on for ever', but Carlyle was not so flattering. He died at Highgate on July 25, 1834, and was buried in a vault of Old Highgate Chapel, which became enclosed in the crypt of the chapel of Highgate Grammar School when its buildings were erected here. The tomb was for long neglected, but in 1961 Coleridge's remains were reinterred in St Michael's church on Highgate Hill (I, D1,28), where he also worshipped. There is a bust of him, the gift of an American admirer, in Poets' Corner.

Charles Lamb, a friend of Wordsworth and Coleridge, was born on February 10, 1775, in Crown Office Row, Inner Temple, destroyed in the last war. He and Coleridge were contemporaries at Christ's Hospital, affectionately recalled in the essay 'Christ's Hospital Five and Thirty Years Ago'. His first employment was in South Sea House, and then for thirty-three years worked in the East India Company's offices, the site of which is now covered by Lloyd's offices, Leadenhall Street. The great tragedy of Lamb's life, when his sister Mary killed her mother in a fit of insanity, occurred at a house whose site is occupied by Holy Trinity Church, Kingsway. During the years 1801-17 Lamb lived in Inner Temple Lane, but the houses he occupied disappeared long ago. There is a memorial to him in Inner Temple Gardens. One London residence of his, though it was in the country in his time, has survived— 64 Duncan Terrace in Islington (I, E3), formerly Colebrook Cottage, and it is marked with a tablet.

Hazlitt, who has recorded the feast of fun and wit at Lamb's Inner Temple lodgings, was married at the church of St Andrew, Holborn, when Lamb was present and Mary Lamb a bridesmaid. A tablet on 6 Bouverie Street marks the site of a house in which he lived before moving to his last London home at 6 Frith Street (I, D3,70), which survives, marked with a tablet. There he died on September 18, 1830, and

Lamb was at his bedside. His last words were, 'Well, I've had a happy life', which one would not have suspected without his testimony. He was buried in the churchyard of St Anne, Wardour Street (I, D3,69).

Leigh Hunt, like Coleridge and Lamb, but a little later, was at Christ's Hospital. An attack on the Prince Regent in his paper *The Examiner* resulted in three years' imprisonment in Horsemonger Lane Gaol, which used to stand on the south side of Trinity Square, Southwark. Leigh Hunt Street in Southwark commemorates him. For some years he lived in the Vale of Health, Hampstead, where he met Shelley for the first time and where Keats and Shelley first met. For seven years he lived at 22 Upper Cheyne Row, Chelsea (I, D4,1, marked with a tablet). Carlyle described Hunt's household there as 'unutterable . . . a poetical Tinkerdom, without parallel even in literature'. In his last years he lived at 32 Edwardes Square, Kensington, a house that survives but is unmarked, and his residence in Kensington evoked a pleasant book on *The Old Court Suburb*. His last home was in Cornwall Road, Hammersmith, where Nathaniel Hawthorne visited him, as recorded in *Our Old Home*. Whilst staying with friends in Putney High Street he died there on August 28, 1859, and was buried in Kensal Green cemetery (I, C3,38).

Byron, who was one of Hunt's visitors in prison, was born in Holles Street (between Oxford Circus and Cavendish Square) on January 22, 1788. After leaving Cambridge, he took lodgings in St James's Street, returning to them after his travels in the Near East, and the site is occupied by a modern building at No. 7 called Byron House. It was here that he awoke to find himself famous after the publication of *Childe Harold*. His only London residence to survive is Albany, Piccadilly (I, D3,75), where he lived at No. 2A before his marriage. However, two houses intimately connected with him have survived. One is Dover House in Whitehall, in use as the Scottish Office (it was Melbourne House in his time), where he all but lived for nine months during his affair with Lady Caroline Lamb. The other is the office, at 50A Albemarle Street (I, D3,82), of John Murray the publishers, where Byron and Scott met for the first time, and where many Byron relics are preserved. His biographer Thomas Moore, who had entered the Middle Temple in 1799, soon forsook law for the softer delights of society drawing-rooms, where he won his way with his singing and playing, as he had done in Dublin. He first met Byron in 1811, after Moore had requested an explanation of a slighting reference in 'English Bards and Scotch Reviewers'. One of Moore's residences, 28 Bury Street (I, D3,76), St James's, has survived and is marked with a tablet.

Shelley took lodgings at 15 Poland Street (I, D3,72) after his expulsion from Oxford; the house, somewhat altered since his day, is still standing, but has no tablet. After separating from his first wife, Shelley lived with Mary Godwin for three months at 26 Nelson Square, off Blackfriars Road (I, E4,60); it is marked with a tablet. In December 1816 Harriet Westbrook's body was found in the Serpentine, and soon afterwards Shelley was married to Mary Godwin at St Mildred's Church, Bread Street, which was destroyed in the last war. He was in London for a brief stay before leaving for Italy, where he remained for the last four years of his life. He was drowned in the Gulf of Spezia in July 1822, and after cremation (Byron and Leigh Hunt were present) his ashes were interred in the Protestant cemetery at Rome, near the grave of Keats.

Keats himself was born above his father's livery stable in Moorfields on October 29 or 31, 1795. A tablet on the Moorgate Tavern, 85 Moorgate, marks the site of his birthplace. Except for Robert Bridges, Keats appears to be the only English poet who studied medicine at a London hospital—Guy's Hospital, Southwark. Among his London residences, the only one to survive is Wentworth Place, now called Keats House and Museum,* Keats Grove, Hampstead (I, D2,22), where he lived most of the time during 1818-20, the period of his greatest work. Early in 1820 Keats's consumption became fully evident, and in September he left for Italy with his friend Joseph Severn, soon became rapidly worse, and died in Severn's arms in Rome on February 23, 1821. He was buried in the Protestant cemetery in Rome. His rooms in Rome are preserved as a memorial.

Thomas De Quincey's acquaintance with London, not a long one, was profoundly important in its results on his work. He first came to

* Open weekdays 10 a.m. to 6 p.m. (closed on Boxing Day). Contains some of Keats's letters and own books, his notebook when a medical student, other personal relics, first editions, and relics of Fanny Brawne.

London when aged fifteen, and two years later, when disappointed of money from guardians, lodged in a miserable room in Greek Street, Soho, where he found 'a poor, friendless child, apparently ten years old'. During the day he wandered about and made friends with outcast women. One, called Ann, was particularly kind to him; he tried, unsuccessfully, to find her after a few days' absence from London, and the memory of her haunted him all his life. The episode provides some of the most moving passages in *The Confessions of an English Opium-Eater*. It was during a vacation spent in London during his Oxford days that he first took opium, to provide relief from toothache. After a long residence in the Lake District he returned to London in 1821 to seek work, and lodged at the premises of Bohn the publisher in York Street (now Tavistock Street), Covent Garden. There he wrote the first version of the *Confessions*, and *Murder Considered as One of the Fine Arts*, both of which appeared in the *London Magazine*.

Another contributor to the same periodical, who became acquainted with De Quincey, was Thomas Hood. He was born at 31 Poultry on May 23, 1799, the son of a tailor, and a tablet marks the site of the house. He was a Londoner all his life, and lived at numerous addresses. Tablets commemorating him at two surviving houses can be seen at 1-3 Robert Street, Adelphi (I, E3,89), and 28 Finchley Road (I, C2). He moved into the latter house in 1844, and died there on May 3, 1845. He is buried in Kensal Green cemetery (I, C3,38). There died the same year, on February 22 in Green Street, Grosvenor Square, the witty and lovable Sydney Smith. During his first period of residence in London, when for a time he was in very straitened circumstances, he lived for three years (1803-6) at 8, now 14 Doughty Street (I, E3,55 marked by a tablet). He became a canon of St Paul's in 1831, and thereafter lived much in London. He is buried in Kensal Green cemetery.

Foreign writers have occasionally stayed in London—we have already mentioned Voltaire—and Heinrich Heine was one of them. In 1827 he stayed three months at 32 Craven Street (I, E3,79, marked by a tablet), two doors away from the house which had been occupied by Benjamin Franklin. Heine found London expensive and somewhat oppressive to his hypersensitive nature.

From a foreign to one of the most English of writers, Jane Austen, who had little acquaintance with London. She knew something about Sackville Street, Piccadilly, and introduced it into *Sense and Sensibility* as the locality of the jeweller's where the Miss Dashwoods accidentally met their brother, a person 'of strong, natural, sterling insignificance'. Miss Austen stayed for a few weeks in 1814 with her brother at 10 Henrietta Street, Covent Garden, a house that has survived but is unmarked. Another and slightly later but very different kind of novelist, Frederick Marryat, was a native of London, being born in Great George Street, Westminster, on July 10, 1792. Whilst at sea Marryat wrote his first book, *The Naval Officer*, which was a very great success and was followed by many other stories. Marryat lived much in London, and one of his residences, 3 Spanish Place, Marylebone (I, D3,50), has survived and is marked with a tablet.

Most of the great Victorian writers were very much connected with London. In his infancy Macaulay's parents lived in Birchin Lane in the City, and then in 1805 moved to 5 The Pavement, Clapham (I, D5). For a long period (1840-56) Macaulay had chambers in Albany, Piccadilly where much of the *History of England* was written, and then moved to Holly Lodge, Camden Hill, Kensington, where he remained until his death on December 28, 1859. He is buried in Poets' Corner. Both 5 The Pavement and Holly Lodge are marked with tablets.

There was uncertainty at one time about Disraeli's birthplace, but eventually 22 Theobald's Road (I, E3, formerly King's Road) was found to be the correct locality, and a tablet marks it. He was born on December 21, 1804, and his birth is recorded in the registry of births at the Spanish and Portuguese Synagogue in the City. When he was Prime Minister he lived at 10 Downing Street. The last house purchased by Disraeli in London, 19 Curzon Street (I, D3,85, marked by a tablet), was where he died on April 19, 1881. There is a memorial to him in the north transept of Westminster Abbey.

Now we turn to two dour social critics, one English and the other Scottish. John Ruskin was born on February 8, 1819, at 54 Hunter Street, Brunswick Square (I, E3,56, the house survives and is marked by a tablet), where he lived until 1823, when his parents moved to Herne Hill, and in 1843 to Denmark Hill, Camberwell, where Ruskin lived until 1872. At Herne Hill he wrote most of the first volume of *Modern Painters*. These last two houses have been demolished; a tablet on a post in the front garden of 26 Herne Hill marks the site of Ruskin's home. He is commemorated by Ruskin Park, near the site of the Denmark Hill home, and there is a tablet monument in the church of St Paul, Herne Hill.

Our other social critic, Carlyle, first visited London in 1824, then again in 1831 to find a publisher for *Sartor Resartus*. He and his wife stayed for six months at 4 (now 33) Ampton Street (I, E3,57, it has a tablet), returning there for a short while in 1834. Later that year, thanks to a suggestion from Leigh Hunt, they went to live at 5 (now 24) Cheyne Row, Chelsea (I, D4,2). Now known as Carlyle's House,* it is one of the great literary shrines of London. There he lived for forty-six years, writing in a sound-proof room at the top of the house; denouncing, prophesying, very rarely laughing—Sydney Smith was one of the few people who made him laugh—a dyspeptic, morose 'sage of Chelsea' (a misnomer, for Carlyle was anything but a sage) visited by a great many distinguished people. Tennyson, Dickens, Thackeray and Emerson were among the large number of writers who called upon him. Oliver Wendell Holmes, who visited the house after Carlyle's death, said that 'the dingy, three-story brick house was far from attractive'. Froude paints a different picture, at any rate of the interior. In that house Carlyle died on February 4, 1881. A statue of him stands in Chelsea Embankment Gardens.

James Anthony Froude, whose revelations of the Carlyle *ménage* shocked the world, came to live in London in 1860, and his residence from 1865 to 1892, 5 Onslow Gardens, Kensington (I, C4,41), is marked with a tablet. The historian W. E. H. Lecky, a friend of Froude (but they differed strongly over the interpretation of Irish history), lived at No. 38 in the same square from 1871 until his death there on October 22, 1903. A tablet marks his residence. Another historian, J. R. Green, was curate of St Barnabas's in King Square, Goswell Road, and then at Hoxton, from 1860 to 1866, when he became vicar of St Philip's,

---

* Open weekdays (except Tuesday) 10 a.m. to 1 p.m., 2 to 6 p.m., Sunday, 2 to 6 p.m. or dusk if earlier. The house is a museum full of personal relics, including fragments of manuscripts.

Stepney. His old vicarage in Newark Street (I, F3,63) is marked by a tablet. Ill health obliged him to give up clerical work in 1869, when he became librarian at Lambeth, and resided at 4 Beaumont Street, Marylebone, where *A Short History of the English People* was written. His house was demolished in 1925, and there is a tablet on the present building.

The love-story of the Brownings is one of the romances of literature and of London life. Robert Browning was born in Southampton Street, Camberwell, on May 7, 1812. The cottage has been demolished, but a tablet at 179 Southampton Way is near the site of the birthplace and of the adjacent cottage to which Browning's family moved soon after his birth. Browning lived in Camberwell until about 1835, when the family moved to Hatcham until 1846. Meanwhile Elizabeth Barrett and her family about 1835 settled in London at 74 (now 99) Gloucester Place (I, D3,53, marked by a tablet). In 1838 they moved to 50 Wimpole Street, (I, D3,51, demolished; tablet is on the present house) though for three years Elizabeth Barrett was away at Torquay. Browning wrote to her at Wimpole Street, declaring his love before he had seen her, and soon afterwards came to visit her frequently. He planned to get her away from her domineering, selfish and ill-tempered father. On September 12, 1846, they were married secretly in the parish church of St Marylebone, Marylebone Road (I, D3,35), and a week later sped away to Paris. After residence in Florence for five years they lived successively in Devonshire Street, Welbeck Street, Dorset Street, and again Devonshire Street, interspersed with residence on the Continent, mainly in Florence. There, at their apartments in the Casa Guidi, Mrs Browning died on June 29, 1861, and was buried in the English cemetery.

Browning returned to London, and after a short spell in lodgings, settled at 19 Warwick Crescent, Paddington (I, C3,49), by the canal (the house is marked with a tablet), where he lived until 1887. His final London home was in De Vere Gardens, Kensington. He died at the Palazzo Rezzonico, Venice, on December 12, 1889, and is buried in Poets' Corner. St Marylebone Parish Church has a Browning Memorial Chapel. The Congregational Chapel in Browning (formerly York) Street, Walworth, now the Browning Settlement, where he was christened, possesses a few relics.

Wimpole Street is associated also with Tennyson, for at the home of Hallam the historian (No. 67, marked with a tablet) Tennyson used to visit his friend Arthur Henry Hallam. For a time Tennyson and his family had rooms at Mornington Crescent, and a later stay of about a year was at 225 Hampstead Road, destroyed in the last war. He first met Wordsworth, at Hampstead, when taken there by his friend Aubrey de Vere. Tennyson's most interesting connexion with London is celebrated in 'Will Waterproof's Monologue', in which he refers to the 'plump head-waiter at the Cock', which however is not the present Cock Tavern in Fleet Street, but a tavern whose site is occupied by the West End Branch of the Bank of England. Tennyson also frequented the famous Cheshire Cheese. A younger contemporary poet, Matthew Arnold, had no particular love of London, but lived for several years until 1868 at 2 Chester Square, Pimlico (I, D4,87), until 'driven out' as he said, 'partly by the number of our children, partly by the necessity of a better school for the boys'.

Only a few of the considerable group of Victorian novelists were born in London, one of them being Edward Bulwer Lytton, who was born in Baker Street on May 25, 1803. He resided much in London, and *The Last Days of Pompeii* was written in Hertford Street, Mayfair. He died at Torquay, and is buried in the chapel of St Edmund, Westminster Abbey.

Mrs Gaskell, whose maiden name was Stevenson, was born on September 29, 1810, in a house called Lindsey Row, now 93 Cheyne Walk, Chelsea (I, D4, marked by a tablet). In the following year her parents moved to Beaufort Street, where her mother died after a few months, and she was moved to the care of an aunt in Knutsford, Cheshire. She paid visits to London in later years, but does not belong to the literary history of the capital.

The London associations of Dickens need a volume to themselves, and indeed several works have been devoted to the subject. In order to know something of the life of the underworld and of the shabby-genteel in central London, the City and the East End during the earlier Victorian period, and the atmosphere and topography of London and its river, it is necessary to be thoroughly acquainted with the work of Dickens. His London residences were numerous, and we must content ourselves with the one survival and the marked sites of some others. When he was ten his parents came to live in Bayham Street, Camden Town (the site is marked by a tablet), moving after two years to Gower Street. Dickens went to school at Wellington House Academy in Hampstead Road (I, D3), which survives though shorn of the actual schoolroom which was demolished when the railway was built. The house, marked by a tablet, is in such a shabby state that it is unlikely to survive for long. During his father's incarceration in the Marshalsea Prison, Dickens was lodging in Lant Street, Southwark. The Charles Dickens School in that street, probably on the site of the boy Dickens's miserable lodging, has a commemorative bust. A tablet on Prudential Buildings, Holborn, records the fact that it stands on the site of Furnival's Inn, where Dickens lodged during 1834-7, and where most of *Pickwick Papers* was written. The George and Vulture tavern (in Castle Court between Cornhill and Lombard Street), so familiar to readers of *Pickwick*, is still in existence, though it has ceased to be a tavern.

From Furnival's Inn Dickens went to 48 Doughty Street (I, E3,55), which is now called Dickens House* and the only survivor of his twenty or so London lodgings and residences. In Doughty Street he completed *Pickwick* and wrote *Oliver Twist* and *Nicholas Nickleby*, and by 1839 was prosperous enough to afford a larger house, 1 Devonshire Terrace, Regent's Park, where he lived for twelve years and which was most unfortunately demolished as recently as 1957. Ferguson House, Marylebone Road, which covers the site, has a mural relief showing a portrait of Dickens and some characters from his novels. Even after he bought Gad's Hill Place in Kent Dickens continued to rent houses in London, but in later years he began to tire of the great city which had been the very stuff of his existence, and said in a letter that 'London is a vile place. . . . I have never taken to it kindly since I lived abroad.' Contrary to his own wishes he was buried in London, and his remains are in Poets' Corner. His collaborator, Wilkie Collins (author of *The Moonstone*, one of the best, if not *the* best, of all detective stories), was

---

* Open weekdays 10 a.m. to 12.30 p.m., 2 to 5 p.m.; closed on Bank Holidays. A veritable museum of Dickens relics, and includes parts of the manuscripts of *Nicholas Nickleby* and *Oliver Twist*.

born in Tavistock Square on January 8, 1824. A tablet marks 65 (formerly 90) Gloucester Place (I, D3,53), where he resided for many years. He died in Wimpole Street on September 23, 1889, and was buried in Kensal Green cemetery (I, C3,38).

As Dickens is the supreme novelist of poorer London, so Thackeray is the supreme novelist of fashionable London. He was born in Calcutta on July 8, 1811, and his first acquaintance with London was when sent in 1822 to Charterhouse School, which appears in *The Newcomes* as 'Greyfriars' and in *Vanity Fair* as 'Whitefriars'. Thackeray had several London addresses before settling at 16 (then 13) Young Street (I, C4,45) in 1846, and soon afterwards he first gained the general public with *The Snob Papers*, which became *The Book of Snobs*. During residence here he wrote *Vanity Fair, Pendennis* and *Henry Esmond*. In 1853 he moved to 36 Onslow Square (I, C4,41), where *The Newcomes* was completed, *The Virginians* written and *Roundabout Papers* begun. In 1861 Thackeray made his final move, to 2 Palace Green (I, C4,44), a house he himself designed in neo-Georgian style long before there was a Georgian revival. There he died suddenly on Christmas Eve, 1863. He was buried, not in Westminster Abbey as one would expect, but in Kensal Green cemetery. All the three houses mentioned above are in Kensington, and are marked with tablets.

Anthony Trollope, who knew Thackeray and considered him the first novelist of his time, was born at 6 Keppel Street, Bloomsbury (the house has not survived) on April 24, 1815. Most of his life until middle-age was spent outside London, but in 1872 he settled at 39 Montagu Square (I, D3,54), which is extant and marked by a tablet. With his usual industry Trollope managed to produce a great deal of work during his eight years in that house, including two of his greatest novels, *Dr Wortle's School* and *The Way We Live Now*, as well as his *Autobiography*. He left in 1880 to live near Petersfield. After a journey to Ireland he was staying at Garland's Hotel in London when he had a stroke; he was moved to a house in Welbeck Street, and died there a month later on December 6, 1882. He was buried in Kensal Green cemetery. Another admirer of Thackeray, Charlotte Brontë, was several times in London, and met Thackeray in 1849. A carved wooden panel on the door of the Cornhill Insurance Company, 32 Cornhill, commemorates the association of Thackeray and Charlotte Brontë with the firm of Smith, Elder, whose offices were at that address.

That peripatetic romantic, George Borrow—who figures among our novelists here, but whose delightful romanticized autobiographic writings are not novels—had a singularly long acquaintance with London. He first arrived in 1824, bent on authorship, and his adventures are described in the early chapters of *Lavengro*. He left about a year later, and revisited London several times before settling in 1860 at 22 Hereford Square, Kensington (I, C4,42, marked by a tablet). His wife died here in 1869. In 1874 Borrow returned to Oulton, where he died, and is buried with his wife in Brompton cemetery (I, C4,30).

Charles Reade, truly a novelist and almost as strange a character as Borrow, entered Lincoln's Inn in 1836, and was called to the Bar, but belongs to that numerous group of writers who have forsaken law for literature. He lived for fourteen years in Knightsbridge, where he helped waifs, strays and necessitous middle-class folk and harboured a menagerie of dogs, gazelles and hares. In 1882 he moved to Shepherd's Bush, where he died on April 11, 1884, and was buried in Willesden cemetery (I, B2,26).

George Eliot, who settled in London in 1851, lived in or near the capital for the rest of her life. During 1859-60 she lived at Holly Lodge, now 31 Wimbledon Park Road, Wandsworth (I, C6,61), a house that survives and is marked with a tablet, and where she wrote *The Mill on the Floss*. The most famous residence connected with her, the Priory in North Bank, St John's Wood, was demolished long ago. The house became one of the great intellectual and literary centres of London, and many brilliant and famous people were gathered there. Much of *Middlemarch*, her greatest novel, was written in that house. Her final residence, where she lived only a few months, was 4 Cheyne Walk, Chelsea (I, D4, marked by a tablet). There she died on December 22, 1880, and is buried in Highgate cemetery (I, D1,27).

The Pre-Raphaelites and their friends were prominent in the artistic and literary life of Victorian London. Of the original three members of the brotherhood, one, Dante Gabriel Rossetti, was a writer as well as an artist. Rossetti was born on May 12, 1828, at 38 Charlotte Street, Portland Place, where his sister Christina was also born on December

15, 1830. The house and the street name have disappeared, and the site is now 110 Hallam Street, on which there is a tablet. For a brief period in 1851 Rossetti had rooms at 17 Red Lion Square (I, E3,32), where William Morris and Burne-Jones shared rooms during 1856-8. A tablet records the associations. After a ten-year residence in Blackfriars Rossetti went in 1862 to 16 Cheyne Walk, Chelsea (I, D4, marked by a tablet), a large house which he filled with quaint oak furniture and many fine ornaments, including a great quantity of blue china. The garden he filled with very strange animals. After several years here his health declined, and when desperately ill in 1882 was removed to Birchington in Kent. His sister Christina, who in spite of her limited range is the greater poet, lived from 1877 until her death on December 29, 1894, at 30 Torrington Square (I, D3,33), which survives and is marked by a tablet. She is buried in Highgate cemetery. William Morris's chief association with London is at Kelmscott House, Upper Mall, Hammersmith (I, B4,24, marked by a tablet), which he took in 1878. There he installed the famous Kelmscott Press in 1890, and died there on October 3, 1896.

There is a somewhat indistinct story that Meredith was invited to join Rossetti at 16 Cheyne Walk, but after one night's residence found Rossetti's Bohemian habits too much for him. Meredith had first come to London in 1844, when he was articled to a solicitor, but before long preferred the prospects of journalism. He lived for a time in Hobury Street, Chelsea, where he completed *The Ordeal of Richard Feverel*. From 1862 until 1894 Meredith was reader to Chapman and Hall, coming up once a week from the country to interview authors.

Swinburne did live on and off for two years (1862-4) with Rossetti at 16 Cheyne Walk. He was born on April 5, 1837, in Chester Street, Grosvenor Square. When an infant he was removed to the family home in the Isle of Wight, and saw little of London until he took rooms near Russell Place in 1860. After leaving the Rossetti *ménage* he lived for some years in Dorset Street, Portman Square, followed by a six-year residence in Great James Street, Bloomsbury. His health failing, he went in 1879 to his friend Theodore Watts-Dunton at The Pines, 11 Putney Hill (I, C5), which is marked by a tablet. By now the volatile, elf-like genius who had shocked the literary world was a spent force, and his poetry a mere imitation of itself. The Watts-Dunton-Swinburne household is delightfully described by Max Beerbohm in his essay 'No. 2 The Pines', and Arnold Bennet in a little-known passage in *Books and Persons* describes the impact that the sight of Swinburne walking on Putney Hill had upon him. Swinburne died at The Pines on April 10, 1909.

Four nineteenth-century American writers have connexions with London. Edgar Allan Poe, whose mother was English, was educated during 1816-17 at a school in Sloane Street, and during 1817-20 at the Manor House School in Stoke Newington. It stood on the north side of Church Street, and the Central Library near by commemorates him with a tablet. Nathaniel Hawthorne stayed in 1856 at 4 Pond Road, Blackheath (I, H5, marked by a tablet), and has recorded his impressions of Blackheath, Greenwich Hospital and English life in the neighbourhood in the chapter on 'A London Suburb' in *Our Old Home*. Bret Harte appears to be a unique case of an American writer—this is not to forget Henry James, a special case—who spent his final years in England. When he retired from the U.S. Consulship at Glasgow in 1885 he settled at Hamilton Terrace, St John's Wood, moving later to 74 Lancaster Gate, Hyde Park Gardens (the house has survived, but is unmarked). A tablet on 23 Tedworth Square, Chelsea (I, D4,3), records Mark Twain's stay there in 1896-7, during the period when he was on a world lecture tour following the loss of all his money.

Henry James was by birth American, acquired British nationality shortly before he died, and was intellectually cosmopolitan. When wandering about Europe he decided that he would settle in Paris, but changed his mind and took up residence in Bolton Street, Piccadilly, in 1876. There he wrote *Portrait of a Lady* and *The Princess Casamassima*. After ten years he moved to 34 De Vere Gardens, Kensington (I, C4, marked by a tablet, and which in his time was 13 De Vere Mansions). In 1898 he took a house in Rye, Sussex, but spent his winters in De Vere Gardens until 1901, when he took up winter quarters at the Reform Club. During this period he produced, among other works, that macabre masterpiece *The Turn of the Screw*. His final winter quarters were in Cheyne Walk, Chelsea, from 1912 until his death there on

February 28, 1916. His body was cremated and a commemorative tablet placed in Chelsea Old Church.

Wits, satirists and humourists are not lacking from the literary associations of later Victorian London. A tablet at 30 Seymour Place, Marylebone (I, D3,52), marks a residence of Edward Lear, who was born at Highgate on May 12, 1812. After much travelling and painting throughout Europe, Asia and Africa he spent his last five years at San Remo, where he died on January 29, 1888, and is buried there. George Du Maurier, author of *Trilby*, was born in Paris on March 6, 1834. In childhood he lived for a few years in Devonshire Terrace in the house later occupied by Dickens. Two of his residences (marked by tablets) have survived: 91 Great Russell Street (I, E3,34), where he lived for four years, and New Grove House, 28 Hampstead Grove (I, C2,23), where he lived during 1874-95. He died at his home in Oxford Square, Paddington, on October 6, 1896, and was buried in the parish church-yard at Hampstead.

W. S. Gilbert was born at 17 Southampton Street, Strand (the house has long disappeared), on November 18, 1836. He graduated at King's College, London University, obtained a commission in the Gordon Highlanders and a post in the Civil Service in the same year, having meanwhile entered the Middle Temple. He was called to the Bar, but found contributions to periodicals more remunerative than the law, and so began the course that was to end in magnificent collaboration with Arthur Sullivan. His London residence of 1883-90, 39 Harrington Gardens, Kensington (I, C4,43), survives and is marked by a tablet. No tablet records the thirty-eight years' residence of Samuel Butler, the master-satirist of the later Victorian era, at Clifford's Inn, Fleet Street. Butler settled there in 1864 on his return from New Zealand, and most of his work was written there. He died on June 18, 1902, in a nursing home in St John's Wood, and his body was cremated at Woking. Butler's chambers were demolished, together with the rest of Clifford's Inn, in 1935.

Among later Victorian writers (and as a novelist he was the last of the great Victorians) Thomas Hardy almost surprisingly has London connexions. He entered the office of Blomfield the architect at 8 Adelphi, in 1862, returning to his native Dorset five years later. This terrace of famous associations was demolished in 1936, and Hardy's name appears among others on a tablet on the present building. Hardy returned to the London area in 1874, when he lived at Surbiton for two years, and again in 1878, when he lived at 172 Trinity Road, Tooting (I, D5, marked by a tablet). Here he wrote *The Trumpet Major* and *A Laodicean*, and left in 1881. His ashes were interred in Poets' Corner.

W. H. Hudson, to whom the English countryside was as dear as it was to Hardy, though he did not regard it as an aspect of mankind's sinister cosmic environment, came to London in 1874 from Argentina, where he was born at Quilmes near Buenos Aires on August 4, 1841. Impoverished and lonely, he married in 1876, and for the next ten years his wife ran boarding houses that failed. In 1886 Hudson moved to 40 St Luke's Road, Paddington (I, C3,47, marked by a tablet), which remained his home until his death on August 18, 1922. He is commemorated in Hyde Park by a bird sanctuary and Epstein's representation of the character Rima from *Green Mansions*. His friend Edward Thomas, a very much younger man, and also a delightful writer on the English countryside, was born in Lambeth on March 8, 1878. He was educated at St Paul's School, and his home from childhood until young manhood, 61 Shelgate Road, Battersea (I, D5), is marked with a tablet.

A very remarkable group of Anglo-Irish writers, varying widely in temperament, descended on London in the later years of the Victorian era. It was in London that Oscar Wilde achieved his finest in writing and in conversational wit. On leaving Oxford in 1878 he came to London, and after marriage in 1884 settled at 34 (formerly 16) Tite Street, Chelsea (I, D4,4, marked by a tablet), which remained his home until 1895. He was a frequenter of the Café Royal, which has seen many famous people in its rooms, and there crossed swords with Whistler, the most famous wit of his day until Oscar asserted his own ascendancy. Alas! all ended in disgrace and imprisonment through his crowning folly in bringing an action against the Marquess of Queensberry. George Moore was the nearest to Wilde in his attitude to life and literature among the group of Anglo-Irish writers we are discussing. He had lived in London on and off since young manhood, and in 1911 went to live at 121 Ebury Street (I, D4, marked by a tablet), where he remained until his death there on January 21, 1933. There he wrote his two finest books, *The Brook Kerith* and *Héloïse and Abélard*. A fine picture of Moore and his domestic surroundings is given in Geraint Goodwin's *Conversations with George Moore*.

Bernard Shaw, at the age of twenty, joined his mother in lodgings in Victoria (now Netherton) Grove, off the Fulham Road. For many years he struggled to gain a bare existence, and it was not until he began to contribute to the *Pall Mall Gazette* in 1885 that he emerged from poverty. He went from one lodging to another—in Fitzroy Street, Osnaburgh Street and Fitzroy Square, until his marriage in 1898, when he took a flat at 10 Adelphi Terrace, which no longer exists, but his name is on a tablet on the present building. In 1906 Shaw acquired a house in Hertfordshire, but continued to use the Adelphi flat and 4 Whitehall Court to which he moved in 1927.

W. B. Yeats, the youngest of this group, had the earliest acquaintance with London; his family moved from Dublin in 1867, when he was only two, to 23 Fitzroy Road, Regent's Park (I, D2,59, marked by a tablet). There he lived for seven years, and the Yeats family continued to live at various addresses in London until 1881, returning six years later. As a young man Yeats met William Morris, Wilde and Shaw, as well as other writers. His 'Lake Isle of Innisfree' was written in London.

The unfortunate Francis Thompson arrived in London in 1885 to seek a living, obtained menial work, was tortured by neuralgia and took to opium. The descent from poverty to destitution was all too easy, but Wilfred Meynell (in whose periodical *Merry England* some of Thompson's work had appeared) befriended him and induced him to enter a hospital. For many years he was out of London, returning in 1907, but had to enter the Hospital of St Elizabeth and St John in St John's Wood, where he died of consumption on November 13, 1907. He is buried in the Catholic cemetery at Kensal Green (I, C3,38). One of Francis Thompson's haunts in his earlier London sojourn was the Skiddaw public house in Elgin Avenue. His friend Alice Meynell, a poet and essayist of great charm, is commemorated by a tablet at 47 Palace Gate, Kensington (I, C4,48), a house in which she lived for fifteen years.

Coventry Patmore, a friend of Francis Thompson and Alice Meynell and one of the first to recognize Thompson's genius, is commemorated by a tablet at 14 Percy Street (I, D3,58), where he lived during 1863-4.

Our final group in this section comprises writers whose careers began towards the end of the Victorian era. The first in birth was Rudyard Kipling, who as a boy used to spend Christmas holidays with Sir Edward and Lady Burne-Jones (the latter was his aunt) at Samuel Richardson's old home in Fulham. After leaving India in 1889 he took rooms at 43 Villiers Street, Charing Cross (I, E3,78, marked by a tablet). Here he wrote *The Light that Failed* and some of the *Barrack Room Ballads* amidst the rumble of the Charing Cross trains and 'the boom of the Strand', and below him 'Harris, the Sausage King . . . for tuppence gave as much sausage and mash as would carry one from breakfast to dinner'. Ill-health obliged Kipling to quit London in 1891. The rest of his life was spent mainly in the country. He died at the Middlesex Hospital on January 18, 1936, and was buried beside Thomas Hardy in Poets' Corner. Brown's Hotel in Dover Street has a Kipling Room in commemoration of his frequent visits to the hotel.

H. G. Wells, whose outlook was strongly antithetical to Kipling's imperialism, had a great deal of connexion with London from early days. In 1884 he began studying at the Normal School (later the Royal College) of Science in South Kensington, under no less a teacher than the great T. H. Huxley, beginning brilliantly but later becoming too much absorbed in literature and politics, recovering, however, to do very well for his B.Sc. degree. Wells lived at several addresses in London: for three years he was at 17 Church Row, Hampstead, then after nearly twenty years in Essex lived in Chiltern Court Mansions in Baker Street from 1930 to 1937, when he moved to 13 Hanover Terrace, Regent's Park. He died at the last address on August 13, 1946, and his body was cremated at Golders Green. Curiously enough, none of these houses (and all have survived) has a commemorative tablet.

Arnold Bennett, often compared with Wells, for both derived from and depicted the same social stratum, arrived in London in 1889 to become clerk to a firm of solicitors in Lincoln's Inn Fields, but a few years later decided to take up journalism. Bennett's second London address, 6 Netherton Grove (now 6 Victoria Grove), where he lived during 1891-7, has survived but is unmarked. It was a formative period in his development, when he was engaged on editorship, contributions to the *Academy*, and when his first published work of fiction appeared. His residence at 75 Cadogan Square, Chelsea (I, D4,5), during 1923-30 is commemorated with a tablet. In his last few months he lived at 97 Chiltern Court Mansions, where he died on March 27, 1931.

In contrast to Wells and Bennett, John Galsworthy depicted later Victorian and Edwardian upper-middle-class commercial society. *The Man of Property*, the first novel of what became *The Forsyte Saga*, was written when he lived in Aubrey Walk, Camden Hill. After residence in Addison Road, Kensington, Galsworthy lived during 1913-18 at 1 Adelphi Terrace House, now part of 1-3 Robert Street and marked with a tablet. Then he moved to Grove Lodge, Hampstead Grove (I, C2,23, marked), where the two latter novels of *The Forsyte Saga* were written. He died at Grove Lodge on January 31, 1933, and his body was cremated at Woking. In the same Adelphi Terrace House as Galsworthy, Sir James Barrie (also noted on the tablet) occupied another flat from 1911 to the end of his life. He had had several earlier lodgings in London (he had come to try his fortune in 1885), and two of these, 133 Gloucester Road and 100 Bayswater Road (I, C3), have survived and the latter is marked with a tablet.

Owing to lack of space some literary figures connected with London have had to be omitted, but before we close this section we must mention those writers on whose former homes tablets have been placed. The tablet on 19-20 Bow Street which mentions Wycherley and Fielding mentions also Charles Sackville, sixth Earl of Dorset, of whom we shall have something to say in the next section. George Grote the historian of Greece lived latterly at 12 Savile Row, where he died, and is buried in Poets' Corner; Sir Leslie Stephen lived latterly at 22 Hyde Park Gate, where he died, and his ashes were interred in Highgate cemetery. Sir Walter Besant's last home, where he died, was Frognal End in Frognal Gardens, Hampstead, and he is buried in the parish churchyard. The once famous and slightly notorious 'Ouida' (Maria Louisa de la Ramée) lived at 11 Ravenscourt Square, Hammersmith, at the time that she was beginning her literary ventures. G. A. Henty, once immensely popular as a writer of adventure stories for boys, lived at 33 Lavender Gardens, Battersea, and is buried in Brompton cemetery.

Austin Dobson, poet and essayist, who wrote pleasantly on some of the literary associations of eighteenth-century London, lived for a time at 10 Redcliffe Street, Kensington. Also in Kensington, at 1 Marloes Road, Andrew Lang, poet, critic, historian and anthropologist, lived from 1876 to 1912. Stéphane Mallarmé in 1863 spent nine months in London, at 6 Brompton Square, in order to improve his English, mainly with the idea of reading Edgar Allan Poe, and with such success as to publish a notable translation of Poe's poems. William De Morgan, ceramic artist, inventor and novelist—he took to writing late in life, his first novel not being published until he was sixty-six—lived the last seven years at 127 Old Church Street, Chelsea, where he died. Olive Schreiner, the South African writer, came to England with the manuscript of *The Story of an African Farm*, which was recommended for publication by George Meredith. She lived at 16 Portsea Place, Paddington. Kenneth Grahame during 1901-8, when he was secretary of the Bank of England, lived at 16 Phillimore Place, Kensington, and wrote much of *The Wind in the Willows* there. Goldsworthy Lowes Dickinson, humanist, historian and a writer of delightful prose, had a London home for many years at 11 Edwardes Square, Kensington. G. K. Chesterton from about the age of five lived for over twenty years at 11 Warwick Gardens, Kensington (I, C4, 46); and Henry Handel Richardson, the expatriate Australian novelist, from 1910 to 1934 made her London home at 90 Regent's Park Road, and there wrote *The Fortunes of Richard Mahony*.

NOTE ON THE LONDON MUSEUMS

The seeker of literary associations should visit three museums in particular. The Manuscript Saloon of the British Museum (I, E3,31) exhibits many holograph manuscripts, including such great treasures as *Alice in Wonderland* with Lewis Carroll's own illustrations, Shakespeare's writing in *The Booke of Sir Thomas More* and his signature on a deed. The Victoria and Albert Museum (I, D4,40), (Room 74 West), has Dickens manuscripts and relics. The Public Record Office in Chancery Lane (I, E3,17) has the signatures of Chaucer and Shakespeare. The National Portrait Gallery in St Martin's Place (I, D3,71, behind the National Gallery) has the portraits of most British writers.

South-East England

London area: East and North
                  North-west
                  West and South-west
Windsor area
Staines area
North and East Kent
West Kent
East Sussex
Brighton area
Horsham area
Epsom to Dorking
Guildford area
North Hampshire and Reading
Winchester
Chichester and Portsmouth area
Haslemere, Midhurst and Petersfield area
Southampton and Bournemouth
Isle of Wight

LONDON AREA: EAST AND NORTH

William Morris, the son of a London broker, was born on March 24, 1834, at Elm House (no longer extant) on Clay Hill, **Walthamstow** (I, G1). About six years later his family moved to **Woodford** only a few miles away, and when Morris was fourteen they returned to Walthamstow and lived at Water House, Lloyd Park, Forest Road, which has survived and is now the William Morris Gallery.* It continued to be Morris's home until he left Oxford. At **Wanstead**, a little east of Walthamstow, there used to exist the great mansion of Robert Dudley, Earl of Leicester, visited by Pepys, Evelyn and Horace Walpole, who have all left descriptions of their visits.

At **Chigwell** (II, F2, off the A113 and about three miles north-east of Wanstead), there is the famous King's Head inn, a gabled seventeenth-century building which is the 'Maypole' of *Barnaby Rudge*, in which the building is fully described and the entire novel centres round the inn.

* Open weekdays 10 a.m. to 5 p.m. (in summer, Tuesday and Thursday times are 10 a.m. to 8 p.m.), and the first Sunday in each month, 10 a.m. to 12 noon, 2 to 5 p.m.; closed on Bank Holidays. Contains textiles, wallpapers, etc., designed by Morris and other artists of his time, but no literary relics.

Dickens knew the inn long before he wrote the novel. Arranging to meet his friend Forster there, in 1841, he said that 'Chigwell, my dear fellow, is the greatest place in the world'.

Going to the west of our present area, at **Muswell Hill** there used to exist, at the bottom of the hill, the cottage in which Thomas Moore lived in 1817. It was later called Lalla Rookh Cottage, under the mistaken impression that that poem was written there. It was, as we record later, written at Mayfield in Staffordshire. At **Southgate** (II, E2), Leigh Hunt was born on October 19, 1784. 'It is a pleasure to me to know that I was born in so sweet a village,' he says in his *Autobiography*, but it has long ceased to be a village. His birthplace was so badly damaged in the last war that it had to be demolished. In Vicarsmoor Lane, **Winchmore Hill** (which is the north-east part of Southgate) is Ross Cottage, occupied by Thomas Hood during 1829-32, and here he wrote his *Comic Almanack*.

Enfield (II, E2) and **Edmonton** (II, E2) are intimately associated with Keats and Lamb. Keats, when eight years old, was sent to a school in Enfield Town, and the station there covers its site. At first a normal boy fond of fun and fighting, after three or four years he was devoured by a passion for serious study, especially classical mythology. After his mother's death in 1810 Keats was articled to a surgeon in Edmonton. He lived with his grandmother in Church Street, and the site of the house is now covered by Keats Parade. He began to write poetry probably in his sixteenth year, and some of his poems written here appeared in his first volume, published in 1817. Keats quarrelled with his employer, and the articles were cancelled by mutual agreement.

Charles and Mary Lamb moved in 1827 to Enfield, where they had stayed before at various times, to a house in Chase Side. Soon afterwards they moved to another house in Chase Side (now called Clarendon Cottage and marked by a tablet) where they lived until 1829. They moved again in 1833, but only next door, 'twenty-five inches further from the town', Lamb said. This cottage has also survived, though altered externally, and is called Westwood Cottage from the name of the 'haberdasher in Bow Lane' with whom the Lambs lodged. Lamb missed his friends and the London he loved, and there are magnificent passages in praise of London in his letters of this period.

However, friends visited him, Coleridge, Wordsworth, Hazlitt, Leigh Hunt and Thomas Hood being among the callers. Carlyle, not exactly a friend, also called on him, and has left some unflattering reminiscences —two more dissimilar characters it were difficult to imagine. The diarist Crabb Robinson brought Landor to meet Lamb for the first time, and before they parted had become very firm friends.

In 1833 came the Lambs' last move, to the house of a Mr and Mrs Walden in Edmonton with whom Mary had stayed whenever she was ill. The house, in Church Street, has survived and is now known as Lamb Cottage. One day when he was walking to the Bell Inn at Edmonton (where John Gilpin's famous ride began) Lamb slipped and fell, wounding his face, which resulted in death from erysipelas five days later, December 27, 1834. He was buried in the churchyard of the parish church. His sister survived him thirteen years, and was buried beside him. He is commemorated inside the church with a medallion portrait, next to a portrait of Cowper, who was never here but is commemorated because of the John Gilpin association.

There are two other literary associations to record in connexion with Enfield. Walter Pater's mother brought her two sons here after her husband's death in 1842. They lived in a house in Chase Side, which has been demolished, until 1857. Frederick Marryat was at a school in Baker Street part of the time that Keats was at another school, and distinguished himself by frequently running away with the idea of going to sea.

Waltham Cross, fifteen miles north of London on the old Cambridge road, and on the route of John Gilpin's famous ride, was the home of Anthony Trollope for twelve years. He took Waltham House in 1859. It stood near the Eleanor Cross, and was demolished between the two world wars. Two of his finest novels, *The Claverings* and *The Belton Estate,* and two or three others nearly as good, including *The Last Chronicle of Barset,* were partly or wholly written here.

Two miles east of Waltham Cross is **Waltham Abbey** (II, E2) in Essex, where John Foxe (of the *Book of Martyrs*) came to reside in 1565. Because of his greater fame in former days, his house was much visited until well into the eighteenth century, but was eventually demolished. Thomas Fuller, an admirer of Foxe, was perpetual curate of Waltham Abbey during 1649-58. Whilst here he wrote much of his *Church History*, the most readable of all ecclesiastical histories, which includes a history of Waltham Abbey. Rather surprisingly we find Sheridan as a resident here, whither he was sent by his father after the affair with Elizabeth Linley in Bath and in France, so that he could pursue his studies well away from the young lady's presence. He did not stay long, arriving in August 1772 and departing for London in the following April.

It has been claimed that it was the bells of the lovely Norman abbey church here that Tennyson had in mind when he composed those magnificent stanzas in *In Memoriam* beginning 'Ring out, wild bells, to the wild sky'. Be that as it may, Tennyson and his mother and sisters lived in Beech House, **High Beech**, in the heart of Epping forest, during 1837-40. The house he lived in, almost completely rebuilt in 1850, is now called Beech Hill Park. Whilst here, Tennyson visited Fairmead, near High Beech, where John Clare was confined, and it is possible that the two poets met. The man who owned this madhouse, Dr Matthew Allen, was of a speculative turn of mind and became interested in a process, called 'Pyroglyphs', for carving wood by machinery. He interested Tennyson in the venture, and the poet invested the entire capital he possessed in it. The scheme failed after Tennyson left High Beech, and he lost all his money.

LONDON AREA: NORTH-WEST

Harrow-on-the-Hill (II, E2), with its great public school, has some remarkable associations. Richard Brinsley Sheridan was at Harrow School during 1762-8, and his name can be seen carved on a panel in the old Fourth Form Room. About ten years after leaving school he returned to live in Harrow, and was here during the earlier part of his career as a brilliantly successful playwright. His house, The Grove, is just by the north side of the churchyard, and has been a school boarding-house since 1820.

Byron, who later came to know Sheridan, entered the school in 1801, and during his first three years was unpopular and unhappy. He was one of the leaders in a revolt at the appointment of a new head-master, whom he satirized later in his *Hours of Idleness*, but a few years later apologized. There is a railed-in tomb in Harrow churchyard—the Peachey tomb, often unfortunately referred to as the Byron tomb—on which he used to while away many hours, and which he commemorated in the 'Lines Written Beneath an Elm in the Churchyard at Harrow', part of which is inscribed on the tomb. Byron left Harrow for Cambridge in 1805. His name can be seen carved on the same panel as Sheridan's, and some thin't that Byron himself carved it. His school books and some relics of his later life are preserved in the school library. Byron's illegitimate daughter Allegra died at the age of five, and Byron wanted her buried in Harrow church, but there were objections to the burial of an illegitimate child inside the church. A compromise was reached whereby she was buried beneath the porch.

By far the unhappiest of the Harrovians we have to record was Anthony Trollope. He entered in 1827, and, as he relates in his *Autobiography*, because he was a day-boarder he was not received on equal terms by the other boys in the Harrow School of those days. He was taught only Latin and Greek, and though nearly nineteen when he left, his education had been so badly neglected that he was woefully ignorant. Trollope lived for seventeen years in or near Harrow. During 1817-27 his family had a fine house called Julians on the south side of Harrow Hill; then for three years they lived in a farmhouse, Julians Hill, near their former home. Both have vanished: Julians Hill was depicted in *Orley Farm* (in which 'Hamworth' stands for Harrow) and Millais drew it for the first edition of the book. When their fortunes declined the Trollope family moved to a farmhouse at **Harrow Weald** three miles away. It was 'a wretched tumbledown farmhouse', says Trollope, and he had to walk through the three miles of dirty lanes twice a day to attend school. It is thought by some that the existing Durrant's Farm at Harrow Weald is the old Trollope home.

C. S. Calverley, a very different character, was a brilliant scholar and noted for his personal charm and athletic feats during his years here (1846-50). Some brilliant Latin verses secured him the Balliol scholarship in 1850. Another brilliant classical scholar, but uninterested in games, was J. A. Symonds, who during his time here (1854-8) studied intensively but without the success attained by Calverley, and was a shy, retiring boy. John Galsworthy, who did not shine particularly in studies, became a monitor, captain of football, and distinguished himself in athletics.

Sir Winston Churchill, with his usual verve and candour, has described his Harrow days in *My Early Life*. Whilst still at Harrow, the late G. M. Trevelyan had determined to become an historian and to write the history of the reign of Queen Anne, which his great-uncle Lord Macaulay contemplated but never carried out. Matthew Arnold, who was not educated at Harrow, lived at Byron House on Byron Hill from 1868 to 1873. He informed his mother that the 'old countryfied look of the house' pleased him. Harrow School life has been depicted in H. A. Vachell's *The Hill*.

W. S. Gilbert lived at **Harrow Weald** on the edge of the common in the fine house and estate (still there) which he bought in 1890. He died there on May 29, 1911, from heart failure after rescuing a young lady from drowning in the lake on the estate. After cremation his ashes were buried in **Great Stanmore** churchyard, a little to the north of Harrow Weald. At Pinner Wood House, **Pinner** (nearly three miles north-west of Harrow), Bulwer Lytton lived during 1831-3, and wrote most of *Eugene Aram* there. Other literary inhabitants of Pinner included Henry Pye, George Gissing and Barry Pain. Pye, a forgotten (it must be confessed, justly) poet laureate, was the first holder of the office to receive a regular salary instead of the customary donation of canary wine. He is commemorated in the parish church.

At **Kingsbury** (I, A1, now part of Wembley), three miles east of Harrow, we have an association with Goldsmith. He took a cottage in Hyde Lane in 1768 for occasional retirement from London, and in 1771 moved to a farmhouse on the west side of the Edgware Road, near the sixth milestone. Sir Joshua Reynolds, Boswell and Johnson were among his visitors. At this farmhouse, which disappeared long ago, he wrote *She Stoops to Conquer*, and it was here that he contracted his fatal fever.

LONDON AREA: WEST AND SOUTH-WEST

Chiswick (I, A4/5, on the A4 leading out of London) is the scene of Becky Sharp's schooling, and where occurred the famous scene when she threw Johnson's *Dictionary* out of the carriage window. An inscription on Boston House in Chiswick Square claims that it is the original of Miss Pinkerton's Academy, but there is little doubt that Thackeray had Walpole House on Chiswick Mall more in mind, and in *Vanity Fair* the school was placed in the Mall. However, Thackeray's illustration of the school incorporates features of both houses—which serves as a reminder that a writer's imagination transmutes experience and locality for artistic purposes. Pope lived at Mawson's Buildings from 1716 to 1719, and his house is now the Fox and Hounds, at the corner of Mawson Row.

At **Brentford** (I, A4) which with Chiswick forms one borough, Shelley was at school from 1802 until he went to Eton three years later. The school was Syon House Academy at Brentford End, past the church over the Brent Bridge. It is now a transport office. The hypersensitive Shelley suffered from the persecution of his schoolfellows, and his friend and biographer, Medwin (who was at school with him), says that life 'was indeed a perfect hell' to Shelley. His experiences there, and at Eton, resulted in a permanent horror of oppression and cruelty. However, Shelley himself sometimes caused alarm, as when he blew up boundary palings with gunpowder.

At Fordhook House (no longer there) on Ealing Common, Henry Fielding spent the last month or two of his life in England before going on a vain search for health in Lisbon. Lady Byron lived in the same house many years later. Near the church at **Ealing** (II, E3) there once existed Great Ealing School (where Louis-Philippe and T. H. Huxley's father were assistant masters) and among its distinguished pupils were Marryat, Newman, Thackeray and W. S. Gilbert. At another vanished school, Ealing House, Bulwer Lytton was educated. R. L. Stevenson was at Burlington Lodge School (now a house called St Vincent's) in Witham Road, **Isleworth** (II, E3) in 1863. Sheridan is also associated with Isleworth, living for a short time by the riverside in Lacy House, no longer there.

Off the A4, at **Cranford** (II, D3), Thomas Fuller is buried in the church where he was rector for the last three years of his life. Two hundred London clergymen attended the funeral of this very popular man. There is a memorial tablet to him on the east wall of the chancel.

Twickenham (II, E3) has a long association with literature. Sir

Francis Bacon in about 1595 secured a house (long vanished) in Twickenham Park, now covered by the district of St Margaret's. He lived there until 1605, and possibly wrote some of his *Essays* there. Bacon's house came into the possession of Lucy, Countess of Bedford, a famous patroness of poets who gathered a brilliant circle about her. Her circle included Ben Jonson, George Chapman, Samuel Daniel, Michael Drayton and John Donne, who all dedicated poems to her. Donne was often here during the years 1605-10, and addressed several poems to his patron. He wrote a poem called 'Twicknam Garden' which has no local allusion or colour.

Sir John Suckling was born in February 1609 in **Whitton**, now part of Twickenham, but nothing appears to be known of his early years.

The two literary figures most closely associated with Twickenham are Pope and Horace Walpole. In 1719 Pope took a house in Crossdeep in which he lived the rest of his life, and where his greatest work was produced. He had five acres of ground in which he could indulge his favourite recreation of gardening. Such was Pope's nature that his enemies called him 'the Wasp of Twickenham', but his acerbity was due, partly at least, to his physical deformity and suffering. Swift, Bolingbroke and Gay were among his visitors; so was Voltaire, who scandalized Pope's mother with his atheism. Lady Mary Wortley Montagu, a resident of Twickenham, took Saville House (no longer extant) in order to be nearer her friend Pope, but subsequently they quarrelled bitterly. Near by her cousin Henry Fielding lived during 1747 and 1748. Pope died on May 30, 1744, and was buried in the parish church, St Mary's. There is a memorial to him in the form of an obelisk with a portrait medallion. Pope's villa was demolished in 1807, and the present building called Pope's Villa is the second building erected approximately on the same site. Pope's famous Grotto, which connected his house and garden, has survived as a subway under the road.

Horace Walpole bought a coachman's cottage in Twickenham in 1747 and called it Strawberry Hill. Then he conceived the idea of erecting a 'little Gothic castle'. The building, furnishing and enlargement of the grounds became the ruling passion of his life. William Beckford, who built a far more fantastic affair in Wiltshire, called it 'a species of Gothic mousetrap'. Walpole set up a printing press, and the first production was a small volume of the 'Pindaric Odes' of his friend Gray, who used to visit him here. Among Walpole's possessions here was the 'lofty vase' inherited from Gray, whose favourite cat was drowned in it, and was celebrated in one of Gray's odes. Most of the famous people of Walpole's day visited him here. Strawberry Hill has undergone alteration since his time, but much of the original building has survived. Walpole also owned a house called Little Strawberry Hill on the Teddington road, but it was demolished in 1883.

Later Twickenham associations include Dickens, who lived in 1838 and 1839 at No. 2 Ailsa Park Villas, which has survived and is opposite the station. He wrote part of *Nicholas Nickleby* there, and a picnic scene in that book is placed on Twickenham Ait, popularly called Eel Pie Island. Tennyson lived at Chapel House (which is still there) in Montpelier Row during 1851-3. Among his friends who visited him were Thackeray, Fitzgerald and Benjamin Jowett, but the continual stream of visitors made him dissatisfied with Twickenham. Whilst here he wrote the great 'Ode on the Death of the Duke of Wellington' which, strange as it seems to us, was almost universally disliked. Also in Montpelier Row lived Walter de la Mare, in South End House, where he died in 1956.

At **Teddington** (II, E3) a little south of Twickenham, there is a connexion with Thomas Traherne, little known until the discovery on a bookstall of the manuscript of his poems and *Centuries of Meditations*, the latter revealing him as one of the great prose writers of the seventeenth century. He was rector of the parish church, St Mary, during the last two years of his short life. He died at Teddington in September or October, 1674, and is buried in his church. Also at Teddington lived R. D. Blackmore, at Gomer House (which has survived) from 1858 until his death on January 20, 1900. *Lorna Doone* and many other novels were written here, and he was, moreover, a very active market-gardener. In Hampton Court near by, Pope sets some of the scene of his *Rape of the Lock*, characterized as a 'structure of majestic frame', where

> *Great Anna! whom three realms obey*
> *Dost sometimes counsel take—and sometimes tea.*

c*

Over on the Surrey side of the river, **Richmond** (II, E3), beloved of artists and celebrated both in prose and verse, has had its literary residents. James Thomson, who spent much of his last years revising *The Seasons* here, in 1736 took up residence at a cottage later called Rosedale House, and what remained of it has been incorporated in the Royal Hospital. He died at his home on August 27, 1748, and was buried in the parish church, St Mary Magdalene, with a memorial tablet. George Eliot lived with G. H. Lewes at Parkshot, Richmond, during 1855-9, and here she wrote *Scenes of Clerical Life* and *Adam Bede*. The site of her house is now covered by the offices of the Medical Officer of Health. Mary Elizabeth Braddon, now remembered for her sensational *Lady Audley's Secret*, though she later wrote better novels which have been largely forgotten, lived the last forty years of her life in Richmond, and died there on February 4, 1915. She is buried in the churchyard of St Mary Magdalene.

At **Wimbledon** (II, E3) there survives Gothic Lodge in Woodhayes Road, where Captain Marryat lived from 1839 to 1843, when he was not at his London house. Near by, at **Kingston Hill**, John Galsworthy was born on August 14, 1867. In **Kingston-upon-Thames** itself Gibbon was at a school where he was bullied by the boys and birched by the master.

WINDSOR AREA

In a small area of country lying west of London there are an astonishing number of associations of the greatest interest. Chaucer has a connexion with Windsor Castle, because he was for a time Clerk of the Royal Works, and may have lived in 1390 in the Winchester Tower there. Henry Howard, Earl of Surrey, when a boy spent two years as the companion at **Windsor** (II, D3) of Henry VIII's illegitimate son, the Duke of Richmond. 'With a king's son my childish years did pass', he says in one of his poems. Fanny Burney obtained the post of second keeper of the robes to the queen of George III, not because she wanted it, but merely to get away from her stepmother in London. From 1786 to 1791 she was 'royally gagged and promoted to fold muslins', as Horace Walpole said, though he was quoting someone else's remark. Macaulay was more trenchant, and said that it was inconceivable how a person called by Burke the first woman of the age 'could endure such a life while there remained a vacant garret in Grub Street, a crossing in want of a sweeper, a parish work house, or a parish vault'. There are excellent accounts of her life at Windsor (and at other royal homes, including what is now known as the Dutch House at Kew) in her *Diary*.

The great public school at **Eton*** (II, D3), the neighbour of Windsor but on the other side of the river, has had some famous men of letters among its scholars. Sir Henry Wotton, poet and diplomat, came home penniless from diplomacy abroad and in disfavour with James I, but managed to secure the provostship of Eton in 1624. He held the position until his death in December 1639, and is buried in the College Chapel. As to the scholars, Edmund Waller was here, but little is known of his activities. Henry Fielding was contemporary with the elder Pitt and Henry Fox, later first Baron Holland. Thomas Gray and Horace Walpole entered in the same year, 1727, and with two other boys formed a circle of friendship called the Quadruple Alliance. 'I was a blockhead,' says Walpole, 'and pushed up above my parts.' He and Gray went up to Cambridge in 1734.

The most famous Etonian among men of letters was Shelley, who entered in 1804, during the provostship of the famous Dr Keate, and was a misfit and frequently unhappy. He had a passion for scientific experiments, one being the destruction of an old willow-tree with a burning glass. There are many stories of his life here, and it is difficult to sift truth from legend. The boys frequently tormented him, and nicknamed him 'Mad Shelley' and 'Shelley the Atheist'. He had, however, his moments of happiness in scientific experiment and boating on the Thames, and recalls the latter in a passage in 'The Boat on the Serchio'. He became a good classical scholar, and his literary proclivities resulted in the composition and publication before he left Eton of *Zastrozzi*, a romance in the style of Mrs Radcliffe's 'horror novels'. He carved his name in Upper School, where it can still be seen.

* The School Yard and Cloisters are open daily 10 a.m. to 5 p.m. (10 a.m. to 8 p.m. during summer); the College Chapel, Lower School and certain other buildings may be visited with a guide (apply at School Office) 11.30 a.m. to 12.30 p.m., 2.30 to 5 or 6 p.m. (from 10.30 a.m. during holidays), from Monday to Saturday.

Dr Keate was still Provost when A. W. Kinglake entered about fifteen years after Shelley. In his *Eothen* he has drawn a remarkable portrait of Keate, and it is a capital example of Kinglake's sly humour. Only one sentence can be quoted here: 'He had such a complete command over his temper—I mean, over his *good* temper, that he scarcely ever allowed it to appear: you could not put him out of humour—that is, out of the *ill*-humour which he thought to be fitting for a head-master.'

Swinburne, who entered in 1849, stood apart from other boys, did not care for games, cultivated only a few friends, and read omnivorously. He laid the foundations of a lifelong love of the English poets and dramatists, and on rambles in Windsor forest with a friend would recite from favourite works at great length. He was regarded as an oddity but, unlike Shelley, was not persecuted by the boys, and in fact they were a little afraid of him, for the diminutive figure possessed boundless courage. Robert Bridges entered Eton in 1854, whilst Swinburne was still there. Unlike Swinburne, he was fond of—and distinguished himself in—games. He became friendly with D. M. Dolben, a distant cousin, younger than himself, whose poems he edited many years later. Dolben, of a religious nature, wished to found an Anglican brotherhood with Bridges as its head.

Slough (II, D3), two miles north of Windsor, has come within the 'Dickens country' of late through the discoveries of Mr Felix Aylmer of facts relating to the novelist's life with his mistress, Ellen Ternan. It appears that Dickens lodged in 1867 in Elizabeth Cottage, in High Street, with Ellen Ternan. The cottage perished by fire in 1889, and its site is covered by the shop of Messrs Dallen.

On an unclassified road between Windsor and London Airport is the village of **Horton** in Buckinghamshire. Milton's father retired there in 1632, at about the time Milton left Cambridge and resolved to devote himself to literature. His six years here were productive of great work: 'L'Allegro', 'Il Penseroso', 'Arcades', 'Comus', and 'Lycidas'. The lyrics for 'Arcades' were written at the suggestion of his musician friend Henry Lawes, who was then attached to the household of the first Earl of Bridgewater, at **Harefield** in Middlesex, about twenty miles to the north of Horton. After five years here Milton's mother died, and she is buried in Horton church. Milton travelled abroad in 1638, and when he returned settled in London. His Horton home was demolished about 1795; its site is covered by the front of the large house called Berkyn Manor.

He returned to Buckinghamshire nearly thirty years later, when the Great Plague was ravaging London. His Quaker friend, Thomas Ellwood, found him 'a pretty box' of a cottage in the village of **Chalfont St Giles** (II, D2, on the A413 leading off the A40 London-Oxford road). Milton's Cottage* here is the only residence of his that has survived. When here he lent Ellwood the complete manuscript of *Paradise Lost*. 'Thou hast said much here of Paradise Lost,' said Ellwood, 'but what hast thou to say of Paradise Found?' Milton acknowledged, says Ellwood, that *Paradise Regained* resulted from his question. Milton returned to London in 1666.

Another poet connected with this area and contemporary with Milton, belonged to the other side (at first) in the Civil War troubles. This was Edmund Waller, born on March 3, 1606, at the manor house at **Coleshill** (at that time in Hertfordshire, but now in Buckinghamshire, off the main road between Beaconsfield and Amersham). He settled at **Beaconsfield** (II, D2) at Hall Barn, which disappeared long ago, in 1631. It was his home for the rest of his life (though away from it when banished from the country between 1644 and 1651). He died at his home on October 21, 1687, and is buried in the churchyard of the parish church, with a large monument over the grave.

Edmund Burke was another resident of Beaconsfield. He bought a house called Gregories, which stood a mile from the town, in 1768, and however stormy his political life, he found peace and happiness here. A much-liked local figure, he helped the poor with food and medicine, and patronized strolling players. He finally retired from London in 1794, badly broken by the death of his son. On the last day of his life he discussed affairs in Europe, and his favourite Addison's essays were read to him. He died on July 9, 1797, and is buried in the parish church. Beaconsfield was the home of G. K. Chesterton from

* Open all the year on weekdays (except Tuesday) 10 a.m. to 1 p.m., 2.15 to 6 p.m., Sunday 2.15 to 6 p.m.; closes at dusk from October to March. Contains personal relics, first editions, portraits, busts, etc.

his marriage in 1909 until his death here on June 14, 1936. He is buried in the churchyard of St Teresa of the Child Jesus, with a monument designed by Eric Gill.

William Penn, the founder of Pennsylvania, is buried with his two wives and five of his children beside the Quaker meeting house of **Jordans** (II, D2), two miles north-east of Beaconsfield. He has his place in English letters, among other writings, for the beautiful little book of aphoristic wisdom entitled *Some Fruits of Solitude*, which no doubt is read by Quakers but scarcely by anybody else. Three miles north-west of Beaconsfield, at the village of **Penn** (II, D2), Emile Zola lived during 1898-9 after he had to fly from France for championing the cause of Dreyfus.

About eight miles west of Beaconsfield, on the A40, is **High Wycombe** (II, D2), and just over a mile north of it is Hughenden Manor,* Disraeli's country house from 1847 until his death. A large Georgian house, much altered to suit his wife's tastes, it contains his fine library, manuscripts of his novels and many other relics. He died in London, and is buried beside his wife in the churchyard of the parish church. The tablet in the church was erected on the orders of Queen Victoria. She sent a wreath of primroses with the inscription: *His favourite flowers, from Osborne, a tribute of affection from Queen Victoria.* The day of his death, April 19, has since been known as Primrose Day.

We meet a curious mixture of personalities in this small area, and pass on to Shelley and Peacock at **Marlow** (II, D3) a few miles north-west of Maidenhead, and on a particularly lovely stretch of the Thames. Before settling at Marlow Shelley had stayed with friends at Bracknell, Berkshire, three miles east of Wokingham, where he had previously stayed with his first wife. He wrote there the lovely 'Stanzas' beginning 'Away, the moor is dark beneath the moon', the first poem to show the characteristic Shelley. Then in the summer of 1815 he and Mary Godwin stayed in Bishop's Gate, near Windsor and on the edge of Windsor forest, in which he loved to wander, and composed *Alastor*. His friend Peacock, already settled at Marlow, came over frequently

---

* Open February to December, Tuesday to Friday 2 to 6 p.m.; Saturday and Sunday 10 a.m. to 1 p.m., 2 to 6 p.m.; also Bank Holiday Mondays; closed on Tuesday after Bank Holidays.

to see him. After a trip to Switzerland with Mary Godwin, marriage, and wanderings between London, Bath and Marlow, Shelley took Albion House in Marlow in February 1817. Albion House, divided since Shelley's time, is in West Street, and a tablet marks his association. The Shelley household included Claire Clairmont and her daughter Allegra, who had Byron for father. Shelley found Peacock's companionship most congenial and they went boating and wandering through the countryside. *The Revolt of Islam* (at first called *Laon and Cythna*) was written during the Marlow residence, whilst boating, says Mary Shelley; in Bisham Wood, says Peacock. Mary Shelley herself wrote *Frankenstein* here. Shelley sold Albion House in February 1818, and after a short stay in London left England for ever. Peacock stayed on at Marlow, undecided on a profession, but he had begun writing his brilliant satirical novels. *Headlong Hall* had been published in 1816, followed by *Melincourt* and *Nightmare Abbey* in successive years. In the last, Shelley is depicted as 'Scythrop'. Then in 1819 Peacock had prospects of a job in London, and left Marlow.

Just over a mile south of Marlow is Medmenham Abbey, an eighteenth-century mansion built on the site of a Cistercian monastery. An eccentric politician and man of the world, Sir Francis Dashwood, founded here about 1745 a fraternity which was variously titled, but best known as 'The Monks of Medmenham' or 'The Hell-Fire Club'. Over the doorway was inscribed *Fay ce que voudras*, taken from Rabelais (it can still be seen), and their motto was 'Love and Friendship'. They parodied, somewhat obscenely, rites of ancient Rome, and drank to heathen deities. The poet Charles Churchill became a member, and, somewhat uncharacteristically, described the club as 'a disgrace to mankind'.

Now to Thomas Gray at **Stoke Poges** (II, D3, off the A332 a few miles north of Slough). After his father's death in 1741, Gray and his mother came to live at a house called West End, which was a mile north of Stoke Poges church, both being within the estate of Stoke Park. Soon afterwards Gray made Cambridge his headquarters, but spent the summers with his mother. He began the famous 'Elegy Written in a Country Churchyard' in 1742, resuming it in 1749. Then it was sent to his friend Horace Walpole, who greatly liked it, and publication followed in 1751. As usual with Gray, he allowed the book-seller to keep all the profits, only once taking money for his poems. He lived on the small fortune left by his father.

The famous yew tree of the poem is still there, but it must be mentioned that the connexion of the 'Elegy' with Stoke Poges church rests on tradition, though a very strong one. It has been suggested that Harefield in Middlesex is the more likely church, and it is certainly very much a church of 'storied urn and animated bust', which Stoke is not. However, it is unlikely that Stoke Poges will lose its cherished association with Gray. His mother died in 1753, and is buried in a vault just outside the east end of the church. Gray composed an inscription to the 'careful tender mother of many children, one of whom alone had the misfortune to survive her'.

After 1759 Stoke ceases to be a home to Gray. His house there was bought by the son of William Penn, and part of the building, including the room in which he wrote, was incorporated in a much larger house about 1845. Gray died at Cambridge and was buried in the same vault with his mother, in accordance with his wishes. Near the church is 'Gray's Field', a National Trust Property, with a large, graceless monument designed by James Wyatt and erected in 1799. On it are extracts from his poems.

STAINES AREA

Laleham, a mile south-east of Staines, was the birthplace of Matthew Arnold. His father, later to become the famous headmaster of Rugby School, was taking pupils here at a house which has been demolished. Its approximate site is marked by the cedar tree in Ashford Road which used to be in its grounds. He was born on December 24, 1822, but was moved to Rugby when his father was appointed head-master. He came back to Laleham in 1830 to become a pupil under his maternal uncle, and was sent to Winchester six years later. Not far away, at **Cobham** (II, D3, on the A3), Arnold lived the last fifteen years of his life at Pain's Hill Cottage, which has survived, but is in danger of demolition. He is buried in Laleham churchyard, where three of his children, who all died young, are also buried.

At **Chertsey** (II, D3, on the A320 between Staines and Woking), the poet Abraham Cowley spent his final years, 1665-7, at Porch House (long since demolished) in Guildford Street. The inscription used to read: *The Porch of this House, which projects Ten Feet into the Highway, was taken down in the year 1786 for Safety and Accommodation of the Public. Here, the last Accents flow'd from Cowley's Tongue.* His house was then in thickly wooded country, and one of his best poems refers to 'old patrician trees, so great and good', which is reminiscent of (and did it inspire?) Keats's magnificent line: 'Tall oaks, the senators of mighty woods'.

Chertsey was the boyhood home of T. L. Peacock, brought here by his mother to her father's house some time after the death of her husband in 1788. The only formal education he ever received was at a school at Englefield Green on Cooper's Hill, by Egham, and overlooking the famous meadow of Runnymede. 'Cooper's Hill' is the title of a poem by Sir John Denham, published in 1643 and the earliest example in English of purely descriptive poetry, but its moralizing reflections have long rendered it out of favour.

About three miles east of Chertsey, at **Lower Halliford** on the Thames, there used to be a cottage that Peacock bought in 1823 for his mother. He spent his week-ends and later his years of retirement there. His death was hastened by a fire (of which, like Gray, he was greatly afraid). 'By the immortal gods,' he said, 'I will not move.' He had to be carried to his bed, in which he remained until he died on January 23, 1866. He is buried in the churchyard of the parish church.

His son-in-law, George Meredith, spent most of his life near by. After his marriage he settled in **Weybridge** in 1850, where he began writing his first novel, *The Ordeal of Richard Feverel*. He was having a hard struggle with poverty, and Peacock invited him in 1853 to live in his house at Lower Halliford, but the two did not hit it off, and Meredith moved to another house near by. In 1859 Meredith and his wife and the only child of this marriage went to live in London, where his wife left him, and later he came to live in High Street, **Esher**, moving soon afterwards to Copsham Cottage between Esher and **Oxshott**. Swinburne and Rossetti were among his visitors here. His wife died in 1861 and he married again in 1864, in **Mickleham** church (II, E4). In 1867 he made his final move, to Flint Cottage on Box Hill (see below, p. 83), the only residence of his in this area that has survived.

Some distance away from our immediate area, at **Croydon** (II, E3), a tablet on the Davidson Secondary Modern School there records that D. H. Lawrence taught at the school from 1908 to 1912. Lawrence was a good schoolmaster, but had to resign his post through ill-health.

NORTH AND EAST KENT

The old Roman road that leads from London to the Kent coast and followed, with one detour, by the pilgrims depicted by Chaucer, takes us through the main Dickens country and several other associations. At the outset, although it is some way off our route, we must take note of H. G. Wells's birthplace at **Bromley** (II, E3). He was born on September 21, 1866, at 47 High Street, over a shop called Atlas House, 'a needy shabby home', as he says in *Experiment in Autobiography*. His father was at various times gardener, professional cricketer and general dealer. Wells's earliest education was at Morley's Academy at Bromley.

Nearer our route, at **Bexley Heath** (II, F3) there survives the Red House which was designed for William Morris by his friend Philip Webb, and where Morris lived during 1860-5. As the result of a severe illness he had to decide between giving up the Red House or his work in London, and reluctantly chose the former.

Returning to our pilgrims, who generally began their journey at Southwark, after passing Dartford they diverged for Gravesend and then rejoined the Roman road just outside Rochester. There are Dickens associations between Gravesend and Rochester to which we shall return shortly. At Rochester and the adjoining town of Chatham we are in the heart of the Dickens country. His first acquaintance with the area was at **Chatham** (II, F3), where, at 2, now 11, Ordnance Terrace his family lived during 1817-21. The house, near the station, is marked with a tablet. Then until 1823 the family lived in St Mary's Place, The Brook (near the Town Hall), and the house survived until demolition in 1952.

In 1823 the Dickens family left for London. Dickens returned to the area when he spent his honeymoon at **Chalk** (II, F3), now part of Gravesend, but the cottage marked as 'the one and only genuine Dickens Honeymoon Cottage' is not where he stayed. The actual cottage was in the same lane, but has vanished within recent years. The old forge in the village is often supposed to be the original of Joe Gargery's forge in *Great Expectations*, but it is more likely that Dickens had in mind the old forge that once existed in **Cooling**, to the north-east, and in the Cooling Marshes are laid the opening scenes of the story.

Whilst he was staying in **Gravesend** in later years Dickens heard that the house he had longed to possess since his boyhood was for sale. This was Gad's Hill Place (II, F3), about half-way between Gravesend and Rochester, and by the spot where Falstaff committed highway robbery. The house was bought in 1857, and he finally settled there three years later. There were extensive grounds attached to the house on both sides of the road, and in 1865 a Swiss châlet, sent by a friend all the way from Paris, was erected in that part called The Wilderness. In the châlet he wrote his last books, and was at work on *Edwin Drood* when he suffered the stroke that resulted in death on June 9, 1870. His wish for burial near his last home was not fulfilled.

Among his many visitors at Gad's Hill was Longfellow in 1868. His house is now a school. The châlet was presented by his family to the Earl of Darnley, who re-erected it in his park at **Cobham** (II, F3), about four miles south of Gad's Hill, where it remained until transferred to the grounds of the Rochester Public Museum in 1961. Dickens often walked to Cobham, and had a key to the park. In the village of Cobham is the Leather Bottle inn made famous in *Pickwick Papers*; it was near the inn that Mr Pickwick discovered the 'Bill Stumps' stone—and a stone has since been placed there!

Rochester (II, F3), which Dickens knew and loved from his childhood—it was, as his first biographer says, 'the birthplace of his fancy'—possesses several buildings that figure so much in his work. Mr Pickwick, who like his creator got around a great deal of the kingdom, stayed with his friends at the Bull, an old coaching inn that survives in High Street. In *Great Expectations* it appears as the 'Blue Boar', and Dickens himself stayed there. Opposite is the old clock of the Corn Exchange, described in *Great Expectations* (in which Rochester appears as 'the Market Town') as 'inexpressive, moon-faced and weak'. In the Maidstone Road is Restoration House★ (so called because Charles II stayed there on his return from exile), the original of Miss Havisham's residence and called 'Satis House' in the novel, but should not be confused with the real Satis House on Boley Hill.

To return to High Street, further eastward there are three picturesque houses, Nos. 150-4 (originally one house) where Uncle Pumblechook ran his corn shop. But Rochester figures, as 'Cloisterham', most prominently in *Edwin Drood*. The cathedral and its precincts and the houses in the High Street are closely interwoven into the texture of the book. The College Gateway in High Street was Jasper's Gate House, and Uncle Pumblechook's corn shop in *Great Expectations* becomes transformed into the dwelling of Mr Sapsea. Opposite is Eastgate House, original of the 'Nuns' House' (in *Pickwick* it appears as 'Westgate House'), now the Rochester Public Museum,† which includes a Dickens collection.

Before leaving High Street we must note Watts's Charity‡ at No. 97, described in 'Seven Poor Travellers'. Founded under the will of Richard Watts in 1579 'for six Poor Travellers, who, not being rogues or proctors, may received gratis for one night lodging, entertainment, and fourpence each', the institution came to an end in 1947. Richard Watts himself lived at Satis House on Boley Hill, where he entertained Queen Elizabeth, but the house has been considerably altered since his time. Below his effigy in the cathedral is a tablet commemorating Dickens. All the buildings in Rochester connected with Dickens are carefully marked with tablets. The city also appears in different guises— 'Dullborough Town', 'Mudfog' and 'Great Wringlebury'—in *Sketches by Boz*.

The pilgrim route continues its straight course eastwards for Canterbury, and at Harbledown (probably the 'Bob-up-an'-down' referred to by Chaucer) the pilgrims caught their first sight of their objective.

★ Admission on application.

† Open daily (except Friday) 2 to 5.30 p.m. Contains letters, other Dickens relics and a special Dickens library.

‡ Open on weekdays 2 to 5 p.m.

At **Canterbury** (II, H4), as we should expect, there are several literary associations. It is thought that Chaucer himself went on pilgrimage, and his pilgrims used to turn from the High Street into Mercery Lane, passing at the corner the Chequers of the Hope inn, which was never mentioned by Chaucer, as is so often stated. The inn (now a tobacconist's shop) was damaged by fire, and the masonry at ground level is all that remains of it.

Canterbury's greatest native was Christopher Marlowe, the son of a shoemaker, born at a house (destroyed in the last war) in St George's Street, in February 1564. He was baptized in St George's Church, another casualty of the war, but the tower has survived. He was educated at King's School, Canterbury, the most ancient school in England, founded as long ago as 598. Marlowe went to Cambridge, and as far as we know never revisited his native city after his university days. There is a memorial to him in the Dane John Gardens. Other writers educated at the King's School are Walter Pater, who entered in his fifteenth and did not leave until his twentieth year, and Mr Somerset Maugham.

Richard Lovelace, a native of Kent, had rich estates in the county, one of them being the first Franciscan friary to be built in England, the remains of which are off Stour Street. An old building in the garden, on the water's edge, was occupied for some time by the poet. Also in Stour Street is St Mildred's Church, in which Izaak Walton married his first wife in 1626. At No. 61 Burgate Street a tablet marks the site of the house in which R. H. Barham was born on December 6, 1788. Canterbury figures often in his *Ingoldsby Legends*.

For many the chief literary association in Canterbury is with *David Copperfield*. Young Copperfield was sent to school in Canterbury, and the prototype is probably the King's School. The Sun Inn, near the cathedral, proudly proclaims its connexion with Dickens, and it was probably in his mind as the inn where David, his aunt, Mr Dick and Traddles stayed when they went to help Mr Micawber unmask Uriah Heep. The House of Agnes (now an hotel) in St Dunstan's Street, near the West Gate, is claimed as the house Dickens had in mind as the residence of Mr Wickfield and his daughter Agnes. Dickens gave a reading from *David Copperfield* in Canterbury in 1861. On another occasion he stayed at the Crown Inn, now known as Queen Elizabeth's Guest Chamber.

Off the A2 and seven miles south-east of Canterbury is the village of **Bishopsbourne** (II, H4). Richard Hooker, author of *The Laws of Ecclesiastical Polity* (the later portions of which were written here), was rector of the old church here from 1595 until his death on November 2, 1600. He is buried in the chancel of the church, with a monument on the wall above. Very near the church, in a house called Oswalds (now the rectory) Joseph Conrad lived from 1920 until his death there on August 3, 1926. (Mr Alec Waugh, the novelist, lived in this house in the early 1930's.) His last books were written there. He is buried in the Roman Catholic portion of Canterbury Cemetery. There is a bas-relief portrait of him in the memorial porch of the British Legion Hall in Bishopsbourne.

About eight miles south-east of Canterbury, on the A260, is the village of **Denton** (II, H4), and two miles south-west of it is the Jacobean mansion called Tappington-Everard, the ancestral home of R. H. Barham. Some of his *Ingoldsby Legends* are derived from local lore, and the very first one was on 'The Spectre of Tappington'. At **Godmersham** (II, G4), on the A28 between Ashford and Canterbury and situated on the River Stour, is the fine eighteenth-century house called Godmersham Park. Jane Austen's brother Edward owned the house, slightly reconstructed since his time, and Jane Austen paid several visits here between 1798 and 1809, with a final one in 1813. Edward Austen's eldest daughter Fanny (who became Lady Knatchbull) was Miss Austen's favourite niece.

Keats stayed in **Margate** (II, H3) for a few weeks in 1816, and again in 1817 when he was at work on *Endymion*, but it is not known where he lodged. He complained that it was a treeless place, and on his second visit got tired of it. Charles and Mary Lamb spent a holiday at Margate in 1821, which resulted in 'The Old Margate Hoy'—hoy is a small coasting vessel—in the *Essays of Elia*. It was their 'first seaside experiment', he says in the essay.

At **Birchington** (II, H3), four miles west of Margate, Dante Gabriel Rossetti spent the last few months of his stricken life. He was attended in his last days by his relatives, Hall Caine and Watts-Dunton the friend of Swinburne. Rossetti died at Birchington on April 9, 1882, and a Celtic cross by the porch of the parish church marks his grave.

Broadstairs (II, H3) was Dickens's favourite holiday haunt, and he was there almost every year for twelve years. His first visit, soon after marriage, was in 1837, when he stayed at 12 (now 31) High Street, and there wrote part of *Pickwick Papers*. At 40 Albion Street (now incorporated in the Albion Hotel) part of *Nicholas Nickleby* was written. He was at Lawn House when at work on *Barnaby Rudge* and *The Old Curiosity Shop*. He was at Chandos Place in 1847 and 1848, and at Fort House overlooking the harbour he completed *David Copperfield*. Fort House has been most unfortunately renamed Bleak House,* though it has no connexion with the novel. The original of Betsey Trotwood, one Mary Strong, lived in Nuckell's Place, now called Dickens House, at the end of Victoria Parade. Dickens's regular visits ceased in 1851, though he paid one visit in 1859. All his associations are marked by tablets. Lionel Johnson was born at Broadstairs on March 15, 1867.

Sandwich (II, H4), at one time the senior Cinque Port, is the 'Sunwich Port' of W.W. Jacobs's lively stories of longshoremen and sailors. A tablet at 20 New Street reminds us that Tom Paine, author of *The Rights of Man*, lived there for a time. At **Deal** the Carter House Hotel has a tablet stating that it was the home of Elizabeth Carter, who translated Epictetus and whose learning was much admired by Dr Johnson. At **Walmer** (II, H4), near by, Robert Bridges was born on October 23, 1844, at Roselands (now a convent), and spent his childhood and boyhood there. He recalls his childhood in the fine poem 'The Summer House on the Mound' as well as in other poems.

Dickens placed the home of Betsey Trotwood, David Copperfield's forbidding but kind-hearted aunt, in **Dover** (II, H4), and one of the most delightful episodes in the novel is Betsey Trotwood's aversion to donkeys, chased from her demesne with the cry of 'Janet, donkeys!' Dover has more sombre associations with two English poets. Charles Churchill the satirist is buried in the churchyard of St Mary's in Cannon

* Open every day from Good Friday until the last Sunday in September 2-5 p.m. ; with additional hours (7-9 p.m.) from mid-June to mid-September, and 10.30 a.m. to 12.30 p.m. on Sunday from Easter to the end of September.

Street. He was on his way to meet his friend John Wilkes at Boulogne, contracted fever and died there on November 4, 1764. On the slab is a line from one of his own poems: *Life to the last enjoyed, here Churchill lies.* There is a monument to him inside the church.

At Dover Byron spent his last two days in England. He had just managed to escape from the bailiffs in London, and his friend Hobhouse thought that they might turn up in Dover, so whilst waiting for a favourable wind took the precaution of putting Byron's carriage on board. Byron and Hobhouse went to see Churchill's grave; the former lay down and measured his length against it, and then gave the sexton five shillings and instructions to returf the grave. A little later, at Diodati in Switzerland, Byron wrote the poem which begins:

> *I stood beside the grave of him who blazed*
> *The comet of a season . . .*

and may sadly have pondered on the fact that until recently he himself had been the very brilliant comet of a season. Next day, his inn packed with sightseers, he sailed, and never returned to England—alive.

At **Postling** (II, H4), about three miles north of Hythe (on an unclassified road running eastwards off the B2068), Joseph Conrad lived from 1898 to 1907. The old farmhouse he occupied, Pent Farm, is still in existence, and there Conrad wrote some of his greatest novels, including *Lord Jim, Youth, Typhoon* and *Nostromo*.

WEST KENT

William Hazlitt was born in Mitre Lane, **Maidstone** (II, F4), in a house that has long since disappeared, on April 10, 1778. In infancy he was taken back to his family home in Shropshire. He is commemorated in the town in a section of the Museum and Art Gallery★ in Chillington Manor, St Faith's Street. At Allington Castle, on the west bank of the Medway and just outside Maidstone, Sir Thomas Wyatt was born in 1503. His father, Sir Henry Wyatt, was one of those who had opposed Richard's III's claim to the throne and suffered for it with two years'

★ Open on weekdays in summer 10 a.m. to 6.30 p.m., in winter 10 a.m. to dusk (closed on Bank Holidays). Contains portraits and personal relics.

imprisonment in the Tower of London. The castle, restored in recent years, is now occupied by Carmelite nuns.

At **Boughton Malherbe** (II, G4, off the A20 about eight miles south-east of Maidstone), there is the manor house (near the church) where Sir Henry Wotton was born in 1568. At **Aylesford** (II, F3), three miles north-west of Maidstone, there is a house called The Friars that is often stated to be the birthplace of Sir Charles Sedley, but it is virtually certain that he was born in London. No doubt he lived in it, inheriting it from his father after the death of his brothers.

'In 1422 I was born and learned my English in Kent, in the Weald, where English is spoken broad and rude,' said William Caxton, and some think that he was born at **Hadlow**, between Maidstone and Tonbridge, but nothing certain is known. Another native of the Weald of Kent was John Lyly of *Euphues* fame, but again the exact locality is unknown.

The great mansion of Knole,* about a mile from the centre of **Sevenoaks** (II, F4), has been in the possession of the Sackville family for hundreds of years. Two of the Sackvilles claim our attention. The first, Thomas Sackville, Lord Buckhurst and first Earl of Dorset, is notable for his share in *Gorboduc*, the first tragedy in blank verse, a work not otherwise distinctive, and he wrote much better poetry in his contributions to *A Mirror for Magistrates*. Charles Sackville, sixth Earl of Dorset and Earl of Middlesex, was a courtier, rake (Pepys mentions his escapades), poet and munificent patron of letters. Wycherley, Dryden, Pope and Prior were among his friends. Dryden, whose pension was paid by the earl after William III had dismissed him as poet laureate, dedicated *An Essay of Dramatic Poesy* to him, and Sackville is the Eugenius of that work. The dining-room at Knole (not shown to the public) is known as the Poets' Parlour because in it Sackville entertained his literary friends and also because so many portraits of English poets adorn its walls. Prior said that 'a freedom reigned at his table which made every one of his guests think himself at home'. Miss V. Sackville-

---

* Open April to October on Wednesday, Thursday, Friday, Saturday, and Bank Holidays, including Good Friday 10 a.m. to 12 noon, 2 to 4.30 p.m.; November, December and March, on Wednesday, Thursday, Friday, Saturday, and Bank Holidays (except Boxing Day) 10 a.m. to 12 noon, 2 to 3.30 p.m.

West (1892-1962), who was born at Knole, wrote a brilliant account of *Knole and the Sackvilles*.

At **Shipbourne**, three miles north of Tonbridge, Christopher Smart was born on April 4, 1722. He came of a north-country family, was first educated at Maidstone, and then his family moved to Durham.

Penshurst Place (II, F4), about four miles north-west of Tunbridge Wells, is another great house rich in associations, the chief being Sir Philip Sidney, born there on November 30, 1554. His father was Sir Henry Sidney, at that time Lord President of Wales and later Lord Deputy of Ireland. Philip Sidney spent his childhood and youth at Penshurst, but did not see much of his home from the time he first went abroad. Long after Sidney's death Ben Jonson, invited by Sidney's brother Sir Robert, was a frequent visitor to Penshurst, and in his poem 'To Penshurst' shows a felicitous appreciation of Sir Robert and Lady Sidney's ample house, grounds and hospitality. Jonson had felt the smart of being treated as a social inferior by patrons, but at Penshurst

> *The same beer, and bread, and self-same wine,*
> *That is his lordship's, shall be mine.*

Sir Philip Sidney's grand-niece, Lady Dorothy Sidney, has secured immortality by being the 'Sacharissa' of Edmund Waller's poems. She was eighteen when she first met Waller at Groombridge, and Waller, after losing his wife, courted her at Penshurst. Aubrey says that he was passionately in love with her, but it was probably a courtship in the Elizabethan literary tradition. When the lady was married, after her father had considered four suitors, Waller's letter of good wishes (to her sister) did not suggest a broken heart. His finest poem, 'Go, lovely rose', does not appear to have been addressed to her. One of the avenues in the park is called 'Sacharissa's Walk'. Penshurst Place has been in the possession of the Sidney family since 1552, and the present owner, Viscount De L'Isle and Dudley, is a collateral descendant of Sir Philip Sidney.

At **Tunbridge Wells** (II, F4) there is an eighteenth-century house

* Open April 5 to October 11 on Wednesday, Thursday, Saturday, and Easter, Whitsun and August Bank Holidays 2 to 5 p.m.; also on the first, third and fifth Sundays in the month, and Whit Sunday.

on the London road called Thackeray House, and there the young Thackeray spent part of his boyhood. His essay on 'Tunbridge Toys' in *Roundabout Papers* refers to one of his school holidays there. Tennyson lived at Tunbridge Wells during 1841-2, and did not care for the place and moved to Boxley, near Maidstone, until 1843. At **Groombridge** (on the A264 about seven miles south-west of Tonbridge), Mark Rutherford lived the last ten years of his life. He died there on March 14, 1913, and is buried in the churchyard.

EAST SUSSEX

In the picturesque little town of **Rye** (II, G5), a Cinque Port, John Fletcher the dramatist was born in December 1579, the son of Dr Richard Fletcher, minister of Rye and later Bishop of London. The vicarage in which he was born was demolished in 1701. Rye in its smuggling days in the eighteenth century is the principal scene of Thackeray's last and unfinished novel, *Denis Duval*. In the High Street is an early seventeenth-century building called Peacock's School which is transformed into 'Pocock's School' in the novel.

Rye's chief literary association is with Henry James, who settled here in 1898 in Lamb House,* West Street. Although he visited London a great deal, Rye was his headquarters for the rest of his life, and all his later work was written here. James knew and disliked his compatriot Stephen Crane, author of *The Red Badge of Courage*, who spent his last years at Brede Place† not far away. It lies a mile east of **Brede** (II, G5), which is on the A28 and seven miles north of Hastings. With little money between them, Crane and his wife rented this little mansion (part of which is of the fourteenth century) and in a Bohemian atmosphere Crane attempted to stave off poverty and the threat of bankruptcy proceedings. Doomed with consumption, he died at Heidelberg, aged only twenty-eight, on June 5, 1900.

The eastern and some of the midland areas of Sussex were made peculiarly her own by Sheila Kaye-Smith, who was born in **St Leonard's** in 1887. She depicted the influence of the Sussex landscape

* One room, with Henry James relics, is open on Tuesday 2.15 to 6 p.m.

† Open March 15 to October 15 on Wednesday and Bank Holidays 3 to 6 p.m. There are relics of Stephen Crane in his study over the porch.

on its inhabitants in *Sussex Gorse* (many of its scenes are in Rye), *Tamarisk Town*, *The End of the House of Alard* and other novels, but the main scene of *Joanna Godden* is in the Romney Marsh area of south-east Kent.

Charles and Mary Lamb spent a holiday in 1823 in **Hastings** (II, G5), staying near the priory. Lamb did not approve of Hastings, which he called 'that detestable Cinque port' in his essay on 'The Old Margate Hoy', but in a letter he praised the 'exquisite views and walks'. Lamb says in the essay that it was written in Hastings. In the church of St Clement in the High Street, D. G. Rossetti was married in 1860 to Elizabeth Siddall. Also in High Street is the Roman Catholic church of St Mary Star-of-the-Sea, built largely from money supplied by the poet Coventry Patmore, who designed it as a memorial to his second wife. Patmore lived in Hastings for many years. Lewis Carroll used to pay frequent visits to **Eastbourne** (II, F5), staying at No. 7 Lushington Road, which has survived.

Burwash (II, F4, on the A265), was the last home of Rudyard Kipling, who lived there for over thirty years. In 1902 he bought a seventeenth-century house called Bateman's,* half a mile south of the village. *Puck of Pook's Hill*, which takes some colour from the locality, and all his later work was written here. There are a number of Pook's Hills in Sussex, but there is a little Pook's Hill (from Dodwell Brook to Burwash Common) visible from the western side of Bateman's, and it appears to have been named from the time Kipling began the book. From about his mid-forties Kipling's health declined, and he was in considerable pain often in the last twenty years of his life. Shortly before his death he was moved to London.

To the north-west of Burwash there is the home of Sir Arthur Conan Doyle in his later years, at **Crowborough** (on the A26). He died at his home, called Windlesham, on July 7, 1930. Richard Jefferies lived at the house called the Downs in 1887.

Half a mile west of the village of **Fletching** (II, E5), which lies on an

---

* Open Wednesday, Saturday and Sunday 2 to 5 p.m.; Bank Holidays 11 a.m. to 6 p.m., Good Friday 2 to 6 p.m. (but from November to February by appointment only). Personal relics are on view, and Kipling's study is as he used it.

unclassified road ten miles north of Lewes, is **Sheffield Park**★ (II, E4), once the seat of Lord Sheffield, the friend of Edward Gibbon. The historian was a frequent visitor to the house. He spent several months here after Lady Sheffield's death in 1793, and on his next visit became unwell and returned to London, where he died. He was buried in the Sheffield Mausoleum in Fletching church.

At **Southover**, a western suburb of **Lewes** (II, E5), John Evelyn lived with his grandparents at the Elizabethan building called Southover Grange from 1625, and during 1630-7 he was educated at Southover Free School. He says that he was 'extremely remiss' in his studies until his last year. At **South Malling**, a northern suburb of Lewes, the church of St Michael was built mainly at the expense of his grandfather, and 'I laid one of the first stones', says Evelyn. In this same church and whilst Evelyn was still resident at Southover, John Harvard of university fame was married in 1636 to the daughter of a Sussex clergyman.

BRIGHTON AREA

Dr Johnson, his friends the Thrales and Fanny Burney were among the early visitors to **Brighton** (II, E5), then becoming popular because a certain doctor had recommended its bracing air and the advantages of sea-bathing. The Thrales had a house (long vanished) in West Street, and they used to worship at the church of St Nicholas (at the west end of Church Street) where the Thrales had a family pew. A tablet on the north wall commemorates Johnson's connexion. 'I do not much like the place,' said Johnson before his visit of 1780, but nevertheless went to oblige Thrale, who was unwell at the time, and died in the following year. When Johnson and Mrs Thrale were here in 1782 Fanny Burney joined them. Her second novel, *Cecilia*, had recently been published with enormous success, and it was being discussed as eagerly in Brighton as in London. Johnson, however, was out of humour, except with his 'little Burney', who reported that people found him such a bear that he was omitted from cards of invitation sent to the Thrale party.

★ The house is not open to the public, but the gardens are open from April to October on Wednesday, Saturday, Sunday and Bank Holidays 2 to 7 p.m. (in October 12 noon to 5 p.m.).

Brighton, originally a fishing village (described by Macaulay in the famous third chapter of his *History*), was made especially fashionable through the patronage of George IV when he was Prince of Wales, and the increase of residents and visitors included notable men of letters. (An excellent picture of Regency Brighton is given in Conan Doyle's *Rodney Stone*.) Dickens was a frequent visitor from 1837 onwards, and stayed at several addresses. One of these, where he stayed in 1848 and some later visits, has survived. It is the Bedford Hotel on the sea-front near West Pier, and commemorates him with a tablet. Captain Cuttle and other characters in *Dombey and Son* are placed as staying at the Bedford, and Dr Blimber's establishment in the novel is given as on the sea-front. Dickens's reading tours also brought him to Brighton, and one reading was given in the Royal Pavilion.

Thackeray has some Brighton scenes in *The Newcomes* and wrote on it in some of his contributions to *Punch*, in one of which he said that at that particular season (October) Brighton was 'London *plus* prawns for breakfast and the sea air'. Surtees the creator of Jorrocks died here on March 16, 1864; so did Thomas Hughes of *Tom Brown's Schooldays* on March 22, 1896, but both are buried elsewhere. At Lansworth House in Brunswick Road Sir Winston Churchill was at school during 1883-5. Richard Jefferies, in his mortal illness, was resident here for a short time in 1887. Harrison Ainsworth, who lived for fifteen years at Brighton, celebrated **Ovingdean**, three miles to the east and within the county borough, in *Ovingdean Grange*. The Grange of the novel is the house at the north-east side of the green.

A little further south-east, is **Rottingdean** (II, E5), on the coast and also within the county borough, where Rudyard Kipling lived during the years 1897-1902. He lived for a short time in the house of his uncle Sir Edward Burne-Jones, North End House, which has survived and where he wrote the poem 'Recessional'. Then he moved to The Elms★ (which has also survived) opposite the church, where he completed *Stalky and Co.*

Three miles west of Worthing, at **Goring-by-Sea** (II, D5), Richard

★ Near the Elms is the Grange (the Branch Museum and Exhibition Gallery) which has portraits, letters and early editions in the Kipling Room. Open on weekdays 10 a.m. to 7 p.m., Sunday 2 to 6 p.m.

Jefferies died, aged only forty-eight, on August 14, 1887, after a short residence there. In the last two years of his life he had been unable to hold a pen. He was buried in the cemetery of the church at **Broad-water**, a mile north of and now within the boundaries of Worthing. In the same cemetery is buried another great lover of the English countryside, W. H. Hudson.

At **Storrington** (II, D5, on the A283 and ten miles north-west of Worthing), Francis Thompson lived for a few years, sent there by his friend Wilfred Meynell. He stayed at Storrington Priory, where the monks looked after the poet, who had endured so much privation and who had taken to opium. Whilst here he wrote most of the poems, including 'The Hound of Heaven', that appeared in his first volume of *Poems* (1893), as well as his essay on Shelley. At **Bury** (II, D5), on the A29 about four miles north of Arundel, is the country house that John Galsworthy lived in a good deal of his later life.

HORSHAM AREA

Just a little north of the village of **West Grinstead** (II, E5), seven miles south of Horsham, is a deer park (open to the public) in which is Pope's Oak, under which Pope is said to have composed the *Rape of the Lock*. He stayed here in 1712 with his friend John Caryll, a country gentleman who liked the company of literary men. Apparently the subject of the poem was Caryll's suggestion, and at the beginning of it Pope says: 'This verse to Caryll, Muse, is due.' Hilaire Belloc is buried at West Grinstead. He lived from 1906 to the end of his life at **Shipley** seven miles south of Horsham, in a house called King's Land, parts of which date from the fourteenth century. After an accident at his home, he died at Mount Alvernia nursing-home in Guildford on July 16, 1953. Sussex was the county he loved so well and whose praises he celebrated both in prose and poetry. Shipley Mill was restored as a memorial to him.

Two miles south-west of **Warnham** (II, E4), just off the A24 and the same distance north-west of Horsham, is a house called Field Place, where Percy Bysshe Shelley was born on August 4, 1792. He was descended from a long line of Sussex squires, and for his very respect-able father, who later succeeded to the baronetcy, his only son turned out an alarming prospective heir. Shelley was first educated at Horsham before being sent at the age of ten to a school in Brentford. Whilst at school and university he was at home for vacations, but very little thereafter. He is supposed to have written part of *Queen Mab* at Field Place.

About two miles south-west of Horsham is Christ's Hospital (the Bluecoat School) where Coleridge, Lamb and Leigh Hunt were educated, but in their time the school was in London, and therefore their schooldays are mentioned under the London section. Mr Edmund Blunden, however, was educated here after the move. Twelve miles south of Horsham, at **Ashurst** (on the B2135), Michael Fairless (pseudonym of Margaret Fairless Barber) is buried. She lived latterly the life of an invalid at Mock Bridge House, near **Shermanbury**, which is a mile and a half east of the A281, about ten miles south of Horsham. There she wrote *The Roadmender* and her other books.

EPSOM TO DORKING

About two miles north-west of **Epsom** (II, E3, on the A24) is Chessington Hall, which has connexions with Fanny Burney, but not the present Hall, although it was built in her lifetime. In the former Chessington Hall lived her father's friend Samuel Crisp, a misanthropic and disappointed dramatist whose taste and learning were much prized by Dr Burney. Fanny Burney paid many visits here in the 1770's. The Hall was to her 'Liberty Hall', and a 'dear, dear place'; and 'Daddy Crisp' profoundly influenced her taste and intellectual development. She was here when her friend Mrs Thrale informed her that Dr Johnson had read her *Evelina*, and she was so delighted that she danced round the mulberry tree in the garden. The tree survived until a few years ago.

About six miles south of Chessington is **Mickleham** (II, E4, on the A24), also intimately connected with Fanny Burney. In 1793 she visited friends at Norbury Park (near Mickleham, and west of the A24) and met General Alexandre D'Arblay, one of the French refugees who were staying at Juniper Hall (on the east side of the A24; it is now a field-study centre held by the National Trust). There was distinguished company at Juniper Hall: Talleyrand and Mme de Staël were there, and D'Arblay himself had been adjutant-general to Lafayette. He and

Fanny Burney fell in love, and in spite of poverty and Dr Burney's objections (which were overcome) were married in Mickleham Church in July 1793, followed by a Catholic ceremony in the Sardinian Chapel, Lincoln's Inn Fields, London. They lived at **Bookham**, a mile or so west of Norbury Park. When Fanny Burney's third novel, *Camilla*, was published in 1796, they were able to build their own house, calling it Camilla Cottage, a little to the south of Mickleham. They lived there from 1797 until 1802, when Fanny Burney joined her husband in Paris. The cottage was burned down in 1919.

Only a few hundred yards further along the A24 is the Burford Bridge Hotel, by the River Mole, and at the foot of Box Hill. Keats stayed here during part of November and December 1817, and completed *Endymion*. 'I like this place very much,' he said in a letter, 'there is hill and dale and a little river—I went up Box Hill this evening after the moon.' R. L. Stevenson, too, was a visitor at this hotel, staying no less than four times, and wrote of 'the inn at Burford Bridge with its arbours and green gardens and silent, eddying river'.

From the grounds of the hotel a track ascends **Box Hill** (II, E4), on which is situated Flint Cottage (National Trust property, but no admission), George Meredith's home for forty years. He took it in 1876, and some years later installed a Swiss châlet, which he used both for bedroom and study, at the foot of the sloping garden. He was deeply attached to Surrey—'the smell of the earth is Elysian,' he said—and joined the informal order of Sunday Tramps founded by his friend Leslie Stephen. Many friends called to see him, among them Stevenson (who is portrayed as 'Woodseer' in *The Amazing Marriage*, J. M. Barrie and James Russell Lowell.

When *Diana of the Crossways* was published in 1885 it secured Meredith for the first time the notice of the wider public. The novel takes its name from Crossways Farm, which survives at **Abinger** (II, D4), five miles south-east of Dorking. Thereafter Flint Cottage became a centre of pilgrimage. Meredith's wife used to ward off sightseers, but she died in 1886. He died at Flint Cottage on May 18, 1909. King Edward VII and the leading men of the time suggested that he should be buried in Westminster Abbey, but it was refused, and he is buried beside his wife in Dorking cemetery.

In **Dorking** (II, E4) there are three claimants as the original of the Marquis of Granby public house kept by Mrs Weller of *Pickwick Papers*. They are the former King's Head (now the post office), a great coaching inn in its heyday, the King's Arms and the White Horse Hotel. A quarter of a mile east of Dorking is the former mansion of Deepdene (now an hotel) in which Disraeli stayed and wrote most of *Coningsby*. George Gissing lived at Dorking in 1891 or 1892, and was one of Meredith's visitors at Box Hill. Meredith had been one of the earliest to appreciate his work. About four miles north-west of Dorking is the Regency mansion of Polesden Lacey, which stands on the site of a seventeenth-century house bought by Sheridan in 1797, towards the end of his career as a brilliantly successful dramatist.

GUILDFORD AREA

Wotton (II, D4, on the A25 between Dorking and Guildford) is the birthplace of John Evelyn. The second son of a man of considerable means, he was born on October 31, 1620, at Wotton House, a red brick building of many styles and gables. Sent away at the age of five he was only a visitor to his home until he came to live here in 1694, three years after his brother had settled the estate on him. He died here on February 27, 1706, and is buried in the church, which is very near the house. About five miles along the A25 nearer Guildford, the A248 leads to Albury Park,* the home of the Dowager Duchess of Northumberland. The gardens here were originally laid out by Evelyn, and Cobbett described them as 'the prettiest garden I ever beheld'.

Guildford (II, D4) was considered by Malory to be the Astolat of Arthurian romance, but we are on firmer ground in noting its connexion with Lewis Carroll. He used to stay with his sister in a house on Castle Hill, called The Chestnuts (marked by tablet on the gateway) and there he died on January 14, 1898. He is buried in Guildford Cemetery, at the top of a steep hill called the Mount.

Just over twenty miles west of Guildford is the busy, pleasant town of **Farnham** (II, D4), situated on the River Wey, and the birthplace of William Cobbett. But first a word about Izaak Walton. Farnham Castle, which stands high above the town, was for long one of the

* Open daily 1.30 to 5 p.m.

residences of the bishops of Winchester, and Walton's friend Bishop Morley is responsible for most of the structure as we see it now. Walton lived latterly at Winchester and used occasionally to stay at this castle with his friend Morley.

William Cobbett, the third son of a publican and farmer, was born on March 9, 1762, at the Jolly Farmer, which is just by the bridge over the River Wey. He had no formal education and spent his early days as a labourer in the fields. One day, when working on the flower beds at Farnham Castle, the head gardener told him about Kew Gardens, and Cobbett (then aged eleven) decided to find employment there. Next morning he set out to walk to Kew, and in a window at Richmond he saw a copy of Swift's *Tale of a Tub*. Tired and hungry, but very curious, he spent his last threepence on it, and read it by a haystack until darkness came and he fell asleep. Many years later he said that that moment was for him the 'birth of intellect'. He often visited his old home in later years. When he died suddenly at Normandy Farm, near Guildford (where he was carrying on his last farming experiment) on June 18, 1835, he was brought to his native town for burial. He is buried in the churchyard of the parish church, St Andrew, and a commemorative tablet and bust are on the south wall. Augustus M. Toplady, who wrote the famous hymn 'Rock of Ages', is also commemorated in the church, and his birthplace in the High Street is marked by a tablet.

Curiously enough, *A Tale of a Tub* was written only two miles away and to the south-east of Cobbett's birthplace. **Moor Park** (II, D4) the seventeenth-century mansion that lies to the south-east of Farnham, was the home of Sir William Temple, diplomat, author and husband of Dorothy Osborne, who is supposed to have been related to Swift's mother. About 1690 Swift came to this house as secretary to Temple, who promised him employment in Ireland, but nothing came of it and the disappointed Swift returned to Ireland in 1694.

He came back two years later and during this second period wrote *The Battle of the Books* and *A Tale of a Tub*. At Moor Park Swift became acquainted with Esther Johnson, who was to play so large a part in his life and who became known as Swift's Stella, and was aged barely ten when he first knew her. It has often been asserted, but not established, that Stella was Temple's illegitimate daughter, and the absurd suggestion has been made that Swift was Temple's natural son. Soon after his employer's death in 1699 Swift left for London. Cobbett, who used to roam over Moor Park in his boyhood, brought his son here many years later and showed him the hill near the house where Swift used to run for exercise. The house is now Moor Park College for adult Christian education.

Very near Moor Park are the ruins of Waverley Abbey, and near the entrance lodge is what is known as Stella's cottage. Scott is supposed to have derived the title of his first novel (subsequently adopted for the whole series) from Waverley Abbey, the first Cistercian house to be built in England. About six miles north-east of Guildford is **Pyrford**, where John Donne and his wife lived from about 1601 for four years or so, after the discovery of their secret marriage and Donne's imprisonment. Bret Harte died at Camberley on May 5, 1902, whilst visiting a friend, and is buried in the churchyard of St Peter at **Frimley** (II, D3), about eight miles north-east of Farnham.

NORTH HAMPSHIRE AND READING

At **Steventon** (II, C4, on an unclassified road ten miles south-west of Basingstoke), Jane Austen, the youngest of a family of seven, was born on December 16, 1775, and there spent the first twenty-five years of her life. Her father, whose forebears were clothiers in Kent, had been rector of Steventon since 1761 (and held the living of Deane near by from 1773) and his old church here contains a memorial tablet to his daughter Jane. The old rectory was unfortunately demolished over a century ago, but its site was in a field where stands a modern pump on the site of the Austen household pump.

Jane and her elder sister Cassandra, the only girls in the family, were sent to schools at Oxford, Southampton and Reading, and Jane's formal education ended when she was nine. The Abbey School at **Reading** (II, C3) was held in the Old Gateway (which can still be seen) of the former Benedictine abbey. She began writing in her early teens. That field in Steventon has a particular importance in English letters, for we know that in the rectory within its bounds Miss Austen wrote the first drafts of *Pride and Prejudice*, *Sense and Sensibility* and *Northanger Abbey* between the ages of twenty and twenty-three. Her knowledge of human nature shows that she led no life of seclusion in an out-of-the-way country vicarage. She was the daughter of a man of culture; she attended the county balls at Basingstoke, and there were other houses she visited in the vicinity. At Deane House (which survives), the manor house of the Harwoods, she met interesting company. Incidentally, it is alleged that a former Harwood was depicted by Fielding (an author much admired by Miss Austen) as Squire Western in *Tom Jones*. In 1800 her father retired and, much to her sorrow, decided to settle in Bath.

In 1808 her brother Edward offered his widowed mother and his sisters a house near either of his residences, Godmersham in Kent and Chawton in Hampshire. They chose **Chawton** (II, C4, a mile south of Alton and at the junction of the A31 and A32), and moved into Chawton Cottage* in July 1809. It was not until after she settled here that Miss Austen's work was published, and here were written the last three novels, *Mansfield Park*, *Emma* and *Persuasion*, in the eight years of life left to her. Whenever her brother's children were at Chawton House (known then as the Great House) she was a frequent and very welcome visitor. Chawton House is only a short distance away, and is occasionally open to the public.

Miss Mitford visited Chawton Cottage in 1812, and said that it was 'all life, all gaiety', and that there was a 'total absence of the vulgar hurry of business or the chilling apathy of fashion'. Writing cannot have been easy for Miss Austen, for most of it was apparently done in the general sitting-room. Her nephew says that 'she was careful that her occupation should not be suspected by servants, or visitors, or any persons beyond her own family party. She wrote upon small sheets of paper which could easily be put away, or covered with a piece of blotting paper. There was, between the front door and the offices, a swing door which creaked when it was opened; but she objected to having this little inconvenience remedied, because it gave her notice when anyone was coming.' During 1816 Miss Austen contracted a fatal disease, and on May 24, 1817, had to be moved to Winchester.

* Open 11 a.m. to 4.30 p.m. throughout the year, including Sundays and Bank Holidays. There are interesting relics of the family, but the only personal relics of Miss Austen are the patchwork quilt she made with her mother, and her donkey cart.

Another woman novelist is connected with this northern part of Hampshire, and that is Mrs Gaskell. She was enchanted with this fine tract of Hampshire and bought a large house in the village of **Holybourne** (II, C4), less than two miles from Alton, but on the London side. The house was bought from the proceeds of her last book, *Wives and Daughters*, and intended as a surprise present for her husband. She had been in the house only a few months when she died suddenly of heart failure on November 12, 1865, aged fifty-five. She had been to service at the old church only that very morning. Her house, called The Lawn, can still be seen. In **Alton** (II, C4) itself there is a house called Swarthmore in the High Street (marked by a tablet) where John Henry Newman lived during the years 1816-19, when he was an undergraduate at Oxford.

Returning to Reading again, we find in London Road the house (marked by a tablet) of Mary Russell Mitford. Her family moved here when she was ten, having recently won a prize of £20,000 in a lottery, and her father used part of the money to build this house. She attended the same Abbey School that Jane Austen had been to, and completed her education in London. An exceedingly precocious child who read enormously, her literary taste now began to develop, but her first work was not published until she was twenty-two.

Her father, an unprincipled but apparently lovable spendthrift, soon brought the family to poverty. 'My mother's fortune was large, my father's good, legacies from both sides, a £20,000 prize in the lottery—all have vanished,' she said, and it is thought that her father ran through £70,000 in his lifetime. The family moved to the village of **Three Mile Cross** (on the A33, about five miles south of Reading), and took a labourer's cottage. Miss Mitford had to redouble her efforts to keep the family going, but it was not until she began in 1819 to produce the sketches of village life at Three Mile Cross entitled *Our Village* that she attained any real success, and the success was enormous. Moreover she created a new genre in English literature, and has been aptly called the Claude of English village life. She became a great celebrity, and was visited by distinguished people. She received a Civil List pension in 1837, and when her rogue of a father died five years later his debts were met by a public subscription. In 1851 she moved to the village of **Swallowfield**, a few miles south of Three Mile Cross, died there on

January 10, 1855, and is buried in the churchyard. Her cottage is still to be seen, 'where three roads meet'.

For her birthplace we must go into the heart of Hampshire. On the A31, about eight miles east of Winchester and not much more from Miss Austen's home at Chawton, is Alresford, divided by the little River Alre into the village of Old Alresford and the small market town of **New Alresford** (II, C4). She was born in the latter in Broad Street (the house is marked by a tablet) on December 16, 1787, and lived there until she was ten, when she won the £20,000 prize which caused the move to Reading.

There is a further and more tragic association to record for Reading, that of Oscar Wilde. He was moved from Wandsworth Prison, owing to the instrumentality of R. B. (later Lord) Haldane in November 1895 to Reading Gaol, near the Old Abbey Gateway where Jane Austen and Mary Russell Mitford had been to school. At first he fared no better than he had done at Wandsworth, but after a change of governors he was much more humanely treated. During his imprisonment he wrote *De Profundis*, a long letter to Lord Alfred Douglas explaining his conduct, in part profoundly moving and in part evincing Wilde's theatricality, and only comparatively recently published in full. Wilde came out of Reading Gaol in 1897 a broken and a ruined man, and except for 'The Ballad of Reading Gaol' (which was not written in prison, as is sometimes supposed) he wrote no more. He went abroad and died in Paris on November 30, 1900, and was buried in the Bagneux Cemetery, but his remains were removed in 1909 to the cemetery of Père-Lachaise, and rest under a tombstone designed by Jacob Epstein.

On the A327 ten miles south-east of Reading is **Eversley** (II, C3), where Charles Kingsley became curate in 1842, and rector from 1844 until his death. He died there on January 23, 1875, and is buried in the churchyard. There is a bas-relief portrait of him at the east end of the church.

Selborne (II, C4) a village beautifully situated at the foot of a hill called The Hanger, is on the B3006 six miles south of Alton, and indissolubly connected with Gilbert White. He was born at the parsonage, and not, as is sometimes stated, at the family home called The Wakes, on January 18, 1720. His grandfather was the vicar, and his father a barrister. He was educated at the grammar school at Basingstoke, and may have had his first schooling in Farnham. He proceeded to Oxford, and was ordained deacon and later priest. His earlier church appointments were at or never far from Selborne, of which he was vicar in his last years. He lived at first either at the parsonage or The Wakes, and the latter came into his possession in 1763, and was his home for most of his life. He lived a life of gentlemanly ease, never married, aspired to no preferment in his profession, travelled frequently, observed Nature closely, and recorded his observations in a quietly captivating style. *The Natural History and Antiquities of Selborne* originated in letters to his friend Thomas Pennant, other correspondents following later, and he finally gave his consent, at first reluctantly, to publication in 1788. Never has a book on natural history been so popular.

He died at The Wakes on June 26, 1793, and is buried in the churchyard, by the north side of the church. The gravestone bears the simple inscription: G. W. 1793. At the entrance to the churchyard is the enormous yew, over 20 ft. in girth and probably well over a thousand years old, which is described in the fifth letter relating to the antiquities of Selborne. The Wakes, for long the Gilbert White Museum, is now the Oates Memorial Library and Museum* and incorporates the former. In the garden is the sundial erected by White.

WINCHESTER

The former capital of Saxon England (II, B4) has some great names connected with it in all walks of life and not least in literature. Its great public school, Winchester College, founded in 1382 by William of Wykeham, Bishop of Winchester, has a very distinguished list of scholars who became eminent in literature. Sir Henry Wotton, Sir Thomas Browne, Thomas Otway, William Collins, Sidney Smith, Anthony Trollope, Matthew Arnold and Lionel Johnson are all old Wykehamists.

The next association is a tragic one. Sir Walter Ralegh was brought here to be tried for alleged complicity in a plot against James I. When

* Open on weekdays (except Friday) April to October 11 a.m. to 1 p.m., 2.30 to 5.30 p.m., Sunday 2.30 to 5.30 p.m.

he arrived—James I had not long been on the throne, and was still popular—the people threw mud, tobacco-pipes and other objects at him. The trial was in Wolvesey Castle, the palace of the Bishop of Winchester. The prosecution by Sir Edward Coke was conducted with the utmost ferocity, and Ralegh was condemned to death, but the capital sentence was not carried out. His estates were confiscated and he was committed to the Tower of London. By a grim irony of fate the trial had begun on November 17, the anniversary of the accession of the great queen whom he had served with such brilliance and courage.

Winchester Cathedral contains the mortal remains of two choice and not entirely dissimilar spirits—Izaak Walton and Jane Austen—both perfectionists in the art of literature and both embodying the virtues of quietism. In 1662, in his seventieth year, Walton came to live with his friend George Morley, Bishop of Winchester, in the palace in which Ralegh had been tried. There are scanty remains of this palace beside the later building erected for Morley, and which was probably designed by Wren. Here Walton lived happily for the last twenty years of his life, wrote the lives of Richard Hooker and George Herbert, fished on the Itchen and Test rivers near by, and went as far afield as Dovedale in pursuit of 'the contemplative man's recreation'. He died on December 15, 1683, aged ninety, in his son-in-law's house (No. 7 The Close, still standing), and was buried in Prior Silkstede's chapel in the north transept of the cathedral. Thomas Ken, whose half-sister was Walton's second wife, wrote the inscription on the tomb. Ken was the author of those famous hymns 'Awake my soul' and 'Glory to Thee, my God, this night'.

Jane Austen was moved to Winchester in May 1817, when she was desperately ill, to a house in College Street, which survives and is marked by a tablet. She lived less than two months, tended to the last by her sister Cassandra, and died on July 18, 1817, aged forty-one. She was buried in the north aisle of the cathedral, and a tablet and memorial window are above her tomb.

Two years after Miss Austen's death Keats and his friend Charles Brown arrived here in August 1819 from the Isle of Wight. 'We removed to Winchester,' he told a friend, 'for the convenience of a library and find it an exceedingly pleasant town, enriched with a beautiful cathedral and surrounded by a fresh-looking country. We are in tolerably good and cheap lodgings'—but unfortunately he does not say where. During the two months he stayed he completed 'Otho the Great' and 'Lamia', worked on 'The Eve of St Mark' and, most important of all, wrote the great 'Ode to Autumn'. Winchester and its 'fresh-looking country' are therefore very intimately connected with some of Keats's greatest poetry.

One of the most beautiful scenes in Thackeray's *Henry Esmond* is laid in Winchester Cathedral. Thackeray's disciple Trollope based his picture of 'Hiram's Hospital' in *The Warden* on the ancient Hospital of St Cross,* which is a mile south of the cathedral. Winchester is definitely the Barchester of the famous series of novels. The matter has been needlessly debated, but we have Trollope's assurance that it is so, and the further assurance that Barsetshire is not Hampshire, but Somersetshire. At Winchester was enacted the final drama in the life of Tess, in *Tess of the D'Urbervilles*, when she was hanged in the gaol of the city called 'Wintoncester' in the novel.

Botley, (II, C5) about ten miles south of Winchester, was the home of the much-travelled William Cobbett from 1804 to 1817. As usual with Cobbett, wherever he settled he carried out his farming experiments. It was whilst he was here that he served a prison sentence of two years for an article in his *Political Register*, and in 1817, when the Habeas Corpus Act was suspended, he had a shrewd idea that he might be imprisoned again, and decided to remove himself to America.

CHICHESTER AND PORTSMOUTH AREA

Sussex is not a county in which we expect to find an association with Cowper, so intimately is he associated with Buckinghamshire and Norfolk. At **Eartham**, off the A285 about ten miles north-east of Chichester, there is Eartham House, once occupied by William Hayley. He was a popular poet in his day, one of his poems reaching at least twelve editions, but Southey has summed up what all but contemporaries thought of him: 'Everything about that man is good except

---

* Visitors are admitted on application at reasonable hours.

his poetry.' He came to know Cowper when both were engaged in different editions of Milton, and in 1792 invited the poet and his friend Mrs Unwin to stay at Eartham. He later became Cowper's first biographer. Cowper was there for six weeks, and was 'a little daunted by the tremendous height of the Sussex hills'. Romney the portrait painter, who had long been a friend of Hayley's and spent his annual holiday here, was present during Cowper's visit. Romney made a crayon portrait of Cowper and illustrated a passage in 'The Task'; Cowper wrote a sonnet to Romney.

Hayley spent his later years at **Felpham** (II, D5), then a village outside but now a suburb of Bognor. He had been introduced to William Blake by Flaxman the sculptor and draughtsman, and suggested that Blake should stay at Felpham. In September 1800 Blake took a cottage (which has survived) next to Hayley's house. Blake liked Felpham at first, and said that 'the sweet air and the voices of winds, trees and birds, and the odours of the happy ground, make it a dwelling for immortals'. But Hayley, unwearied as he was in trying to please Blake, and incapable of understanding Blake's genius, soon began to grate on him, and Blake did not wish any longer to be 'pestered with Hayley's genteel ignorance and polite disapprobation'.

Just before he was due to leave Felpham, Blake turned a drunken soldier out of his garden. The soldier accused Blake of uttering seditious and treasonable matter. Blake was tried at Chichester on a ridiculous charge of high treason, and acquitted. The trial took place in the church of the Greyfriars (the chancel survives) in Priory Park. Whilst at Felpham he began his prophetic poem 'Milton' (the great lyric 'And did those feet in ancient time' comes from the preface), and did some work for Hayley, including illustrations for the latter's life of Cowper. Blake left Felpham in 1804.

Chichester (II, D5) has a native poet in William Collins, born on Christmas Day, 1721, though exactly where is now unknown. He was the son of a hatter who was twice Mayor of Chichester. He was at first educated locally and then sent to Winchester and Oxford. His hardships and disappointments in London resulted in melancholia and madness, and for the last few years of his life he lived in Chichester, where he died on June 12, 1759. A monument designed by Flaxman was erected in the cathedral in 1795. At 11 Eastgate Street a tablet commemorates the fact that Keats stayed there with friends in 1819, and in that house wrote 'The Eve of St Agnes'.

Hampshire's greatest literary native, Charles Dickens, was born at 1 Mile End Terrace, Portsea, now 393 Commercial Road, **Portsmouth** (II, C5) on February 7, 1812. His birthplace, which fortunately survived the bombing of the last war, is now the Charles Dickens Birthplace Museum.* His father John Dickens was a clerk in the Navy Pay Office, and his mother the daughter of a Naval lieutenant. About two years after his birth his father moved to Hawke Road in Portsmouth, but very soon afterwards the family had to move to London when John Dickens was transferred to Somerset House. Dickens visited Portsmouth in 1838 to secure local colour for the Crummles scenes in *Nicholas Nickleby*, and paid other visits later. His first English provincial reading tour ended here in 1866, and he visited the street in which he was born, but was unable to remember the house.

At 73 High Street (the house was destroyed in the last war) the father of George Meredith practised as a tailor until business declined and he moved to London. Meredith was not born there, as formerly supposed, but spent the first ten years or so of his life there. After a little schooling in Southsea he was sent for further education in Germany. Portsmouth figures as 'Lymport' in his novel *Evan Harrington*. Sir Walter Besant, the novelist and historian of London, was born in St George's Square on August 14, 1836, the son of a merchant. He described much of his boyhood in his novel *By Celia's Arbour*.

Rudyard Kipling's first home in England was in **Southsea** (II, C5). Born in Bombay on December 30, 1865, he was sent to a family here in 1871, and found them pious but disagreeable. He disliked his life here, and was glad to get away for Christmas holidays to his aunt's, Lady Burne-Jones's, home in London. H. G. Wells at the age of fifteen was apprenticed at Hyde's Drapery Emporium in King's Road, Southsea, where he served for two years. The experience was utilized in *The History of Mr Polly*. Sir Arthur Conan Doyle practised as a doctor in Southsea for eight years, and during that time wrote his first four

* Open on weekdays, summer 10 a.m. to 7 p.m., winter 10 a.m. to 5 p.m. Contains first editions, portraits, holograph letters and other personal relics.

novels, the very first being *A Study in Scarlet*, which introduced Sherlock Holmes to the world. As one would expect, Portsmouth figures a great deal in the novels of Marryat; and part of the scene of Jane Austen's *Mansfield Park* is laid in Portsmouth. She derived her knowledge of the port and of sailors from her two sailor brothers.

HASLEMERE, MIDHURST AND PETERSFIELD AREA

At **Witley** (II, D4) a few miles south of Godalming, on the A283, is a house called The Heights which George Eliot and G. H. Lewes acquired in 1876, with ideas of permanent settlement. She resided there at intervals until 1880, and there wrote her last novel, *Daniel Deronda*. Also connected with her is the house called Brookbank at **Shottermill**, near Haslemere, about eight miles south-west of Witley, and on the A286. She occupied it for a short time in 1871.

Haslemere (II, D4) lies under the northern slope of **Blackdown**, and on the slope itself is Aldworth, famous as the last home of Tennyson. The house was erected for him in 1868, and the foundation stone was laid on the traditional day of Shakespeare's birth, April 23. He alternated between here and his home in the Isle of Wight, until he gave up the latter. He died here on October 6, 1892. The house is now the home of H. H. the Gaekwar of Baroda. A footpath that circles the crest of Blackdown is called Tennyson's Walk.

Further west, about five miles beyond Midhurst on the A272 is **Trotton** (II, D5), where Thomas Otway was born at his father's vicarage on March 3, 1652. Soon afterwards his father moved to **Woolbeding** (II, D4), a short distance north of Midhurst, where Otway spent his boyhood years. He has left a curious memorial of himself in scribblings of Latin quotations with his signature in the parish register.

In the area round **Petersfield** (II, C4) there are several associations. The cottage of Edward Thomas, a fastidious and delightful poet and essayist, is at **Steep**, a village situated at the foot of the finely wooded Stoner Hill. Thomas was killed at Arras on April 9, 1917, and there is a memorial to him on the hill.

Off the A3, and three miles south of Petersfield, is the village of **Buriton** (II, C5), where the old manor house north of the church was the home of Edward Gibbon. Gibbon's father settled here after his first wife's death, and Gibbon joined him on his return from the Continent in 1759. Father and son joined the Hampshire militia, and although the company of brother officers was not to young Gibbon's taste, he remarks sententiously in his *Memoirs* that his military experience was 'not useless to the historian of the Roman Empire'. His duties took him to many parts of southern England, but he was able to lead the life of a country gentleman's son, and made good use of his father's library to pursue his studies. He inherited the house on his father's death in 1770, and sold it two years later.

Three miles east of Buriton, at **South Harting**, Anthony Trollope spent the last two years of his life, and here began *The Landleaguers*, but died before the novel was completed. A mile and half to the south, and five miles south-east of Petersfield, is the late seventeenth-century mansion of **Uppark**,* (II, C5) where the mother of H. G. Wells was a housekeeper, and in which he lived as a boy. It figures in the partly autobiographical novel *Tono-Bungay*, as 'Bladesover', but the housekeeper in the novel is not modelled on his mother. The library there proved a boon to Wells, who later during holidays was able to imbibe Voltaire, Tom Paine and other writers to his liking. He was for a time apprenticed to a pharmaceutical chemist in **Midhurst** (II, D5) (depicted as 'Wimblehurst' in *Tono-Bungay*) and took Latin lessons from Horace Byatt, who had been Arnold Bennett's headmaster. The expense of qualification cut short Wells's career as a pharmacist. After some experience as a draper's apprentice he returned to Midhurst and became a student assistant under Byatt at the grammar school.

George Meredith, until recent years regarded as a native of Portsmouth, was born in a farmhouse near Petersfield on February 12, 1828. The house has not been identified, and may not have survived.

SOUTHAMPTON AND BOURNEMOUTH

Southampton (II, B5) possesses three native writers. The first in time, Izaac Watts, is the author of perhaps the most sung of all hymns, 'O God, our help in ages past'. He was born at 21 French Street on July 17,

* Open April 6 to September 28 on Wednesday, Thursday, Sunday and Bank Holidays 2.30 to 6 p.m.

1674, the son of a clothier who was imprisoned for nonconformity. Watts began writing hymns when about twenty, and his first efforts were sung in the Above Bar Chapel (no longer extant) from manuscript copies. He is commemorated by a statue in West Park. Charles Dibdin, dramatist and song-writer, especially of sea-songs—the only one remembered nowadays is 'Tom Bowling'—was born on or just before March 4, 1745, but exactly where is not known. George Saintsbury, one of the greatest of modern critics, was born in Southampton on October 23, 1845. His father was secretary and superintendent of the docks. After early years Saintsbury spent only a few months in Southampton on his retirement in 1915, but is buried in the Old Cemetery.

After a royal visit in 1750 Southampton achieved great popularity as a spa. Assembly rooms were built and famous visitors flocked here, among them Pope, Swift, Voltaire, Gray and Cowper. Horace Walpole came too, and with his usual flair for commenting on anything and everything, said that the town was crowded in 1755, and that sea bathing, something of a novelty then, was established there. It was beginning to decline as a spa when Jane Austen came with her mother to stay with her brother Frank. From his lodgings they moved to a house of their own in Castle Square, where they stayed until April 1809. Neither dwelling has survived.

Between Southampton Water and the Hampshire Avon lies the New Forest, the scene of Marryat's historical romance of *The Children of the New Forest*. In the New Forest, at **Lyndhurst** (five miles south-west of Southampton) is the grave of Mrs Reginald Hargreaves, formerly Alice Liddell and the original of *Alice in Wonderland*. It is surprising to find an Elizabethan dramatist turned clergyman, but John Marston was rector of **Christchurch** (II, A5, on the east side of Bournemouth) from 1616 to 1631, when he resigned, maybe from ill-health. In the beautiful priory church there is, below the tower, the monument to Shelley, represented as supported on the knees of his wife. It was placed here after being rejected by Westminster Abbey. His son lived at Boscombe near by.

At **Mudeford** (II, B5), at the mouth of the Avon and Stour, and a little east of Christchurch, is a rotunda-like little building known as

Scott's House, where he stayed in 1807 and wrote part of *Marmion*. **Burton**, less than two miles north of Christchurch on the road to Ringwood, was where Southey lived during the summer of 1797. Lamb called, just for a night, with a friend of theirs whose love-affair they were trying to disentangle. Southey's cottage may still be in existence, but it seems impossible to identify.

In the churchyard of St Peter's at **Bournemouth** (II, A5) Mary Shelley is buried, and Shelley's heart, snatched from the flames by his friend Trelawny, is buried with her. R. L. Stevenson lived at Bournemouth for three years, the last two (1885-7) in a house called Skerryvore (destroyed in an air raid in 1940) in Alum Chine Road. There he completed *Kidnapped*, and wrote *Dr Jekyll and Mr Hyde* in three days without stopping. Then he read it aloud to Lloyd Osbourne and his wife: the former was enthusiastic, but the latter's praise was qualified, and Stevenson in anger threw the manuscript into the fire. However, he took his wife's criticism to heart, and rewrote the story as we have it in another three days. Bournemouth is the 'Sandbourne' of Hardy's *Tess of the D'Urbervilles*, characterized as 'a Mediterranean lounging-place on the English channel', where Tess murdered Alec D'Urberville.

ISLE OF WIGHT

The island has associations with three great English poets, Keats, Tennyson and Swinburne, and one American, Longfellow. Keats's first visit was a short one, when he stayed at Canterbury House, Castle Road, **Carisbrooke** (II, B6), in April 1817, and paid a visit to **Shanklin** (II, C6). He was enchanted: 'the Island ought to be called Primrose Island,' he said. For the next visit he stayed the whole of July and part of August at Shanklin. His health had begun to decline, and some of his passionate letters to Fanny Brawne are written from Shanklin. He found the air too relaxing, and after six weeks moved to Winchester. His visit is commemorated by a tablet on Eglantine Cottage (which is not the house he stayed in) in the 'Old Village'. His favourite walk on the cliff-top has been named Keats Green. Longfellow, on his visit of 1868 to England, stayed in Shanklin part of the time, and left a memorial of himself in the form of verses for the drinking-fountain near the Crab Inn and not far from the top of the Chine.

The road southwards from Shanklin passes along the lovely Under-cliff to **Bonchurch** (II, C6), about four miles away, and nestling below the Downs. The house, called East Dene (now a hostel), was the boy-hood home of Swinburne. Like Keats, he loved the island and went rambling, climbing and swimming, and describes the difficult climb he had on Culver Cliff,* at the eastern tip of the island. Dickens stayed in Bonchurch in 1849, and his own boys played with the 'golden-haired lad of the Swinburnes'. When Dickens went to congratulate Swin-burne on *Atalanta in Calydon*, he reminded the poet of their first meeting. Dickens did not like the air of this part of the island, and left for Broadstairs. Swinburne is buried in the churchyard above the village, where members of his family are also buried.

At the western tip of the island, on the outskirts of **Freshwater** (II, B6), and a mile west of Freshwater Bay, is Tennyson's old home called Farringford, now an hotel. He leased it in 1853, and from the profits of *Maud* bought it two years later. Subsequently, when he built a house in Sussex, he used annually to cross the Solent, and on one of these crossings composed 'Crossing the Bar'. After more than thirty years there Tennyson found the island growing too fashionable and he him-self being lionized too much for his taste, and retired to his Sussex home. The hotel preserves letters, books and other relics of the poet. Part of High Down above the gleaming white cliffs has been named Tennyson Down, and on it stands the Tennyson Memorial in the form of a cross.

* It appears from his description that he climbed the easier eastern face of the cliff. The present writer, intoxicated with Swinburne's poetry when a boy, decided to climb the western and more difficult side, but has to confess that he was helped at certain points by the old cable that used to run from that point across the Channel.

South-West England

Dorsetshire
Salisbury and South Wiltshire
North Wiltshire
Bath
Bristol
Somersetshire
North Devonshire
South Devonshire
Cornwall
The Channel Islands

Dorsetshire

The county is the very heart of Thomas Hardy's Wessex, and most of his life was spent in it, but there are several other notable associations. **Wimborne,** or **Wimborne Minster** (II, A5) is probably the birthplace of Matthew Prior, though he has been claimed as a native of Westminster. The library of the very beautiful minster possesses a copy of Ralegh's *History of the World* with a hole burned through more than a hundred pages, and tradition says that Prior was the culprit, and furthermore that he repaired the book carefully. Thomas Hardy lived in Wimborne during the years 1881-3, but the house does not appear to be known. It figures as 'Warborne' in his *Two on a Tower*. **Shaftesbury** (III, H3 on the A30) is the 'Shaston' of *Jude the Obscure*.

Four and a half miles west of Shaftesbury is **East Stour**, where Fielding's family moved when he was three, but their manor house has gone. Fielding received his early education from the curate of Motcombe, only a few miles away, when the latter lived for a time at East Stour. Parson Trulliber (in *Joseph Andrews*), an ignorant lazy and selfish man, is supposed to have been modelled on him. At the end of his Eton school-days Fielding was involved in a love-affair with a young lady of Lyme

Regis. Her guardian objected, and was apparently threatened by Fielding and his manservant, whose doings or manner thoroughly frightened the guardian. The young lady was sent away, and married another. A year or two later Fielding went to London, but returned to live for a short time at East Stour after his marriage.

About twelve miles south-west of Shaftesbury, on the A357, is **Sturminster Newton**, where Hardy lived during 1876-8, and it appears as 'Stourcastle' in *Tess of the D'Urbervilles*. North-west of Sturminster Newton lies the Vale of Blackmore, and in the hamlet of **Rushay** (parish of **Bagber**) William Barnes the Dorsetshire poet revered by Hardy was born on March 20, 1801. He was educated at Sturminster Newton, and then entered a solicitor's office there, leaving in 1818 for **Dorchester** (III, H4), where he applied himself to learn wood-engraving, the acquisition of languages, and contributing poems to a local paper. His first volume of poems was published in 1822. After a spell of schoolmastering in Wiltshire he returned in 1835 to Dorchester, and by now had mastered several languages and become a lover and protagonist of the Dorset dialect. He settled in Durngate Street, running his own little school, moving later to a larger house in South Street, then again to No. 40 opposite (marked by a tablet) where he lived during 1847-62. He became rector of **Winterborne Came** (off the A352 and about two miles south-east of Dorchester) in 1862 and remained there until his death on October 7, 1886. He was buried in the churchyard there, and is commemorated in Dorchester by a statue outside St Peter's Church in the High Street. On the pedestal is a quotation from one of his own poems in the Dorset dialect.

Thomas Hardy, the son of a builder, and of Dorset stock on both sides, was born on June 2, 1840, in the hamlet of **Higher Bock-hampton*** (III, H4) in the parish of **Stinsford** (off the A35 and about three miles east of Dorchester). The parish of Stinsford, apart from being Hardy's birthplace, was made famous by him in the idyllic *Under the Greenwood Tree, or the Mellstock Quire* (written at Bock-hampton), Stinsford being 'Mellstock'. The Hardys had been keen musicians for generations, and the instrumental music they and others

* The cottage in which he was born is open on Thursday, Saturday and Sunday 2 to 6 p.m. (closed from November to end of January).

provided for the services in Stinsford Parish Church was famous for many miles around in their time. As a boy Hardy often played the fiddle at local dances. He was born on the edge of 'Egdon Heath', the name he gave to the expanse of heathlands stretching from Dorchester to Bournemouth. A description of it marks the opening of *The Return of the Native*, and throughout the novel it is like a great brooding presence. 'Egdon Heath' seems to symbolize (or so it appears to the present writer) Hardy's tragic view of life, and once *The Return of the Native* has been read the heath is a hovering presence in nearly all Hardy's novels. For artistic purposes Hardy placed the hill called Rainbarrow in the centre of the heath, though in fact it lies near the western edge.

Hardy was first educated at the village school, and later at a private school in Dorchester, where he received an excellent grounding in Latin and French, and after leaving school he studied Greek and German. At the age of sixteen he entered an architect's office in Dorchester. Whilst there he met William Barnes and—more important for his future development—Horace Moule, a classical scholar of Queens' College, Cambridge, who encouraged him to write.

In 1862 Hardy sought work in London, and five years later returned to the architect's office in Dorchester. He now decided to devote himself to writing though not as yet giving up architectural practice. His first story was rejected by Macmillan but accepted by Chapman and Hall, whose reader (no less a person than George Meredith) advised Hardy against publication and to concentrate on plot in his novels. His second novel, *Desperate Remedies*, was also rejected by Macmillan but appeared under another imprint in 1871. In the following year *Under the Greenwood Tree*, which showed his real power, was published. Leslie Stephen was impressed by it, and invited Hardy to write a serial for the *Cornhill*. The result was *Far from the Madding Crowd*, the first of his really great novels, and completed at Bockhampton. Much of the scene is laid at Waterston Manor (now a farmhouse and on the A35 five miles north-east of Dorchester), which as 'Weatherbury Farm' is the dwelling of Bathsheba Everdene. The 'Weatherbury' of the novel is Puddletown.

Soon after the appearance of this novel Hardy married, and lived in various places until he settled in 1885 in a house of his own design, called Max Gate,* on the Wareham road just outside Dorchester. There he lived the rest of his long life. Later it became a centre of pilgrimage, and he was visited by many notable people. At Max Gate he completed *The Mayor of Casterbridge* and wrote *The Woodlanders, Tess of the D'Urbervilles* and *Jude the Obscure*, as well as the bulk of his poetry. *The Mayor of Casterbridge* is Hardy's greatest novel, and its main action is in Dorchester ('Casterbridge'). Part of the action of *Tess* is also laid in Dorchester, and the town recurs in other novels, but references in other parts of this book testify to the fact that his *mise en scène* is almost as extensive as the ancient Saxon kingdom. Hardy died at Max Gate on January 11, 1928; his heart was interred in the churchyard at Stinsford and his ashes in Westminster Abbey. A statue of him by Eric Kennington stands in The Grove on the north side of Dorchester.

About seven miles south of Dorchester, at **Weymouth** (III, H4), the main action takes place of Hardy's *The Trumpet Major*, a fine story of the Napoleonic wars, only a little inferior to Hardy's greatest and less popular than it should be. The town figures also in *The Dynasts* and other works by Hardy. *The Dynasts* mentions Gloucester Lodge (now the Gloucester Hotel) where George III used to stay, and when Fanny Burney was in royal service she stayed there too, as recorded in her *Diary*. Thomas Love Peacock was born in Weymouth on October 18, 1785, though exactly where is not known. His father, a London glass merchant, died in 1788, and not long afterwards he was taken by his mother to live with her father at Chertsey.

Bere Regis (III, H4, at the junction of the A31 and A35 and about ten miles north-east of Dorchester) is the 'Kingsbere' of *Tess of the D'Urbervilles*. It contains tombs of the ancient Dorset family of Turbeville, which no doubt suggested the name of D'Urberville. Three and a half miles south-west of Bere Regis, on the unclassified Puddletown road, is **Clouds Hill†** (III, H4), the cottage where T. E. Lawrence

* Not open to the public, but Hardy's study there has been reconstructed in the Dorset County Museum in High Street, Dorchester, open weekdays 10 a.m. to 1 p.m., 2 to 5 p.m. (closed Boxing Day and Good Friday). Among the relics is the manuscript of *The Mayor of Casterbridge*.

† Open Sunday, Wednesday and Thursday 2 to 6 p.m. in summer, and 12 noon to dusk in winter.

(Lawrence of Arabia) lived in his later years. He died at Bovington Camp Hospital near by on May 19, 1935, after an accident, and is buried in the churchyard at **Moreton**, about eight miles east of Dorchester. A sculptured figure of him by Eric Kennington is in St Martin's Church, **Wareham**, and in St Paul's Cathedral is the same artist's bronze bust of Lawrence. In the same area, at **Wool** (III, H4) off the A352, five miles west of Wareham, is Woolbridge Manor (now a guest house), the 'Wellbridge House' of *Tess of the D'Urbervilles*, and formerly the manor-house of the Turberville family. The mural portraits of the 'horrid women' that frightened Tess are now very faded. The ruins of Bindon Abbey are near by, where Angel Clare laid Tess in the empty stone coffin of the abbott, and where she made her confession.

Sherborne (III, H3, off the A30), appears as 'Sherton Abbas' in three of Hardy's works, *The Woodlanders*, *Far from the Madding Crowd* and *A Group of Noble Dames*, and the town has many earlier associations. Whilst on his way from London to meet the imperial ambassador at Falmouth Sir Thomas Wyatt contracted fever, stopped at Sherborne and died there on October 11, 1542. He is buried in the Wickham Chapel of Sherborne Abbey.

Sherborne has a monumental reminder of its association with Ralegh. In 1592, shortly before getting into disgrace over the affair of Elizabeth Throgmorton, he had acquired from the Bishop of Salisbury a ninety-nine year lease of the castle here. Then he came down with his bride and began to alter the castle. The central portion of the building is that built by Ralegh. For the next year or two he divided his time mainly between London and the castle. It remained in his possession until 1603, when he made it over to his son, but on Ralegh's disgrace James I took advantage of a technical flaw in the document to give it to a court favourite.

Thomas Fuller, who is our only authority for the story of Ralegh's cloak, was rector of **Broadwindsor** (III, G4), about five miles south of Crewkerne, from 1634 to 1641. The Jacobean pulpit in the church is no doubt the one from which he preached. Whilst here he wrote his *Holy and Profane State*.

It is a little surprising to find Wordsworth living in Dorset. Only a few miles from Broadwindsor, near the road between Crewkerne and

Lyme Regis, is **Lewesdon Hill** (III, G4). On its north-west slope is Racedown Lodge, now a farmhouse, where Wordsworth and his sister lived for two years. In 1795 a friend allowed him the use of it rent-free, with a fee of £50 for acting as tutor to his son. Here he wrote the tragedy of 'The Borderers', rejected by Covent Garden. Coleridge, whose acquaintance he had made fairly recently, came over to see him. Each read his poetry to the other; Wordsworth and his sister repaid the visit, and in order to be nearer Coleridge, moved in the summer of 1797 into Somersetshire.

The pleasant little seaside town of **Lyme Regis** (III, G4) has an interesting association with Jane Austen. The Austen family were in the habit of taking an annual jaunt to the coast of Dorset or South Devon, and probably in the autumn of 1803 they were in Lyme Regis. Jane Austen was enchanted with the place, as is evident from the enthusiastic references in her letters. Bay Cottage, at the end of the parade nearest to the harbour, is claimed as the house in which the Austen family stayed. The stone pier known as the Cobb, where the Duke of Monmouth landed on his ill-fated expedition, is now more often remembered as the place where Louisa Musgrove (in *Persuasion*) had such an unpleasant accident. There used to be Assembly Rooms at Lyme, mentioned in Miss Austen's letters, but these disappeared early in this century. Tennyson, when he visited Lyme in 1867, was brusque with friends who wanted to show him where Monmouth landed. 'Don't talk to me of the Duke of Monmouth,' he said, 'show me the exact spot where Louisa Musgrove fell.'

SALISBURY AND SOUTH WILTSHIRE

The city of **Salisbury** (II, A4), dominated by the tallest spire in England and set among fine meadows depicted by Constable, is in the midst of an area rich in associations. Pepys and his wife stayed at the Old George Inn, which is still there, during their holiday jaunt of 1668. He slept 'in a silk bed', and had 'very good diet'. Then he toured the city and the vicinity and found it 'a very brave place'. The cathedral was 'most admirable', the market-place 'most capacious', but when he returned to the inn to pay the reckoning he found it 'so exorbitant' that he left in high dudgeon. In The Close, the loveliest in England (and Pepys admired it), is a house, No. 14, in which Fielding when a boy used to stay with his maternal grandmother. Salisbury figures in *Martin Chuzzlewit*, but Dickens was not very familiar with this part of England, but when here on one occasion explored Winterslow. It was whilst he was 'wandering about the purlieus of Salisbury Cathedral' that the idea of writing *The Warden* (which opens the Barchester series of novels) first came to Trollope's mind, but Salisbury is *not* 'Barchester', that honour belonging to Winchester. The city is the 'Melchester' of Hardy's *Tess* and more particularly of *Jude the Obscure*.

Six miles before reaching Salisbury by the London road (A30) is the Pheasant Inn, just two miles north of the village of **Winterslow** (II, B4). Hazlitt's first wife owned some cottages in the village, and in one of them they came to live after their marriage in 1808. In the following summer Charles and Mary Lamb paid them a visit. They took long walks to Wilton, Stonehenge, Salisbury and other places. The Lambs paid another visit in 1810. Hazlitt and his wife, requiring more income, moved to London in 1812. After he divorced his wife he often stayed at the Pheasant Inn, sometimes still called Winterslow Hut. A posthumous volume of his work is entitled *Winterslow: essays and characters written there*.

At **Boscombe** (II, A4, on the A338 about five miles north-west of Salisbury), Richard Hooker was rector during 1591-5. He was responsible for the building of the north transept of the church, and whilst here wrote the first four books of his *Laws of Ecclesiastical Polity*. At **Amesbury Abbey** (II, A4), seven miles north of Salisbury, John Gay wrote *The Beggar's Opera* in a stone room rather like a cave, known as the Diamond, on a bank overlooking the River Avon. It was then the seat of the Duke of Queensberry, who with his wife lodged and looked after Gay in his later years, spending their time between their town house in London and the Abbey.

About two miles north of Amesbury and off the A345, is **Milston** (II, A4), where Joseph Addison was born on May 1, 1672. His father's old rectory has gone, but the church in which he was baptized on the day of his birth (he was considered delicate) is still there. He was educated in schools at Amesbury and Salisbury, and then moved to Lichfield when his father became dean there. Another two miles or so further north is

Netheravon (II, A4), where Sydney Smith was curate during 1794-6, and became tutor to the squire's son, Michael Hicks-Beach. Smith helped to provide elementary education for the villagers, and was popular with them. The same Hicks-Beach was visited in 1822 by Cobbett, who records in his *Rural Rides* that he had previously seen there 'an acre of hares' in an area now given over to the Royal Air Force.

George Herbert, a kinsman of the Herbert family of Wilton, first came to Wiltshire when he stayed with his stepfather's brother, the Earl of Danby, at **Dauntsey**, four miles north-east of Salisbury. There he met Jane Danvers, related to Danby, fell in love with her and married her in the beautiful church at Edington, near the western boundary of Wiltshire, in 1629. The third Earl of Pembroke, his kinsman, persuaded Charles I to present Herbert with the living of **Bemerton**, a mile and a half to the west of Salisbury. Herbert hesitated; he visited the Earl at Wilton; the Earl informed Laud, then Bishop of London, of Herbert's doubts, and Laud said that it was sinful to refuse. He accepted, and performed his duties with the truest Christian devotion, and his poems were written here. It was a 'good and more pleasant than healthful parsonage', said Izaak Walton in his exquisite life of Herbert, and Herbert soon contracted consumption and died late in February or early in March 1633. He was buried beneath the altar of the church, with the simple inscription, *G. H.* 1633, above his remains.

His old parsonage has survived, and a poem he wrote and which was engraved in his time above the hall chimney has been reproduced on the outside wall. The medlar tree that Herbert planted is still in the garden of the parsonage, and the old fig-tree against the wall is traditionally ascribed to Herbert's time.

The great mansion of **Wilton House** ★ (II, A4) three miles west of Salisbury is associated with Sir Philip Sidney and other great names. His sister had married, as his third wife, the second Earl of Pembroke in 1577, and soon afterwards Sidney paid the first of several visits to

★ Open April 1 to October 15 daily 10 a.m. to 6 p.m.; October 16 to March 31, Wednesday, Saturday and Sunday only 10 a.m. to 4 p.m. (but sometimes open on additional days). The gardens are open all the year, daily 9 a.m. to sunset.

Wilton, but the present buildings are after his time. When he was in disfavour at Court he paid the most fruitful of his visits. According to John Aubrey, he and his sister retired during the summer to a small house in Ivy Church near by, and there, at her suggestion, he began writing *Arcadia*. In any case most of the book was written at Wilton or Ivy Church. A woman of remarkable accomplishments, the Countess of Pembroke is remembered chiefly as the patroness of men of letters, some of them being her brother Philip's protégés. Samuel Daniel was engaged as tutor for her son, later the third Earl of Pembroke, who became the patron of William Browne, Ben Jonson and Philip Massinger, and is still regarded by some as the 'W. H.' of Shakespeare's *Sonnets*. Daniel dedicated his sonnet series *Delia* to her. She eventually lived mainly in London, where she died, and is buried in Salisbury Cathedral with a beautiful epitaph by William Browne.

Philip Massinger spent his boyhood here, where his father was a house steward to the Herbert family. There is good reason for supposing that Shakespeare was at Wilton House when *As You Like It* was performed there in 1603 and James I was present. Tradition connects Spenser and Ben Jonson with visits to Wilton; and certainly in a later era Izaak Walton was a visitor. So was John Aubrey, that wonderful antiquary and gossip who is frequently quoted in these pages, and who provided us with interesting (and in one case horribly salacious) details of the Sidney family. He lived for some periods at **Broad Chalke** (his house is not extant), eight miles south-west of Salisbury. Five miles west of Wilton, at the village of **Dinton**, the great Earl of Clarendon was born on February 18, 1609. Hyde's House beside the church is probably on the site of his birthplace.

The remains of **Fonthill Abbey** (II, A4), two miles south of **Fonthill Bishop** on the B3089 and about fifteen miles west of Salisbury, remind us of a fantastic character and a fantastic building. William Beckford, author of *Vathek*—written, so he said, at a single sitting of three days and two nights—inherited a million of money and an income of £100,000 a year at the age of ten. Born in a large house on this site on September 29, 1759, he was educated and travelled abroad for many years, and finally settled here in 1796. He rebuilt, then demolished his father's house, and then commissioned the architect Wyatt to build a 'convent partly in ruins and partly perfect'. Hazlitt, who saw it, said that it was 'a glittering waste of laborious idleness, a cathedral turned into a toyshop'. He filled the house with curios, works of art and an enormous library. What with his vast expenditure, the decline of investments and expensive lawsuits, after twenty years he decided to sell the property, retaining the best paintings and his books. All that remains of Fonthill Abbey is one of the smaller towers.

About a mile to the east, at **Tisbury**, Sir John Davies was born, the exact date being unknown, but he was baptized in the church there on April 16, 1569. Anthony Wood said that his father was a wealthy tanner, but he was probably a country gentleman. Some eight miles farther west, at **Mere** (II, H3, on the A303) William Barnes became the master of a small school in 1823. Four years later he moved the school to the Chantry House which lies a little to the south-west of the church, and taught there until 1835.

The great estate of Stourhead* by the village of **Stourton** (III, H3), three miles north-west of Mere, has a connexion with Pope. In a grotto on the north-west side of the lake are two statues by Rysbrack, 'Neptune' and the 'Sleeping Nymph', the latter being the 'nymph of the grot' celebrated by Pope in lines carved on the basin below the statue.

NORTH WILTSHIRE

At **Marlborough** (II, B3), an ancient town with a chequered history, there are several associations. Francis Lord Seymour, who defended the town for Charles I, built here a fine mansion which early in the eighteenth century was the home of Frances Countess of Hertford, a patroness of poets. In her grounds were 'picturesque' sham ruins, artificial cascades and a grotto much in the same style as Pope's at Twickenham. The writers associated with her were sometimes

---

* The house is open all the year on Wednesday, Thursday, Saturday, Sunday and Bank Holidays (except Boxing Day) 2.30 to 6 p.m. or dusk. The pleasure grounds are open from April to September at 2 to 7 p.m. on Friday and Sunday, on other days and on Bank Holidays 11 a.m. to 7 p.m.; October to March, Sunday 2 to 7 p.m. or dusk, Monday, Wednesday, Thursday, Saturday and Bank Holidays 11 a.m. to 7 p.m. or dusk.

referred to as 'grotto poets'. James Thomson was one of them, and possibly during his stay here wrote 'Spring', part of his *Seasons*, which was dedicated to his hostess. Isaac Watts the hymn-writer was another visitor.

The Countess of Hertford's house at Marlborough became one of the most famous inns in the heyday of the coaching era. This Castle Inn was taken over as the first building in which Marlborough School was housed on its foundation in 1843. William Morris was educated there from 1848 to 1851. The earlier story of the old house is well told in Stanley Weyman's *The Castle Inn*.

One of Lady Hertford's protégés was Stephen Duck, the 'thresher poet'. He was born in 1705 at **Charlton** (II, A3) in the Vale of Pewsey (off the A342 and seven miles south-west of Marlborough). The son of poor parents, he became an agricultural labourer, read whatever books he could find and wrote verses in his spare time. He began to attain fame locally, was recommended by a clergyman to Queen Caroline, who patronized him, granting him a pension and a position at court. In 1746 he was ordained priest and became rector of Byfleet in Surrey in 1752, but his mind became deranged soon afterwards, and he drowned himself at Reading on March 21, 1756. His success at court had stirred the envy of far abler writers, and Swift was thoroughly contemptuous:

> *Thrice happy Duck! employed in threshing stubble,*
> *Thy toil is lessened, and thy profits double.*

The first Lord Palmerston gave a piece of land, the rent from which provides for an annual commemoration of the poet at his native Charlton, and on June 1 the 'Duck Feast' is held at the Charlton Cat, the village inn.

The Waggon and Horses inn at **Beckhampton** (II, A3), on the A4 midway between Marlborough and Calne, is the one Dickens probably had in mind when describing the inn where Mr Pickwick and his friends stayed on their way to Bath, and it is the scene of 'The Bagman's Story' in *Pickwick Papers*. The Bear Hotel at **Devizes** (II, A3) was where Fanny Burney and her friend Mrs Thrale stayed in 1780. It was kept by the father of the painter Sir Thomas Lawrence, then a boy of ten, 'the wonder of the family, [and] of the times, for his wonderful skill in drawing', noted Fanny Burney, who saw the boy's drawings.

George Crabbe became rector of **Trowbridge** (II, A3) in 1814, just after he had lost his wife. The majority of the parishioners, desiring another man as rector, demonstrated against him, but gradually his friendliness and kindness, especially towards the poor, and his homely sermons made him respected and popular. In his early days here his outspokenness occasionally startled his congregation. He had already criticized George IV in his poetry, and on the king's death preached a sermon with the text 'the sting of death is sin'. During one very acrimonious election a mob threatened to tear him to pieces if he voted, and he replied that they could kill him if they wished, but no threats would deter him. He wrote the *Tales of the Hall* here, and the lovely gabled old rectory in which he lived has survived. He died on February 3, 1832, and is buried in the chancel of the church; his statue is above the grave.

At **Bromham** (II, A3, off the A342 and five miles north-west of Devizes), Thomas Moore spent most of the last thirty-five years of his life. He took Sloperton Cottage (about a mile north-west of Bromham) in 1817, but was not long settled when he had to fly abroad because his deputy in Bermuda had defalcated and rendered him liable for £6,000. He was able to return in 1822 after reaching an agreement with the Admiralty, whose agent he had been appointed many years earlier. He wrote Byron's life here. He died on February 25, 1852, and is buried in Bromham churchyard. A Celtic cross marks the grave, and he is commemorated in the west window of the church.

Coleridge lived at **Calne** (II, A3, on the A4 five miles south-east of Chippenham), from 1814 to 1815, before he settled finally in London. A hopeless opium addict by now, an old friend of Bristol days gave him a home and looked after him. He probably completed *Biographia Literaria* here.

John Aubrey was born at **Easton Piercy**, in the parish of **Kington St Michael** (II, A3, off the A429 three miles north-west of Chippenham), on March 12, 1626. His birthplace is now a farmhouse. Early he developed a great interest in the past. He was at first educated privately by the rector of Leigh Delamere, near Malmesbury, and later at Blandford Grammar School in Dorset. On his father's death he inherited property in four counties, but when evil times came upon him he was obliged to sell Easton Piercy and most of his other holdings. There is a memorial window to him in the church at Kington St Michael.

Aubrey's tutor had earlier been the tutor to Thomas Hobbes, the 'philosopher of Malmesbury', who was born at **Westport** (now part of **Malmesbury**) on April 5, 1588, son of the vicar of Charlton and Westport. He was a premature child because his mother was frightened by the rumours then circulating about the Spanish Armada, but he lived to the age of ninety-one. At **Charlton** (II, A2, on the B4040 some two miles north-east of Malmesbury), is a modernized Jacobean mansion where Dryden stayed from May 1665 to the end of 1666. It was the seat of his father-in-law, and Dryden had left London because the theatres were closed on account of the Great Plague. Here he wrote *Annus Mirabilis* and the *Essay of Dramatic Poesy*.

Richard Jefferies, who wrote so delightfully about Wiltshire, was born at Coate Farm* on November 6, 1848. The hamlet of **Coate** (II, A4) is just over a mile south-east of Swindon, off the A345 (the Marlborough road). The farmhouse, marked by a tablet, is a short distance beyond the entrance to Coate Reservoir. His childhood and youth here are idealized in his *Bevis* and *The Story of My Heart*. Much of the Wiltshire he loved is described in *Wild Life in a Southern County*. One of his favourite haunts (which figures in that book) is the prehistoric camp called Barbary Castle, about five miles south of Swindon, set on the Marlborough Downs and overlooking the Vale of the White Horse. Another favourite haunt was Burderop Park at **Wroughton** (on the A361 two miles south of Swindon), which appears as 'Oketowne Chase' in his *Round About a Great Estate*.

Four miles north-west of Swindon, at **Purton**, there exists the Church Farm, a building that once belonged to the Hyde family. In his youth the Earl of Clarendon came to stay during a spell of bad health, and at the church here he married his first wife in 1629. Going outside Wiltshire and into Gloucestershire, there is at **Little Sodbury** (III, H1, off the A46 and ten miles north-east of Bristol) the sixteenth-century

* A ground-floor room houses the Richard Jefferies Museum, open Wednesday and Saturday 2 to 5 p.m. Contains manuscripts and personal relics.

manor-house where William Tyndale stayed when tutor to the children of the lord of the manor here. Tyndale preached the reformed doctrine at villages around and on College Green at Bristol. He was soon in trouble with and persecuted by the local clergy. To one who opposed him he made the famous remark that 'ere many years I will cause a boy that driveth the plough shall know more of the scripture than thou doest'. His translation of the Bible was begun here. After about a year Gloucestershire was becoming unsafe for Tyndale, and he left for London in 1523.

BATH

The social history of **Bath** (III, H2) is a brilliant one, and though its great period was the eighteenth century it had been fashionable for centuries before. Evelyn in 1654 and Pepys in 1668 visited the city. Both were impressed by the stone houses but remarked on the narrow streets. Pepys went to the baths, and thought 'it cannot be clean to go so many bodies together in the same water'; nevertheless he was 'parboiled' for two hours, carried home in a sheet and sweated in bed for an hour. Then 'comes musick to play to me, extraordinary good'. The next day he attended service at the Abbey Church, but was angered by 'a ridiculous, affected sermon'.

The modern history of Bath begins with Ralph Allen (1694-1764) and Beau Nash. Allen, who was for some time deputy postmaster of Bath, gained a large fortune by inventing a system of cross-posts for England and Wales, and was a munificent benefactor to the city. He built at Prior Park, **Widcombe**, three miles from the centre of the city, a large mansion where he entertained many notable people. Pope and Fielding were his friends. The latter depicted him as 'Squire All-worthy' in *Tom Jones*. He is said to have sent Fielding £200 before he met him, and was a good friend to Fielding's children (one of whom was named after him) after their father's death. He helped to bring them up and provided them with money. Nash, for fifty years master of ceremonies and the 'King of Bath', established the Assembly Rooms. His reign made Bath very fashionable, and among the throng of visitors were many men and women of letters.

Henry Fielding was in or near Bath on several occasions. He first came in 1734, and in November of that year was married at the church of St Mary, **Charlcombe**, just over a mile north of the city. He and his wife were given as resident in the parish of St James, Bath, but where exactly is unknown. Later he paid visits to Ralph Allen at Prior Park. He also stayed on more than one occasion at **Twerton**, a western suburb of Bath, where his later residence, at the top of Widcombe Hill and near the church, has survived. There he began writing *Tom Jones*. At Widcombe, below the slopes of Prior Park, there is a fine Georgian house called Widcombe Manor, next to which is Widcombe Lodge, where Fielding stayed about 1748 and probably wrote part of *Tom Jones* there. The Squire Western of the story is alleged to have been modelled on the then owner of Widcombe Manor.

Another eighteenth-century novelist, Smollett, first visited Bath in 1751 or 1752, hoping to do better as a doctor here than in London, but he did not succeed. He paid two subsequent visits for the sake of health, one in 1762, and another in 1766 when he stayed in Gay Street. It is possible that on the latter occasion he began writing *Humphry Clinker*, part of the scene of which is laid in Bath, and it probably owed something to Anstey's famous *New Bath Guide*. Sterne, no lover of Smollett, also came in search of health in 1765, and called on Ralph Allen at Prior Park. He stayed at an inn called the Three Black Birds that was formerly in a passage between New Bond Street and North Gate Street. Gainsborough, who lived here, painted Sterne's portrait at a single sitting.

Dr Johnson was here in 1776 with his friends the Thrales, but where they stayed is not known, possibly in North Parade where the Thrales stayed on later visits. Johnson wrote to Boswell to join them, and Boswell put up at the Pelican Inn, demolished long ago. Several of Dr Johnson's circle of friends were visitors or residents. Goldsmith came in 1762 during a spell of bad health and whilst he was engaged on a life of Beau Nash, who had recently died. Where he stayed is not known, but he was here again in 1771 with his friend and patron Lord Clare at 11 North Parade (marked by a tablet). One morning when Goldsmith was returning from a walk he went absent-mindedly into the neighbouring house, which happened to be that of the Duke of Northumberland. The duke and duchess talked amiably to him,

Goldsmith supposing them to be guests of Lord Clare's, but when asked to breakfast he realized his error. The duke and duchess said that it was a most fortunate error for them, and made him promise to come to dinner.

Goldsmith's countryman and friend, Edmund Burke, visited Bath when in bad health and at the invitation of his physician, Dr Nugent, in whose house (Circus House, Circus) he stayed. He fell in love with the doctor's daughter, and married her in the city in 1756. He was again in Bath when his health was declining rapidly, and lived during 1796-7 in the same house, 11 North Parade, in which Goldsmith had stayed.

Gibbon paid his first visit as a sickly boy of twelve, and was restored to health. He paid other visits, but the only one for which a residence can be ascertained (10 Belvedere) was to his stepmother in 1793, the year before he died. In a letter of 1790, written from abroad, he said: 'Should I ever return to England, Bath, not the metropolis, would be my last retreat,' but it turned out otherwise.

Richard Brinsley Sheridan's residence in Bath was linked largely with romance. His father settled in 1770 at 9 New King Street (marked by a tablet) and taught elocution. Young Sheridan was pursuing his studies with a future career as yet undecided, and with some bent towards literature. He wrote two poems which were published in the *Bath Chronicle*. Meanwhile the Sheridan children became friendly with the children of Thomas Linley, a composer and teacher of music. Elizabeth Linley, wishing to escape from the attentions of a suitor (Major Mathews) she disliked, asked Sheridan to escort her to France, where she wished to enter a convent. Her sisters were in the secret, but no one else, and from their residence, 11 Royal Crescent, the young couple left for France in March 1772. By the time they were in France Sheridan was in love, and the young lady was turned (she did not need much pressure) from the convent to the altar. Although the marriage was valid, both parties looked upon it as a betrothal only. Meanwhile the bride's father pursued them, and took the young lady back to Bath. Sheridan went on to London and fought two duels with Major Mathews.

Fanny Burney came to Bath in 1780 with her friends Mr and Mrs Thrale, not long after the publication of *Evelina*, when she heard her book being discussed on all sides. They stayed at 14 South Parade, which is marked by a tablet. She did not return to Bath until 1815, having married in the interval, and she and her husband stayed in Rivers Street for a short time, and then settled at 23 Great Stanhope Street. She met Mrs Thrale (now Mrs Piozzi) again; they had quarrelled many years before over the matter of Mrs Piozzi's second marriage, and now concluded a somewhat uneasy reconciliation. She met the Queen, whom she had served in former days at Windsor. Her husband died in 1818, and soon afterwards she left to spend the rest of her life in London, where she died. Her body was brought to Walcot church-yard for burial in her son's grave.

Horace Walpole, who admired her work, had been a visitor in 1766, staying at the north-east corner of Chapel Court (marked by a tablet). 'I am tired to death of the place,' he said, and only stayed on for the sake of health. 'These watering places, that mimic a capital, and add vulgarisms and familiarities of their own, seem to me like abigails in cast gowns, and I am not young enough to take up with either,' and so 'it does one ten times more good to leave Bath than to go to it.'

No. 6 Green Park Buildings (marked by a tablet) was the home during 1796-9 of Thomas De Quincey whilst he was at Bath Grammar School. He lived here with his mother. He was a brilliant scholar, known for his ability to write Latin verse, and by the age of fifteen could converse in Greek. An accident led to his removal. One of the masters, in attempting to strike a boy with his cane, misdirected the blow and struck De Quincey on the head. A long illness resulted, and when he was recovering the headmaster called on his mother to request that her son might remain at school, making most flattering references to him. Such was his mother's 'moral austerity', says De Quincey, that she was shocked to hear him so complimented, and decided to remove him to a school in Winkfield, Wiltshire, about seven miles south-east of Bath. He was there for about a year.

Robert Southey lived much of his boyhood and young manhood in Bath with a rich aunt of imperious temper, at 108 Walcot Street (marked by a tablet). She had a good library, and by the time Southey was eight years old he had read all the plays in it. He was apparently dependent upon her for money after his father's death, by which time he had formed radical opinions of which she disapproved. When in 1794 he became engaged to be married she threw him out of her house, which he never entered again. In later years he was one of the many visitors to Landor.

When Jane Austen's father decided to retire from the rectory at Steventon he chose Bath as the future home of the family. He first sent his wife and Jane to the former's brother in Paragon in May 1801, and in the autumn they all settled in a house of their own at 4 Sydney Terrace (now Sydney Place) just by the gardens (marked by a tablet). Although Jane Austen had regretted leaving her native Hampshire, she was soon interested in Bath and its high life, and her first letter describes a walk with her uncle to the Pump Room, where he took 'his second glass of water'. It was whilst she was at Bath (according to her niece, Caroline Austen) that 'she declined the addresses of a gentleman', because he did not possess 'the subtle power of touching her heart'. At Sydney Place she wrote the short work *Lady Susan*, began *The Watsons* (never completed) and completed or revised *Northanger Abbey*. The last was sold in 1803 to a publisher for £10, but it was never published in her lifetime. The family moved in 1804 to 27 Green Park Buildings, where Miss Austen's father died in January 1804, leaving the family reduced in circumstances. The sons helped, and for a time they lived in lodgings, first at 25 Gay Street, then in Trim Street, and finally quitted Bath in 1806. Two of Miss Austen's novels are a capital source for the social scene in the Bath of her time: *Persuasion* presents the typical social round, and *Northanger Abbey* deftly satirizes visitors to Bath.

Walter Savage Landor had visited Bath several times before settling there for a long residence. It was here in 1811 that he saw Julia Thuillier at a ball, and said to a friend, 'that's the nicest girl in the room, and I'll marry her', which he did a month or two later. After more than twenty-five years of a peripatetic life and quarrels with many people (including his wife, from whom he separated in 1835) he settled at 35 St James's Square in 1837, staying there until he moved to 3 Rivers Street in 1849. Both are marked by tablets. He left England in 1858, and died in Florence on September 17, 1864. Landor could rarely keep out of quarrels and on one occasion had to pay £1,000 damages in a libel case. However, he had many admirers and friends who called on him, including Longfellow, Hawthorne, Dickens and Wordsworth.

Dickens (one of the few people Landor wholeheartedly admired) stayed three days with him in 1840, when the unfortunate idea first occurred to him of creating the character of 'Little Nell' (*Old Curiosity Shop*). Landor is reported to have said that he never regretted anything so much as failing to buy the house in St James's Square and burning it to the ground so that 'no meaner association should ever desecrate the birthplace of Little Nell'. There are some characteristics of Landor in the character of 'Boythorn' in *Bleak House*. Dickens had been a frequent visitor from 1835 onwards, and it is therefore not surprising that there are six chapters devoted to Mr Pickwick and his party in Bath. They are placed as staying at the White Hart Inn (no longer there) opposite the Great Pump Room.

Of all the literary characters known to Bath the strangest was William Beckford, whose doings at Fonthill we have already mentioned. He came to reside in Lansdown Crescent (Beckford House, marked by a tablet) in 1822, and lived as secluded a life as he had done at Fonthill, collecting works of art, curios and books. As before, he had a passion for building towers, and built one on Lansdown Hill in 1827. He lived in extraordinarily good health up to the age of eighty-four, and died on May 2, 1844. He was at first buried in Bathwick Cemetery, and then his remains were moved a short distance to a mausoleum beside the tower he built, now known as Beckford's Tower. He is commemorated by Beckford Road near by.

Poets are not as prominent as prose writers among Bath associations. Shelley, when a boy, had stayed at 3 Miles Buildings, and in 1816 with Mary Shelley he stayed at No. 5 Abbey Churchyard (now the Roman Pavement) and 6 Queen Square. George Crabbe is recorded for a short visit in 1826, when he stayed at 23 Brock Street. Wordsworth, during his annual holiday in 1841, stayed at 9 North Parade (marked by a tablet).

Two nineteenth-century historians were here, Froude at 16 Lansdown Place East in 1848, and Macaulay at 2 Pulteney Street in 1859. Bulwer Lytton, after a stay at 9 Royal Crescent in 1866, was at Macaulay's former address in 1867 and 1872, and is recorded on a tablet there.

Thackeray, who as a boy had sometimes stayed with his aunt in the Circus, was a visitor to 16 Lansdown Place East in 1857.

Among more modern writers, W. H. Hudson stayed at 22 New King Street in 1898-9, and Ella Wheeler Wilcox at 8 Upper Church Street in 1919. George Saintsbury settled at 1 Royal Crescent on his retirement in 1915, and his impressive figure was a familiar sight, still remembered by some, up to his death on January 28, 1933. Among the fruits of his retirement were *The Peace of the Augustans*, *Notes on a Cellar-Book* and the *Scrap Books*.

BRISTOL

Bristol (III, H1) is the native city of Thomas Chatterton, 'the marvellous boy', a curious case of a genius, perhaps a supreme genius, whose gifts were devoted to the writing of poetry (which it undoubtedly is) attributed to a mythical fifteenth-century monk. The posthumous son of a poor schoolmaster of a charity school, he was born in a tenement at the back of the school on November 20, 1752. His birthplace has been preserved, and another room to the front of it is now the museum of Chatterton House* in Redcliffe Way. In the year after his birth his mother moved to Redcliffe Hill and opened a dame school, soon afterwards moving to another house in the same street.

When five years old, Chatterton was sent to school, but was such a dunce that he was sent home, and his mother thought him 'an absolute fool'. One day he saw his mother tearing up an old French music folio; something stirred within this apparently dull boy, who suddenly began to read, and by the age of eight was a voracious reader. He spent hours in a lumber-room at home, and haunted the great church of St Mary Redcliffe where he had been baptized. At the age of seven he went to Colston's Hospital, Bristol's Bluecoat school, and after school hours retired to the lumber-room, drawing heraldic designs, churches, castles, knights in armour, and writing poems. His first poem appeared in a Bristol paper when he was ten.

One day he was interested in a piece of old parchment he found at

* Open Wednesday and Saturday 3 to 5 p.m.; other times can be arranged by writing to the caretakers, Mr and Mrs Hambling. Contains manuscripts, wax model of Chatterton, photographs, etc.

home. It was among other pieces that his father had obtained (through his brother-in-law the sexton at St Mary Redcliffe) from old oak chests that lay unguarded in the muniment room over the great porch of the church. At the age of eleven Chatterton began writing poetry purporting to be 'antique', and later invented a monk named Thomas Rowley as the real author. George Catcott, a pewterer, eagerly patronized the young wonder and collected whatever Chatterton handed over to him. He wrote to Horace Walpole and sent manuscripts on 'The Rise of Peynctynge in Englande' and other pieces, but Walpole kept them so long and did nothing, much to Chatterton's bitter disappointment. He worked off his feelings on all the leading people of Bristol, including those friendly towards him. Meanwhile he had been apprenticed to an attorney, who soon came to disapprove of Chatterton scribbling away whilst he should have been at work, and burned some of the boy's compositions. Chatterton contemplated suicide; and when one day his employer found on Chatterton's desk the latter's 'Last Will and Testament', he was dismissed. With money raised by friends he set off for London. He is commemorated outside St Mary Redcliffe with a statue.

Dr Johnson and Boswell went to Bristol in 1776 after their visit to Bath 'to enquire upon the spot into the authenticity of "Rowley's Poetry" '. They met the George Catcott who had patronized Chatterton: a heated discussion followed, Catcott being 'zealous for Rowley', and Johnson not convinced. So they adjourned to St Mary Redcliffe in order that Johnson might see the 'ancient chests in which the manuscripts were found', but Johnson remained unconvinced. Johnson's friend Edmund Burke was Member of Parliament for Bristol from 1774-1780, and one of his finest compositions is his address to the electors here.

The man who became a champion of Chatterton, and issued his poems for the benefit of the family—Robert Southey, was born at 9 Wine Street (which has survived) on August 12, 1774. He was the son of a linen-draper, and was first educated at Corston and Bristol before being sent to London. Corston Manor in Somerset, three miles west of Bath, is now a farmhouse. Southey settled in Bristol in 1794, after he had met Coleridge at Oxford and had been converted to

Pantisocracy, Coleridge's scheme for a republican community in America. With another Pantisocratist they settled at 48 College Street, which has survived. They came to know a Bristol publisher by the name of Cottle who was useful in various ways to these ardent republicans, and deserves honour as the publisher of *Lyrical Ballads*. Love and money shortage were disturbing elements in their schemes: Southey became interested in Edith, and Coleridge in Sara Fricker, two of five sisters. Cottle advanced fifty guineas to Southey for a play on Joan of Arc; Coleridge was offered payment for poetry, but did little about it, got engaged to Sara Fricker and went off to London. Southey went after him to recall him to his lady-love, though meantime his ardour for an older love revived, and he did not *wish* but out of duty *would* marry Sara.

After a quarrel Southey threatened to throw up Pantisocracy, much to Coleridge's disgust. Just about this time they met Wordsworth and his sister, who had been attending one of Coleridge's lectures, for the first time. Wordsworth called at College Street, and later they all met at 7 Great George Street, which is now called Georgian House and is a museum of furniture. Coleridge married Sara Fricker in the church of St Mary Redcliffe, and went to Clevedon (see opposite page) for the honeymoon. A few weeks later Southey was married in the same church, but having been invited to Spain by an uncle, left his wife the day after marriage. He returned in 1797 with his revolutionary ardour spent, and when a friend settled £160 a year on him, went off to London to study law, but soon gave that up. Cottle published his *Letters Written in Spain and Portugal* and two volumes of *Minor Poems*, and Southey began to compose his longer poems. Soon he left for **Westbury-on-Trym**, just outside Bristol, where he lived for a short time, and then left the district for ever.

Meanwhile Coleridge (who amongst his other activities was a preacher in Unitarian chapels), after the failure of Pantisocracy, decided to propagate his ideas in a paper called *The Watchman*. After a tour in Birmingham and elsewhere to attract subscribers (amusingly described in *Biographia Literaria*) and ten issues of the paper, the project was dropped. After his return his son Hartley Coleridge was born, in Bristol and not Clevedon as is generally asserted. In 1796 Coleridge moved to Nether Stowey, though he reappeared in Bristol when he lectured on Shakespeare in 1813.

On the **Clifton** side of Bristol Thomas Lovell Beddoes was born at 3 Rodney Place (which is extant) on July 20, 1803. His father was a physician famous in his day, and his mother a sister of Maria Edgeworth, who sometimes visited the family. After his earlier university vacations Beddoes never returned to Clifton. Another physician's son, J. Addington Symonds, was born on October 5, 1840, at 7 Berkeley Square, Bristol, which is extant. After education elsewhere and a short residence abroad and in London he settled in 1868 in Victoria Square, Clifton. Whilst here he wrote the essays for periodicals that later formed the *Sketches in Italy and Greece* and the first volume of *The Renaissance in Italy*. After 1878 most of his life was spent at Davos in Switzerland, where he came to know Stevenson, who depicted him as 'Opalstein' in *Memories and Portraits*. Symonds died in Rome on April 19, 1893, and is buried in the Protestant cemetery where Keats and Shelley are interred.

At **Clevedon** (III, G1) on the Bristol Channel, and eight miles west of Bristol, there is a cottage in Old Church Road and near the station, marked by a tablet as that which Coleridge occupied during his honeymoon, but this is not certain. At Clevedon Court,* a fine mansion parts of which date from the fourteenth century, Thackeray was a frequent visitor. He wrote part of *Henry Esmond* there, and in the book Clevedon Court is depicted as 'Castlewood', though placed in Hampshire. In Clevedon Church is buried Arthur Henry Hallam, the friend Tennyson commemorated in *In Memoriam*. Soon after the publication of the poem, Tennyson at his wife's request paid a visit to the church.

SOMERSETSHIRE

At Sharpham Park, two miles south-west of **Glastonbury** (III, G2), Sir Edward Dyer was born, but even the approximate year of birth is unknown. He was a courtier and minor Elizabethan poet now remembered chiefly for a lovely lyric found in most anthologies, and beginning, 'My mind to me a kingdom is'. There was born in the same house on April 22, 1707, Henry Fielding, the son of an army officer. He

* Open Thursday 11 a.m. to 1 p.m.

and Lady Mary Wortley Montagu were second cousins, both being descendants of the first Earl of Denbigh. The Fielding family moved in 1710 into Dorsetshire. Fielding's birthplace is now a farmhouse.

Samuel Daniel was born near **Taunton**, 'so am I certified by some of his late surviving acquaintance', said Thomas Fuller, and that should settle the matter, for there is no other evidence on the point. His father, continues Fuller, was 'a master of music, and his harmonious mind made an impression on his son's genius'. After a successful career in London he returned to his native county, and 'in his old age he turned husbandman and rented a farm in Wiltshire near to the Devizes'. The farm wasactually inside the Somerset border, near **Beckington** (III, H2, on the A361), between Frome and Trowbridge, and at Beckington he died in October 1619, and was buried in the north aisle of the church there. Many years later his old pupil Lady Anne Clifford, now the Dowager Countess of Pembroke, erected the bust over his grave.

A. W. Kinglake was born in Wilton House, High Street, Taunton, on August 5, 1809, the eldest son of a local banker and solicitor. Trained as a barrister, he was much more interested in military history and travel. He wrote a detailed history of the Crimean War, and much more important, *Eothen, or Traces of Travel brought Home from the East.* Its pellucid and brilliant style has not saved it from neglect in this century.

At **Combe Florey** (III, F3, on the A358 six miles north-west of Taunton), Sydney Smith was rector from 1829 until his death. In 1831 he made the famous speech at Taunton on the resistance of the House of Lords to reform, and told the story of Mrs Partington who, armed with a mop, tried during a great storm at Sidmouth to keep back the great Atlantic surges—'she was excellent at a slop or puddle, but should never have meddled with a tempest'. Sydney Smith had to be moved to London when he fell ill in 1844, and there he died. He is commemorated in the east window in Combe Florey church.

Nether Stowey (III, F2), a village on the A39 about ten miles west of Bridgwater, is a place of particular importance in the lives of Coleridge and Wordsworth, and in the development of English literature. Coleridge and Southey, when engaged on Pantisocratic schemes in Bristol, were advised by a friend to call on Thomas Poole of Nether

Stowey, a rich merchant of radical views, altogether unorthodox and not liked in his neighbourhood. Poole was impressed by the two young poets, especially Coleridge, and sympathetic towards their views. Coleridge saw him again later, and in 1796 asked Poole to find him a house in Nether Stowey, which Poole did. Coleridge and his wife and child settled at the cottage* in the winter of 1796, and was provided moreover with an annuity raised by Poole and other friends.

In 1797 Wordsworth and his sister Dorothy rented the manor house at **Alfoxden**(III, F2) only three miles to the west (the house, off the A39 and half a mile west of the village of Holford, is now an hotel). In the grounds there is a cottage in which, it is claimed, Wordsworth did most of his writing. Together the friends wandered over the Quantock Hills and other parts of the county, discussing theories of poetry which led to collaboration over *Lyrical Ballads*, published at Bristol in 1798. It attracted little attention at the time, but it inaugurated the Romantic revolution in English literature. It contains Wordsworth's 'Tintern Abbey', and Coleridge's 'Ancient Mariner' and 'Kubla Khan'. The birth of the last poem is a fascinating story. Coleridge had wandered off on his own to a lonely farm above **Ashley Combe** in the Culbone Hills, about twenty miles to the west. One day, whilst reading Purchas's *Pilgrims*, in which are told, among other things, the doings of the great Kublai Khan, he fell asleep, possibly under the influence of opium. On waking he began to write down what he had dreamed, but before he could complete it, 'a man from Porlock' knocked at the door, and afterwards Coleridge was unable to recapture the rest of the dream. What Coleridge did manage to write before the unfortunate interruption from the caller is quite the most entrancing fragment in English poetry.

Coleridge stayed only about two years at Nether Stowey. A welcome addition to his annuity enabled him to carry out the cherished idea of a visit to Germany to study philosophy. Wordsworth and his sister decided to join him, and they all started off towards the end of 1798.

* Coleridge's Cottage Museum, as it is called, is open daily (except Saturday) 11 a.m. to 1 p.m., 2 to 5 p.m. Thomas Poole is commemorated in the church (where he is buried) by a tablet as the friend of Wordsworth, Davy (Sir Humphrey Davy), Southey and Coleridge.

There had been interesting visitors to Nether Stowey. Charles and Mary Lamb spent a week there in July 1797, and met Wordsworth for the first time. Hazlitt also first met Wordsworth when he stayed for a few weeks in the following summer. At **Porlock** (III, E2), already mentioned, there is the Ship Inn where Southey once stayed and wrote the poem about Porlock's 'verdant vale'. 'Southey's Corner' is pointed out to visitors.

Exmoor, most of which lies in Somersetshire, is in literature pre-eminently the *Lorna Doone* country. The story is not based on an actual family, as is often supposed, although it is set in the period of Charles II and James II. The Doone Valley, just over the Devonshire border (III, E2), is named after the book, and the descriptions of the valley are dramatically heightened. The natural defences of the valley are not 'sheer rock' but gentle moorland hills. In the little church at **Oare** (III, E2) Blackmore placed the marriage of Lorna Doone to John Ridd and her shooting by Carver Doone. There is in the church a medallion portrait of Blackmore, who spent some of his youth in Devon. His father was curate at Ashford near Barnstaple and then at Culmstock eight miles east of Tiverton. Blackmore was educated first at Bruton in Somerset and then at Blundell's School, Tiverton, where ill-treatment by older boys made him subject to epilepsy in later life.

NORTH DEVONSHIRE

Lynmouth (III, E2) was to Southey 'the finest spot, except Cintra and the Arrabida', that he ever saw. Shelley, whom Southey came to know, stayed here with his first wife in June 1812. He was as enthusiastic as Southey regarding the place, and found his 'myrtle-twined' cottage to his taste. In his passionate desire for the betterment of mankind Shelley had had printed at Dublin a pamphlet entitled the 'Dedication of Rights', and sent copies out to sea in bottles and boxes. The local authorities brought the matter to the attention of the Home Secretary, and after a few months Shelley prudently removed himself. Shelley's cottage was destroyed by fire in 1907, and another built on the site; this and another cottage stake claims as 'Shelley's Cottage'.

Barnstaple (III, D3) is the birthplace of John Gay, who came of an ancient but latterly impoverished Devonshire family. He was born in

1685 (the exact date is unknown) at what is now 35 High Street, and baptized on September 16 in St Peter's Church. In the churchyard is the fourteenth-century St Anne's Chapel, which was for three hundred years the Grammar School, where Gay was educated.

Just over ten miles south-west of Barnstaple is 'the little white town of **Bideford** [III, D3], which slopes upwards from its broad tide-river', as Charles Kingsley said, who during an extended stay here in 1854 wrote part of *Westward Ho!* He is said to have written in an old house, part of which is incorporated in the Royal Hotel, and the particular room in which Kingsley wrote, the old parlour with the finely decorated plaster ceiling, is shown to visitors. Bideford commemorated him with a statue facing the quay. It is said that Froude, who married a sister of Kingsley's first wife, began his *History of England* at Bideford.

Kingsley was a deep lover of the scenery of north Devon, which he knew well. He had spent much of his boyhood at the village of **Clovelly** (III, D3), where his father was rector. **Westward Ho!** (III, D3) some twelve miles west of Bideford in Barnstaple (or Bideford) Bay, was named after his novel, a fact he deplored. In Westward Ho! there used to be the United Services College, at which Rudyard Kipling was educated from 1878 to 1882. His life there forms the staple of *Stalky & Co.* He is commemorated by the near-by Kipling Tors.

SOUTH DEVONSHIRE

Ottery St Mary (III, F4) seven miles south-west of Honiton, is the birthplace of Coleridge. The B3171, which diverges off the A30, leads to it. Samuel Taylor Coleridge, the thirteenth and last child of the rector of Ottery St Mary (he was also headmaster of the King's School there) was born on October 21, 1772. The rectory in which he was born has disappeared. His father was an unaffected man of considerable learning, likened by his son to Parson Adams in Fielding's *Joseph Andrews*, and died when Coleridge was nine. The boy was exceedingly precocious—he said that he 'never thought as a child, never had the language of a child'—and was educated first at a dame school, but it is not known if he ever attended his father's school. On his father's death a judge and local squire (and former pupil of his father's) obtained for him entry to Christ's Hospital in London. He saw very little of his old home thereafter, though once when he wished to call on his brother, when his unorthodox opinions were becoming known, he was told he would be unwelcome.

Ottery St Mary is also associated with Thackeray, whose mother and stepfather settled at the house called Larkbeare (still there) in 1825, and during his school holidays Thackeray lived there. The house figures as 'Fairoaks' in *Pendennis*, his mother as Helen, and a cousin who lived here as Laura Bell. His stepfather was the prototype for Colonel Newcome in *The Newcomes*. Ottery St Mary becomes Clavering St Mary in *Pendennis*, and the near-by towns of Exeter and Sidmouth as 'Chatteris' and 'Baymouth' respectively. Elizabeth Barrett Browning lived at **Sidmouth** (III, F4) with her father during the years 1832-5, but the exact locality is not known.

Just over a mile west of the pretty village of **East Budleigh** (III, F4, on the A376 three miles south-west of Sidmouth), is the old farmhouse of Hayes Barton,* where Sir Walter Ralegh was born about 1552. His father was a country gentleman who originally came from Plymouth. Ralegh was the child of his third wife who, by her first husband, was the mother of Sir Humphrey Gilbert. We do not know where Ralegh went to school, but it is possible that his love of adventure was implanted early by associations with sailors at Budleigh Salterton near by, and Millais' famous picture of 'The Boyhood of Ralegh' depicts him listening to them on the sea shore. Throughout his life he retained the Devonshire accent.

George Gissing lived at **Exeter** (III, E4) for two years, and the setting of his *Private Papers of Henry Ryecroft* is in the countryside round the city, but exact localities cannot be deduced. Richard Hooker was born in March 1554 in **Heavitree**, now a suburb of Exeter, and educated at Exeter Grammar School. He is commemorated by a statue in the Cathedral Close.

During 1834-41 Elizabeth Barrett Browning sought health in **Torquay** (III, E5), and lived at Bath House, now the Regina Hotel, by the harbour. Whilst she was here her brother was drowned in Babbacombe Bay, a tragedy that deeply affected her throughout life. Bulwer Lytton died in Torquay on January 18, 1873. About two miles north

* Open June to September on weekdays 10.30 a.m. to 1 p.m., 2 to 6.30 p.m.

of Torquay, Kipling lived at Rock House, **Maidencombe** (III, F5), during 1896-7, a period of his life he remembered with distaste, but it resulted in the writing of part of *Stalky & Co.*

At **Ilsington** (III, E4) on the edge of Dartmoor and about three miles south-west of Bovey Tracey, John Ford the dramatist was born about 1586. He came of a Norman family who for long had a mansion here called Bagtor, and on its site the present house of the same name was built in the seventeenth and eighteenth centuries.

About ten miles further south, on the A38, is the beautifully situated village of **Dean Prior** (III, E5), near Totnes, where Robert Herrick became vicar in 1629, but being a Royalist was ejected in 1647 by the Parliamentarians. He was reinstated in 1662 and remained there until his death. He never cared for Devonshire, where he was, in his own words,

> *. . . by hard fate sent*
> *Into a long and irksome banishment.*

He said that his parishioners—some of his epigrams were directed at them—were 'a people currish'. Yet he confesses that Devonshire inspired his Muse, and it is ironic that one who disliked 'this dull Devonshire' is the greatest of English pastoral lyrics. He never married:

> *Chaste I lived, without a wife,*
> *That's the story of my life—*

and in a distich averred that

> *Suspicion, discontent and strife,*
> *Come in for dowry with a wife.*

Was that his real belief? Nevertheless he was enraptured by a pretty face, and no other English poet has captured as successfully as Herrick a purely pagan delight in life. And so he lived out his 'banishment', looked after by his maid Prue, who is commemorated in some of his poems.* The exact date of his death is unknown, but he was buried in the churchyard in October 1674. No tombstone marks his grave, but

---

* Herrick's life in Devonshire is depicted with brilliant insight in the late Rose Macaulay's novel *They Were Defeated.*

'here, here, tomb of Robin Herrick is'. A window and a tablet commemorate him in the church. Part of his old vicarage is incorporated in the present building.

Only about five miles north-west of Dean Prior, at **Holne**, finely situated high above the River Dart, Charles Kingsley was born at the vicarage on June 12, 1819, and baptized in the old church there. Whilst he was still a small boy his father was moved to another living. James Anthony Froude, who later became his brother-in-law, was born at **Dartington** two miles north of Totnes, on April 23, 1818, at the rectory of his father, 'a learned and cultured antiquary, and an accomplished artist'. He returned to his native country in his later years and lived at **Salcombe** (III, E6, at the end of the A381, and three miles south of Kingsbridge). His first residence was The Moult and the second Woodcot; both have survived, and he died at the latter on October 20, 1894. He was buried in Salcombe cemetery.

Robert Stephen Hawker, more famous for his connexion with Cornwall, was born at **Stoke Damerel** (now part of Plymouth and Devonport), on December 3, 1803. His father was at the time practising medicine, and later became curate and vicar of Stratton in Cornwall. Towards the end of his life, when his health was failing, he was living in Plymouth, and died in Lockyer Street on August 15, 1875. Shortly before he died he was formally received into the Roman Catholic Church. He was buried in Plymouth cemetery.

William Browne, author of *Britannia's Pastorals*, was born at **Tavistock**, beyond the western fringe of Dartmoor, about 1591. He was educated at the grammar school there and then sent to Oxford. Very little is known of him, and the date of his death, which may have occurred at Tavistock, is conjectured to be about 1643. Except for the beautiful epitaph on the Countess of Pembroke, he is remembered chiefly for his influence on Milton, Keats and other poets, but deserves better, and there is fine poetry in *Britannia's Pastorals*, in which there is much allusion to the country round Tavistock.

The desolate tract of **Dartmoor**, though one might expect it, is not depicted in Hardy's Wessex. It has been excellently described in *Cristowell*, a forgotten novel by R. D. Blackmore, and Eden Phillpotts made the area very much his own. *Children of the Mist*, *The River* and

The Portreeve are among the notable novels in which he has depicted Devonshire life and character in the setting of Dartmoor.

CORNWALL

The Duchy of Cornwall is the legendary land of King Arthur, and our first association is that of a man steeped in Arthurian lore—Robert Stephen Hawker, who has himself become a legend in Cornwall. When ordained priest in 1831 he was appointed to the living of North Tamerton in Cornwall, and in 1834 was transferred to **Morwenstow** (III, C3), by the rocky and inhospitable coast in the north-east. Morwenstow lies three miles west along an unclassified road off the A39. Through Hawker's intervention a school was founded in this secluded village, and a new parsonage house was built (it survives, but not as a parsonage, and has a quaint inscription over the door). Hawker was deeply interested in the people and antiquities of Cornwall, and his *Cornish Ballads* are simple, direct and have the flavour of antiquity. He was a strange man who wore a claret-coloured coat with long tails, belonged in spirit to the Middle Ages and believed in witchcraft and the evil eye.

Tennyson, during a tour of the west country in 1848, called on him. Asking the way to the remote vicarage, Tennyson happened to speak to Hawker's brother-in-law, did not disclose who he was, and was taken to see Hawker. They found a common interest in King Arthur. Tennyson remarked on the isolation of Hawker's life, and Hawker quoted 'Locksley Hall'. 'That man appears to be your favourite poet,' said Tennyson. 'Not mine only, but all England's,' replied Hawker, and then Tennyson disclosed himself. They went out to wander on the shore and talked of Arthur and legends of Cornwall. When he departed, Tennyson was loaded with Hawker's books and manuscripts on Arthurian lore.

About fifteen miles lower down the coast is **Boscastle** (III, C4) the westernmost point connected with Hardy's Wessex. It is the 'Castle Boterel' of his *A Pair of Blue Eyes*; and just over two miles up the River Valency is **St Juliot** (III, C5), the 'Endelstow' of the novel. In 1872 Hardy was employed as architect in the restoration of the church here, and he fell in love with the rector's sister, whom he married two years later. There is a tablet to her memory in the church, and on its walls are the sketches made by Hardy for his church restoration plans.

In South Cornwall, **Fowey** (III, C5) was the home for many years of Sir Arthur Quiller-Couch, who had made it famous as 'Troy Town', in a series of novels. His home was The Haven, where he died on May 12, 1944. A granite monolith on Hall Walk, over-looking the harbour, commemorates him. He was born at Bodmin on November 21, 1863, and educated at Newton Abbott and Clifton College. Sir Hugh Walpole used **Truro** as 'Polchester' in his novels *Jeremy* and *Jeremy and Hamlet*, and it is prominent in the scene of *The Old Ladies*, but in *The Cathedral* Truro appears as part of a composite background.

At Mount's Bay, in which Penzance lies, Ralegh and Spenser landed in 1589 on their way back from Ireland, the latter carrying the first three books of his *Faerie Queene* to present to Queen Elizabeth. Spenser described their approach to the coast in 'Colin Clout's Come Home Again'. In **Penzance** (III, A6) the *fin-de-siècle* poet John Davidson lived during the last year of his life, depressed by ill-health and poverty. He drowned himself on March 23, 1909, and when his body was recovered some months later it was buried at sea.

THE CHANNEL ISLANDS

In the middle of the bay at **St Helier** (III, H6), capital of Jersey, is Elizabeth Castle, and inside it is the house occupied by the Earl of Clarendon during 1646-8. He came here with the young Prince Charles (later Charles II) under his care, but the latter was soon sent to France on his mother's orders. 'I resolved to write the history of these evil times,' said Clarendon in a letter to a friend, and so the *History of the Great Rebellion* was begun here.

Victor Hugo, banished from France because of his opposition to Louis Napoleon, fled to Brussels and then to Jersey, where he lived from 1852 to 1855 at the Maison Victor Hugo (now an hotel) at **St Luke's**, just outside St Helier and overlooking the Grève d'Azette. Here he wrote *Les Châtiments*, which satirizes the Second Empire. In 1855 Hugo moved to **St Peter Port** (III, H6), capital of Guernsey, and lived first at 20 Hauteville, moving in 1856 to Hauteville House,* where he remained until able to return to France on the fall of the Second Empire. Some of his finest poetry was written here, in his study at the top of the house, as well as *Les Misérables* and *Les Travailleurs de la Mer*, a story set in Guernsey. There is a statue of Hugo in Candie Gardens. About three miles east of Guernsey is the small island of **Jethou**, which Sir Compton Mackenzie owned and lived on for some years.

* Open weekdays (except Thursday afternoon) 10 a.m. to 12.30 p.m., 2 to 4.30 p.m. Contains portraits and personal relics.

Eastern England

Hertfordshire
Essex
Suffolk
Cambridgeshire and Huntingdonshire
Bedfordshire and North Buckinghamshire
Northamptonshire
Norfolk
Lincolnshire

HERTFORDSHIRE

Gorhambury House,* two miles north-west of **St Albans** (II, E2 on the A5), is the eighteenth-century seat of the Earl of Verulam. In it are portraits, books and other relics of Francis Bacon. In the park can be seen the remains of the mansion that was erected by Bacon's father, and in which he lived at various times from his fall until his death. Bacon was buried in St Michael's Church, St Albans, and is commemorated by the seated marble figure placed there soon after his death. He is represented with his eyes closed—*Sic sedebat* (thus he sat) says the inscription.

According to Anthony Wood, James Shirley the dramatist became a minister in or near St Albans, possibly during the period 1619-23. He then became a Roman Catholic, and obtained the mastership of King Edward VI's Grammar School here in 1623, leaving for London two years later. The unfortunate William Cowper was lodged in a private madhouse in St Albans for eighteen months (1763-5) after he had attempted suicide in London, when he suffered from religious terrors

* Open on Thursday only from May 1 to September 25, 2 to 6 p.m., but daily (except Sunday) during August.

and became mad. He was born not far away from here, in the former rectory at **Berkhamsted** (on the A41), on November 15, 1731. He lost his mother when he was six, and was then sent to a school (no longer there) in Market Street, Hertford, where he was badly treated by one of the boys and was taken away two years later.

North of St Albans, and about three miles north-west of Welwyn Garden City, is **Ayot St Lawrence** (II, E2), where at the house now known as Shaw's Corner* Bernard Shaw lived from 1906 until his death there at the age of ninety-four on November 2, 1950. He was cremated and his ashes, mingled with those of his wife, were scattered in the garden. The contents of the house are just as they were during Shaw's lifetime.

About six miles to the north-east of Hertford is **Widford**, associated with an early love-affair of Charles Lamb. He became enamoured of Ann Simmons here; nothing is known of the affair, but it is possible that disappointed love had something to do with the fact that Lamb was in a madhouse for a short time not long afterwards. He contributed some sonnets to Coleridge's first published volume of poetry (it was Lamb's first appearance in print) and two of the sonnets refer to Ann Simmons. Lamb became acquainted with her through his visits to his grandmother at **Blakesware**, only a mile or so away from Widford, and the 'Blakesmoor' of one of the finest *Essays of Elia*.

There is another Lamb association hereabouts just over a mile west of the village of **Westmill** (II, E1), which is on the A10 two miles south of Buntingford. The little seventeenth-century cottage there called Button Snap was owned but never occupied by Lamb. He inherited it from his godfather in 1812, and three years later sold it for £50. He informed his tenant of the sale, and with characteristic generosity waived the last instalment of rent due to him. 'I forgive it you,' he said, 'as you may have been at some expenses in repairs.' The cottage is now owned by the Charles Lamb Society, who hope one day to open it as a memorial to Lamb. Mackery End, a fine seventeenth-century house with Dutch gables, celebrated by Lamb in his famous

* Open in summer from Wednesday to Saturday, and Bank Holidays 2 to 6 p.m., Sunday 11 a.m. to 1 p.m.; in winter on Saturday and Sunday only, 2 to 4 p.m.

essay, lies a mile and a half north-east of **Harpenden** (II, E2) and about six miles north of St Albans. Lamb says in the essay that it was the oldest thing that he remembered, being taken by his sister to visit relations there.

Knebworth House (II, E1),* just over a mile north-west of Knebworth (on the A1 and about eight miles north-west of Hertford) was the home of the first Lord Lytton. It has been the family seat since Tudor times, and one wing has survived of the Tudor mansion. Lytton came into possession in 1843, and had the exterior remodelled on Victorian Gothic lines. Dickens, Disraeli and other literary figures were among Lytton's visitors here.

Further northwards, at **Hitchin** (II, E1), George Chapman was born about 1559, and tradition connects his birth with Tilehouse Street. There are a few sixteenth-century houses in the street, and it is possible that his birthplace, though unidentifiable, has survived. Also in the street is the Salem Chapel, which possesses a chair presented by John Bunyan.

ESSEX

There used to exist near **Harlow** (ten miles north-east of Waltham Abbey) the estate of Matthew Prior, who purchased it from the handsome profits derived from his collected works, supplemented by an equal sum from his patron the Earl of Oxford. Prior's first visit to his estate is described in the ballad of 'Down Hall', the name of his house, but he was in failing health, and enjoyed his retirement for only about a year. Tradition has long ascribed **Witham**, about seven miles northeast of Chelmsford, as the birthplace of Thomas Campion, born in 1567. There is no certainty on the point, and nothing is known of his parentage.

Just about a mile west of **Saffron Walden**, off the A11, is the great Jacobean mansion of **Audley End**† (II, F1), where Queen Elizabeth was entertained in the former mansion here in 1578 during one of her

* Open May 1 to September 28 Wednesday to Sunday inclusive, 2 to 5 p.m., and at the same time on Whit Monday and August Bank Holiday. Contains manuscripts, portraits and other relics.

† Open from April 20 to October 5 on Thursday, Saturday, Sunday and Bank Holidays 9.30 a.m. to 5.30 p.m.

progresses, and Sir Philip Sidney was in attendance upon her. John Evelyn has recorded that he visited the present mansion on three occasions, and described it as 'a mixed fabric, betwixt antique and modern'. Later, in 1721, when the house was in the possession of the Earl of Suffolk, Sir John Vanbrugh was called in for advice. This resulted in the demoliton of three sides of the old quadrangle or western court, and the erection to Vanbrugh's designs of lodges at the north and south of the west front. Audley End is the seat of Lord Braybrook, descendant of the first editor of Pepys's *Diary*.

At **Thorpe-le-Soken** (II, H1, at the junction of the A1033 and A136, about ten miles east of Colchester), there is a house called Comarques once owned by Arnold Bennett. He returned from France in 1912, famous as the author of *The Old Wives' Tale* and *Clayhanger*, and bought this Queen Anne house which he restored and then furnished in Second Empire style. He did not use the house much after the outbreak of the First World War, and sold it in 1921 after separating from his wife.

SUFFOLK

At the Great White Horse hotel in Tavern Street, **Ipswich** (IV, G5), Mr Pickwick had his remarkable adventure with 'the middle-aged lady in the yellow curl papers'. Dickens may have stayed at the hotel in 1835, when he was a parliamentary reporter, and he certainly did in 1859 and 1861 when he gave readings in Ipswich. The museum and art collection at Christchurch Mansion* in Christchurch Park has some personal relics of Edward Fitzgerald, who spent nearly the whole of his life in Suffolk.

He was born on March 31, 1809, at Bredfield House (destroyed quite recently) at **Bredfield** (on an unclassified road off the A12 about three miles north of Woodbridge), and lived there until about 1825, having been sent in 1821 to King Edward VI's Grammar School, Bury St Edmunds. From 1825 for ten years the family lived at Wherstead Lodge (no longer extant) near Ipswich, and then in 1835 moved to Boulge Hall (destroyed by fire in 1923) just about a mile west of

* Open weekdays 10 a.m. to 6 p.m. (10 a.m. to 4.30 or 5 p.m. in winter), Sunday 3 to 5 p.m. (2.30 to 4.30 p.m. in winter).

Bredfield. Two or three years later Fitzgerald decided to live in a small cottage (which has survived) near the park gates of Boulge Hall, and remained there until 1853. In 1853 he went to live with a friend at a farmhouse called Farlingay Hall (no longer in existence) just outside Woodbridge (IV, G5), seven miles north-east of Ipswich. He married the daughter of his friend Bernard Barton, the Quaker poet of Woodbridge, and separated from his wife six months later. Here his friend Carlyle visited him, and here he produced the first version of his translation of *The Rubá'iyát* of Omar Khayyám.

In 1860 he moved to lodgings on the Market Hill at Woodbridge, and then in 1874 into his own house called Grange Farm, which he renamed Little Grange. It has survived and is on the main road leading northwards out of the town. Tennyson visited him at this house, which Fitzgerald occupied for the rest of his life. He died in Norfolk and is buried in the churchyard at Boulge (IV, G5). In 1893 a rose-bush from the tomb of Omar Khayyám was planted beside his grave, and though that particular bush died in 1932 its descendants are flourishing.

A Suffolk story that deserves revival is that of *Margaret Catchpole* by Richard Cobbold, a native of Ipswich descended on his mother's side from Edmund Waller. The story is based on an actual Ipswich adventuress whose benefactor had been Cobbold's father.

What Olney and Weston were to Cowper, Aldeburgh (IV, H5) was to George Crabbe, who was born there, the son of a collector of salt duties, on December 24, 1754. The Aldeburgh of his day was very different from the town of today, and consisted largely of two unpaved and parallel streets lined with the cabins of seafaring folk and fishermen. Crabbe was mainly self-educated, worked in a warehouse after some schooling and then became apprenticed first to a doctor and then to a surgeon. He set up in practice, unsuccessfully; took to writing poetry with no better result until he wrote to the great Edmund Burke in 1781. Burke read his work, persuaded a publisher to undertake *The Library*, and invited Crabbe to his Beaconsfield home. He advised him to take holy orders as offering a safer career. *The Library* was successful; he took holy orders, and married the girl who had originally inspired him to write poetry. He became curate at Aldeburgh, then chaplain to the Duke of Rutland at Belvoir Castle for three years, followed by various other livings until he settled finally in Wiltshire.

There is now no visible reminder of Crabbe in Aldeburgh, but the quiet descriptive poetry of *The Borough* reminds us of the town, the quay, the river and the moods of Nature as he saw them. There has been a revival of interest in his work, helped by the fact that the libretto of Benjamin Britten's *Peter Grimes* is founded on one of the episodes in *The Borough*. Among other Aldeburgh associations are those of Wilkie Collins, who lived here for a time and placed the setting of his novel *No Name* here, and Edward Fitzgerald and George Meredith as visitors.

At **Theberton** (IV, H5) five miles north of Aldeburgh, C. M. Doughty, author of *Arabia Deserta*, was born at Theberton Hall on August 19, 1843. Quite near at **Framlingham** (IV, H5), about seven miles north of Woodbridge, the church has memorials and tombs of the Howard family, among them the tomb of the ill-fated poet Henry Howard, Earl of Surrey. At **Stowmarket** (IV, G5) on the A45 and ten miles north-west of Ipswich), there is the Old Vicarage in Milton Road which was the home of Dr Thomas Young, tutor to John Milton. Young taught Milton in London before the latter was sent to St Paul's School, and in later years Milton almost certainly visited Young here. A mulberry which was supposed to have been planted by the poet was blown down within recent years.

Jocelin of Brakelond, a twelfth-century monk of **Bury St Edmunds** (IV, F5), wrote an account of the great abbey there under the administration of Abbot Samson, and on this Carlyle based the first part of his *Past and Present*. Carlyle, not much given to praise, regarded Bury as 'a prosperous, brisk town beautifully diversifying', and Dickens, whose connexion with it was more intimate, regarded it as a 'bright little town'. He stayed at the Angel Hotel opposite the Abbey Gateway, during his reading tours of 1859 and 1861, and in that hotel he placed Mr Pickwick and his friends when they were chasing Mr Jingle. Besides Jocelin of Brakelond, the great abbey (now merely a ruin) produced another distinguished monk in John Lydgate, born at **Lydgate** near Stowmarket about 1370, and who entered the abbey when he was about fifteen. A disciple of Chaucer, he has been called a 'voluminous, prosaic and drivelling monk', though he produced one passage of pure poetry. It appears that he was not long a monk, but returned to Bury towards the end of his life. In the famous King Edward VI's Grammar School at Bury, Edward Fitzgerald was educated from 1821 to 1826.

Honington (IV, F4), about six miles north-east of Bury, was the birthplace of Robert Bloomfield, the 'Suffolk Poet' and author of *The Farmer's Boy*. He was born on December 3, 1766, the son of a tailor, and turning out too diminutive to be of use as a farmer, was sent to London to learn shoemaking.

Thomas Nash (or Nashe), the Elizabethan poet and miscellaneous writer, was born in **Lowestoft**, where his father was apparently the curate of the parish church, St Margaret's, in the register of which is recorded Nash's baptism in November 1567. The coastal area north of Lowestoft is the setting of the East Anglican portions of Theodore Watts-Dunton's romance of *Aylwin*, in which the East Anglian gypsies are prominent. Watts-Dunton knew George Borrow, who when he married in 1840 settled at his wife's house on the north side of Oulton Broad, only a short distance from Lowestoft. Though he was often away for considerable periods, this was his permanent home to the end of his life. This great lover of the gypsies welcomed their camping on his land, and any others except those professing gentility were welcome to call upon him. His house has gone, so has the summer-house in which he wrote *The Bible in Spain* and *Lavengro*. He died in his house in August 1881. There is a memorial of him in Oulton church.

Blundeston (IV, H4), three miles north-west of Oulton, was visited by Thomas Gray, but is more memorable as the 'Blunderstone' of *David Copperfield*. It was the birthplace of the hero, and Dickens says in a letter that during a visit in 1848 to this area he 'chose Blunderstone for the sound of its name'. The curious round-towered church at Blundeston has been restored as a memorial to Dickens. Much of the scene of *David Copperfield* is laid at **Yarmouth** (IV, H3, in Norfolk, but only a short distance north of our present area), where Mr Peggotty and his family lived on the seashore. And at Yarmouth George Borrow lived during the years 1853-60 on account of his wife's health.

CAMBRIDGESHIRE AND HUNTINGDONSHIRE

Pepys, though London-born, came of fenland stock, and one branch of his family owned Impington Hall (IV, E5), the Elizabethan building three miles north of Cambridge. Pepys has recorded his visit to his cousin Roger Pepys there in 1661. At **Trumpington** (IV, E5, on the A10 just over three miles south of Cambridge) there used to be a mill connected with Chaucer's 'Reeve's Tale', which tells the story of the unsatisfactory miller of Trumpington. Wordsworth, who was fond of rambling, came here in his undergraduate days and says:

> *Beside the pleasant mills of Trumpington*
> *I laugh'd with Chaucer.*

The successor of Chaucer's mill is supposed to have inspired Tennyson's 'The Miller's Daughter', and that mill was destroyed by fire in 1928.

Less than a mile to the west is **Grantchester**(IV, E5), where Rupert Brooke took lodgings in 1909 and then in the two following years lived at the Old Vicarage, which is still there and made famous in one of his best poems. D. H. Lawrence, in one of his letters, says that Brooke used to read poetry in his pyjamas 'at Granchester upon the lawns where the river goes'. At Grantchester too is Byron's Pool, named after Lord Byron, and in the poem just referred to Brooke evokes the association:

> *His ghostly Lordship swims his pool,*
> *And tries the strokes, essays the tricks,*
> *Long learnt on Hellespont, or Styx.*

About seven miles south-west of Cambridge, off the A603, is Wimpole Hall, formerly the seat of Robert Harley, Earl of Oxford, patron and friend of Matthew Prior. The poet was on a visit to Harley when he died on September 18, 1721.

In **Huntingdon** (IV, D4), in the High Street, is the restored Grammar School attended by Samuel Pepys, the same school that Oliver Cromwell had been to thirty years before. Also in the High Street is the house, marked by a tablet, where William Cowper lodged during

1765-7 with the Unwins, whom he met here, after he had been released from a private madhouse at St Albans.

At **Brampton** (IV, D4, off the A604 two miles west of Huntingdon) there is the cottage that belonged to the Pepys family, and often visited by Samuel Pepys in connexion with family affairs. In 1667, when the Dutch ships came up the Medway and surprised the English horribly, Pepys took fright and sent his wife and father to hide his money in the garden at Brampton. The foolish pair buried the money by daylight, contrary to Pepys's instructions, and he was very annoyed. Later he had a most trying time digging for it—his wife and father had forgotten where they buried the money.

About six miles north of Huntingdon, the B660 road crosses the A1 (Great North) Road, and the western arm leads to **Little Gidding** (IV, D4). Here Nicholas Ferrars, an Anglican divine who had at one time been active in the affairs of the Virginia Company, founded in 1626 a little self-supporting religious community. Among the visitors were his friends George Herbert and Richard Crashaw. Ferrars died in 1637, and the community was broken up by the Parliamentarians in 1647. The church in which they worshipped was damaged but has been restored. The community is well described in J. H. Shorthouse's *John Inglesant*, and T. S. Eliot was influenced to write 'Little Gidding', one of his *Four Quartets*. Some ten miles beyond Huntingdon on the A1 is **Norman Cross**, where George Borrow met the gypsy Jasper Petulengro, one of the most colourful personalities in *Lavengro*.

BEDFORDSHIRE AND NORTH BUCKINGHAMSHIRE

The great glory of the county of Bedfordshire is John Bunyan, who was born at **Harrowden**, a mile and a half east of **Elstow** (IV, D5, on the A6 two miles south of Bedford). His baptism on November 30, 1628, appears in the parish record at Elstow. His birthplace at Harrowden disappeared long ago, but the house he occupied after his first marriage, though somewhat changed, is still there. Bunyan had no formal schooling, learning what little he did from a primer and copy-book at home, and helped his father to make and mend pots and kettles. After soldiering in the Civil War, he married a godly wife, and the gay young fellow fond of games and given to swearing began to change his habits. A few years of inner spiritual conflict was resolved by his finding true peace in the Christian faith. It is all magnificently described in the simple highly nervous style, of which he was a supreme master, in *Grace Abounding*.

He joined a dissenting body, preached at **Bedford** (IV, D5), whither he had moved, and elsewhere. After the Restoration, when repressive measures against nonconformists were revived, he was arrested—he could have avoided arrest—refused to give an undertaking to refrain from public preaching and was committed to the county gaol in Bedford. There he spent twelve years, preaching to fellow-prisoners and writing, among other works, *Grace Abounding* and *The Pilgrim's Progress*. After his imprisonment he was pardoned under a recent measure suspending penal laws against nonconformists and Roman Catholics. The site of the Bedford gaol is marked by a stone slab in the pavement at the corner of High Street and Silver Street.

Bunyan became pastor of the nonconformist congregation in Bedford. Repressive measures against nonconformity were reintroduced, but he continued preaching and was never arrested again. The site of a barn in which he preached in Mill Street is now covered by the Bunyan Meeting Library and Museum,* which contains the largest number of Bunyan relics to be found anywhere. The Public Library† in Harpur Street also contains personal relics. The medieval Moot Hall at Elstow‡ has a collection illustrating life in the England of Bunyan's time.

Bunyan was one of the chief influences on the mind of William Hale White (who adopted the pseudonym of Mark Rutherford), born on December 22, 1831, in the High Street, Bedford. He was, like Bunyan, brought up in a dissenting household. Educated at Bedford Modern School, thereafter his life was lived elsewhere, but he has given us remarkable and sensitive pictures of the dissenting community of the

---

* Open Tuesday to Friday 10 a.m. to 12 noon, 2.30 to 4.30 p.m., and can be visited at other times by special arrangement.

† Weekdays 10 a.m. to 8 p.m. (Thursday 10 a.m. to 1 p.m.).

‡ Open Tuesday to Saturday 11 a.m. to 5 p.m., Sunday 2.30 to 5.30 p.m., and on summer Bank Holidays.

Bedford of his day in several novels and autobiographical works now most undeservedly neglected. The town of **Ampthill**, eight miles south of Bedford, was depicted by Mark Rutherford as 'Cowfold'. Near Ampthill are the ruins of Houghton House (formerly the home of the Countess of Pembroke, Sir Philip Sidney's sister) which may have suggested the 'House Beautiful' of *Pilgrim's Progress*. In Ampthill Park itself there is a memorial cross with an inscription composed by Horace Walpole stating that it marks the site of Catherine of Aragon's residence.

Five miles west of Ampthill and standing away from the main roads, there is **Chicksands Priory** (IV, D5), where Dorothy Osborne who wrote the beautiful letters to Sir William Temple was born in 1627. Near by is **Shefford**, where Robert Bloomfield the 'Suffolk Poet' lived in his last years, which were marked by hypochondria, semi-blindness and poverty. He died there on August 19, 1823, and is buried in the churchyard at **Campton**, a mile to the south-west.

Olney (IV, C5) in Buckinghamshire (on the A509 and twelve miles west of Bedford), is particularly associated with William Cowper. Here he wrote his finest poetry and most of the letters that place him among the great English letter writers. It was at the suggestion of the Rev. John Newton, curate of Olney, that Cowper and his friend Mrs Unwin came to live here in 1767, and they occupied the western half of a house called Orchard Side in the market-place. It is now the Cowper Memorial Museum.* The garden at the back contains the little summer-house that was later built for Cowper. The poet helped in the work of the parish and with Newton composed the famous Olney hymns. One of Cowper's friends, Lady Austen, suggested that he should try blank verse; he replied that he could not think of a subject; 'you can write upon any subject, write upon this sofa', said Lady Austen, and soon afterwards Cowper began 'The Task', his finest poem. Its publication in 1785 established Cowper as the greatest poet of his time.

Next year he and Mrs Unwin moved to **Weston Underwood**, a village about two miles south-west of Olney, where they remained until the move to Norfolk in 1795. At Weston, during one of his fits

* Open on weekdays 10 a.m. to 5 p.m.

of insanity, he tried to hang himself, and was just saved in time by Mrs Unwin. The scenes and features of his life at Olney and Weston are often minutely described in his letters, which are full of playful humour. About a quarter of a mile outside Olney, on the road to Weston, a track on the right leads to a hillock frequented by Cowper and Mrs Unwin. The visits to the hillock and the scene from it are described in a striking passage near the beginning of 'The Task'.

NORTHAMPTONSHIRE

John Clare, the eldest son of a poor labourer, was born on July 13, 1793, at the village of **Helpston** (IV, D3) between Peterborough and Stamford. The tenement in which he was born is marked by a tablet. He was tending sheep and geese at the age of seven, and later became under-gardener at the great Burghley House a few miles away. He got into bad company, whose brutality made him run away and enlist as a soldier for a short period, and then was employed at a limekiln. A few years before, he had bought a copy of Thomson's *Seasons*, which inspired him with a desire to write poetry, and writing poetry instead of attending to work resulted in his dismissal from the limekiln. A chance sight by a Stamford bookseller of one of Clare's poems led to publication in 1820 of *Poems Descriptive of Rural Life and Scenery*, 'by John Clare, a Northamptonshire Peasant'.

He visited London, met celebrities and was lionized, and dined at grand houses—in the servants' halls. His former employer, the Marquess of Exeter, gave him a small annuity for life. Three more volumes of poetry followed in the next fifteen years, but public curiosity about the peasant poet had been sated by the first volume, and he returned to a life of poverty. A nobleman built him a better home (which survives) at **Northborough** (IV, D3), three miles north-east of Helpston, to which Clare and his wife—he married after his initial success—moved in 1832. His health was breaking; he began to have hallucinations about evil spirits, was sent to a private asylum in Epping from which he escaped after a few years, and then after a few months at home he was certified and sent to Northampton County Asylum, where he died, and is buried in the churchyard at Helpston.

Near by is **Barnack** (IV, D3), two miles south-east of Stamford, where at the rectory Charles Kingsley spent some of his boyhood, and where his brother Henry (author of *Ravenshoe*) was born in 1830. At **Aldwinkle** (IV, C4, on an unclassified road off the A605 and four miles south-west of Oundle) Thomas Fuller was born at the rectory of St Peter's in June 1608. The old rectory has gone; Fuller is commemorated in the church by a window. He was educated at the village school under the Rev. Arthur Smith, who may have been related to John Smith of Virginia fame, but his father was dissatisfied with his progress and taught the boy himself. In the adjoining parish of **Aldwinkle All Saints**, John Dryden was born on August 9, 1631, in his maternal grandfather's rectory, which has survived though no longer the rectory. Dryden's home was actually at **Tichmarsh** (IV, D4, only two miles away on the other side of the A605). A great elm tree in the village is on the site of his old home. A bust of him in the church was erected by Elizabeth Creed, daughter of his first cousin Sir Gilbert Pickering, and she was also a cousin of Samuel Pepys, in whose *Diary* she figures. Part of her inscription below Dryden's bust says: . . . *we boast he was bred and had his first learning here, where he has often made us happy by his kind visits and most delightful conversation.* At **Cotterstock** (IV, D4), about a mile to the north-west of Oundle, there is a seventeenth-century building where Dryden sometimes stayed in later life with another cousin.

Laxton Hall, six miles north-west of **Oundle** (IV, D4), formerly the seat of the Earls of Carbery (and now the Cardinal Howard School), has an association with De Quincey, but the predecessor of the present building is the one in which he actually stayed in 1800. Lady Carbery had met the De Quincey family in Bath, and was greatly impressed by his ability. He was then only fifteen, but was virtually her tutor in Greek and theology for three months.

John Clare, as we have seen, was confined in 1841 in the County Asylum (now St Andrew's Hospital for Mental Diseases) in **Northampton** (IV, C5), and there he spent the rest of his life. For the first ten years or so he was allowed to wander about Northampton when he pleased, and used to sit for hours in the portico of All Saints Church. He continued writing poetry, and his greatest poem—beginning, 'I am, who knows, who cares?'—was written here. He died on May 20, 1864. Among his visitors was Mary Russell Mitford, who has left an account of him in her memoirs. There are relics of him in the Public Library in Abington Street. The library commemorates two other native writers of Northampton, Thomas Fuller and John Dryden, with statues in the front. Anne Bradstreet the American poet was born probably in Northampton in 1612. She was the daughter of Thomas Dudley, who later became Governor of Massachusetts. Anne, her husband and father left for New England in 1630, settling eventually at Ipswich, Massachusetts. Oliver Wendell Holmes and R. H. Dana were descendants of Anne Bradstreet. Jerome K. Jerome died in Northampton General Hospital on June 14, 1927, after he was taken suddenly ill when on a motor tour of England. After cremation his ashes were buried at Ewelme in Oxfordshire.

Easton Maudit (on an unclassified road off the A509 seven miles east of Northampton) was the home for twenty-nine years of Bishop Percy. He was appointed vicar in 1753, and here his main work on the *Reliques of Ancient English Poetry* was done. Among his visitors were Burke, Goldsmith and Johnson, the last spending part of a summer here. The holly walk in the village is still referred to as Johnson's Walk.

NORFOLK

John Skelton was probably a native of Norfolk, and may have been born in **Diss** (IV, G4), about fifteen miles south-east of Norwich, where he became rector in 1498. The church here is substantially as it was during his very irregular incumbency. He acted the buffoon in the pulpit, and lived with a woman by whom he had many children. He retained the living until his death, though he appears to have spent much if not more time in London and elsewhere than in Diss.

Robert Greene the dramatist and pamphleteer was born in **Norwich** (IV, G3) about 1560, of parents, as he himself says, respected for their gravity and honest life. By far the greatest literary figure associated with Norwich is Sir Thomas Browne. After practising medicine in Oxfordshire and travel and study abroad he finally settled here in 1637. Engaged in antiquarian studies and writing that magnificent prose every sentence of which rings like an epic, he lived out his remaining forty-five years in the city; but his first and most famous book, *Religio Medici*, was probably written elsewhere. John Evelyn visited him in

1671, and records the astonishing collection of objects in Browne's house—books, medals, plants and many other 'natural things' including birds' eggs. Browne took Evelyn on a conducted tour of the city. He died on his birthday, October 19, 1682, at a house (no longer there) near Lamb Inn Yard, almost opposite the church of St Peter Mancroft in which he was buried. In 1840, when workmen were digging in the chancel, his coffin lid was broken by a pick-axe. His skull was presented to the Norfolk and Norwich Hospital, where it remained until returned to the grave in 1922. There is a statue of Browne outside the church.

A now forgotten Victorian blue-stocking, Harriet Martineau, was born in Norwich on June 12, 1802. She wrote on an astonishing number of subjects and, somewhat uncharacteristically, a charming children's story called *Feats on the Fjord*, which appears to be almost unknown to children of today. She was a friend of Wordsworth, was famous in her day, and consulted by cabinet ministers on social questions.

George Borrow, born not far from Norwich, spent part of his early years in the city, whither his family moved after having been in many parts of Britain and Ireland. They settled in a house, now called Borrow House,* in Willow Lane. Borrow completed his education at the Grammar School, and whilst there renewed acquaintance with the gypsy Jasper Petulengro, whom he had met in Huntingdonshire, and now encamped near Norwich on Mousehold Heath. In 1818 Borrow was articled to a solicitor, 'a gentleman lawyer of the old school', as he says in *Lavengro*. But law did not interest him; he was much more interested in the study of languages, and his interest was fostered by William Taylor, who taught him German. When his father died in 1824 he gave up law, and went to London, hoping there to earn a living through literature. Later he stayed at various times with his mother at the house in Willow Lane. In his last years, when he was living at Oulton, he used to visit the city, staying at a house in Lady Lane.

His birthplace is at **Dumpling Green**, a mile south of East Dereham

* It used to be open to the public, but is now in private occupation. The tenant, Mrs Baker, is willing to show the house to visitors if arrangements are made with her *in advance*. The manuscripts and other relics that used to be at Borrow House are now in the Central Public Library.

(on the A47 about fifteen miles north-west of Norwich). The farm-house in which he was born in 1803 is still there, in a lane which runs off the Yaxham road. Owing to his father's occupation as a recruiting officer, the family was constantly on the move, and at a very early age Borrow was removed from Dumpling Green, though the family returned there for short periods in 1809 and 1810.

At **East Dereham** (IV, G3) William Cowper spent the last melancholy years of his life. He came here with his friend Mrs Unwin in 1795; she died a year later, and friends and relations tried to relieve the effects of his melancholia by encouraging him to continue writing. He did some work on his translation of Homer, and wrote that tragic poem 'The Castaway'. He died on April 25, 1800, and is buried in the north transept of East Dereham church. The site of his house in the market-place is now covered by the Cowper Memorial Chapel.

At the rectory at **Merton** (IV, F4), nearly ten miles south-west of East Dereham, Edward Fitzgerald died suddenly on June 14, 1883, when on a visit to his friend the Rev. George Crabbe, grandson of the poet. At **Weeting** (now **Weeting-cum-Bromehill**), a mile north of Brandon, Thomas Shadwell was born in 1640 or 1642. His birthplace, no longer in existence, was a farmhouse built on the site of Bromehill Priory. Fanny Burney was born either in Chapel Street or High Street (probably the former), **King's Lynn** (IV, E3), on June 13, 1752. Her father at that time was organist at the church of St Margaret. Fanny spent the first nine years of her life here, and then the family moved to London.

Fanny Burney was later to find an admirer of her work in Horace Walpole, who came of a Norfolk family. Twelve miles north-east of King's Lynn, off the A148, is the enormous mansion called **Houghton Hall** (IV, F3), with a façade 450 feet long. It is the seat of the Marquess of Cholmondeley, and was built in 1722-31 for Sir Robert Walpole, born in Houghton village, and the father of Horace Walpole. In a letter of 1761 Horace Walpole describes with tender nostalgia his feelings about the house, now falling into decay under the ownership of his nephew. 'I loved this garden,' he says, 'as now, with many regrets, I love Houghton; Houghton, I know not what to call it, a monument of grandeur or ruin! . . . For what has he built Houghton? for his grandson to annihilate, or his son to mourn over.' This nephew (whom he succeeded as Earl of Orford) sold the wonderful art treasures to Catherine the Great, and Horace Walpole said that it was 'the most signal mortification to my idolatry of my father's memory it could receive. It is stripping the temple of his glory and his affection.' The old church where his father was buried lies in the park, and in the earlier letter quoted above he says: 'Every clock that strikes tells me that I am an hour nearer to yonder church,' and in that church he was buried, but there is no monument to him or to his father.

Going towards the northern seaboard of the county, there is the village of **Langham** (IV, G2), off the A149 and two miles south of Blakeney. Here Captain Marryat settled at Manor Cottage (a modern house occupies the site) in 1843, and spent his years here mainly on writing stories for children. Eventually the amount of literary work he did undermined his strength, and he thought that a return to naval service would restore his health. The refusal of the Admiralty to reinstate him so angered him that he broke a blood-vessel in his lungs, and six months later the death of his eldest son proved his death-blow. He died on August 9, 1848, and is buried in the churchyard. In the church there is a memorial window by Burne-Jones and a commemorative tablet.

LINCOLNSHIRE

John Foxe the martyrologist was born in this county in 1516, but beyond this, and the fact that his father died when he was young, nothing is known of his early years here. Another native of Lincolnshire, to whom no exact locality is assignable, is the dramatist Thomas Heywood, born about 1575. The poet Jean Ingelow was born in **Boston** (IV, D2) on March 17, 1820, the daughter of a banker. She spent her early years here, and her fenland upbringing is reflected in some of her poetry. Much of her work is of no great merit, but there are a few excellent poems, especially 'High Tide on the Coast of Lincolnshire', though modern neglect suggests otherwise.

Dickens is associated with **Grantham** (IV, C2). He stayed at the George Hotel, which is still there (Sir Isaac Newton had stayed there too) on his way up to investigate Yorkshire schools in 1838, accompanied by his illustrator 'Phiz'. Writing to his wife he said that it was 'the very best inn I have ever put up at', and is probably the one he had in mind when praising a Grantham inn in *Nicholas Nickleby*. **Horncastle** (IV, D1), some twenty miles east of Lincoln, and on the A153, figures in Borrow's *Lavengro*, and its annual horse fair, still held, has a chapter to itself.

About ten miles north-east of Horncastle, on an unclassified road, is **Somersby** (IV, D1), the birthplace of Tennyson. He was the fourth child of the rector of Somersby, and born in the old rectory, which is still there, on August 6, 1809. At the age of seven he was sent to live with his grandmother at **Louth**, about ten miles to the north, and educated at the old Grammar School there, where John Smith of Virginia fame had been educated. The school, in Schoolhouse Lane, was rebuilt on the same site in 1869. He returned to Somersby in 1820, and received further education from his father until sent to Cambridge, which he had to leave in 1831 because of his father's bad health. His father died soon afterwards. Meanwhile in 1827 he and his brother Charles had published *Poems by Two Brothers*—Tennyson had begun writing verse at the age of eight.

His great friend Arthur Hallam frequently visited him at Somersby, and together they took a journey abroad. Hallam's death in 1833 was to evoke from Tennyson many years later one of the greatest elegies in English poetry—*In Memoriam*. Shortly before Hallam's death there had appeared a small volume of *Poems*, savagely attacked in the *Quarterly Review*, the same periodical that had attacked Keats with equal venom, with the result that Tennyson was to publish nothing for nearly ten years. The incoming rector had allowed the Tennyson family to stay on at the rectory until 1837, when they moved into Essex. Tennyson remembers Lincolnshire in much of his poetry, and in one of the earliest poems, 'Ode to Memory', he recalls the rectory with

> *The seven elms, the poplars four*
> *That stand beside my father's door.*

From Tennyson back to the eighteenth century, and we find Dr Johnson in Lincolnshire. Two miles north-west of **Partney** (IV, E1, situated at the crossing of the A16 and the A158), is the Elizabethan building called Langton Hall, where his friend Bennet Langton lived. Here Johnson visited him in 1764, and here he was fully convinced that he could not endure life in the country, although always happy to visit his friends there. George Eliot, whose 'country' is Warwickshire and Derbyshire, strayed into Lincolnshire for some of the setting of *The Mill on the Floss*, where **Gainsborough** appears as 'St Oggs'. In the novel her brother Isaac is portrayed as Tom Tulliver.

Cambridge

The City
The University

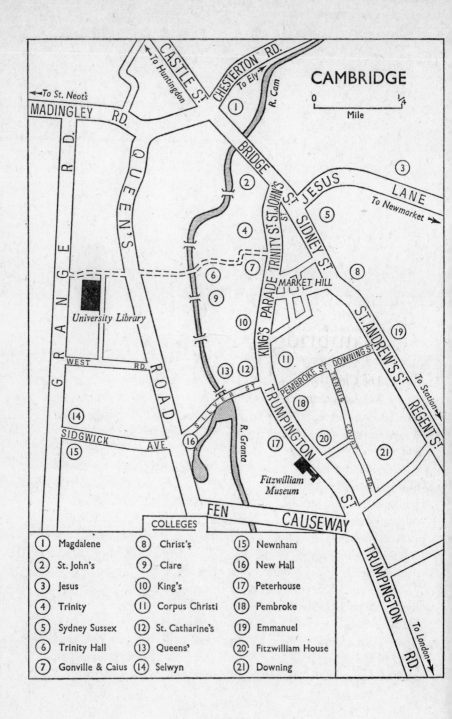

CAMBRIDGE

0   ¼
Mile

To St. Neot's
MADINGLEY RD.
CASTLE ST.
To Huntingdon
CHESTERTON RD.
To Ely
R. Cam
BRIDGE ST.
QUEEN'S ROAD
GRANGE RD.
WEST RD.
University Library
TRINITY ST.
ST. JOHN'S ST.
JESUS LANE
To Newmarket
SIDNEY ST.
MARKET HILL
KING'S PARADE
ST. ANDREW'S ST.
To Station
SIDGWICK AVE.
SILVER ST.
R. Granta
PEMBROKE ST.
DOWNING ST.
TENNIS COURT RD.
REGENT ST.
TRUMPINGTON ST.
Fitzwilliam Museum
FEN CAUSEWAY
TRUMPINGTON RD.
To London

COLLEGES

①	Magdalene	⑧	Christ's	⑮	Newnham
②	St. John's	⑨	Clare	⑯	New Hall
③	Jesus	⑩	King's	⑰	Peterhouse
④	Trinity	⑪	Corpus Christi	⑱	Pembroke
⑤	Sydney Sussex	⑫	St. Catharine's	⑲	Emmanuel
⑥	Trinity Hall	⑬	Queens'	⑳	Fitzwilliam House
⑦	Gonville & Caius	⑭	Selwyn	㉑	Downing

THE CITY

Its most eminent literary native is Jeremy Taylor, the son of a barber, who was born in August 1613, exactly where is not known, but it must have been within the parish of Trinity Church, where he was baptized. A contemporary churchman, Thomas Fuller, having been at Queens' and Sidney Sussex colleges, was appointed in 1630 by Corpus Christi College to the perpetual curacy of St Benet's, in Benet Street. In the following year he preached the funeral sermon of Thomas Hobson the University carrier, eponymously famous in 'Hobson's choice', who is celebrated also in two poems by Milton. Fuller resigned his curacy in 1634. Abraham Cowley, a Royalist supporter during the Civil War, was residing in Cambridge during 1643-4 when the Parliamentarians gained control, and was ejected, whereupon he moved to Oxford.

Pepys visited Cambridge several times after his undergraduate days, the first occasion being when his brother had just taken up residence in his old college. He spent one afternoon drinking immoderately at the Three Tuns. In 1667 he took his wife with him, conducting her round some of the colleges and to King's College Chapel, 'to see the outside only'. Charles Lamb visited the city on a few occasions. It did not, unhappily, draw from him a complementary essay to 'Oxford in the Vacation' (which was written during a visit to the rival university) though he wrote a sonnet in which he imagines himself walking gowned. It was at Cambridge that he and Mary Lamb first met Emmy Isola, whom they decided to adopt.

THE UNIVERSITY

Cambridge, as well as Oxford, has its connexions with the Protestant reformers. Tyndale, who had had his troubles at Oxford, removed to Cambridge about 1515, drawn thither no doubt by the influence of the University as a centre of humanism, and where the great Erasmus had recently distilled the New Learning. Tyndale, Cranmer, Latimer and others used to meet at the White Horse Inn, and discussed eagerly doctrines abhorrent to the Establishment. The inn was demolished in 1828, and the other White Horse Inn (which became the Folk Museum) has no connexion with it. It may be that from these discussions Tyndale derived the inspiration that urged him on to translate the Bible, and his glorious cadences were echoed by the translators of the Authorized Version. It was due to the influence of these Cambridge reformers that we owe the Prayer Book of Edward VI, whose beautiful language was mainly the work of Cranmer. Latimer preached in the church of St Edward, in St Edward's Passage, and the pulpit he used is still there.

Among those educated at the University who, for lack of precise information, cannot be assigned to their respective colleges, are John Lyly, who had obtained his B.A. at Oxford, and then became M.A. at Cambridge in 1579; George Chapman, alleged to have been also at Oxford; Thomas Heywood, who may have been a fellow of Peterhouse; Thomas Campion; and Samuel Butler the author of *Hudibras*. For the special case of John Skelton we have something to say under Oxford.

When James I paid a state visit to Cambridge in 1615, he requested the university to confer the degree of D.D. on his chaplain, John Donne. Apparently the authorities had some objection, the nature of which is unknown, and conferred the degree unwillingly, taking care to make no record of it in the University register. Cambridge has been an astonishing nursery of great poets, and no other university in Britain, or beyond, can match the greatness of this group of six: Spenser, Milton, Wordsworth, Coleridge, Byron and Tennyson.

Before we proceed to discuss the literary associations of the colleges, a word about the University Library,* which is in Burrell's Walk. It is one of the great libraries of the world, with many great treasures in books and manuscripts, and should be visited. The Fitzwilliam Museum in Trumpington Street should also be visited. It has a small collection of manuscripts.

CHRIST'S COLLEGE:† John Leland the antiquary graduated at this college in 1522, and Francis Quarles the author of *Emblems* in 1608. The greatest son of the college was John Milton, who entered as a pensioner in 1625. Two years later he was joined by Edward King, whose death on his way to Ireland inspired Milton's 'Lycidas'. Milton graduated B.A. in 1629 and M.A. in 1632. Handsome to the point of femininity, he was known as 'the lady of Christ's'. He was out of sympathy with the scholasticism of the fellows, and there are stories of difficulties with them, but there is no doubt of the superb grounding in the classics that he gained here. Among the poems he wrote whilst at college are the sonnet on Shakespeare and the 'Hymn on the Morning of Christ's Nativity', and was already thinking of a poem on an epic theme. He occupied a first-floor room on the north side of the first court, and above the entrance to the chapel.

Over a hundred and fifty years later Wordsworth called to pay his respects when the same room was occupied by a friend of his. In *The Prelude* he relates how they drank to Milton's memory:

> . . . till my brain reel'd,
> Never so clouded by the fumes of wine
> Before that hour, or since.

* Open weekdays 9.30 a.m. to 6.30 p.m., Saturday 9 a.m. to 1 p.m., but visitors must be accompanied by a graduate or undergraduate in academic dress.

† Visitors should remember that the colleges are private foundations, and admission to them is by courtesy of the respective authorities. During vacations the halls, chapels and gardens are open during reasonable hours of the day; during term-time the hours are of course more restricted, and inquiries can be made at the porters' lodges at the college gates.

Another poet at this college was Charles Stuart Calverley, who entered in 1852 after removal from Balliol College, Oxford. Noted for social graces rather than academic ardour, Calverley's friends used to drag him out of bed and sometimes lock him in his rooms to make sure that he worked. He won prize after prize, and in 1856 was elected a fellow. He lectured, took pupils, published *Verses and Translations*, and then in 1865 left to take up study of law.

CLARE COLLEGE: The original foundation was University Hall, refounded as Clare Hall in 1338 and the name changed to Clare College in 1856. According to tradition Chaucer is connected with Clare Hall, and some have sought to identify the 'Solere Hall' of 'The Reeve's Tale' with this college. Hugh Latimer was a member of the college, but little is known of him here until he obtained a fellowship in 1510, and then proceeded to graduate. Robert Greene migrated from St John's College and became M.A. in 1583.

CORPUS CHRISTI COLLEGE: Christopher Marlowe entered with a Matthew Parker scholarship in 1581, became B.A. in 1584 and M.A. in 1587. One of his tutors was Francis Kett, later consigned to the flames for heresy. It is possible that Kett's unorthodox views had some bearing on the fact that Marlowe was later suspected of being an atheist. Another dramatist, John Fletcher, may have been a member of this college, but the evidence is inconclusive.

EMMANUEL COLLEGE: This was the college of John Harvard and of some of the Pilgrim Fathers. The prototype of Captain Lemuel Gulliver was educated here too, but unfortunately the college has no record of him.

GONVILLE AND CAIUS COLLEGE: Thomas Shadwell the dramatist entered Caius College (as it was then) in 1656 as a pensioner, and left without a degree. Jeremy Taylor entered in 1628, graduated B.A. in 1631, then took holy orders, and obtained his M.A. in 1634. James Elroy Flecker, after graduating at Oxford, became a member of the college in 1908 in order to study oriental languages for two years before entering the consular service.

JESUS COLLEGE: Thomas Cranmer entered the college about 1503, becoming B.A. in 1512, M.A. three years later, and then was elected a fellow. However, when he married not long afterwards he lost the fellowship, and in order to resume studies lodged his wife at the Dolphin inn, whose hostess was related to Mrs Cranmer. The fact was perverted many years later, when it was stated that Cranmer was an ostler. A very different type of churchman was Laurence Sterne, who was admitted as a sizar in 1733. He secured the exhibition instituted by his great-grandfather, Archbishop Sterne, who had been master of the college. His studies were somewhat desultory, though he acquired a considerable knowledge of the classics, but none of mathematics. He became friendly with a younger student whose coarseness and delight in obscene literature had some influence on Sterne, and in later years both attended the orgies of the Demoniacs Club. They are alleged to have studied under a walnut tree in the inner court, and one of them composed this distich:

This should be the Tree of Knowledge,
As it stands in so very wise a college.

Sterne graduated B.A. in 1736, leaving soon afterwards under a cloud, having run into debt, and became M.A. in 1740.

Coleridge took up residence in 1791. He won the Browne medal for a Greek ode, and then became one of four chosen to compete for the Craven scholarship, two of the others being Keate (the successful competitor, later provost of Eton in Shelley's time), and Samuel Butler who became the father of the author of *Erewhon*. After a time Coleridge's studies became irregular. He was interested in radical politics, became a pacifist and Unitarian, was still in love with the girl he met when at school, and ran seriously into debt. In 1793 he 'fled to debauchery' in London, enlisted and when discharged returned to college, when he was formally admonished and confined to college for a month, after which he left without a degree. In *Biographia Literaria* he bewails that 'in an inauspicious hour I left the friendly cloisters and the happy grove of quiet, ever honoured Jesus College'. Sir Arthur Quiller-Couch was elected a fellow of Jesus when he was appointed

King Edward VII Professor of English Literature in 1912, and during term resided here for the rest of his life.

KING'S COLLEGE: Giles Fletcher the elder entered in 1565 and graduated in 1569. His son Phineas, author of *The Purple Island* and a much better poet, entered in 1600, and before graduating in 1604 had already acquired reputation as a poet. Edmund Waller was in residence during 1620-2, and left without a degree. Horace Walpole entered his father's college in 1735. Little is known of his life here, though we know from his letters that his professor of mathematics told him that he seemed incapable of learning anything of the subject. He preferred the classics and French and Italian studies. He left in 1739 without a degree. Rupert Brooke, who entered in 1906, was an enthusiastic undergraduate who joined the University Fabian Society (becoming its president) and helped to found the Marlowe Society. Though officially studying the classics, he found the Elizabethan writers more to his taste, and made a favourite of John Donne when he was neglected by most readers. Brooke graduated in 1909, and in 1912 secured a fellowship with his dissertation on 'John Webster and the Elizabethan Drama'.

MAGDALENE COLLEGE: Samuel Pepys, migrating to Magdalene from Trinity Hall in 1651, was soon elected a scholar. He graduated B.A. in 1653. Little is known of his college life, though once he was admonished before all the fellows 'for having been scandalously over-served with drink ye night before'. He bequeathed his library* and the manuscript of his *Diary* to his old college, and subscribed in 1677 towards the new buildings. Charles Kingsley entered in 1838, soon gaining a scholarship, and graduated in 1842. The course of study was somewhat distasteful to him, and he found much more delight in rowing, walking, boxing and other recreations. He returned to Cambridge as Professor of Modern History in 1860, holding the post until 1869, and engaged in the famous controversy with Newman which evoked from the latter the magnificent *Apologia pro Vita Sua*.

* The Pepysian Library is open Monday to Saturday during term, 2.30 to 3.30 p.m.

PEMBROKE COLLEGE: This is very much a college of poets. Edmund Spenser entered Pembroke Hall (as it was then) as a sizar in 1569. He was poor and in ill-health during his university days, but read avidly Latin, Greek, French and Italian literature, and became M.A. in 1576. He came under the influence of Gabriel Harvey, a fellow of Pembroke, a great but cantankerous scholar who believed that English poetry should be based closely on Latin models. Spenser remembered Cambridge with gratitude in his *Faerie Queene*:

> *My mother, Cambridge, whom, as with a crown,*
> *He doth adorn, and is adorn'd of it*
> *With many a gentle muse and many a learned wit—*

'he' referring to the River Ouse.

Richard Crashaw entered Pembroke Hall as a pensioner in 1632. He had a gift for languages, and mastered Greek, Latin, Hebrew, Spanish and Italian; was fond of music, and deeply religious. He went daily for hours to St Mary's Church, praying and composing religious poetry. He graduated in 1634, and in the same year published, in Latin, his first book of verse. In 1637 he went to Peterhouse. Thomas Gray's was the reverse process, coming from Peterhouse to Pembroke in 1757. He was offered the post of poet laureate in the following year, but declined. In 1759 he went to London to carry out research, and paid short visits to the college until 1761. He applied unsuccessfully for the professorship of history and modern languages, but obtained the appointment in 1768. At about that time he had a narrow escape from a fire that destroyed part of the college. As at Peterhouse, he lived a secluded life, and did not dine in hall. People who were curious to see him watched for him when he turned up at the Rainbow Coffee-house to order circulating-library books. In 1771 he returned from a visit to London feeling ill, and got gradually worse. He was attended by his cousin Mary Antrobus, who lived in Cambridge, and his last words were addressed to her: 'Molly, I shall die', and did so on July 30, 1771.

Christopher Smart was admitted in 1739 and graduated in 1742. Elected a fellow in 1745, he secured as well the position of praelector in philosophy, but he was much too fond of tavern life to perform his duties satisfactorily. Gray reported his activities: his debts were mounting; he had written a play and 'acts five parts himself' (it was later performed in the college); and 'all this, you see, must come to a jail or a bedlam'. Gray was prophetic. Smart was deprived of his college posts and creditors confined him to his room. He gained the Seatonian prize in 1750 for a poem on the Supreme Being, was confined for madness for a short time in London in 1751, and then got married. When the authorities heard of the marriage he was in trouble, but they agreed to extend his fellowship on certain conditions. However, shortly afterwards he left for London.

PETERHOUSE: Richard Crashaw migrated here from Pembroke College in 1637, was elected a fellow and then graduated M.A. He considered taking holy orders, but revolted by increasing puritanism in the Anglican Church, gave up the idea. Moreover he was increasingly attracted by Roman Catholicism. He pursued for several years a life of scholarship, devotion and the writing of poetry until the Parliamentarians destroyed the chapel at Peterhouse, and required all fellows to take the Solemn League and Covenant. Crashaw was one of those who refused and was ejected. He went to Oxford and London for a short period, then to Paris, where he met Abraham Cowley, whom he had known at Cambridge. He became a Roman Catholic. He was very poor, and Cowley introduced him to Henrietta Maria, who gave him introductions to influential people in Rome. He obtained employment, but died soon afterwards, and was buried at Loreto.

Thomas Gray entered the college in 1734. A shy, retiring student, he was shunned by others as a fop. He left in 1738 without a degree, but returned in 1742 and became LL.B. a year later. A recluse, he quietly pursued his scholarly way. He was very afraid of fire, especially after his London house was burned, and kept a rope-ladder in his room. In 1756 some mischievous students one evening placed a tub of water under his windows, and then called out 'Fire!' Gray escaped by his rope-ladder and landed in the tub. When he found that the authorities (who probably enjoyed the joke) had not treated the perpetrators with enough severity, he left and took up residence in Pembroke College. His rooms in the Fellows' Building can be recognized easily by the iron bars he placed against the windows.

QUEENS' COLLEGE: Thomas Fuller entered Queens' in 1621, soon after his uncle, Dr John Davenant, had resigned the presidency of the college to become Bishop of Salisbury. He graduated B.A. and M.A. in due course. His uncle's attempt to obtain a fellowship for him was unsuccessful, and Fuller passed on to Sidney Sussex College. Many years later Fuller wrote a most readable *History of the University of Cambridge*.

ST CATHARINE'S COLLEGE: James Shirley was a migrant to this college from Oxford, and graduated here about 1618. He took holy orders and obtained his M.A.

ST JOHN'S COLLEGE: Sir Thomas Wyatt was admitted to this college at the age of twelve, but nothing is known of his life here beyond the fact that he obtained his B.A. in 1518 and M.A. in 1520. Robert Greene the dramatist entered as a sizar in 1575, and after graduating led a dissolute life on the Continent, and then returned to the University, but to another college, Clare Hall. Thomas Nash followed Greene to this college, and they were to become acquainted later. He graduated in 1585 or 1586, says that he was at Cambridge for seven years, and claimed that he could if he had so desired become a fellow. Gabriel Harvey said that Nash gained a bad reputation for insulting the townsmen, and left before his time; but Harvey was a virulent controversialist who quarrelled with Greene, Nash and others, and cannot be trusted in this context. Nash later described his old college as 'the sweetest nurse of knowledge in all that university'.

According to Thomas Fuller's *Worthies of England*, Ben Jonson was for a time at St John's College, but Jonson himself stated that he was 'taken from school and put to a trade', which disposes of Fuller's assertion. Robert Herrick, who became a friend and worshipper of Ben Jonson, entered the college in 1613. He was always petitioning his uncle for more money, and said that shortage of money resulted in neglect of studies. He went in 1616 to Trinity Hall, apparently to effect economy and to pursue legal studies. Matthew Prior came up with a scholarship from Westminster School in 1682, and graduated in 1686. In the following year he produced his first literary work, a reply to

Dryden's *The Hind and the Panther*. He obtained a fellowship, and wrote a tribute in verse to one of the college's benefactors, the Earl of Exeter, as a result of which he became tutor to the earl's sons.

The college has great names, literary and otherwise, but none greater than Wordsworth, who entered in 1787. Lectures, examinations 'I did not love, nor do I love them now', he says in *The Prelude*. The tutors left him much to his own devices. He studied Italian under a man named Isola (whose granddaughter was adopted by Charles and Mary Lamb), and in his last two years did a great deal of miscellaneous reading. Spenser, a Cambridge man, was honoured by him—'I call'd him Brother, Englishman and Friend'; and as to Milton, 'our blind Poet', we have already recorded what Wordsworth did at Milton's own college. His reactions to Cambridge can be studied in the third book of *The Prelude*, and it reveals some pharisaism in his attitude. He graduated in 1791. In addition to the third book of *The Prelude*, Cambridge evoked other poems from Wordsworth, including three sonnets on King's College Chapel and a sonnet on the occasion of his portrait being presented to his own college.

Henry Kirke White entered as a sizar in 1805 and distinguished himself in classical studies, but consumption cut short a career that promised outstanding academic and possibly poetic achievement. He died in his college rooms on October 19, 1806, and was buried in All Saints Church. Samuel Butler entered in 1854, destined for the ministry, and graduated brilliantly in classics. When an undergraduate he did some writing, including an amusing parody of a typical 'crib' of the time, entitled 'The Shield of Achilles, an Homeric Picture of Cambridge Life'.

SIDNEY SUSSEX COLLEGE: Thomas Fuller migrated to this college from Queens', having failed to secure a fellowship, and a similar attempt here also failed.

TRINITY COLLEGE: This college has a formidable list of men of letters, and in great names bears down all other colleges, whether of Oxford or Cambridge. The first, in point of time, is Francis Bacon, who entered in 1573, and left in 1575 without a degree. Many years later he represented the University in Parliament. Giles Fletcher the younger, whose father and brother have already been noticed under King's College, entered about 1603, graduating in 1606, and later became reader in Greek grammar and language.

George Herbert had a very distinguished academic career. He entered with a scholarship in 1609, graduated B.A. and M.A. and was elected a fellow. He lectured on the classics, and tried to secure the position of public orator, but obtained instead the deputy oratorship, though succeeding to the higher position when its occupant retired. Thereby he came into contact with the court and men of influence, including Bacon. Finally 'the painted pleasures of a court life' conflicted with his conscience, and he took holy orders, though it was ill-health that forced him to resign as public orator. A man who took readily to 'painted pleasures' was Sir John Suckling, who entered about 1625, and appears to have departed within a year or so.

Abraham Cowley entered with a scholarship in 1637, and in due course obtained his degrees. Having already written poetry at school, he continued to do so here, and a Latin comedy of his was acted by members of the college before the University. When Prince Charles (later Charles II) was at Cambridge in 1641 a comedy by Cowley was acted for his entertainment.

Andrew Marvell entered as a sizar in 1633. A story, impossible to verify, says that he came under the influence of Jesuits, who persuaded him to go to London, where his father found him in a bookseller's shop and induced him to return to Cambridge. He graduated in 1638. Like George Herbert and Abraham Cowley before him, Dryden entered in 1650 with a scholarship from Westminster School. He appears to have got into some kind of trouble for which he had to apologize. His academic career is obscure, but it is known that he obtained his B.A. in 1654.

Byron entered in 1805. In between somewhat desultory studies he rode, shot, boxed and swam. He read a great deal unsystematically, and wrote poetry, which was published as *Poems on Various Occasions* and *Hours of Idleness* (an exquisitely apt title), both appearing in 1807. The latter was criticized severely in *The Edinburgh Review*, which provoked Byron to reply with the stinging satire of 'English Bards and Scotch

Reviewers', begun at Cambridge and published in 1809, the year after
he received the degree of M.A. Byron's rooms are thought to have been
in Nevile's Court, on the first floor on the north side, next to the
library. His statue by Thorvaldsen, originally commissioned for Westminster Abbey, was refused, and is now in the library.

Macaulay entered in 1818, lodging at first in Jesus Lane and then
took the rooms on the ground floor beside the chapel. Unusually
brilliant though he was, his regular course of studies was sometimes set
aside for the discussions he loved on questions of the day. He just
managed to pass in mathematics, which he disliked intensely. He failed
twice to secure election to a fellowship, but obtained it in 1824. Meanwhile his father's business had declined, and he took pupils. He used to
spend many of his vacations at Cambridge.

A remarkable group of contemporaries here—Tennyson, Fitzgerald
and A. W. Kinglake—were all born in the year 1809, and Thackeray
only two years later.* Tennyson entered in November 1827, but never
lived in college. At Trinity, he first met Arthur Henry Hallam, and in
Hallam's rooms (in New Court, D Staircase, set 3) he spent many
happy hours:

> *Where once we held debate, a band*
> *Of youthful friends, on mind and art,*
> *And labour, and the changing mart,*
> *And all the framework of the land.*

Tennyson worked hard at his poetry, and won the Chancellor's medal
for his poem 'Timbuctoo', and in 1830 published *Poems, Chiefly
Lyrical*. He benefited greatly from his intellectual contacts, but had a
poor opinion of the dons, and in a sonnet written in 1830 said that they
'taught him nothing, feeding not the heart'. He had to leave in 1831
without a degree because of his father's ill-health. Edward Fitzgerald,
whom Tennyson came to know more intimately in later days, had
entered two years earlier, and took his degree in 1830.

Thackeray, who entered in 1829, did not shine as a scholar, his

* It was an astonishing year for the birth of genius. In addition to those
mentioned above, there are Lincoln, Darwin, Gladstone, Mendelssohn, Oliver
Wendell Holmes and Edgar Allan Poe, five out of the nine being writers.

interests being more social and literary. He founded an 'Essay' club, contributed to a paper called *The Snob*, was very fond of literary talk, and developed a passion for the poetry of Shelley. His habits began to get rather expensive, and some of his experiences are distilled in *Pendennis*. After little more than a year he decided to leave because he felt that his studies would be of no use to him in later life. His rooms were on the ground floor on the north side of the Great Gateway. Kinglake, who knew both Thackeray and Tennyson at college, entered in 1828 and graduated in 1832.

G. Lytton Strachey, after two years at Liverpool University, entered in 1899, and had for contemporaries E. M. Forster and Sir Desmond MacCarthy. He gained the Chancellor's English medal, graduated in history in 1903, but failed to secure a fellowship. It was largely through Cambridge contacts that the famous Bloomsbury Group, to which Strachey belonged, was formed. A. E. Housman, on election as Professor of Latin at Cambridge, was elected a fellow of Trinity College, and lived here until his death in a Cambridge nursing home on April 30, 1936. One of the greatest classical scholars that England has produced, he was noted for his caustic comments on other scholars. Of one, fortunately dead long before Housman assailed him, he said that 'Stoeber's mind, though that is no name to call it by, was one which turned as unswervingly to the false, the meaningless, the unmetrical, and the ungrammatical, as the needle to the pole'.

Trinity College has had some very distinguished masters, among them G. M. Trevelyan, himself educated at this college. The College Library* possesses some remarkable treasures, including manuscripts of Milton, Byron, Tennyson, Thackeray (the complete manuscript of *Esmond*) and A. E. Housman.

TRINITY HALL: Raphael Holinshed, whose *Chronicles* are famous chiefly because Shakespeare found them a useful quarry, may have been at this college. Herrick, who came here after an unsatisfactory spell at St John's College, graduated in 1617. Pepys was admitted as a sizar in 1650, but in the following year migrated to Magdalene College. The fourth Earl of Chesterfield, famous for his *Letters* and his con-

* Open weekdays 1 to 4 p.m.

nexion with Dr Johnson, was greatly addicted to classical studies, but left in 1714 after only a year's residence. Bulwer Lytton had entered Trinity College in 1822, but not caring for the lectures, and thinking that a tutor had insulted him, moved in the same year to Trinity Hall. Whilst here he published a volume of poems, and won the Chancellor's medal for a poem entitled 'Sculpture' in 1825, the year in which he graduated.

The Midlands

The Thames Valley
Gloucestershire
Worcestershire
Stratford-on-Avon
Warwick area and Rugby
Coventry and Nuneaton area
Leicestershire
Nottinghamshire
Derbyshire
Staffordshire

THE THAMES VALLEY

At **Shiplake-on-Thames**, four miles south of Henley-on-Thames, Tennyson was married in the parish church in 1850. The choice of place was owing to the fact that he and his bride met here for the first time after ten years' separation. The marriage had been indefinitely postponed because of Tennyson's poverty, but now, with handsome profits from *In Memoriam*, he was able to embark on marriage. At **Henley-on-Thames** (II, C3, on the London-Oxford road) William Shenstone wrote a poem at an inn, and, tradition says, on the window, adding further that it was the old Red Lion inn that is still there. The last verse is famous:

> *Whoe'er has travell'd life's dull round,*
> *Where'er his stages may have been,*
> *May sigh to think he still has found*
> *The warmest welcome at an inn.*

Ipsden House, the manor house at **Ipsden** (II, C2, off the B479, five miles south of Wallingford, is the birthplace of Charles Reade, who was born on June 8, 1814.

A mile or so beyond the point where the B4027 runs off the A40 a few miles east of Oxford, there is **Forest Hill**, where Milton was first married. How he came to know the lady is a matter of guesswork, but he suddenly left London about Whitsuntide in 1642 to come up here, where Mary Powell lived. His father was born at **Stanton St John** just a mile farther up the road, and the families were probably acquainted. Anyhow, Milton returned to London a married man.

Littlemore (II, C2), three miles south-east of Oxford, was part of J. H. Newman's parish when he was vicar of St. Mary's, Oxford, but possessed neither church nor parsonage. He lived in a cottage which is now the George Inn; when the church was being built he lived in the house now called St George's, later moving to the new parsonage. Newman retired from Oxford to Littlemore in 1842, agonized over religious doubts, and three years later, at Littlemore, was received into the Roman Catholic Church.

The Thames has often been sung by the poets, but its course in this part of Oxfordshire and Berkshire is peculiarly the country of Matthew Arnold's 'Scholar Gipsy', who crossed 'the stripling Thames at Bablockhithe', or was to be found 'at some lone alehouse in the Berkshire moors', or on 'the skirts of Bagley wood', or with his 'face towards Hinksey and its wintry ridge'. Arnold himself had often 'moor'd to the cool bank in the summer heats' and watched 'the warm green-muffled Cumnor Hills' amidst which is set the village of **Cumnor** (II, B2) made famous by Scott in *Kenilworth*.

Lying four or five miles west of Oxford, there once existed here Cumnor Place, the home of Robert Dudley, Earl of Leicester, and where occurred the tragedy of his wife Amy Robsart. She was buried in St Mary's Church, Oxford, and there are memorials of her in Cumnor church. Scott originally called his novel *Cumnor Hall*, but changed it at his publisher's request.

At **Stanton Harcourt** (V, H6), six miles west of Oxford, there are three surviving portions of the former manor-house* of the Harcourt family. The first Lord Harcourt was a friend of Alexander Pope, and in one part of the building known as Pope's Tower the fifth volume of the translation of the *Iliad* was completed. The manor-house had

* Open daily.

already been abandoned by the Harcourt family when Pope stayed here in 1717-18. They had moved to **Nuneham Courtnay**, near Oxford, where there used to be a pane of red glass on which Pope recorded the completion of this fifth volume. Pope did not know, or was unaffected by the grisly associations of the tower, which is supposed to be haunted by the ghost of a Lady Alice Harcourt alleged to have been brutally murdered there in the fifteenth century.

Another seat of the Harcourt family used to exist at **Cockthorpe**, where John Gay was a guest of Lord Harcourt, and he used to visit Pope at Stanton Harcourt. On one of his visits two lovers were struck dead by lightning near the manor house. Both Pope and Gay wrote varying accounts of the incident to their friends. Goldsmith was impressed by the story and introduced it into *The Vicar of Wakefield*. Outside the south side of the church is their memorial stone, with an epitaph by Pope.

At **Longworth**, ten miles south-west of Oxford, R. D. Blackmore, author of *Lorna Doone*, was born on June 7, 1825; and at **Uffington**, twenty miles south-west of Oxford and in the Vale of the White Horse, Thomas Hughes was born on October 20, 1822. The Vale is described in the opening chapters of *Tom Brown's Schooldays*.

At **Kelmscott** (V, H6, off the B4449 twenty miles west of Oxford) is the famous manor-house of late Elizabethan or early Jacobean date which was William Morris's country home for the last twenty-five years of his life. He bought it in 1871, and said later that 'it has come to be to me the type of the pleasant places of the earth'. Much of his writing was done here, including parts of his longest poem, the epic of *Sigurd the Volsung*. Here, as elsewhere, Morris practised what he preached, that art should not be divorced from life, and most of the wallpaper, needlework and furniture were designed by him. His *News from Nowhere* contains descriptions of the countryside round the manor. The house contains many relics of Morris and his friend Rossetti, but is not open to the public, and is the property of the University of Oxford. Morris is buried in the churchyard of Kelmscott village.

At **Boar's Hill** (II, C2), four miles south of Oxford, is Chilswell House where Robert Bridges lived from 1907 until his death there on April 21, 1930. Four miles north-east of Oxford there is **Elsfield** manor (II, C2), purchased by John Buchan (Lord Tweedsmuir) in 1919 and it remained his home for the rest of his life, though in his last years he was Governor-General of Canada. He died at Montreal on February 11, 1940, and is buried in Elsfield churchyard.

In the historic town of **Woodstock** (V, H6, seven miles north-west of Oxford on the A34), there is a building called Chaucer's House. It is not, as far as is known, connected with the poet, but was granted to Thomas Chaucer, who was speaker of the House of Commons and probably his son. According to tradition, Chaucer was a visitor to Woodstock. Scott placed the main action of his story of cavalier and puritan, *Woodstock*, in and around the town.

The great Blenheim Palace* at Woodstock, built at the nation's expense for the first Duke of Marlborough, was designed by the dramatist and architect Sir John Vanbrugh. There was a most un-dignified squabble about the building, too long to relate here, but the upshot was that after the duke's death the duchess took the matter into her own hands and directed the completion of the building without Vanbrugh's help, but she kept to his design. When Vanbrugh and his wife called in 1724 to view the building, the duchess gave orders that Lady Vanbrugh was not to be allowed within the park, gardens or buildings. Marlborough's descendant, Sir Winston Churchill, was born at Blenheim Palace on November 30, 1874. Sir Winston's biography of his ancestor is considered by some to be his finest work.

At **Ditchley** (V, H6, a few miles north-west of Woodstock, and off the A34) John Wilmot, second Earl of Rochester, was born on April 10, 1647. The house in which he was born, described by John Evelyn as 'a low ancient timber house with a pretty bowling green', was pulled down in 1722, and the present mansion designed by James Gibb built on the site. Wilmot, who succeeded to his father's title at the age of ten, was educated at the old Grammar School at **Burford** (it is still there), one of the most beautiful of the Cotswold towns. After Oxford

* Open March 24 to July 31 Monday to Thursday, and on Easter Saturday, Sunday and Monday, but closed at Whitsun week-end; from August 2 to September 18 daily except Friday, but including August Bank Holiday week-end; from September 22 to October 30 Monday to Thursday. Hours of opening 1 to 6 p.m. November 7 to March 20 Thursday only, 1.30 to 4.30 p.m.

and a period of foreign travel he spent most of his time at the court of Charles II. His licentious life undermined his health; conscience began to prick him and he asked to see Gilbert Burnet, Bishop of Salisbury. Getting weaker, he journeyed up to High Lodge, Woodstock Park (as it was then), and from there wrote to Burnet asking him to be present to hear his dying repentance. Two days after Burnet left he died, on July 26, 1680. High Lodge, where his bed is preserved, is on the far side of the lake in Blenheim Park. He was buried in the north aisle of Spelsbury church (five miles south-east of Chipping Norton) without monument or inscription.

GLOUCESTERSHIRE

William Tyndale's connexion with the county we have noted in an earlier section of this book. At **Cirencester** (V, G6) there is the fine early eighteenth-century mansion, Cirencester House,* where Pope and Swift visited their patron Lord Bathurst, a man who enjoyed the society of wits and poets, and Sterne has given a sketch of him in his *Letters to Eliza*. At **Nailsworth**, (V, G6) three miles south of Stroud, W. H. Davies the 'super-tramp' and poet lived in his later years, and died there on September 26, 1940.

At **Gloucester** (V, G6) John Taylor the 'Water Poet' was born on August 24, 1580. He was educated at the grammar school, but says that he was 'mired' in his Latin accidence, and instead of completing schooling became apprenticed to a London waterman. W. E. Henley was born at No. 2 Eastgate Street, Gloucester, the son of a bookseller. He was educated at the Crypt Grammar School under T. E. Brown the poet, who was headmaster.

Cheltenham (V, G6) became popular as a spa when visited in 1788 by George III, and in his entourage was Fanny Burney. The royal party stayed at Fauconberg House, predecessor of the present house of the same name. Fanny Burney's *Diary* has vivid descriptions of what went on during their five-week stay. Tennyson, during a phase of illness, came in 1843 to live at 6 Belle Vue Place, and then went for treatment to a hydropathic hospital near by. Later he moved to 10 St James's

* Not open to the public, but the park and woods of the estate are open daily, 10 a.m. to 6.30 p.m. (Sunday 2 to 6.30 p.m.)

Square. Probably part of *In Memoriam* was written during his Cheltenham stay.

WORCESTERSHIRE

Samuel Butler, author of *Hudibras*, was born in 1612 at **Strensham**, (V, G5) just over four miles south-west of Pershore. His father was a farmer. He was educated at the King's School, Worcester, and spent some years of his early manhood at **Earl's Croome** near by as secretary to Thomas Jeffery, a justice in these parts. Jeffery's house, a sixteenth-century half-timbered building near the church, has survived though considerably altered.

The Malvern Hills were familiar to William Langland, author of *Piers Plowman*, and so was the great priory church (at any rate the interior, for the exterior was remodelled after his time) at **Great Malvern** (V, G5). He was educated at the Benedictine monastery there, of which the only relic is the church, and on the Malvern Hills saw the vision of Truth and Wrong and the 'fair field full of folk' which inspired the poem of *Piers Plowman*—if we accept this somewhat shadowy William Langland as the author of that poem, which is by no means a certainty.

Martley, (V, F4) six miles north-west of Worcester, was where C. S. Calverley, son of the rector, was born on December 22, 1831. A. E. Housman, the son of a solicitor, was born on March 26, 1859, at Valley House (now called Housmans) in **Fockbury**, about two miles north of **Bromsgrove** (V, G4). Later his family moved to the neighbouring Clock House. He was educated at Bromsgrove School and after taking his degree at Oxford taught for a short time at his old school and studied at home for the civil service examination.

Richard Baxter, author of *The Saint's Everlasting Rest* and of one of the more remarkable autobiographies in the English language, was assistant preacher at **Kidderminster** (V, G4) during 1641-2. He returned about 1647 and remained until 1660, during which time he was a great spiritual and moral influence. He is commemorated with a statue in the Bull Ring, and his pulpit is preserved in the Unitarian Chapel.

Halesowen (V, G4), ten miles south-west of Birmingham, is the birthplace of William Shenstone, a minor poet of whom Horace

Walpole said that he laboured all his life to write a perfect song, and never once succeeded. He was born on November 13, 1714, in Halesowen, and spent most of his life in or near the town. In 1745 he came to possess Leasowes, a house that stands just over a mile east of the town. He sedulously cultivated the property, and is more remarkable as a landscape gardener than a poet. 'In time,' says Dr Johnson, 'his expenses brought clamours about him, that overpowered the lamb's bleat and the linnet's song; and his groves were haunted by beings very different from fauns and fairies.' He died on February 11, 1763, and is buried in Halesowen churchyard. In the church there is a monument in the form of an urn.

At **Stourbridge** (V, G4), ten miles north-west of Kidderminster (at the end of the A451), Dr Johnson completed his schooling. He was sent here from Lichfield Grammar School, and acted as assistant to the master who taught the younger boys. He found the master able, but idle, and severe towards himself. Many years later he said of his schooling in two grammar schools: 'At one [Lichfield], I learnt much in the school, but little from the master; in the other, I learnt much from the master, but little in the school.' He returned to Lichfield after a year. Stourbridge Grammar School, in the High Street, has been rebuilt on the same site since Johnson's time.

STRATFORD-ON-AVON

An so to bardolatry at **Stratford-on-Avon** (IV, A5). William Shakespeare, the son of a prosperous glover (who later became bailiff, or in modern terms, the mayor of Stratford), was born in Henley Street in April 1564. The exact date of birth is unknown, but he was baptized on April 26 in Holy Trinity Church by the river, where the register is always open at the appropriate entry. The celebration of his birth is always held on April 23, which is St George's Day. Shakespeare's mother was Mary Arden, who came from **Wilmcote*** (IV, A5, on the A34, the Birmingham road, three miles north-west of Stratford).

* Mary Arden's Cottage at Wilmcote is open April to October on Monday, Tuesday, Thursday, Friday 9 a.m. to 12.45 p.m., 2 to 6 p.m., Wednesday and Saturday 9 a.m. to 6 p.m. (9 a.m. to 7 p.m. in August), Sunday 2 to 6 p.m.; November to March, weekdays only, 9 a.m. to 12.45 p.m., 2 to 4 p.m.

His Birthplace* in Henley Street was originally two separate but related buildings, one being the home and the other his father's shop. An upper room of the dwelling has been assigned by a very old tradition as the actual room in which Shakespeare was born. Until the visitors' book was instituted visitors were allowed to scratch their names on the window panes in this room, and the names of Isaac Watts, Sir Walter Scott, Thomas Carlyle, Henry Irving and Ellen Terry can be seen. Although there is no documentary evidence, it is virtually certain that Shakespeare was educated at the Grammar School† in Church Street.

There is no knowledge of Shakespeare's life thereafter until his marriage at the age of eighteen to Anne Hathaway, daughter of Richard Hathaway, a yeoman farmer of **Shottery**.‡ There is a mystery about Shakespeare's marriage that has given scholars plenty of scope for disagreement and conjecture. In the bishop's register at Worcester there is an entry dated November 27, 1582, stating that a marriage licence was issued to William Shaxpere [sic] and Anne Whateley of Temple Grafton. On the following day two sureties (as Shakespeare was a minor he had to provide these) agreed to pay forty pounds should anything arise to prevent the marriage of William Shaxpere and *Anne Hathaway*. What happened? Was young Shakespeare playing fast and loose? Anyhow, the little village of **Temple Grafton**, about four miles west of Stratford, is now among the localities associated with Shakespeare.

A story that began circulation nearly a hundred years after Shakespeare's death says that soon after marriage he left Stratford to avoid prosecution for deer-stealing at Sir Thomas Lucy's estate of

* Same times as previous note except that the extension to 7 p.m. applies during the whole summer. The Birthplace has a Museum devoted to early editions, records of the house, etc.

† Open weekdays 10 a.m. to 12 noon and 2 to 4 p.m. during the Easter and summer holidays only, but closed during special summer courses.

‡ Anne Hathaway's Cottage is open from April to October on Monday, Tuesday, Thursday, Friday 9 a.m. to 12.45 p.m., 2 to 6 p.m., Wednesday and Saturday 9 a.m. to 6 p.m. (9 a.m. to 7 p.m. in summer), Sunday 2 to 6 p.m.; from November to March the hours are 9 a.m. to 12 noon, 2 to 4 p.m., weekdays only.

Charlecote Park near Stratford. The story has been effectually disposed of by the fact that there was no deer-park at Charlecote at that time.

The next phase of Shakespeare's life is dealt with under our London section. He was prosperous enough by 1597 to purchase New Place,* the second largest house in Stratford. The date of his final retirement to Stratford has not so far been ascertained: he was certainly writing plays up to 1610 or 1611, and probably divided his time between London and Stratford before finally settling in Stratford about 1610. He died on St George's Day, April 23, 1616, aged fifty-two, and was buried in the chancel of Holy Trinity Church. According to a local tradition, he died as the result of a fever contracted by hard drinking at a 'merry meeting' with Michael Drayton and Ben Jonson. Above his grave is the bust, executed possibly from a life- or death-mask by Gerrard Janssen or Johnson, and erected not later than 1623. Some scholars consider that the engraved portrait in the First Folio was copied from the bust.

In spite of reminders of Shakespeare in every street and corner, there are other literary associations in Stratford. The Red Horse in Bridge Street, 'Washington Irving's Hotel', was where he stayed on his visit to Stratford. The room in which he wrote his account of Stratford (included in the delightful *Sketch-Book of Geoffrey Crayon, Gent.*) preserves his chair and poker, 'Geoffrey Crayon's Throne and Sceptre', in a cupboard by the fireplace. Dickens stayed at the same hotel in 1848, the year he joined the committee formed to purchase Shakespeare's Birthplace.

Mrs Gaskell was educated at the Avonbank School (long demolished) during the years 1824-7. Her first published work was a contribution to Howitt's *Visits to Remarkable Places* in which she described a visit to

---

* Destroyed in 1759 by the owner, Rev. Francis Gastrell, who had previously destroyed the mulberry tree, said to be planted by Shakespeare, because so many people wanted to see it. The gardens of New Place are open on summer weekdays 9 a.m. to 9 p.m., Sunday 12 noon to 9 p.m.; in winter closing time is at 4 p.m. New Place Museum contains portraits of Shakespeare's contemporaries, Shakespearian curios, etc. It is open April to October, Monday, Tuesday, Thursday, Friday 9 a.m. to 12.45 p.m., 2 to 6 p.m. (2 to 7 p.m. during August), Wednesday and Saturday 9 a.m. to 6 p.m., Sunday 2 to 6 p.m.; November to March 9 a.m. to 12.45 p.m., 2 to 4 p.m.

Clopton House. Marie Corelli, the most popular writer of her time, lived for many years at Mason Croft in Church Street. She was a benefactor to Stratford, helping to save among other buildings the home of the mother of John Harvard, but her meddlesome and tactless ways antagonized many people. Finally, we must mention that Dr G. M. Trevelyan was a native of Stratford. The son of Sir George Otto Trevelyan and a grand-nephew of Macaulay, he was born on February 16, 1876, and spent his early years at Welcombe House (now an hotel) on the Warwick Road.

WARWICK AREA AND RUGBY

The great castle at **Warwick** (IV, A5) was granted in 1605 to Fulke Greville, Lord Brooke, poet, courtier and friend of Sir Philip Sidney. It was in a ruinous state, and Brooke spent a huge sum in restoration. Brooke was stabbed to death in London by a servant, and was buried in the church of St Mary at Warwick. The church contains a bust of Walter Savage Landor, who was born in Warwick on January 30, 1775, in a house near the East Gate which is now the High School for Girls. After education at **Knowle**, about ten miles north-west of Warwick, and Rugby, he was sent to Oxford, but a quarrel with his father terminated his university career. He disliked the idea of taking up any profession and left for London.

Dickens, Landor's friend of later days, stayed at Copp's Royal Hotel (long since demolished) in **Leamington Spa** (IV, A5) in 1838 on his way up to Yorkshire, and gave readings here in 1858 and 1862. He places a scene or two of *Dombey and Son* at Leamington and Warwick. No. 10 Lansdown Crescent, near the Town Hall, was where Nathaniel Hawthorne stayed frequently during the years 1853-7, when he was American consul at Liverpool. It was to him 'a small nest of a place ... one of the coziest nooks in England or in the world' and there he wrote some of his *English Notebooks*. There are descriptions of Warwick, Leamington and Stratford in his *Our Old Home*.

Kenilworth Castle* at **Kenilworth** (IV, A4), now a splendid ruin, is more notable in military and political history, but it has connexions

* Open weekdays 9 a.m. to 6 or 8 p.m. (4 p.m. in winter); Sunday 2 to 6 or 8 p.m. (2 to 4 p.m. in winter).

with Sir Philip Sidney and Scott. Connected with the great names of Simon de Mont-fort and John of Gaunt, the castle was conferred by Elizabeth I on her favourite the Earl of Leicester. During the queen's famous visit of 1575 there was splendid and sumptuous entertainment. Sidney, Leicester's nephew, was present at the revels depicted with gusto in Scott's *Kenilworth* which, as already mentioned, is more closely connected with Cumnor in Berkshire. Scott's chronology is somewhat reckless: Amy Robsart did not meet Queen Elizabeth here, and in fact had been dead some six years.

Two miles east of Kenilworth is **Stoneleigh Abbey★** (IV, A4), one of the great mansions of England, and once visited by Jane Austen. Soon after her father's death Miss Austen and her mother, before settling at Southampton, visited their relatives the Leighs at Adlestrop in Gloucestershire. Thomas Leigh had just inherited Stoneleigh Abbey, and the party arrived there in August 1806. Mrs Austen was impressed, charmed and puzzled by the great eighteenth-century mansion built amidst surviving portions of a great Cistercian monastery. She is very amusing about it all: 'We cannot find our way about it,' she writes, 'I mean the best part; as to the offices, which were the Abbey, Mr Leigh almost despairs of ever finding his way about them. I have proposed setting up direction posts at the angles.'

At the famous school at **Rugby** (IV, B4), housed in modern buildings, we find some famous names. Landor was sent here at the age of ten, and his irascibility, which grew worse with the years, began to show itself. After five or six years he was removed, at the headmaster's request, and sent to a private tutor at Ashbourne in Derbyshire. Arthur Hugh Clough entered the school in 1829, the year after the famous Thomas Arnold became headmaster, and gained the Balliol scholarship in 1837, just before Matthew Arnold was transferred from Winchester College. Arnold won a prize for his poem 'Alaric at Rome' and secured a classical scholarship for Balliol. The year after he left his father died, and is commemorated in the poem 'Rugby Chapel'. Arnold returned to the school for a short time as a master in 1847.

His contemporary, Thomas Hughes, became the author of *Tom*

★ Open daily from Good Friday to mid-October, including Sunday and Bank Holidays 2.30 to 5.30 p.m.

Brown's Schooldays, the most famous of all school stories. He declared that Tom Brown was not a portrait of himself. Lewis Carroll, who entered in 1846, may have been taught by Matthew Arnold; he distinguished himself in mathematics and divinity, and cared little for games. Finally we come to Rupert Brooke, who was born in Hillmorton Road on August 3, 1887, and educated at the school where his father was a master. He began writing verse at school, though as yet showing no marked poetic gift.

Just two miles south-west of Rugby (on the A427) is Bilton Hall (IV, B4), purchased by Joseph Addison in 1711 and in which he resided at various times until his death. The author of *Morte d'Arthur*, Sir Thomas Malory, has always been a somewhat shadowy figure, but the discovery of a manuscript of his work in Winchester Cathedral library has rendered him a little less obscure. He was almost certainly the lord of **Newbold Revel**, five miles north-west of Rugby, sat in Parliament for Warwickshire, and for various offences spent about twenty years in prison. Whilst in captivity he wrote *Morte d'Arthur*, which now joins that select group of great books—*Don Quixote, Pilgrim's Progress*, Marco Polo's *Travels*—composed in prison.

COVENTRY AND NUNEATON AREA

The road (A444) between **Coventry** (IV, A4) and **Nuneaton** (IV, B4) passes through the heart of the 'George Eliot country', but first a word about Michael Drayton. He was born at **Hartshill**, near Nuneaton, in 1563, and Aubrey says (as he did of Shakespeare) that he was the son of a butcher, but Drayton claims that he was 'nobly bred'. How he spent his early years we do not know; he may have been a page, and then, like Shakespeare, went off to seek his fortune in London. A contemporary of Drayton's, John Marston, is sometimes claimed as a native of Coventry, but he may have been born in **Wardington**.

George Eliot, whose maiden name was Mary Ann (or Marian) Evans, was born on November 22, 1819, at South Farm on the estate of **Arbury Hall**★ (IV, A4), two miles south-west of Nuneaton. Her birthplace has not survived, and the parish church of **Chilvers Coton** in

★ Open from April 5 to October 5 on Thursday, Saturday, Sunday, on Bank Holidays and the Tuesday following 2.30 to 6 p.m.

which she was baptized was destroyed in an air raid in 1941, but has since been rebuilt. In 1820 her family moved to Griff House, which has survived and is about a mile north of her birthplace. Both South Farm and Griff House were part of the Newdigate family estate of Arbury Hall, of which her father was agent. She drew some of his characteristics as Adam Bede and as Caleb Garth in *Middlemarch*. She said that 'there is not a single portrait in the book' (*Adam Bede*), nor would there be in any future book of hers, but the disclaimer has not convinced posterity.

She was educated at schools at Attleborough, Nuneaton and Coventry. The Coventry school has survived and is now a residence called Nantglyn, 29 Warwick Row, on the west side of Greyfriars Green. In 1841, some years after her mother's death, she moved with her father to Bird Grove in Foleshill Road, Coventry, and the house is still there. She began to write, her first considerable literary effort being the completion of a friend's translation of Strauss's *Life of Jesus*. Latterly she resided with friends at Rosehill in Coventry, and left for London in 1851. In *Scenes of Clerical Life* her native county is depicted as 'Loamshire', her native parish of Chilvers Coton as 'Shepperton', Nuneaton as 'Milby', and Arbury Hall as 'Cheverel Manor'. The 'Treby Magna' of *Felix Holt* and *Middlemarch* is probably Coventry. However, she used three other counties for her backgrounds, as is recorded in other parts of our survey. There is a memorial garden to George Eliot in Nuneaton.

It was through his residence in **Birmingham** (V, G4) that Dr Johnson first achieved publication. He came from a first miserable experience as an usher in a school to see his former Lichfield schoolfellow Edmund Hector, who lived in Old Square. The house has long disappeared, but the original panelling of the house is preserved at Aston Hall,★ the magnificent Jacobean mansion just beyond the north-east side of Birmingham. He stayed for six months with Hector, and then moved to lodgings in another part of the city. He must have had a difficult time subsisting. He had happened to mention to Hector that he had read the Jesuit Lobo's *Voyage to Abyssinia*. Hector suggested that Johnson should translate it, and aided and abetted by the bookseller over whose shop

★ Open in summer on weekdays 10 a.m. to 5 p.m., Sunday 2 to 5 p.m.; in winter on weekdays only, 10 a.m. to dusk.

Hector lodged, Johnson agreed. It was published in 1735, and he was paid a mere five guineas. It was at Birmingham that he was introduced by Hector to a mercer called Porter, who died soon afterwards, and his widow in the following year became Johnson's wife.

Dickens was frequently in Birmingham, on one occasion with his company of players raising money for the endowment of Shakespeare's birthplace, and gave several readings in later years. Mr Pickwick and his friends journeyed to Birmingham to see Mr Winkle senior to mollify him regarding his son's amorous adventure. There is 'an old red-brick house with three steps before the door' in Easy Row that is supposed to be the original of Mr Winkle's house, but there was another house with the same claims that was pulled down many years ago. Also demolished is the house in Easy Row where Washington Irving stayed in 1818, and where he wrote 'Rip Van Winkle'. Alston Hall, mentioned above, is probably the original of his *Bracebridge Hall*.

In Hagley Road, Edgbaston, is the Oratory of St Philip Neri established by Cardinal Newman in 1847, at first in Alcester Road and later moved here. This was where Newman spent most of the rest of his life, and there he died on August 11, 1890. He was buried in the graveyard beside the country-house of the Oratory Fathers on **Rednal Hill** (on the A38 and about eight miles south-west of Birmingham).

LEICESTERSHIRE

Tennyson was a visitor on several occasions in the 1840's at the old rectory at **Shawell** (off the A5 and five miles north-east of Rugby). The wife of the rector had been a ward of Tennyson's father. It is probable that some of *In Memoriam* was composed here, for Tennyson worked on the poem for seventeen years, and he said that parts of it were composed wherever he happened to be. About two miles further north (on the A426) there is **Lutterworth** (IV, B4) with the famous little church where John Wyclif was rector from 1374 until his death in 1384. Here he inspired and possibly took a part in the first English translation of the Bible. He died and was buried in Lutterworth, but by order of the Council of Constance his body was disinterred, burned and thrown into the River Swift.

Two miles beyond Nuneaton (just east of the intersection of the A444 and A5) is the site of Lindley Hall, where Robert Burton was born on February 8, 1577. He was educated at the Free School at Sutton Coldfield and the Grammar School at Nuneaton before proceeding to Oxford. He became rector of **Seagrave** (off the Fosse Way, now traversed by the A46) from 1630 until his death, but since he spent most of his life as a recluse at Oxford he cannot have given much, if any, personal attention to his duties, which no doubt were performed by a curate.

In the small quiet old-world town of **Market Bosworth** (IV, B3), within two miles of which Richard III staked all and perished, Dr Johnson spent an unhappy few months as an usher. It was at the old Grammar School, still there, in the market-place. The patron of the school was Sir Wolstan Dixey, in whose house (which has survived) Johnson acted as a kind of domestic chaplain, in addition to his school duties. His life here he described as being 'unvaried as the note of the cuckoo'; he was treated with harshness, and dislike of the drudgery and a disagreement with his employer drove him to give up the post after a few months. It was his first employment, and now, without money or prospects, he decided to go to Birmingham to see a former school-fellow.

At **Leicester** (IV, B3) it is perhaps surprising to find a connexion with Swift, whose mother was a native of the city. He joined her here in 1688 or 1689 after he left Trinity College, Dublin, and continued to visit her until her death in 1710. She is buried in St Martin's Church. Six miles north of Leicester (off the A6) is the Elizabethan mansion of **Rothley Temple** (IV, B3), where Macaulay was born on October 25, 1800. His father, Zachary Macaulay, was a West Indies merchant and philanthropist who later devoted himself to the abolition of the slave-trade. He was on a visit to his sister, who had married into the ancient family of the Babingtons, the owners of Rothley Temple.

Loughborough was the birthplace of John Cleveland (1613-58) a cavalier poet who led a chequered career, falling into the hands of the Parliamentarians at one time and at another reduced to beggary. He was popular in his day. Five miles north-west of Loughborough (on the A6) is **Kegworth** (IV, B3) where Thomas Moore lived for some months in

1811 just after his marriage. His house, The Cedars, on the Lough-borough Road, is still there.

Off the A50 between Leicester and Burton-upon-Trent, some six miles north of Coalville, are the ruins of the Augustinian priory of Grace Dieu in the village of **Belton** (IV, B3). Amidst these ruins there once stood the manor-house in which Francis Beaumont the dramatist was born in 1584. He was the third son of a judge, and his elder brother Sir John Beaumont was a well-known poet of the period.

Only a short distance away to the west, at **Coleorton** (IV, B3, on the A512, four miles east of Ashby de la Zouch) is Coleorton Hall. Now in the hands of the National Coal Board, it was once the home of Sir George Beaumont, a patron of art and amateur painter who had known Dr Johnson, and became the friend and patron of Coleridge and Wordsworth. Wordsworth's cottage at Grasmere was proving too small for his family, and whilst he was looking for a larger house Sir George Beaumont in 1806 offered him the use of the Hall Farm (no longer there) in the grounds of Coleorton Hall. Coleridge and his son Hartley joined them for a time.

The estate was undergoing considerable alterations when Words-worth was there; the garden was laid out according to his ideas, and the layout is as he planned it, but the inscriptions he wrote for the trees and seats have disappeared. Wordsworth left in 1807, but revisited Coleorton several times. Beaumont died in 1827, and left Wordsworth an annuity of £100 for an annual holiday.

NOTTINGHAMSHIRE

At **Nottingham** (IV, B2) and the district lying to its north we are in the midst of Byron associations. Byron succeeded to the title and estates of his great-uncle, the 'wicked Lord', at the age of ten. The financial position was far too precarious to allow of Byron and his mother living at Newstead Abbey, the ancestral home, and lodgings were taken in 1798 in Nottingham, first in Pelham Street and later in St James Street. The Unitarian Chapel in High Pavement (in which Coleridge had preached two years earlier) was attended by Byron. (When the Luddite riots broke out in this area, they were most violent at Nottingham, and Byron's first speech in the House of Lords was on behalf of the rioters.)

He was sent to school in Dulwich in 1799, and spent school holidays at various places with his mother until they returned to this area in 1804, when they settled until 1807 in **Southwell** (IV, C2) at Burgate Manor, now a youth hostel. Meanwhile Newstead had been let to Lord Grey de Ruthyn, who kept a room free for Byron's use. He used often to visit his cousin Mary Chaworth at **Annesley Hall** (IV, B2), three miles south-west of Newstead, and fell violently in love with her. Two years older than Byron, she did not take him seriously, but her marriage to a local squire greatly agitated Byron for several years.

When he left Cambridge in 1808 he settled at **Newstead Abbey**★ (IV, B2, off the A60 nine miles north of Nottingham). He invited his Cambridge friends to a house-warming and later visits. The famous skull-goblet (still there) was passed round. Soon after, he was absent for two years on a tour in the Near East, and on his way home his mother became ill, but he arrived too late to see her alive. He lived on and off at Newstead until he left England, and sold it in 1818. His bedroom is preserved as it was when he used it. The drawing-room contains manuscripts and other relics of Byron. Near the north-east corner of the house is buried his favourite retriever, 'Boatswain', with a typically misanthropic inscription by Byron. Byron's body was brought from Greece and buried in the church at **Hucknall Torkard** (IV, B2, on the A611 about eight miles north of Nottingham). His mother and daughter are also buried there.

In 'English Bards and Scotch Reviewers' Byron bewailed the fate of Henry Kirke White, a minor poet born in Exchange Alley, Nottingham, on March 21, 1785. He was the son of a butcher, and after elementary education worked at a stocking loom. Then he was employed by lawyers who advised him to study languages. He was determined to go to Cambridge and take holy orders, and tried to raise money by a volume of verse which failed, but an introduction to a don at Cambridge fulfilled his wish. At the corner of Parliament

★ Open from April 4 to September 30 daily at 2 to 5 p.m., and there are conducted tours at each hour. If admission is desired between October 1 and Easter, apply to the Corporation of Nottingham. The gardens are open throughout the year: in summer, weekdays 10 a.m. to 8 p.m. (or dusk if earlier); in winter 10.30 a.m. to dusk, on Sunday 2 to 8 p.m. or dusk.

Street and Newcastle Street in Nottingham there used to be a chemist's shop kept by William Howitt, an author in his spare time, and his books (in which his wife Mary sometimes collaborated) were popular in the nineteenth century. His best known work was *Visits to Remarkable Places*.

Going outside Nottingham again, there is at **Eastwood** (IV, B2, on the A610 eight miles north-west of Nottingham), the birthplace of D. H. Lawrence. The son of a coal-miner, he was born on September 11, 1885, at 8A Victoria Street (which is extant). When he was ten the family moved to The Breach, a house in the same street, described as 'The Bottoms' in Lawrence's greatest book, *Sons and Lovers*. Because he was liable to consumption from childhood he could not follow his father's calling. He won a scholarship to Nottingham High School, and obtained a teacher's certificate at Nottingham University. The education he received was due to the devotion and self-sacrifice of his mother.

Another iconoclast, Samuel Butler, who like Lawrence believed that machines were degrading to the soul of man, was born in the same county. The son of the rector of **Langar** (IV, C2, on an unclassified road ten miles south-east of Nottingham and nearly four miles south of Bingham), he was born at the rectory there on December 4, 1835. He was destined for the ministry, but after leaving Cambridge began to doubt his faith, quarrelled bitterly with his father, who also opposed his wish to become a painter, and emigrated to New Zealand in 1859. Butler's bitter views on family relationships found its expression in the posthumously published novel *The Way of All Flesh*. At the parish church at **Shelford** (IV, B2), six miles east of Nottingham, the fourth Earl of Chesterfield is buried.

DERBYSHIRE

Dr Johnson was married at **Derby** (IV, A2) in St Werburgh's Church (at the beginning of Friar Gate) to Mrs Elizabeth Porter, on July 9, 1735. He had first met his lady in Birmingham, and 'I know not for what reason the marriage ceremony was not performed at Birmingham', says Boswell. Over forty years later, Johnson and Boswell twice visited Derby, and it is strange that the latter did not inquire about the church where the former was married. Derby is the 'Stoniton' of George Eliot's *Adam Bede*. Apart from Warwickshire, Derbyshire and the north-eastern part of Staffordshire and Lincolnshire form the background of her novels. *Adam Bede* was founded on a story told to George Eliot by her aunt Elizabeth Evans (the Dinah Morris of the book), whose husband is probably the original of Seth Bede. The aunt is commemorated by a tablet in the Ebenezer Methodist Church at **Wirksworth**, the 'Snowfield' of the novel, about seven miles north-east of Ashbourne, depicted as 'Oakbourne'. **Norbury**, as 'Norbourne', also figures in the novel, but its main setting is at **Ellastone** ('Hayslope'), just over the Staffordshire border and about fifteen miles north-west of Derby.

At **Mayfield** (IV, A2), on the Staffordshire bank of the River Dove (on the A52 just two miles west of Ashbourne) there is Mayfield Cottage, in which Thomas Moore lived from 1811 to 1817. When his family began to increase, Moore was anxious for more income, and asked Longman the publisher for the highest price (£3,000) ever paid for a poem. Not a line had been written, nor had he chosen a subject, eventually choosing an eastern tale, and *Lalla Rookh* was the result. It was mostly written here, proved immensely popular, but is now unread—and unreadable. A little farther off, at **Ashbourne** (IV, A2), there is a house opposite the old Grammar School where Dr Johnson used to stay with his friend Dr John Taylor, and on two occasions Boswell came with him.

The beautiful **Dovedale** (IV, A2), which is in both Derbyshire and Staffordshire, becomes, by a very strange transformation, the 'Eagledale' of *Adam Bede*. After where Dovedale proper ends there are some very beautiful glens, the first being Milldale, in which is Viator's Bridge, on which Izaak Walton and his friend Charles Cotton used to stroll on their angling expeditions. The last is Beresford Dale, at the end of which is the fishing lodge built by Cotton in 1675 and used by him and Walton.

Thomas Hobbes the philosopher has connexions with the great ducal houses of Chatsworth* and Hardwick.† He was tutor and secretary to

* Open March 30 to October 12: Wednesday and Thursday 11.30 a.m. to 4 p.m., Saturday and Sunday 2 to 5.30 p.m., Bank Holidays and Good Friday 11.30 a.m. to 5.30 p.m.

† Open April 2 to October 5: Wednesday, Thursday, Saturday, Sunday and Bank Holidays 2 to 5 p.m.

the second and third Earls of Devonshire from about 1610, and was often at these two houses. The present Chatsworth House, however, is a residence built after his time. He finally settled at these two houses in 1675, and died at Hardwick Hall on December 4, 1679, aged ninety-one. **Chatsworth** (IV, A1), near Bakewell, is approached by the A623 which runs off the A6 between Matlock and Bakewell. **Hardwick Hall** (IV, B2), near Chesterfield, is two miles south of the A617 between Mansfield and Chesterfield. About a mile north of Hardwick (off the A617), there is **Ault Hucknall**, where Hobbes is buried. The Latin inscription on the marble monument records his great erudition and his faithfulness to the two Earls of Devonshire he served.

About a mile south of **Eckington** (IV, B1) there is the fine sixteenth-century Renishaw Hall, the residence of Sir Osbert Sitwell and Dame Edith Sitwell. Sir Osbert's autobiography, *Left Hand Right Hand*, gives a brilliant account of his early life here.

STAFFORDSHIRE

Walsall(V, G3), ten miles north-west of Birmingham, was the birth-place of Jerome K. Jerome. The house in which he was born on May 2, 1859, in Bradford Street has been swept away in recent redevelopment schemes.

Lichfield (IV, A3), ten miles north-east of Walsall, is pre-eminently associated with Dr Johnson. The son of a bookseller, he was born on September 18, 1709, above his father's shop at the corner of Market Street, and the house has been preserved as Dr Johnson's Birthplace.* The site of the dame school where he was first educated is marked in Dam Street. Later he went to the Grammar School in St John Street, and the old building is still there, but the school itself is now at Borrow-cop Hill, just outside Lichfield. Joseph Addison, whose father was Dean of Lichfield, had been educated at the same school. After further education at Stourbridge Johnson 'loitered, for two years, in a state very unworthy his uncommon abilities', but read a great deal and helped to lay the foundations of his massive knowledge of literature. When he

* Open daily April to September 10 a.m. to 6 p.m. (Monday 10 a.m. to 1 p.m.); October to March 10 a.m. to 4 p.m. (Monday 10 a.m. to 1 p.m.). Contains personal relics, portraits, etc.

married he went to live in **Edial**, three miles south-west of Lichfield, and took pupils. He had very few, one of them being David Garrick, who had been to Lichfield Grammar School. The Edial venture failed, and Johnson resolved to try his luck in London. Armed with a letter from Gilbert Walmsley, an influential friend who was impressed by the three acts of the tragedy of *Irene* which had been written at Edial, he set out in 1737, taking Garrick with him. He said jokingly later that he had twopence-halfpenny in his pocket and Garrick three halfpence, and in fact they could not have had much more.

Johnson frequently revisited Lichfield. He was there with Boswell in 1776, and they stayed at the Three Crowns Inn, which has survived and is next door to the Birthplace. 'I went through the house where my illustrious friend was born,' says Boswell, 'with a reverence with which it doubtless will long be visited.' Statues of Johnson and Boswell stand in the market-place, and Johnson's bust is in the cathedral. Two inns at Lichfield must be mentioned, both in Bird Street: the Swan, where Johnson stayed with the Thrales in 1774, and the George, in which part of the scene of Farquhar's *Beaux' Stratagem* is laid.

Off the A513 and about four miles north-east of Lichfield, there is **Croxall Hall★** (IV, A3), an Elizabethan building damaged in 1942 and since then partly rebuilt. Dryden used to visit the Hall when it belonged to the Earl of Dorset, one of his patrons.

Stafford (V, G3) is Izaak Walton's native town. He was born on August 9, 1593, in Eastgate Street (the house has disappeared) and baptized in the Norman font of St Mary's Church, where he is commemorated by a bust. Sheridan was Member of Parliament for Stafford from 1780 to 1806, and sometimes stayed at Chetwynd House (now the post office) in Greengate Street. When proposing the toast of Stafford, whose staple industry is bootmaking, the said: 'May the trade of Stafford be trod underfoot by all the world.' Also in Greengate Street is the Swan Hotel, where George Borrow served as an ostler in 1825—at least, that is what is generally believed on the evidence of certain chapters in *Romany Rye*. Dickens may have stayed at the Swan: in *Reprinted Pieces* he describes the 'Dodo Inn', possibly this particular hotel.

★ At reasonable times admission can be gained on application.

At **Shallowford** (V, G2), about five miles north-west of Stafford, we return to Izaak Walton. He had a country cottage here at Half head Farm which he bequeathed for a charitable purpose. The half-timbered cottage has been restored and preserved as the Izaak Walton Cottage and Museum.*

At **Uttoxeter** (V, G2) Dr Johnson underwent his famous penance in the market-place. 'I refused to attend my father to Uttoxeter market,' he said in 1784. 'Pride was the source of that refusal, and the remembrance of it painful. A few years ago, I desired to atone for this fault; I went to Uttoxeter market in very bad weather, and stood for a considerable time bareheaded in the rain, on the spot where my father's stall used to stand. In contrition I stood, and I hope the penance was expiatory.' A bas-relief on the conduit in the market-place commemorates the incident. Nathaniel Hawthorne, after making a pilgrimage to Lichfield, came to the scene of penance, as he describes in *Our Old Home*.

The six towns of the Potteries, which Arnold Bennett for artistic purposes chose to call the Five Towns, have since 1910 been united in the city of **Stoke-on-Trent** (V, G2). The Five Towns are the scene of his most enduring work. Bennett was born on May 27, 1867, at 90 Hope Street, **Hanley**, but the house was demolished in 1961. His father was by turns potter, schoolmaster, pawnbroker (90 Hope Street was used as pawnbroking premises) and solicitor. Bennett was educated at the Wesleyan Infants School on Swan Bank (now a Sunday school), the Burslem Endowed School (in his time in the Wedgwood Institute, Queen Street) and at the Middle School, Newcastle-under-Lyme, which has been transferred and has become the Wolstanton Grammar School. With schooling completed he entered his father's office to prepare for London University, but in 1889 struck out on his own by becoming a clerk in a London firm of solicitors.

His family lived in various houses during Bennett's time in the Potteries: Dain Street (in his time Ward Street), 1875-6, but the house is not identifiable; 175 Newport Lane, 1876-8; 198 Waterloo Road, 1878-80, and 205 Waterloo Road, **Burslem**, from 1880. This last is

* Open daily, except Tuesday, 10 a.m. to 4 p.m. Shallowford is near Norton Bridge Station.

now the Bennett Museum.* Waterloo Road is the 'Trafalgar Road' of his novels; Burslem Town Hall appears in *Clayhanger*, in which his father appears as Darius Clayhanger, and the Hill Pottery ('Sytch Pottery') is still there. The original of John Baines's shop in *The Old Wives' Tale* is the shop at 15 St John's Square, Burslem. The Five Towns appear under the following names: Tunstall, 'Turnhill'; Burslem, 'Bursley'; Hanley, 'Hambridge'; Stoke, 'Knype'; and Longton, 'Longshaw'. Many of the suburbs and near-by towns also appear under disguised names.

Bennett died and was cremated in London, and his ashes were placed in his mother's grave in Burslem cemetery. A plaque of Bennett, presented by Joseph Wedgwood and Sons, was placed in 1962 in the public gardens in Burslem.

Another writer who is a native of Stoke-upon-Trent is Dinah Maria Mulock, author of *John Halifax, Gentleman*, who was born on April 20, 1826, and lived there until she left for London in 1846.

* Open on Monday, Wednesday and Saturday 2 to 5 p.m.; Thursday 2 to 7 p.m. Contains personal relics and some manuscripts, but not of Bennett's principal works.

Oxford

The City
The University

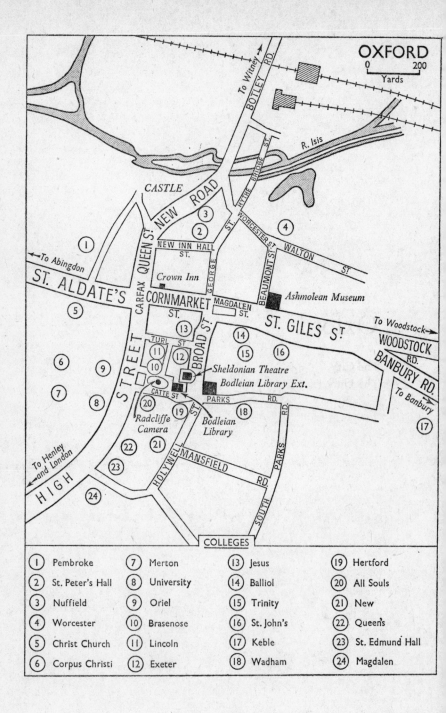

OXFORD

0   200
Yards

To Witney

BOTLEY RD.

R. Isis

CASTLE

NEW ROAD

QUEEN ST.

CARFAX

ST. ALDATE'S

← To Abingdon

③
②
New Inn Hall St.
Crown Inn

GEORGE ST.

HYTHE BRIDGE ST.

WORCESTER ST.

④

BEAUMONT ST.

WALTON ST.

CORNMARKET ST.

MAGDALEN ST.

Ashmolean Museum

ST. GILES ST.

To Woodstock →

WOODSTOCK RD.

BANBURY RD.

To Banbury →

①

⑤

⑬

TURL ST.

⑪
⑫
⑩

BROAD ST.

⑭
⑮
⑯

Sheldonian Theatre
Bodleian Library Ext.

STREET

⑥
⑨
⑦
⑧

CATTE ST.

⑳
⑲
Radcliffe Camera

PARKS RD.

⑱

PARKS RD.

⑰

Bodleian Library

HOLYWELL ST.

㉒
㉑

MANSFIELD RD.

SOUTH PARKS RD.

㉓

HIGH

㉔

COLLEGES

①	Pembroke	⑦	Merton	⑬	Jesus	⑲	Hertford
②	St. Peter's Hall	⑧	University	⑭	Balliol	⑳	All Souls
③	Nuffield	⑨	Oriel	⑮	Trinity	㉑	New
④	Worcester	⑩	Brasenose	⑯	St. John's	㉒	Queen's
⑤	Christ Church	⑪	Lincoln	⑰	Keble	㉓	St. Edmund Hall
⑥	Corpus Christi	⑫	Exeter	⑱	Wadham	㉔	Magdalen

To Henley and London

THE CITY

Owing to one of Aubrey's bits of gossip, Shakespeare cannot be excluded from Oxford. 'Mr William Shakespeare,' says Aubrey, 'was wont to go into Warwickshire once a year, and did commonly in his journey lie at this house [i.e. the Crown Inn] in Oxon, where he was exceedingly respected. . . . Now Sir William [Davenant] would sometimes, when he was pleasant over a glass of wine with his most intimate friends—e.g., Sam. Butler, author of *Hudibras*, etc.—say, that it seemed to him that he writ with the very spirit that did Shakespeare, and seemed contented enough to be thought his son. He would tell the story as above, in which his mother had a very light report.' The Sir William Davenant referred to was the poet and dramatist whose father was proprietor of the Crown Inn* in Cornmarket Street, and he was probably born there in February 1606. A later antiquary added another detail, to the effect that Shakespeare was Davenant's godfather.

Aubrey himself, after his undergraduate days, was a frequent visitor

---

* The guest-chamber of the Crown Inn, known as the Painted Chamber, is open from Monday to Friday, 9.30 a.m. to 12.30 p.m., 2.30 to 4.30 p.m., the times subject to slight variation.

to Oxford, where he says that he 'enjoyed the greatest felicity of his life'. According to tradition, he was on his way to stay with a friend in Wiltshire when he was suddenly taken ill and died here, in June 1697, and was buried in the church of St Mary Magdalen.

Aubrey knew a fellow-antiquarian, Anthony Wood, who was born on December 17, 1632, in a house (no longer there) opposite the gate of Merton College. He was a strange man and refused to take up any profession, preferring to dabble in history and antiquarian studies. He inherited from his father two garrets in the family house, and in one of them built a large chimney to provide a cell in which he could work undisturbed. When he was collecting material for his *Athenae Oxonienses* (from which we derive so much knowledge about Oxford men, and often quoted in this book), Aubrey sent him much information, but found him a difficult man with whom to deal. When the first volume of the *Athenae* was published, a story Aubrey had supplied about the great Earl of Clarendon was considered to be libellous. Wood had to appear before the court of the Vice-Chancellor, was found guilty and expelled from the University. He died at his house on November 29, 1695, and was buried in the outer chapel of Merton College.

Pepys spent a day sight-seeing at Oxford in June 1668. 'A very sweet place,' he says, and saw the Schools, the Library, All Souls, Christ Church and Brasenose. At the last he visited the butteries, curious about the giant called the Child of Hales, whose portrait and the picture of whose hand (seventeen inches long) are preserved there. Lamb has a famous essay on 'Oxford in the Vacation', written during a visit to Cambridge. He visited Oxford in 1800, and again several years later with Hazlitt, who says that Lamb and 'the old colleges were hail-fellow well met, and in the quadrangles he "walked gowned" '.

Like Anthony Wood, John Richard Green was born at Oxford—in 1837—but neither the exact date nor locality are known. From the time he learned to read he was hardly ever without a book, and very early took an interest in the history of the University and city. He was sent to Magdalen College School, where at the age of fourteen he annoyed his masters by writing an essay on Charles I in which he argued that the king was in the wrong. Only a little later he had reached the head of the school, and on the advice of the authorities was removed for further education to private tutors. We shall have something to say of him under Jesus College.

Oxford is the 'Christminster' of Hardy's *Jude the Obscure*, in which Christ Church appears as 'Cardinal College', the name under which it was originally founded by Wolsey. Oxford's High Street, which has called forth praise from many quarters, was to Nathaniel Hawthorne 'the noblest old street in England'.

THE UNIVERSITY

One of the outstanding events in the history of the University was the burning at the stake of the Protestant bishops, Thomas Cranmer, Hugh Latimer and Nicholas Ridley. After Mary Tudor came to the throne they were examined over a considerable period by a commission composed of the learned men of the universities of Oxford and Cambridge. The commission sat either at the Divinity School or in St Mary the Virgin, the University church. Ridley and Latimer stood firm, were condemned for heresy and burned on October 16, 1555, in the City Ditch (now Broad Street) just outside Balliol College. The spot is marked by a metal cross. Cranmer wavered, and recanted, and to complete his humiliation was ordered to recant publicly in the church of St Mary the Virgin, but when the time came with supreme courage repudiated his recantation. He suffered the same fate and in the same spot as the others, on March 21, 1556. The Martyrs' Memorial in St Giles's near by was erected to them in 1841. Cranmer and Latimer have their places in English literature, one as the author of the magnificent prose of the Prayer Book, and the other as author of sermons in a direct, simple yet eloquent style.

The literary associations of the various colleges follow below, but there are two writers educated at Oxford who, for lack of evidence, cannot be assigned to any college. The poet John Skelton appears to have been educated both at Oxford and Cambridge. Caxton says that he was created poet laureate at Oxford sometime before 1490; and he himself claimed that he received the degree from the senate. In 1493 he received the same title at Cambridge. The title was not a degree as then understood, but appears to have been an academical honour bestowed, with a wreath of laurel, on a graduate who had gained particular distinction in rhetoric and poetry. Cambridge repeated the honour some years later. Skelton claimed also that he had been created poet laureate by the king; if this were so, it appears to have been a mere title, and there is little or no foundation for regarding him as the first poet laureate. George Chapman is also supposed to have been at Oxford, but on him there is even less evidence than on Skelton.

Oxford has been unduly disparaged as a nursery of poets when compared with Cambridge, and on a merely quantitative assessment she appears inferior, though appreciably more Oxford than Cambridge men have attained eminence in literature. It is surprising to find a former president of Magdalen College stating that 'Oxford—most poetical of universities and cities—has produced, strangely enough, few poets'. We need not go through the list, for they are mentioned under their respective colleges, but merely point out that Sidney, Ralegh, Donne, Shelley, Matthew Arnold and Swinburne were all Oxford men.

The University figures a great deal in literature, and we cannot do more than indicate some of it under appropriate references, but three books dealing with University life must be mentioned here. A certain Cuthbert Bede's book entitled *The Adventures of Mr Verdant Green*, published in 1853, famous in its time and long forgotten, gives a good picture of life in the mid-nineteenth century. Quiller-Couch said that 'the novel of university life has not been written yet and perhaps never will be', but considered *Verdant Green* the nearest approach to it. Certainly it is a better book than Thomas Hughes's *Tom Brown at Oxford*, which secured the fame it did largely through the great success of *Tom Brown's Schooldays*. Finally Max Beerbohm in *Zuleika Dobson* has described, with the almost indefinable Beerbohm deftness of touch, the effects of a very beautiful young adventuress on the undergraduates of Oxford.

A visit to Oxford is not complete without a visit to the Bodleian Library,* the oldest existing library in the world, and the Bodleian

* The Bodleian Library is open on weekdays 9.30 a.m. to 6.30 p.m., on Saturday 9.30 a.m. to 12.30 p.m. (except holidays and the week beginning the first Monday in August).

Library Extension,* which contain very great treasures in books and manuscripts. In the exhibition rooms of the latter can be seen manuscripts, exceptionally rare first editions (including the Bay Psalm Book, the first English book printed in America), portraits and other exhibits.

BALLIOL COLLEGE:† John Wyclif, who has a place in English literature because he inspired the first translation into English of the entire Bible, became fellow and later Master of Balliol, the exact dates being uncertain, but it was in the period 1356-61.

John Evelyn was admitted as a fellow commoner in May 1637. He says that until his last year at school he was 'extremely remiss' in his studies and 'went to the university rather out of shame of abiding longer at school, than for any fitness'. His tutor was George Bradshaw, probably a relation of the regicide, and neglected Evelyn, who left in 1640 without a degree. Evelyn records that in his time a certain Nathaniel Conopios from Greece came to the college and was the first man he ever saw drinking coffee, 'which custom came not into England till thirty years after'. In later life Evelyn paid several visits to Oxford, which are recorded with particularity in his *Diary*.

Robert Southey, expelled from Westminster School, was refused by Christ Church, but secured entry to Balliol at Michaelmas 1792. His tutor was not impressed with him, and told him: 'Mr Southey, you won't learn anything by my lectures, so if you have any studies of your own, you had better pursue them.' He was undecided about his future, and to make matters worse his father died soon after he came up, leaving him in dire straits for money. His mother and uncle wished him to take holy orders, but being unorthodox in religious opinions it did not

* The Bodleian Library Extension (the exhibits of the Exhibitions Rooms are changed at intervals) is open Monday to Friday 10 a.m. to 12.30 p.m., 2.30 to 5 p.m.; on Saturday 10 a.m. to 12.30 p.m.

† Visitors should remember that the colleges are private foundations, and admission to them is by courtesy of the respective authorities. During vacations the halls, chapels and gardens are open during reasonable hours of the day; during term-time hours are of course more restricted, and inquiries can be made at the porters' lodges at the college gates. There is an Information Office open during summer at Carfax Tower 10 a.m. to 1 p.m., 2 to 5 p.m.; Thursday 10 a.m. to 1 p.m.

appeal to him. Coleridge, on a visit to Oxford in 1794, was introduced to him by a friend, and Coleridge's brilliant talk converted him to Unitarianism and 'Pantisocracy', a scheme they were to pursue later at Bristol. Soon afterwards he left without a degree, and came to much the same conclusions about his university life as did Gibbon about his. 'All I learnt was a little swimming and a little boating,' he says, and 'with respect to its superiors, Oxford only exhibits waste of wigs and want of wisdom; with respect to the undergraduates, every species of abandoned excess.'

Arthur Hugh Clough came with the Balliol scholarship from Rugby in 1837, and was noted for a lovable nature, high principle and a fine intellect. To his friends' surprise he obtained only a second-class degree in 1841. Matthew Arnold, who was also at Rugby, and who was to commemorate Clough in the great elegy 'Thyrsis', came up with a classical scholarship in 1841. Singularly little is known of his time at Balliol. He gained the Newdigate prize for his poem 'Cromwell' in 1843, and graduated in the following year. He returned to Oxford as Professor of Poetry during 1857-67, and some of his lectures have become classics of criticism. One of the most famous passages in Arnold's works is the passage on Oxford in the preface to *Essays in Criticism*, in which the 'beautiful city' is characterized as 'whispering . . . the last enchantments of the middle ages' and as the 'home of lost causes'.

Charles Stuart Calverley, coming up from Harrow in 1850 with a reputation for Latin versification (which secured him the Balliol scholarship) and for high spirits, won also the Chancellor's prize for Latin verse, but the authorities found his recklessness and indiscipline too much for them, and he was removed in 1852. A very different character, Swinburne (who entered in 1856) also troubled the authorities. He wrote poetry, became a republican, and was considered by some as 'dangerous'. Towards the end of his time he lodged in Broad Street, and his landlady complained of his late hours and spirited activities. Benjamin Jowett, his tutor, was interested in Swinburne and did not wish Balliol to make itself as ridiculous 'as University had made itself about Shelley', and apparently advised Swinburne to leave before official action was taken. So he left in 1859 without a degree.

Jowett, who translated Plato into more beautiful English than any one else has ever done, is a legend in Oxford. He had secured the distinction of being elected a fellow whilst still an undergraduate, and became Master of Balliol in 1870. A clergyman of the Church of England, his orthodoxy was suspect. When appointed Professor of Greek he was asked to sign the Thirty Nine Articles, to which he replied that he would sign forty if necessary—and there are many other stories told of him. One of his pupils, J. Addington Symonds, was here 1858-62 and achieved brilliant success as a classical scholar. In 1860 he secured the Newdigate prize with a poem on 'The Escorial'.

Gerard Manley Hopkins, whose poetry has only comparatively recently come to be admired, partly because he was ahead of his time, entered Balliol in 1863, and obtained a first-class degree in 1867. Whilst an undergraduate he was converted to Roman Catholicism. Another Catholic, Hilaire Belloc, who entered Balliol in 1893 shortly before Jowett's death, had a very brilliant academic career and secured a first-class degree in history in 1895. 'Balliol made me, Balliol fed me,' he says in one of his poems. He was one of the most brilliant speakers the Oxford Union has ever known, and became its president.

BRASENOSE COLLEGE: John Foxe the martyrologist entered this college about 1532, and attended Magdalen College School at the same time. He graduated B.A. in 1537, M.A. in 1543, having been elected fellow in 1539. Being inclined towards the stricter form of Protestantism, he was in trouble with the authorities, and resigned his fellowship in company with others of the same persuasion in 1545. John Marston, the dramatist, entered in 1591, and graduated in 1594. Robert Burton of *The Anatomy of Melancholy* entered in 1593, but of his activities here, as with Marston, nothing certain appears to be known. In 1599 he was elected a student (fellow) of Christ Church. R. H. Barham of *Ingoldsby* fame was also of this college, but details of his life here are scanty.

Walter Pater became a fellow in 1864, and except for about five years in London spent the rest of his life in his rooms during term time or at his Oxford residences, the first being 2 Bradmore Road, and the second at 64 St Giles's. As a tutor and writer the apostle of 'art for art's sake' (a term he coined, but of wider application than some of his critics allowed) lived his secluded life, and was a considerable intellectual influence. He died suddenly after apparently recovering from rheumatic fever, on July 30, 1894, at his St Giles's house, and was buried in St Giles's churchyard.

John Buchan gained a scholarship to the college in 1897, won the Stanhope historical prize essay with an effort on Sir Walter Ralegh and the Newdigate prize with a poem on the Pilgrim Fathers. Whilst still an undergraduate he was commissioned by a publisher to write a history of his college. He secured a first-class degree in 1899.

CHRIST CHURCH: Sir Thomas More entered Canterbury Hall (later absorbed in Christ Church) about 1492, aged about fourteen. He learned Greek from Thomas Linacre, one of the great humanists of the time, and another tutor was William Grocyn. He left in 1494, without a degree, to take up the study of law in London. Many years later, when the winds of Reformation were sweeping through England, Oxford was divided into those who called themselves Greek (favourers of the new learning) and Trojans (favourers of the old learning, who were in the majority). More was requested by Henry VIII to write to the governing body of the University to rebuke the fanaticism of the Trojans.

Sir Philip Sidney entered in 1568, and pursued his studies with the same ardour that he had shown since he was a small boy, and impressed all with his unusual charm, proclivity for learning and evident genius. His tutor, Robert Thornton, wished it to be recorded on his tombstone that Sidney had been his pupil. In 1571 plague broke out in Oxford, and Sidney left and did not return to take his degree. One of Sidney's friends at Christ Church was William Camden, who entered about 1566. Little is known of his life here, but Wood says that 'he perfected himself in grammar learning'. He wished to secure a demyship, but failed, and the same Thomas Thornton who was Sidney's tutor secured his entrance to Broadgates Hall (Pembroke College).

Another friend of Sidney's here was Richard Hakluyt, who was elected to a studentship in 1570, graduated B.A. in 1574, and became M.A. in 1577. His taste for geography and discovery had already been formed at school, and at Oxford he pursued his studies with great enthusiasm, reading in seven languages everything that he could lay his hands on. George Peele migrated from Broadgates Hall (Pembroke College) and graduated at Christ Church in 1577. According to Wood, he was noted as a poet and appears to have combined successfully a high standard of scholarship and a somewhat uproarious social life.

John Marston graduated in 1594, but hardly anything is known of him at Oxford. One of the very strangest figures in the history of Oxford is that of Robert Burton. Elected student in 1599 (migrating from Brasenose), he obtained the degree of B.D. in 1614. Two years later the Dean and Chapter of Christ Church presented him with the living of St Thomas's Church (which has disappeared). In 1621 appeared that extraordinary and fascinating work, *The Anatomy of Melancholy*, culled from every known source on the subject, but the whole farrago is closely knit and suffused with the pawky humour of a scholar of genius. As he says in the preface, he lived at Christ Church 'a silent, sedentary, solitary, private life'; but according to Bishop Kennet 'he would be extremely pleasant, and raise laughter in any company', and yet 'nothing at last could make him laugh, but going down to the bridge foot in Oxford, and hearing the bargemen scold and storm and swear at one another, at which he would set his hands to his sides and laugh most profusely'. Some years before he died he had foretold the exact day of his death, which occurred on January 25, 1640, having spent forty-seven years in Oxford. He was buried in the north aisle of Oxford Cathedral, and his brother William (author of a history of Leicestershire) erected a monument over the grave. The Latin epitaph, in which he is called Democritus Junior, is Robert Burton's own composition.

In the summer of 1619 Ben Jonson was the guest at Christ Church of Richard Corbet, the poet and at this time senior student (fellow) of the college, and subsequently Dean of Christ Church and Bishop of Oxford. Whilst here Jonson received the degree of M.A., 'by their favour, not his studie', as he informed Drummond of Hawthornden. William Penn, the founder of Pennsylvania, matriculated in October 1660, but his independence and noncomformity soon got him into trouble with the authorities, and after a year he was sent down.

Thomas Otway entered in May 1669. He was more interested in the theatre than in his studies, and left in 1672 without a degree.

Richard Steele matriculated in March 1690, but migrated to Merton College a year later.

Ruskin took up residence in January 1837. He confessed that he was the worst Latinist in the University, but developed a veneration for Plato and Greek literature. He wrote much poetry, and competed thrice for the Newdigate prize, being successful at the last attempt. When studying hard for his degree it was found that he had consumption, and he had to leave the university in 1840. He returned in 1842 to graduate B.A., and became M.A. in 1843. When a Professorship of Fine Arts was endowed in 1870 by the bequest of Felix Slade, Ruskin was appointed Professor, holding the position until 1879, and was reappointed 1883-4.

Christ Church has another recluse who, like Robert Burton, spent all his working life here, and this was Lewis Carroll. He took up residence in January 1851, and distinguished himself in mathematics and classics. He graduated B.A. in 1855, when he was appointed mathematical lecturer, and M.A. in 1857. In 1861 he was ordained deacon, but never took priest's orders, probably due to excessive shyness and a tendency to stammer. He lived very much the life of a solitary, and his friendships were largely maintained through correspondence. *Alice in Wonderland* originated in a story told to Alice Liddell, daughter of the Dean of Christ Church, during a river excursion at Oxford.

CORPUS CHRISTI COLLEGE: Richard Hooker, through influence, obtained admission in 1568 as a humble student, and five years later was elected a scholar. He graduated B.A. in 1574 and M.A. in 1577, when he was elected a fellow. He was expelled for a month in 1579, possibly because he had offended the puritan Vice-President, and then returned to his studies until 1581, when he took holy orders. Robert Bridges entered as a commoner in 1863, and soon came to know Gerard Manley Hopkins of Balliol, whose work later he came to admire profoundly, and edited the first collected edition of Hopkins's poems. He graduated in 1867.

EXETER COLLEGE: John Ford the dramatist was a member of this college, but for only about a year (1601-2), and then he left to study law in London. William Browne of Tavistock entered about 1603 and left without a degree. About twenty years later he returned to the college to become tutor to a nobleman's son, and was granted the degree of M.A.

J. A. Froude became a fellow in 1842, and took deacon's orders in 1844. He knew J. H. Newman (see under Oriel College) and at the latter's invitation contributed the life of St Neot to his *Lives of the English Saints*, but came to regard the miracles of the saints as nonsense and refused any further collaboration. Froude was moving towards scepticism, and in his book *The Nemesis of Faith* (1849) showed his complete break with orthodoxy. The book was denounced by a college tutor who, on hearing that one of his pupils possessed a copy, seized it and after tearing it to pieces threw it in the hall fire. Froude resigned his fellowship. Many years later he returned to Oxford as Regius Professor of Modern History. He said that 'the temptation of going back to Oxford in a respectable way was too much' for him. He succeeded E. A. Freeman, with whom he had been in furious controversy. His lectures on *The English Seamen of the Sixteenth Century* are magnificent reading.

R. D. Blackmore entered in 1844 and became a good classical scholar, graduating in 1847. William Morris entered in 1853 and graduated 1855. He was perplexed by religious difficulties and very nearly joined the Roman Catholic Church. With Burne-Jones and others he formed a circle known as The Brotherhood. A few years later he returned and with Burne-Jones and Rossetti was engaged on the decorations of the new debating hall of the Union Society. They entered into the work with gusto, joking, laughing and posing as models for each other.

HERTFORD COLLEGE: William Tyndale entered Magdalen Hall (dissolved in 1874 and absorbed by Hertford College) in 1510 and, according to John Foxe, 'improved himself in knowledge of tongues and other liberal arts', made a special study of theology and 'read privily to certain students and fellows . . . some parcel of divinity, instructing them in the knowledge and truth of the scriptures'. After obtaining his master's degree in 1515, he continued study at Cambridge.

Samuel Daniel entered Magdalen Hall in 1579. 'He improved himself much in academical learning by the benefit of an excellent tutor,' says Anthony Wood, 'but his glory being more prone to easier and smoother studies than in pecking and hewing at logic, he left the university without the honour of a degree.' John Donne was admitted in 1584 to Hart Hall, which became Hertford College in 1740. For a time he shared a room with Henry (later Sir Henry) Wotton, the poet and diplomatist. Donne appears to have spent three instead of the customary four years at that period and left without a degree, but became M.A. in 1610.

Thomas Hobbes entered Magdalen Hall in 1603. The old scholastic methods of teaching repelled him and, according to Aubrey, he spent much time snaring jackdaws and reading travel-books, in spite of which he graduated in 1608. Many years later the University authorities, disapproving of his *Leviathan*, publicly burned it in the Schools Quadrangle. Edward Hyde, later first Earl of Clarendon, who entered in 1622, says in his *Life* that his natural ability was not developed by assiduous study, but managed to graduate in 1626. During the Civil War, when Charles I's headquarters were at Oxford, Clarendon was one of the king's principal advisers, and lived at All Souls College. He was Chancellor of the University from 1660 to 1667. His great-grandson left Clarendon's manuscripts to the University, and the profits from the *History of the Great Rebellion* were used to establish the Clarendon Press. Robert Stephen Hawker had entered Pembroke College in 1823, but soon afterwards, at the age of nineteen, married a lady of forty-one. On returning to Oxford he migrated to Magdalen Hall, won the Newdigate prize with a poem on Pompeii, and graduated in 1828.

JESUS COLLEGE: Henry Vaughan 'the Silurist', being a Welshman, came in 1638 to the college that has always had a close connexion with Wales. However, hardly anything is known of his days in Oxford except that he left without a degree. John Richard Green competed successfully for a scholarship to this college in 1854, when he was sixteen, but was too young to take up residence immediately. Most of his fellow-students were Welsh, and Green did not fit in well. He led a solitary life; the college authorities did not understand him; and this brilliant student graduated in 1859 without distinction. Whilst still an undergraduate he wrote some essays on Oxford history for the Oxford *Chronicle*. T. E. Lawrence ('Lawrence of Arabia'), who entered in 1906, graduated first class in history in 1910. A thesis he wrote for his degree was later published as *Crusader Castles*. His college granted him a senior demyship for four years' travel.

LINCOLN COLLEGE: Sir William Davenant was educated at Lincoln College, entering about 1620, but he appears to have been here only a short time. In 1643 Thomas Fuller, flying from London during the Civil War troubles, joined the Royalists in Oxford and resided in the college for seventeen weeks, and preached before Charles I. Thereafter he became chaplain to one of the Royalist generals, and followed the fortunes of war.

MAGDALEN COLLEGE: John Foxe entered the college about 1532, and hardly anything is known of his life here until he became a fellow in 1539. Being a strong Protestant, he objected to the college statutes requiring fellows to attend chapel regularly, to take holy orders within seven years and to remain celibate, and with others of a like mind resigned his fellowship in 1545. William Camden was here, apparently as a servitor, but soon migrated to Broadgates Hall (later Pembroke College).

John Lyly entered in 1567, but did not matriculate until 1571. According to Anthony Wood, he disliked 'the crabbed studies of logic and philosophy . . . his genius being naturally bent to the pleasant paths of poetry', and was esteemed 'as a noted wit, rare poet, comical and facetious'. He graduated B.A. in 1573, and requested Lord Burghley to obtain a fellowship for him, but nothing came of it. He became M.A. in 1575 and then proceeded to Cambridge.

Addison, securing a demyship (scholarship) here in 1689, was transferred from Queen's College. He graduated M.A. in 1693, and became a fellow in 1698. A brilliant classical scholar, he wrote Latin verse which soon gained high praise, and took pupils. He was noted for his shyness, delicacy of perception and studies late into the night. His favourite stroll in the Water Walks is still known as 'Addison's Walk'. He resigned his fellowship in 1711, but had given up regular residence when he went on foreign travel in 1699. William Collins migrated from Queen's, as did Addison, on being elected a demy, and graduated B.A. in November 1743. Whilst here he published a volume of verse, and became acquainted with Gilbert White, who was at Oriel.

Edward Gibbon entered the college in April 1752, aged nearly fifteen, 'with a stock of erudition', as he says in his *Memoirs*, 'which might have puzzled a doctor, and a degree of ignorance of which a schoolboy might be ashamed'. However, 'I felt myself suddenly raised from a boy to a man . . . and my vanity was flattered by the velvet cap and silk gown, which distinguish a gentleman commoner from a plebeian student'. He was apparently something of a prig, and complains that the 'Monks of Magdalen' would not discuss the Early Christian Fathers with him after dinner. Soon 'the irksomeness of cloistered life repeatedly tempted me to wander', and he 'eloped' to London, Bath and Buckinghamshire.

Oxford was lax in his time: the professors gave up all pretence of teaching, and the tutors left the young gentlemen to their own devices. He sums it all up: 'To the university of Oxford I acknowledge no obligation; and she will as cheerfully renounce me for a son as I am willing to disclaim her for a mother. I spent fourteen months at Magadalen College; they proved the fourteen months the most idle and unprofitable of my whole life.' At the end of the lamentable fourteen months he was expelled for having become a Roman Catholic.

Charles Reade entered with a demyship in 1831 and graduated in 1835. He was elected a fellow after graduating M.A. in 1838, and later became Bursar of the college. He also became Dean of Arts, when he shocked the graver members of the University by going about in a green coat and brass buttons. He became Vice-President of the college, but gradually took less part in University life, although he retained his fellowship to the end of his life. J. Addington Symonds became a fellow of the college in 1862, and in the following year won the Chancellor's prize for an essay on 'The Renaissance'. Six months later, through overwork, he broke down after developing consumption and left for Switzerland.

Oscar Wilde, who entered in 1874 with a demyship from Trinity College, Dublin, spent four happy and brilliantly successful years here. He came under the influence of Ruskin and Pater, was constantly reading poetry, especially the work of Keats and Swinburne, and was always a leader in conversation. He was considered by many a poseur and effeminate aesthete, and on one occasion four undergraduates tried to 'rag' him. When they began to invade his rooms he dealt with them so effectually that it was the first and last time that he was 'ragged'. Wilde's impertinence frequently disconcerted the authorities. He won the Newdigate prize with a poem 'Ravenna', and in the same year secured a first-class degree. His rooms were on the kitchen staircase, overlooking the River Cherwell.

MERTON COLLEGE: There are traditions connecting John Wyclif and Chaucer with this college, but they are very shadowy indeed. Philip Massinger, the dramatist, entered St Alban Hall (incorporated in Merton College in 1882) in May 1602. Wood says that 'he applied his mind more to poetry and romances for about four years or more than to logic and philosophy', and whether that was the reason, or whether it was because his father died in 1606, he left in that year without a degree. This same Anthony Wood matriculated at this college in 1647, becoming soon a postmaster. The term postmaster, originally applied to poor scholars, is the equivalent at Merton of the term scholar used at other colleges. Wood graduated in 1652.

Richard Steele, who had been at Christ Church, became a postmaster in August 1691. He was noted for his scholarship, and tried his hand at literature, but the comedy he wrote was, on the advice of a friend, consigned to the flames. He was popular, and it was with general regret that he left in 1694 without a degree and volunteered in the Life Guards. J. H. Newman, so much connected with Oxford (see under Oriel and Trinity Colleges), was Vice-Principal of Alban Hall during 1825-6.

George Saintsbury, who entered in 1863 as a classical postmaster, graduated in 1866. He tried unsuccessfully to obtain a fellowship, but many years later was elected an honorary fellow of his old college. He retained throughout his long life a great affection both for the University and the city, and considered 'the most fortunate man in the history of English letters to be Robert Burton; for he lived all his days in Oxford and he wrote the *Anatomy of Melancholy*'. Max Beerbohm said with impish humour that he was 'a modest, good-humoured boy', and that it was Oxford that made him 'insufferable'.

Beerbohm did not take his degree, but before he left Oxford in 1892 had already achieved prominence as an essayist. There is now a Beerbohm Room in 'Mob Quadrangle' with his drawings, letters and books.

NEW COLLEGE: Sir Henry Wotton the poet and diplomatist entered in 1584, but two years later migrated to Queen's College. Sydney Smith entered in 1789, and managed to secure a fellowship in his second year, but strangely enough hardly anything else is known of the Oxford days of this brilliant and witty man. Lionel Johnson entered in 1886, became something of a literary dictator in his own set and formed his prose style on that of another literary dictator, Dr Johnson. He was much influenced by the writings of Walter Pater, then the darling of the aesthetes. He graduated in 1890. John Galsworthy was contemporary with Lionel Johnson, but they do not appear to have known each other. He studied jurisprudence and graduated in 1889.

ORIEL COLLEGE: Beyond the fact that Sir Walter Ralegh was a member of this college during 1568-9 and did not take a degree, we have no certain knowledge of his life at the University. Wood asserts that 'his natural parts being strangely advanced by academical learning under the care of an excellent tutor, he became the ornament of the juniors, and was worthily esteemed a proficient in oratory and philosophy'.

Gilbert White entered in 1740. He graduated in 1743, was elected a fellow in the following year, and proceeded M.A. in 1746. He took holy orders in 1747, and retained his fellowship to the end of his life. He was sometimes at loggerheads with the authorities. When offered the living of Moreton-in-Pinkney, Northamptonshire, he insisted on serving it in a non-residential capacity (no uncommon thing in those days) but it did not please the Provost of Oriel. Retention of his fellowship and continued residence at Selborne (though he was frequently at the college) did not please the authorities either.

John Henry Newman became a fellow of Oriel in 1822, was ordained deacon two years later and appointed curate of St Mary's, the University church, becoming rector in 1829. He was appointed tutor at Oriel but resigned later owing to differences with the provost. Newman became prominent in the Oxford Movement and in fact the leading figure, but by 1839 had serious doubts about Anglicanism, and a few years later joined the Roman Catholic Church. He was away from Oxford during the years 1842-5, and except for a brief stay in 1846 was not at Oxford again until 1878, after his college (Trinity) elected him an honorary fellow. Also prominent in the Oxford Movement was Richard Hurrell Froude, fellow and tutor of Oriel, whose youngest brother the historian James Anthony Froude entered the college in 1835 and graduated in 1842. Newman had hoped that Froude, like his brother, would join the Tractarians, but he was not attracted. He had already begun to be influenced by Carlyle through reading his *French Revolution*, and later became Carlyle's friend and biographer.

Arthur Hugh Clough became a fellow of Oriel in 1842, and was appointed tutor soon afterwards, resigning in 1848 because of family troubles. In his last year he was connected with an extraordinary *jeu d'esprit*. With four others he circulated a 'revolutionary manifesto' headed 'Liberty, Equality, Fraternity', announcing that the Vice-Chancellor had fled, that the University was no more, etc., and that a provisional government had been established. It created a tremendous sensation, especially because of the clever adaptation of terms made familiar by the revolutions in Europe during that year. Thomas Hughes entered in 1842, and secured his degree in 1845. He gives a picture of the Oxford of his time in *Tom Brown at Oxford*.

PEMBROKE COLLEGE: Francis Beaumont the dramatist entered Broadgates Hall (which became Pembroke College in 1624) in 1597, and nothing is known of his career here. He left in 1598 when his father died, and never returned to the university. Sir Thomas Browne entered Broadgates Hall as a fellow-commoner in 1623, and graduated in 1626. He took up the study of medicine and practised at first in Oxfordshire, but precisely where is not known.

Samuel Johnson was entered as a commoner in October 1728. His father, who was very proud of him, accompanied him, and 'told the company he was a good scholar, and a poet and wrote Latin verses'. The beginning of his university career is best recorded in his own words as reported by Boswell. 'The first day after I came to college I waited upon him [Dr Jorden, his tutor], and then stayed away four. On the sixth, Mr Jorden asked me why I had not attended. I answered I had been sliding in Christ Church Meadow. And this I said with as much *nonchalance* as I am now talking to you. I had no notion that I was wrong or irreverent to my tutor. Boswell: "That, Sir, was great fortitude of mind." Johnson: "No, Sir, stark insensibility." '

However, the Master of Pembroke, Dr Adams, said that he attended lectures regularly, and the authorities were impressed by the width of his reading. In spite of the deep melancholia he inherited from his father, he gave the appearance of being jovial, but Johnson said that they mistook his bitterness for frolic; he was 'miserably poor'. He says that he disregarded all power and authority, but this is not quite borne out by the testimonies of others. A fellow-collegian (who is sure of lasting fame for his remark that 'cheerfulness was always breaking in') said that Johnson was delicate in language, and feared by all. Poverty, presumably, brought Johnson's academic career to an untimely end. It is uncertain at what precise date this occurred, but he was taken off the college books in 1731.

He retained an affection for his old college, and revisited it in later life. On a visit in 1754 he was received coldly by the Master, from whom Johnson expected a subscription for his *Dictionary*, then being prepared for publication, but did not get it. '*There* lives a man,' he said, 'who lives by the revenues of literature, and will not move a finger to support it.' He was there with Boswell in 1776, and pointed out to Boswell that he used to play draughts in the common-room. His final visit was in November 1784, within a few weeks of his death. During his visits, he always prided himself on being 'accurately academic in all points, and he wore his gown almost ostentatiously'. Johnson's rooms in college were over the gateway, on the second floor. The college possesses his old desk, his portrait by Reynolds, and his teapot.

William Shenstone the poet has sometimes been mentioned as a contemporary of Johnson's at Pembroke, but it seems that he was here just after Johnson's time. His status was that of a servitor. A fellow-collegian reports that he refused to comply with the convention then prevailing that every student must cut off his hair and wear a wig, which exposed him to ill-natured remarks. He left without taking a degree.

Thomas Lovell Beddoes entered as a commoner in May 1820, and soon made a mark by rebelliousness, eccentricity and the profession of democratic opinions. He published at Oxford in 1821 a pamphlet called *The Improvisatore*, followed by publication in London in 1822 of a drama called *The Bride's Tragedy*, which had been written when he was at Charterhouse and shows something of his real powers. He made a journey to Italy in 1824 to see his dying mother, and made the acquaintance of Landor and Mary Shelley, and eventually took his Bachelor's degree in 1825. He returned three years later to take his M.A.

QUEEN'S COLLEGE: Thomas Middleton was educated at Queen's, but nothing is known of his life here; and very little of another contemporary, Sir John Davies, who entered about 1585 and graduated in 1590. Sir Henry Wotton, migrating here from New College in 1586, graduated in 1588. William Wycherley was here probably in 1659, but left apparently without matriculating. Addison came to his father's college in 1687, and his classical learning attracted the attention of a fellow, who secured him a demyship at Magdalen. William Collins entered as a commoner in 1740 and, as with Addison, secured a demyship at Magdalen.

Walter Pater entered in 1858, and latterly was taught by Benjamin Jowett of Balliol. He graduated in 1862, and in the same year had taken rooms in the High Street, where he had private pupils. Pater joined a literary society called Old Mortality and came to know Swinburne, also a member. His later association with Oxford is mentioned under Brasenose College.

ST JOHN'S COLLEGE: James Shirley entered in 1612, intended for holy orders. William Laud, recently appointed President of the college, was (according to Wood) impressed by Shirley's talents, but advised against his taking holy orders because he was disfigured by a mole on the left cheek. Whatever the reason, Shirley left without a degree and continued his studies at Cambridge. Abraham Cowley, who was ejected from Cambridge during the Civil War, settled at this college during 1644-6. During the Protectorate he became M.D. at Oxford, possibly as a cloak for Royalist activities. A. E. Housman entered with a scholarship in 1877 and obtained first-class honours in his first public examination, but failed to secure honours when graduating in 1881, and it was a bitter disappointment to him.

TRINITY COLLEGE: Thomas Lodge, the poet, has a rather shadowy connexion with Trinity. He proceeded to Oxford about 1573, and became servitor to Edward (later Sir Edward) Hoby, the courtier. He graduated B.A. in 1577. Sir John Denham matriculated at the college in November 1631. Wood says that he was regarded as 'a slow and dreamy young man, given more to cards and to dice than to study; his seniors and contemporaries could never in the least imagine, at that time, that he would be able to enrich the world with his fancy, or by the issue of his brain, which he afterwards did'—which may account for the fact that there is no record of his ever receiving a degree. John Aubrey entered in May 1642, but he contracted smallpox and with the coming of the Civil War to Oxford he left in 1643.

Walter Savage Landor entered as a commoner in 1793 and, in keeping with his character, indulged in highly unorthodox conduct. He adopted revolutionary principles, was the first undergraduate to attend hall with his hair unpowdered, and wrote satires and an ode to George Washington. To crown all, he fired a gun at the windows of a man he described as an 'obnoxious tory'. This was too much for the authorities, and on Landor refusing to give adequate explanation he was expelled for a year. The authorities were impressed with his abilities, and intimated that he could return, but a quarrel with his father put an end to his university career.

John Henry Newman entered in 1817. He was a sensitive and exceptionally hard-working student, and when called for his *viva-voce* examination a day earlier than he had expected, broke down completely.

He managed however to obtain his degree. He took pupils until he competed successfully for a fellowship at Oriel. Sir Arthur Quiller-Couch entered in 1882 and graduated 1886. He paid tribute, in his dedication to *The Oxford Book of English Verse*, to his old college as 'a house of learning, ancient, liberal, humane, and my most kindly nurse'. James Elroy Flecker entered in 1902 with a classical scholarship, enjoyed the social life, especially conversation, and wrote a great deal of poor verse. He graduated in 1906.

UNIVERSITY COLLEGE: Lord Herbert of Cherbury, elder brother of George Herbert, entered as a gentleman-commoner in 1596. Marriage, at the age of sixteen, interrupted his studies, and it is not known when he left or if he took a degree. Dr Johnson paid a visit to this college in 1776, when with Boswell he dined in hall, and it is probably to this occasion he alludes when he said two years later that he had 'drunk three bottles of port without being the worse for it. University College has witnessed this.'

Shelley was the greatest English poet to have been at Oxford. He entered University College in 1810. 'They are very dull people here,' he said of the tutors to his friend Thomas Jefferson Hogg, and Shelley proved, alarmingly, that he himself was anything but dull. He had a passion for extraordinary chemical experiments, and 'his hands, his clothes, his books and his furniture were stained and corroded by mineral acids', said Hogg in *Shelley at Oxford*, the most revealing portrait of Shelley in his youth. He used to love wandering over the countryside with Hogg, and indulged in shooting with duelling pistols at anything except living beings, and in making and floating paper boats. He and Hogg published some burlesque verses which they attributed to the mad Margaret Nicholson, who was in prison for an attempt on the life of George III.

Shelley's downfall came when he sent to the heads of colleges a pamphlet on *The Necessity of Atheism*. When questioned by the authorities he refused to answer, and was expelled less than a year after taking up residence. Hogg protested to the authorities, and was also expelled. The rooms occupied by Shelley are on the first floor by the stairs to the right of the hall. He is commemorated by the Shelley Memorial (beyond the north-west corner of the great quad), which takes the form of a marble representation of the drowned Shelley.

WADHAM COLLEGE: Sir Charles Sedley the dramatist entered the college as a fellow in 1656, but did not take a degree, and it is not known when he left. A fellow-rake at the court of Charles II, John Wilmot, Earl of Rochester, was admitted as a fellow-commoner in 1660. He was only fourteen when created M.A. in the following year. Whilst at Oxford he began writing poetry. The college possesses four silver pint pots presented by Rochester.

WORCESTER COLLEGE: Richard Lovelace entered Gloucester Hall (which became Worcester College in 1714) in 1634. He was accounted, says Anthony Wood, 'the most beautiful and amiable person that ever eye beheld . . . of innate modesty, virtue and courtly deportment . . . much admired and adored by the fair sex'. In 1636, when Charles I was in Oxford, one of the great ladies of the court was so taken with him that she persuaded the Chancellor, who happened to be William Laud, Archbishop of Canterbury, to confer prematurely the degree of M.A. on Lovelace. He had already begun writing, and his comedy *The Scholar* was performed at Gloucester Hall in 1636. He returned to Oxford when it was a Royalist stronghold in the Civil War, but on the capture of the city by the Parliamentarians in 1646 he went soldiering abroad.

De Quincey entered Worcester College in 1803, and his career whilst here is somewhat obscure. The provost appears to have been impressed with his attainments, but judging from what De Quincey said many years later he appears to have disliked the system of teaching. He distinguished himself in Latin, but suddenly disappeared before the examination in Greek because (so he said later) the authorities abandoned a new system which allowed candidates to answer in Greek upon Greek subjects. 'Oxford, ancient Mother !' he says in his *Autobiographic Sketches*, 'I owe thee nothing . . . [but] at this moment when I see thee called to thy audit by unjust and malicious accusers—even with the hearts of inquisitors and the purposes of robbers—I feel towards thee something of filial reverence and duty.'

Wales and the Border Counties

South Wales
Herefordshire
Shropshire
Cheshire
North Wales

SOUTH WALES

Walter Savage Landor had a somewhat troubled connexion with Wales. He visited Tenby and Swansea, and at the latter place made the acquaintance of Lord Aylmer, whose daughter Rose Aylmer inspired one of his most beautiful lyrics. Later he came to own **Llanthony Priory** (V, E5, on the B4423, about ten miles north of Abergavenny), situated in the beautiful Vale of Ewyas. Having inherited his father's estate, and finding it insufficient for his needs, he decided in 1809 to buy the estate comprising the ruins of the old Augustinian priory and some modern buildings. Intending to become a model squire, he built new houses and roads. He spent a great deal of money, settled in an uncompleted house, though after his marriage in 1811 he lived in the prior's house (now part of an hotel) and got into all kinds of trouble with the bishop, the tenantry and the neighbours. After about five years he left for Jersey, and the estate was managed by his mother, who made a much better job of it.

Wordsworth and his sister Dora made a tour of the Wye Valley in 1793, and a further visit in 1798 inspired the 'Lines Written above Tintern Abbey'. In a few of Wordsworth's poems there are traces of the influence of Henry Vaughan, whose birthplace is not far from here. He was born, with a twin brother, on April 17, 1622, at **Newton-by-Usk** in the parish of **Llansantffraed** (V, E6, off the A40 about twelve miles north-west of Abergavenny). He came of an ancient Welsh family, and John Aubrey was his cousin. Aubrey said that 'their grandmother was an Aubrey: their father, a coxcomb, and no honester than he should be—he cosened me of 50s. once'. Vaughan was first educated privately then sent to Oxford, after which he studied medicine in London. About 1645 he practised as a physician, first in Brecknock for a few years, then for many years, possibly to the end of his life, in his native Llansantffraed. He died there on April 23, 1695, and is buried outside the east wall of the church. In his second volume of poems, *Silex Scintillans*, he called himself 'the Silurist' because, says Aubrey, 'the Silures (a tribe of Britons who fiercely opposed the Romans) contained Brecknockshire, Herefordshire, etc.'

W. H. Davies was born at the Church House Tavern, which belonged to his paternal grandfather, at **Newport** (III, G1) on July 3, 1871. After a somewhat wild life at school and apprenticeship to a picture-frame maker, he emigrated to the United States, and began the life of the 'super-tramp' he describes in his *Autobiography*. At the former mansion of Golden Grove, which stood on the site of the present mansion (off the B4300 and about twelve miles east of Carmarthen), Jeremy Taylor lived during 1645-54. He was chaplain to the second Earl of Carbery, owner of the mansion, and to whom he was related. Whilst here he wrote *Holy Living* and *Holy Dying*. Near by, on the north bank of the River Towy, there is **Grongar Hill** (V, C6), celebrated by John Dyer in a poem of that name. Dyer was born on August 13, 1699, at **Llanfynydd**, about four miles north of Grongar Hill.

Sir Richard Steele, desperately pressed with debts in London, retired in 1724 to Hereford, then shortly afterwards to **Carmarthen** (V, C6), to a house in King Street (now the Ivy Bush Hotel) derived from his second wife. Then he decided to move to a farmhouse he also possessed called Tygwyn, which is still there, at **Llangunnor** (V, C6) a mile away to the east. After a visit to Hereford he became seriously ill, and his relatives moved him to the Carmarthen house for proper medical treatment. He died there on September 1, 1729, and was buried in

St Peter's Church, where there is a memorial tablet to him. He was paralytic in his final years, and much harassed by London creditors. He was known in these parts for his kindness, and he loved to watch the country people at their recreations. There is a memorial to him in the church at Llangunnor.

Coming to our own day, Dylan Thomas, who was born at **Swansea** on October 27, 1914, lived for several years at **Laugharne** (V, B6), at the mouth of the River Taff and about eight miles south-west of Carmarthen. The town is depicted in *Under Milk Wood*. Dylan Thomas died on November 9, 1953, whilst on a visit to the United States, and is buried in St Martin's churchyard in Laugharne.

HEREFORDSHIRE

In **Ross-on-Wye** (V, F6), beautifully situated on a bend of the river, there once lived John Kyrle, a worthy who followed the simple life and devoted all his considerable spare income to charitable works. Pope gave him fame by celebrating him in the third of his *Moral Essays*— 'Rise, honest Muse! and sing the Man of Ross!' Kyrle's house in the market-place, now a shop and marked by a bust of him, later became the King's Arms Inn. Coleridge, passing this way in 1794 on his tour of Wales, stayed at the inn and wrote on the window-shutter some lines which begin:

> *Richer than miser o'er his countless hoards,*
> *Nobler than kings or king-polluted lords,*
> *Here dwelt the man of Ross.*

In the hall of the Royal Hotel in Ross there is a tablet commemorating the fact that Dickens and his biographer met there in September 1867 to discuss the projected American tour of 1867-8. Dickens's manager for the reading tours, a native of Ross, was in favour of the tour; Forster opposed it, but Dickens decided to go.

William Langland, author of *Piers Plowman*, about whom so little is known, may have been born in **Ledbury** (V, F5) about 1332. However, a claim is made for him elsewhere. Just under two miles north of the town there used to be a house called Hope End on Oyster Hill, whither Elizabeth Barrett Browning was moved when an infant and spent the first twenty-eight years of her life. Her genius flowered precociously, and at eight years of age could read Homer in the original and began to write poems. At thirteen she wrote 'The Battle of Marathon' which her father published for her. Her father's pecuniary embarrassments and her mother's death obliged him to move, and his daughter deeply regretted having to leave a countryside she loved dearly.

Ledbury is the native town of the present poet laureate, John Masefield, who was born at a house called The Knapp on June 1, 1878. Some of his earlier narrative poems contain allusions to the countryside. Thomas Traherne was born at **Hereford**, some time during the years 1637-9, but nothing is known of his parentage and early years.

SHROPSHIRE

That William Langland was born in the West Midland area seems virtually certain, but there is more than one claimant for his birthplace. One of them is **Cleobury Mortimer** (V, F4, on the A4117 about ten miles east of Ludlow). The church there has a *Piers Plowman* window commemorating the author.

At **Ludlow** (V, F4) itself we have, among other associations, two seventeenth-century writers who were on opposing sides in the Civil War, and both associated with Ludlow Castle. Milton's masque of *Comus*, with music by his friend Henry Lawes, was performed in the now roofless Great Hall of the castle. The occasion was when the Lord-Lieutenant of Wales, the first Earl of Bridgwater, took up official residence in 1634. Milton, as far as we know, was not present. Samuel Butler the satirist, who for a time was secretary to the Lord President of Wales, took up residence in Ludlow Castle in 1660, and occupied the rooms over the fourteenth-century gateway that leads to the Castle Green. He did not hold the post for long, giving it up when he married a lady who had some money. Part of his *Hudibras* was written here.

We associate Shropshire very much with A. E. Housman, who has sung of the county with moving classical simplicity in *A Shropshire Lad*, though himself no native of the county. It is the area round Ludlow that he celebrates, and some of the familiar features and villages figure in the poems: Wenlock Edge and the beautiful village of Hughley lying under it, and then a cluster of names with which he makes fine play:

> Cluntun and Clunbury,
> Clungunford and Clun,
> Are the quietest places
> Under the sun.

The Bredon Hill of one of his best poems is, however, in his native Worcestershire. He wrote of Ludlow, and it is appropriate that his remains lie in the churchyard of St Lawrence.

Richard Baxter, who was born in November 1615 at **Rowton**, six miles west of Shrewsbury, was during 1640-1 assistant minister of the parish church of St Leonard at **Bridgnorth** (V, F4). His little house, opposite the church, is still there. Near the bridge, in Cartway Friars Street, is the sixteenth-century gabled house where Bishop Percy of the *Reliques* was born, the son of a grocer, on April 13, 1729. It was about 1760, when he was visiting a friend at **Shifnal**, about eight miles north of Bridgnorth, that Percy discovered an old folio manuscript in the house, used by the servants for lighting fires, which contained many old poems. He begged it of his friend, and it inspired him to collect many other old poems.

Very near the border of Shropshire is **Montgomery Castle** (V, E3), about sixteen miles south-west of Shrewsbury, and only scanty ruins survive. It was the birthplace of George Herbert, born there on April 3, 1593. His father was formerly Sheriff of Montgomeryshire; his mother became a lifelong friend of John Donne, who addressed to her one of his most beautiful 'Elegies'; and his elder brother became the first Lord Herbert of Cherbury. He was at first educated at home and then sent to Westminster School.

The historic town of **Shrewsbury** (V, F3) finely situated on sloping ground that forms a peninsula, possesses one of the great public schools of England, in which Sir Philip Sidney, Fulke Greville (Lord Brooke) and Samuel Butler (of *Erewhon*) were educated. Sidney and Fulke Greville were contemporaries and the latter became a poet and the biographer of his friend. Samuel Butler's grandfather had been headmaster for nearly forty years. The school now occupies buildings erected in 1882: the old buildings, opposite the castle entrance, are now the museum and public library. The Elizabethan writer Thomas Churchyard was born in Shrewsbury about 1520. George Farquhar's play *The Recruiting Officer* was written at the Raven Hotel (demolished in 1954) which stood in Castle Street. The play gives a very good picture of certain aspects of Shrewsbury at that time (1705), and was dedicated to 'all friends round the Wrekin'.

Mary Webb, whose novels spring from the soil of Shropshire, was born on March 25, 1881, at **Leighton-under-the-Wrekin**, ten miles south-east of Shrewsbury. She spent part of her married life in Spring Cottage, Lyth Hill, died at St Leonard's in Sussex on October 8, 1927, and is buried in Shrewsbury cemetery. Bomere Pool, three miles south of Shrewsbury, is the 'Sarn Mere' of her *Precious Bane*, published three years before her death and the first book to bring her wider recognition.

About eight miles north of Shrewsbury, off the A9, is **Preston Brockhurst** (V, F3), and just over a mile west from this village is Clive Hall, the birthplace of William Wycherley. Born in 1640, he was the eldest son of a man who became steward to the Marquess of Winchester, and was alleged to have made over some of his employer's money to his own use. Young Wycherley was sent when fifteen to France before proceeding to Cambridge. He was frequently at Clive Hall, which he inherited on his father's death in 1697.

A few miles farther north there is **Wem** (V, F3), where, in Noble Street, there once existed the home of William Hazlitt. This was the family home, but the elder Hazlitt was a travelled man and his son William had been born in Maidstone. The family went to America in 1783 and returned here three years later. Young Hazlitt was educated mainly at home, spent a few years in London training as a Unitarian minister but threw that up and took art lessons from his brother, who was a pupil of Sir Joshua Reynolds. He spent a few months in Paris during 1802-3 and then took up portrait painting in London and the Lake District. Meanwhile he had heard of Coleridge as a poet and Unitarian preacher, and trudged the twelve miles or so to hear him preach at Shrewsbury in 1808—it turned out to be Coleridge's last sermon, for soon afterwards he gave up Unitarianism. Hazlitt was deeply impressed by Coleridge, who later visited the Hazlitts at Wem. Hazlitt, interested in metaphysical speculation, was encouraged by Coleridge, and moreover invited him to visit his home at Nether Stowey. Hazlitt spent most of his time between Wem and London, studying and writing on philosophical questions, and falling in and out of love a few times. He became engaged to Sarah Stoddart in 1807, and in the following year left home to get married to her in London.

CHESHIRE

Knutsford (V, FI, on the A50 about fifteen miles south-west of Manchester), is forever associated with Mrs Gaskell and her idyllic novel *Cranford*. When just a year old her mother died, and she was brought from London to her maternal aunt Mrs Lumb, who lived in Heath House on the edge of Knutsford heath, and it is still there. The journey appears to have been used by her in *Mary Barton*, in which the two grandfathers fetched their motherless granddaughter from London to Manchester. Until marriage, Mrs Gaskell's entire life was spent in Knutsford and the neighbourhood, and she came to know it well. Many of the people she knew are depicted in *Cranford*, but Knutsford appears as 'Duncombe' in the short story 'Mr Harrison's Confessions', as 'Eltham' in *Cousin Phyllis*, and provided some of the material for *Wives and Daughters*. She was married in the parish church of Knutsford to the Rev. William Gaskell in 1832, and they settled in Manchester. Mrs Gaskell died in Hampshire and is buried in the cemetery of the Unitarian Chapel in Knutsford. There is a medallion portrait of her on the wall of the Gaskell Memorial Tower.

In the year that Mrs Gaskell was married there was born not far away at **Daresbury** (V, FI, on the A56 five miles south-west of Warrington), Charles Lutwidge Dodgson, much better known by his pseudonym of Lewis Carroll. He was born on January 27, 1832, in the parsonage, his father being the rector of Daresbury. A precocious boy, his precocity took a curious form: he kept snails and toads as pets, and armed earthworms so that they could fight better; but presaging future development, wrote and acted marionette plays and was curious about logarithms. He lived at Daresbury until sent at the age of twelve to school at Richmond in Yorkshire. The parish church commemorates him with a stained-glass window depicting characters from *Alice in Wonderland*.

Sir John Vanbrugh used to be claimed as a native of **Chester** (V, E1), but it is now established that he was born in London. However, his father set up here as a sugar-baker in 1667, and Vanbrugh was probably educated at the King's School, but after his early days he passes out of Chester. His contemporary Dean Swift passed through Chester sometimes on his journeys between London and Dublin, and once stayed at the Yacht Inn, at the corner of Nicholas Street. His great *Journal to Stella* begins at Chester in 1710. His friend the poet Thomas Parnell was on his way to Ireland when he was taken ill and died in Chester, the exact date of death being unknown. He was buried, without a monument, in the churchyard of Holy Trinity, on October 24, 1718.

Dr Johnson came to Chester with the Thrales in 1774. He perambulated the city pretty thoroughly, going right round the walls, and was impressed with them, but the cathedral he did not consider 'of the first rank'. He made Mrs Thrale a little angry by keeping Miss Thrale 'beyond her hour of going to bed', and risking the young lady's neck, and his, by being on the wall at night.

De Quincey, as a youth, stayed with his mother and uncle for a short time in a house that once existed in the churchyard of St John's, the fine Norman church near the landing-stages on the river. He had run away from school, and was calling on his mother on his way to Wales. The news of his flight was already known to his mother, who must have disapproved, but De Quincey's uncle took his side and said that he should be allowed to go to Wales, with an allowance of a guinea a week. After Wales and the 'impassioned parenthesis' of his experiences in London, he rested from 'dreadful remembrances in the deep monastic tranquillity of St John's Priory'. The house was supposed to have once belonged to the antiquary Sir Robert Cotton, whose library became the nucleus of the British Museum. There is a fine description of it at the end of De Quincey's *Autobiographic Sketches*. After this second visit De Quincey's guardians sent him to Oxford.

The ubiquitous George Borrow was in Chester, probably in 1825, and praises Chester ale. Thomas Hughes, author of *Tom Brown's*

Schooldays, spent his final years in Chester, at 16 Dee Hills Park, but
died in Brighton. Charles Kingsley was a canon of Chester from 1869
to 1873, and founded the Chester Natural History Society. There are
few more beautiful cities or towns in England than Chester, and it drew
from Henry James a memorable passage.

NORTH WALES

The beauty of North Wales has drawn literary men hither and Coleridge in 1794, when it was fashionable to tour Wales, set out on foot
with a friend. He described his wanderings in an appendix to *Biographia
Literaria*.

De Quincey, after he ran away from school in 1802, led the life of a
'homeless vagrant' for a fortnight, slept nine nights in the open, fed
sometimes at hospitable farmhouses, and began to undermine his
constitution. He felt the need of books, and 'had the unpardonable
folly to quit the deep tranquillities of North Wales, for the uproars, and
perils, and the certain miseries of London'. It is all described in his
Confessions of an English Opium-Eater. George Borrow went wandering
in his own fashion in 1854, and his delightful *Wild Wales* describes the
tour in the typical Borrovian manner of romanticized fact.

Some well-known novels have their settings in North Wales.
Peacock's *Misfortunes of Elphin*, which parodies Arthurian romance,
tells the legendary story of the submergence of a great tract of land
beneath the waters of Cardigan Bay. Some of the scenes of his *Headlong Hall* are laid in Snowdonia, and it is possible that Hafod House
(demolished in 1958) in the Ystwyth valley, and about sixteen miles
south-east of Aberystwyth, was the building Peacock had in mind.
Built by Thomas Johnes, the translator of Froissart, the hall was visited
by Peacock in 1811. Kingsley's *Two Years Ago* has a thrilling episode
in and magnificent description of Snowdonia. The once popular
romance of *Aylwin*, by Swinburne's friend Theodore Watts-Dunton,
is partly laid in the same district.

It is unfortunate that Borrow did not visit **Llangollen** (V, E2) in the
time of the delightfully eccentric 'Ladies of Llangollen', for he would
probably have drawn amusing character sketches of them. These Irish
ladies, Lady Eleanor Butler and Miss Sarah Ponsonby, settled in Plas

Newydd★ just outside Llangollen in 1779, and many were the celebrities who visited them, among them Scott and Wordsworth, the latter writing a sonnet in their honour. Robert Browning stayed at the Hand Hotel (which survives) in Llangollen for some weeks in 1886. Two miles north-west of the town, at **Llantysilio**, there is a tablet in the church to mark the spot where Browning was to be seen every Sunday afternoon during his stay in Llangollen.

At **Glyn** (or Glynceiriog, V, E2) on the B4500 and about two miles south of Llangollen, George Borrow is commemorated by a window at the Ceiriog Memorial Institute. The Institute and library here are a memorial to John Ceiriog Hughes, known as the Robert Burns of Wales, and her greatest lyric poet.

Dr Johnson went on a tour of Wales from July to September in 1774 with his friends the Thrales. There was a fairly long stop at **Llewenny** in Denbighshire, but the most interesting memorial of the journey is at **Gwaenynog**, near **Denbigh** (V, D1). A little distance south-west of Denbigh is a farmhouse called Galch Hill, and just beyond it a dingle (called Dolhyfryd) in which is a cottage with eight lines of verse attributed to Johnson. He was the guest of a Colonel J. Myddelton (descendant of the Sir Hugh Myddelton who carried through the New River Scheme) at Gwaenynog near by. The date below the verses, 1768, makes one suspect that it is not Johnson's work. However, in a field at Gwaenynog Johnson's host commemorated his visit with an inscription on a Grecian urn. It reads: *This spot was often dignified by the presence of Samuel Johnson LL.D., whose moral writings, exactly conformable to the precepts of Christianity, gave ardour to Virtue and confidence to Truth.* On this spot Johnson used to stand and recite poetry. He did not seem too pleased with the idea of the memorial. It 'looks like an intention to bury me alive', he wrote to Mrs Thrale, 'let him think, for the present, of some more acceptable memorial'.

In the cathedral at **St Asaph**, six miles south-east of Rhyl, a tablet in the south aisle and part of the east window commemorate Mrs Hemans, who lived just outside St Asaph during the years 1809-27. A house of the same name, Bronwylfa, is on the site of her old home, south of St Asaph. In the village of **Pantasaph** (off the A55 and about

★ Open every day, except on Sunday during winter, 11 a.m. to 4 p.m.

eight miles east of St Asaph) Francis Thompson lived during 1893-7 near the Franciscan monastery. Nearly all the poems in his volume of *New Poems* (1897) were written there.

The seaside resort of **Llandudno** (V, D1), has a most interesting association with Lewis Carroll. On the West Shore Bay side of the town a statue of Lewis Carroll overlooks the Model Yacht Pond, and about this spot he used to amuse his child friends. Near the pond is the church of St Saviour where he is commemorated by the alabaster font. Outside the west gate of the Marine Drive (which goes nearly all the way round Great Orme's Head) is the Gogarth Abbey Hotel, which is on the site of the house of Dean Liddell, the father of the original of *Alice in Wonderland*. The book, or part of it, was possibly written at Dean Liddell's house.

Shelley managed to get over a great deal of Britain and Ireland in the twenty-one years assigned to him before he left these shores, and lived for short periods in three houses in Wales. Soon after his expulsion from Oxford he came to stay with a cousin at a house called Cwm Elan in the **Elan Valley** (V, D4), a little south-west of **Rhayader**. He received pitiful letters from Harriet Westbrook, who threatened to commit suicide, so he hurried to London. A little time after his marriage to Harriet he returned to Cwm Elan, and then took another house near by called Nantgwylt. These houses were submerged when the valley was dammed and the present lakes formed, an unfortunate but perhaps not inappropriate fate for the dwellings of one who was himself drowned in the Gulf of Spezia.

He and his wife returned to Wales for six months during 1812-13, when they lived on the estate called Tan-yr-allt near **Portmadoc** (V, C2). The estate belonged to W. A. Madocks, a philanthropic Member of Parliament who reclaimed 7,000 acres of Traeth Mawr by building a mile-long embankment across the mouth of the estuary. Shelley was interested in the scheme and quixotically went to London to raise funds. According to Shelley he left the house here (which was demolished many years ago) because in February 1813 he was attacked by an assassin, but the probable explanation is that he was suffering from hallucination.

Many years later than Shelley there is another association with the area. T. E. Lawrence ('Lawrence of Arabia') was born at the house called Woodlands on the south side of **Tremadoc**, on August 15, 1888. He was a precocious boy and could read books as well as newspapers at the age of four, and was able to enter the Oxford High School when only eight.

Northern England I

South Lancashire
East Riding of Yorkshire and the York area
West Riding of Yorkshire
North Riding of Yorkshire and County Durham

SOUTH LANCASHIRE*

It is generally stated that Thomas De Quincey was born in a house called Greenhay, which then stood outside **Manchester** (VI, C6), on August 15, 1785. According to De Quincey's own statement, this house was not built until about five or six years after his birth. In any case, he was baptized in St Ann's Church, St Ann Street, where the font in which he was christened may still be seen. His father was a merchant of literary tastes who died when his son was in his seventh year. The boy was then sent to Salford to be educated by one of his guardians. In his *Autobiographic Sketches* he records his thankfulness that his home training was under 'the gentlest of sisters' and not under 'horrid pugilistic brothers', the eldest of whom nevertheless made him engage in fights with factory children in the district.

De Quincey was sent to schools at Bath and at Winfield in Wiltshire, and then in 1800 to Manchester Grammar School. He was now a brilliant scholar, and in his spare time studied Hebrew together with Lady Carbery, whom he first met in Bath. But his health was bad; he

* Other Lancashire associations are recorded under the succeeding section on the Lake District.

disliked the monotonous routine of the school, and asked his guardians to remove him. They refused, and he decided to run away. He borrowed £10 from Lady Carbery and made his way to Chester, where his mother was living, *en route* for Wales.

After her marriage Mrs Gaskell settled in Manchester—her husband was the minister of Cross Street Unitarian Chapel—first in Dover Street, then in Rumford Street (neither residence has survived), and finally in 1850 at 84 Plymouth Grove, which survives. *Mary Barton*, her first novel (a very great success), and *North and South* (together with Dickens's *Hard Times*) give a vivid idea of Manchester factory life at that period. She is commemorated in Manchester by a mural tablet in the Cross Street chapel. Charlotte Brontë, who used to visit Mrs Gaskell at Plymouth Grove, began *Jane Eyre* when in lodgings at 59 Boundary Street (which has been demolished), off the Oxford Road.

Two natives of Manchester became novelists. One, Harrison Ainsworth, was born in King Street (the house has disappeared) on February 4, 1805, and like De Quincey was educated at the Grammar School. He was articled to a solicitor, and then migrated to London. The other, Frances Hodgson Burnett (author of *Little Lord Fauntleroy*), was born on November 24, 1849, at 141 Cheetham Hill Road, and spent her early years at 19 Islington Square, Salford. Both houses survive.

The city has a native poet in Charles Swain (1801-74). In the leisure hours of a long business career he wrote much poetry. Of his many lyrics set to music, one, 'I cannot mind my wheel, mother', was for long very popular. He is buried at **Prestwich**, and has a memorial in the Church.

George Gissing and Francis Thompson were students of Owens College (since their time incorporated in Manchester University) and both were destined to die of consumption. Gissing did brilliantly in English studies, but overwork and amorous troubles led to disgrace. Francis Thompson for six years studied medicine, which he detested, and thrice failed to secure a degree, after which he drifted helplessly. He read eagerly, and among his books was his mother's gift of De Quincey's *Confessions of an English Opium-Eater*—a fatal gift, for, like De Quincey, Thompson began to take opium for neuralgia and other troubles. Failing to earn a living, he migrated to London.

Liverpool (VI, B6) has two native poets. Mrs Hemans, the daughter of a merchant, was born at 118 Duke Street (marked by a tablet) on September 25, 1793. Her family left Liverpool in 1800. A precocious child, she wrote verse early, and her father had a volume of her poems published when she was fourteen. The other poet was Arthur Hugh Clough, the son of a cotton merchant, born in 1819 at 9 Rodney Street (marked by a tablet, which also commemorates the birth of his sister Anne, who became the first Principal of Newnham College, Cambridge). Clough's friend Matthew Arnold, who commemorated him in 'Thyrsis', died at Liverpool on April 15, 1888, when visiting his sister to welcome the return of his daughter from the United States. Mention of the United States takes us on to Nathaniel Hawthorne, who was U.S. Consul at Liverpool during the years 1853-7. In his days the consulate was in Brunswick Place. He has described his experiences amusingly in *Our Old Home*.

At **Hurstwood** (VI, D5), three miles east of Burnley, there is an Elizabethan building that is reputed to be the house in which Edmund Spenser stayed with relatives after leaving Cambridge in 1576. He was certainly in or near Hurstwood, and fell in love with a lady he called Rosalind. She did not return his love, and his disappointment is reflected in some of his poems. It is probable that his 'Shepherd's Calendar' was begun here, but unrequited love and the need to earn a living drove Spenser to London.

EAST RIDING OF YORKSHIRE AND THE YORK AREA

At the village of **Winestead** (VI, H5), near Patrington and about ten miles south-east of Hull, Andrew Marvell was born in his father's rectory on March 31, 1621. He was educated at the Grammar School (near the church of Holy Trinity) at Hull. He was to become Member of Parliament for Hull from 1659 until his death, and was noted for the interest he took in his constituents. There is a statue of him at the corner of Savile Street and George Street.

York (VI, F4) was a city well known to Daniel Defoe, who describes it in his *Tour through the Whole Island of Great Britain* as 'pleasant and beautiful'. Robinson Crusoe, as stated in the first sentence of his adventures, was born in York, though Alexander Selkirk, his prototype, was not a native of the city. Earlier, that diverting character John Taylor, the 'Water-Poet', had in 1622 sailed from London to York in an open boat, and came to the same conclusion as Defoe did about York: ''Tis large, 'tis pleasant, and magnificent.'

Taylor stayed at the Bull Inn (later the George Inn) in Coney Street, where Sir John Vanbrugh stayed in 1710 when up on business in connexion with **Castle Howard*** (VI, F4), which was being built to Vanbrugh's designs for the third Earl of Carlisle. The castle lies on an unclassified road, six miles west of Malton. Later, at the age of fifty-four, Vanbrugh married a Yorkshire lady in St Lawrence's Church (no longer there) in York. He appears to have approached marriage some-what cynically, and when at Castle Howard during the cold winter of 1718, wrote to the Duke of Newcastle, 'I have almost a mind to marry to keep myself warm,' but his marriage turned out well.

The chief literary associations of York, together with certain villages lying to the north of it, are with Laurence Sterne. His great-grandfather had been Archbishop of York; Sterne came to York from school at Halifax soon after his father's death and with no money. A cousin who possessed an estate near York provided money for his education at Cambridge, but Sterne wasted two years in idleness (probably at his cousin's house) before proceeding to the university. After Cambridge he took holy orders, was ordained priest in 1738, and obtained the living of **Sutton-on-the-Forest** (VI, F4, on the B1363 eight miles north of York). Later he acquired a prebendal stall in York Minster, and some-times preached there, only to find that half the congregation gradually disappeared. He married Elizabeth Lumley of York, and through her connexions acquired the living of **Stillington** (VI, F4), three miles farther north on the same road as Sutton, preaching on Sunday mornings at the latter and on Sunday afternoons at the former. He did not care for his parishioners, nor they for him, and for over twenty years led a life that was irksome to him. His wife bored him; she was jealous, not without cause, became insane and was confined. Sometimes he visited

---

* Open from April 6 to September 28 on Wednesday, Thursday, Sunday 1.45 to 5.15 p.m.; Bank Holiday Mondays 11.30 a.m. to 5.30 p.m., and Bank Holiday Tuesdays 1.45 to 5.15 p.m.

a friend at Skelton (five miles north-west of York) and there joined in the coarse merriment of the Demoniacs Club.

At Sutton he began writing *Tristram Shandy*, the first two volumes of which were refused by a London publisher, who however took it up after successful publication in York at Sterne's expense. He pilloried local characters, including Dr John Burton of York, who appears as 'Dr Slop, the man-midwife'. After a spell in London enjoying his fame he obtained in 1760 the living of **Coxwold** (VI, F3) in the Hambleton Hills (off the A19 about twenty miles north-west of York). There was no parsonage house, so Sterne took a cottage near the church and named it Shandy Hall, which has survived and is marked by a tablet. After her recovery his wife returned to him, but they led a troubled existence and finally separated. Further instalments of *Tristram Shandy* were written at Shandy Hall, where also *A Sentimental Journey* was written. Sterne was much away from Coxwold, either on the Continent or in London, where he died.

A very different kind of clergyman of the Church of England was in these parts some time later. This was Sydney Smith, who in 1806 became rector of **Foston-le-Clay** (VI, F4, eight miles north-east of York on an unclassified road off the A64). He was non-resident for three years, then administered his parish from Heslington near by until 1814, when he built a house of his own design a mile from the church. The house is still there, near Thornton-le-Clay to the west of Foston. Smith bought a very old green chariot he named 'Immortal' in which he drove to church. He took to farming, bred horses, became a magistrate (and was noted for leniency towards poachers), opened a dispensary and became a village doctor (he had attended medical lectures in his Edinburgh days) and was kind to poor folk by allowing them gardens at a very tiny rent. The villagers were sorry to see such a parson go after twenty years, and in the church is an inscription recording that *he was a faithful friend and counsellor, a seeker of peace, a wit who used his powers to delight and not to wound.*

Near **Appleton Roebuck** (VI, F4), six miles south-west of York, there is a mansion called Nun Appleton Hall where Andrew Marvell lived when he was tutor to the daughter of Lord Fairfax, the Parliamentary general. He was here from about 1650 until 1653, and wrote here some of his finest poems, including 'The Garden'. He wrote also a long poem on Nun Appleton House.

WEST RIDING OF YORKSHIRE

In **Wakefield** (VI, E5) George Gissing was born at 30 Westgate (marked by a tablet) on November 22, 1857. His father was a pharmaceutical chemist with literary and scientific tastes. After attending private day schools Gissing was sent to a Quaker boarding school at Alderley Edge in Cheshire. At **Bardsey**, about six miles north-east of Leeds, William Congreve was born in February 1670. His father was an army officer, who moved into Ireland soon after the birth of his son.

Getting towards the moors of the West Riding of Yorkshire the Brontës come immediately to mind, for the moors and the Brontës are inseparable. The two eldest children, both daughters, of the Rev. Patrick Brontë had been born at **Hartshead**, near Heckmondwicke, Yorkshire. Three more daughters and a son were born at the parsonage (marked by a tablet) in Market Street, **Thornton** (VI, D5, on the B6145 four miles west of Bradford): Charlotte on April 21, 1816; Patrick Bramwell on July 23, 1817; Emily Jane on August 20, 1818, and Anne on March 25, 1820. Soon after Anne's birth the family moved to **Haworth*** (VI, D5, on the A6033 four miles south-west of Keighley and about eight miles north-west of Bradford). At Haworth the Brontë children spent the rest of their all-too short lives; indulged, as children, in their world of make-believe; and wrote their books.

All died tragically young, and all, except Anne, at Haworth parsonage. The two eldest girls died after contracting fever at school; Patrick Branwell Brontë, after brilliant promise, turned to evil courses and took to opium and drink and died in September 1848. Emily died in the same year on December 19, and the sofa on which she breathed her last is on view *in situ* in the museum. She was buried in the parish church, but the present building, except for the tower, is not the church that the Brontës knew. After Anne's death Charlotte, sole survivor of six children, was left alone with her father. She married in 1854, but

---

* The parsonage at Haworth is now the Brontë Museum, open weekdays 11 a.m. to 6 p.m. (11 a.m. to 5 p.m. in winter), Sunday 2 to 5 p.m. Contains manuscripts and other relics.

survived marriage less than a year, succumbing on March 31, 1855, to the family disease of tuberculosis, and is buried near Emily in the parish church.

One does not need to know the Yorkshire moorland to appreciate the work of the Brontës, but contact with the moors makes one realize forcibly how closely this bleak countryside was woven into the texture of their lives, especially of Emily, who was the greatest both as poet and novelist. A flagstone bridge that spans Sladen Beck near Haworth was one of their favourite haunts.

Three miles west of Haworth there is Withens, the weather-beaten old house on the brow of a moor that became Heathcliff's residence, 'Wuthering Heights'. The residence as portrayed in the novel is probably a composite picture deriving features from Ponden House (which also suggested the 'Thrushcross Grange' of the novel), from High Sunderland (a seventeenth-century mansion near Halifax), and from Withens. Ponden House is a mile across the moors westwards of Stanbury, and two and a half miles from Haworth. Near by are the Brontë Waterfalls. Another two miles and Withens is reached, and about three miles beyond Withens are the ruins of Wycoller Hall, the original of 'Ferndean Manor' in *Jane Eyre*.

About ten miles south-east of Haworth there is **Heckmondwike** (VI, E5), in the district of Charlotte Brontë's *Shirley*: Hartshead, about a mile south-west of Heckmondwike, is 'Nunnely Church'; Birstall, two miles to the north-east, is 'Briarfield'; the Red House at Gomersal, half a mile west of Birstall, is 'Briarmains'; and under a mile north-west of Birstall is Oakwell Hall, which is 'Fieldhead'. Two miles south-west of Heckmondwike there is Roehead, where the three girls were at school, and where Charlotte returned to become a teacher.

Emily was an unhappy teacher at Law Hill—the school building, somewhat altered, has survived—very near the great clothing town of **Halifax** (VI, D5), which has other literary associations. Defoe mentions its ancient wool trade, and describes the law against cloth-stealing that gave the town at one time so unsavoury a reputation for severity, which found expression in the proverb: 'From Hell, Hull and Halifax, Good Lord deliver us.' Defoe stayed in Halifax, and is reputed to have written part of *Robinson Crusoe* at the Rose and Crown in Back Lane.

Another resident was Laurence Sterne, who was at school here during 1723-31. At **Guiseley** (VI, E4, on the A65 five miles north-east of Bradford) the parents of the Brontës were married in the old church in 1812. In the churchyard are buried several generations of Longfellow's ancestors.

Further north, at Skipton Castle*, **Skipton** (VI, D4)—magnificent both in architecture and situation—there is a connexion with the poet Samuel Daniel. He was for a few years, late in the 1590's, employed as tutor here to Lady Anne Clifford, daughter of the third Earl of Cumberland. Unhappy in her two marriages, she gave herself, 'wholly to retiredness . . . and made good books and virtuous thoughts' her companions, and no doubt her tastes had been largely formed by Daniel.

About ten miles north-west of Skipton there is the upland lake called **Malham Tarn** (VI, D4) at the head of which is Tarn House, now a field study centre and formerly the home of Walter Morrison, an eccentric Yorkshire millionaire. Among his guests were Ruskin, Darwin and Kingsley. The last derived the setting of the opening chapters of *The Water Babies* from the scenery of Malham and of Wharfedale, which he also visited in the same year (1858). Kingsley may have written part of *The Water Babies* at Tarn House.

NORTH RIDING OF YORKSHIRE AND COUNTY DURHAM

Scarborough (VI, G3), prominent in Sheridan's *A Trip to Scarborough* and Smollett's *Humphry Clinker*, was where Anne Brontë died on May 28, 1849. She was buried in the 'old town' on the southern slope of the castle hill, in the detached part of the churchyard of St Mary.

Seventeen miles farther up the coast the town of **Whitby** (VI, G2) commemorates the poet Caedmon, whose work is generally considered to mark the beginnings of English literature, with a large cross in the churchyard of St Mary's. He was a monk of Whitby Abbey, which was destroyed by the Danes. The present ruins are of the later medieval abbey. Whitby appears in Mrs Gaskell's *Sylvia's Lovers* as 'Monkshaven'.

* Open daily (except Good Friday and Christmas Day) 10 a.m. to sunset weekdays and 2 p.m. to sunset Sundays.

At the little village of **Sockburn** (VI, E2, off the A167 about eight miles south-east of Darlington) there is a farmhouse where Wordsworth and his sister and Coleridge stayed in 1799 with the Hutchinson family, to whom the Wordsworths were related. Wordsworth later married one of the Hutchinson daughters, and Coleridge—already married—flirted with another. About eight miles south of **Darlington** is **Halnaby Hall** (VI, E2, also off the A167 but to the west of it) where Byron spent his honeymoon, which Byron later referred to as his 'treaclemoon'. On the very first day he asked his wife why she had married him, and according to her account his behaviour throughout was well-nigh demonic. After three weeks they left, and within a year were separated.

To come to a very different character, Lewis Carroll, there is a boyhood home of his at **Croft** (VI, E2, on the A167 five miles south of Darlington). His father was rector here, and the parsonage in which Lewis Carroll lived has survived. He was at school at Richmond, about ten miles to the south-west, from the age of twelve until fourteen, when he was sent to Rugby.

Dickens's connexion with Yorkshire is well known because of his castigation of 'the rascalities of those Yorkshire schoolmasters', as he says in a letter. He made a trip to the north in 1838 with his illustrator 'Phiz'. **Bowes** (VI, D2, at the junction of the A66 and A67) was one of the places he visited in order 'to see a schoolmaster or two'. He saw William Shaw, who kept the Bowes Academy, and in his diary notes that it was in this man's school some boys went blind from neglect, for which Shaw was tried and fined £300. The academy run by Shaw can be seen at the west end of the village and it is generally assumed to be the prototype of 'Dotheboys Hall' in *Nicholas Nickleby*, and that Bowes is 'the delightful village of Dotheboys'. He visited the churchyard, and saw the grave of a boy who had died suddenly at Shaw's academy: 'I think his ghost put Smike into my head, upon the spot,' says Dickens.

Only five miles or so north-eastwards from Bowes is **Barnard Castle** (VI, D2), just over the border in County Durham, and Dickens put up at the King's Head inn there in the market-place, still carrying on under the same name. Nearly opposite there used to be the shop of a clockmaker named Thomas Humphrey, in whose doorway there stood a curious tall clock. There is a story, not fully authenticated, that Dickens called to inquire the time, and that the shop and its owner suggested the title of his periodical *Master Humphrey's Clock*, which provided the framework for *The Old Curiosity Shop* and *Barnaby Rudge*. On the station platform at Barnard Castle there is a clock with the inscription: *This is a genuine Master Humphrey's clock.*

About three miles south-east of Barnard Castle is **Greta Bridge** VI, D2, ont he A66) where a friend of Sir Walter Scott lived. This was J. B. S. Morritt, traveller, classical scholar and politician, who owned Rokeby Hall* there, and with whom Scott stayed in 1809 and 1812. His poem *Rokeby* is a story of the time immediately after the battle of Marston Moor, and the scene is laid chiefly at Rokeby Hall. The beauty of the estate and district add much to the topographical colour of the poem. Brignall Banks, a short distance away in the Greta valley, is commemorated in *Rokeby* in the song, 'O Brignall Banks are wild and fair'. About a mile east of Rokeby Park there is the hamlet of **Wycliffe**, from which the family of John Wyclif may have derived their name, though the reformer himself was born probably at **Hipswell**, two miles south-east of Richmond.

About three miles south-west of Richmond, at **Halfpenny House** (VI, D3, on the A6108), is Hartleap Well, the scene of Wordsworth's narrative poem. Proceeding north-eastwards, we find Thomas Gray as a visitor to his friend Dr Thomas Wharton at Old Park Hall, now a modernized farmhouse (off the A6074) about five miles beyond **Bishop Auckland**. At **Coxhoe** (VI, E2, on the A177 about seven miles south-east of Durham) is Coxhoe Hall (now owned by the National Coal Board) in the parish of **Kelloe**. Elizabeth Barrett Browning was born there on March 6, 1806, and very soon afterwards her parents moved into Herefordshire. She is commemorated in Kelloe church with a tablet.

Durham (VI, E1) was the boyhood home of that unfortunate poet Christopher Smart, whose family moved here from his native Kent, the precise date being unknown, nor is it known whereabouts they lived. Young Smart continued his education here at Durham School, which was then at Palace Green. One day he was invited to Raby Castle

* The Hall is not open to the public, but the grounds can be viewed occasionally on written application to the owner, Major H. E. Morritt.

(twenty miles south-west of Durham), the home of the Duchess of Cleveland, and his brightness so enchanted the duchess that she decided to allow him £40 a year. It was paid regularly until her death in 1742, and it was through her influence that he was educated at Cambridge.

R. S. Surtees, the creator of Jorrocks, was also educated at Durham School, which he left in 1819 and became articled to a Durham solicitor. (Another writer educated at this school was Sir Hugh Walpole.) Surtees is stated by some to have been born (in 1803) in Durham and by others in **Milkwell Burn**, which is in the parish of **Ryton** on the River Tyne, and eight miles west of Newcastle-upon-Tyne. From about 1825 until 1838 he was in London, when his father died and he succeeded to the estate of **Hamsterley Hall** (VI, D1). This is situated a short distance south of the junction of the A694 and B6310, near **Ebchester** and about twelve miles south-west of Newcastle-upon-Tyne.

He had already created, when in London, the character of Jorrocks, the cockney sportsman, in some sketches in the *New Sporting Magazine*, and it was due to a suggestion of Sir Walter Scott's son-in-law, Lockhart, that he turned his hand to the writing of novels. In the first and second, *Handley Cross* and *Hillingdon Hall*, Jorrocks appears again, and Hamsterly Hall is probably depicted in the latter. Surtees died in Brighton on March 16, 1864, and is buried in the churchyard at Ebchester. The late Viscount Gort, V.C., was his grandson.

We noted, a few pages earlier, Byron's honeymoon at Halnaby Hall, and at **Seaham** (VI, E1) there is Seaham Hall where he was married on January 2, 1815. He had been courting Anne Isabella Milbanke, daughter of Sir Ralph Milbanke, since 1812. The lady had an interest in poetry, theology and mathematics, and Byron called her the 'Princess of Parallelograms'. The wedding ceremony took place in the drawing-room of Seaham Hall. 'I shall never forget the 2nd of January 1815!' he wrote some years later, 'Lady Byron was the only unconcerned person present; Lady Noel, her mother, cried; I trembled like a leaf, made the wrong responses, and after the ceremony called her Miss Milbanke.' After the honeymoon they returned to Seaham for a short time, and then departed to settle in London.

Newcastle-upon-Tyne (VII, H6, in Northumberland) was the native town of Mark Akenside. The son of a butcher, he was born on November 9, 1721, in Butcher Bank, now called Akenside Hill. At the age of seven, when playing in his father's shop, a butcher's cleaver fell on his foot and lamed him for life. At school he showed poetic gift; the dissenting community of Newcastle (his parents were Presbyterians) were proud of their youthful poet and raised money to send him to Edinburgh University to train for the ministry. He changed his mind and took up medicine and returned the money raised for him.

Right up at the border, at **Cornhill** (VII, G4, on the A698, and about fifteen miles south-west of Berwick-upon-Tweed), a tablet on the old bridge records that over this bridge Robert Burns entered England for the first time.

Northern England II

The Lake District
Areas round the Lake District

THE LAKE DISTRICT

We associate the Lake District particularly with certain poets of the Romantic era, but there are a considerable number of other associations. Some earlier literary figures, among them Addison, Johnson and Gray, had been in the district, though there is no visible reminder of them. Gray has recorded the pleasures of his visit of 1769 to Keswick, Grasmere and elsewhere, and how alarmed he was at the 'impending crags' of Borrowdale. It is Wordsworth above all others that we connect with the Lakes, and he was the chief of the Lake Poets, a term first used in the *Edinburgh Review* in 1817. He was born at **Cockermouth** (VI, A2) on April 7, 1770, and his famous sister Dorothy in the following year. Their father was the estate and law agent of the first Earl of Lonsdale. The River Derwent flows by his birthplace, now called Wordsworth House,* and he had an especial affection for the river:

> *Behind my father's house he passed, close by,*
> *Along the margin of our terrace walk.*

His schooling began in 1778 (the year his mother died), learned very

* Open Monday and Saturday 2 to 5 p.m., and on other days on application.

255

little at the schools in Cockermouth and Penrith, but at the Grammar School* at **Hawkshead** (VI, B3) he received an excellent education. His desk is still there with his name on it, cut possibly by Wordsworth himself. He lodged at the cottage of Ann Tyson, the 'old dame so motherly and good' whom he recalls in a long passage in *The Prelude*. The cottage is still there, in a lane off the square opposite the Red Lion Hotel. His father died before he left school, and guardians raised money to send him to Cambridge. His later school holidays and part of the Cambridge long vacations were spent with his sister at their maternal grandfather's house in Penrith; but thereafter Wordsworth was absent from the Lake District until he stayed with a friend at Windy Brow near Keswick. This friend, Raisley Calvert, had great faith in Wordsworth's gifts, and dying soon afterwards left him a legacy of £900.

It was in 1798 that Wordsworth and his sister settled in **Grasmere** (VI, B2) at a cottage called Town End, now known as Dove Cottage,† and henceforth dedicated his life to poetry. He married in 1802. In the following year Coleridge came from Keswick on his way to Malta, fell ill and was nursed for a month here. Before he left, Wordsworth (knowing the state of Coleridge's affairs) bludgeoned him into accepting a loan of £100. Another distinguished visitor, Sir Walter Scott, came to visit him in 1805. Needing a larger house, Wordsworth moved in 1808 to Allan Bank (which has survived) at the other end of the town. Soon afterwards De Quincey took over Dove Cottage, and Coleridge was again a visitor. The latter thought of settling in London with a friend; Wordsworth warned the friend about Coleridge's opium-taking and other habits, which greatly riled Coleridge, who refused to call on Wordsworth when on a visit to Keswick, in 1812. They were later reconciled.

Meanwhile in 1811 Wordsworth had moved again, this time to the

* No longer a school, and admission on application.

† Open weekdays from April to October 10 a.m. to 6 p.m.; from October to March 10 a.m. to 4.30 p.m. (closed on Thursday). There are manuscripts, a complete set of first editions, portraits and personal relics, including the bed in which he died at Rydal Mount. The Wordsworth Museum across the lane, illustrating rural life in his time, is open from April to October only, on weekdays (except Friday morning) 10 a.m. to 6 p.m.

parsonage, which is still there, opposite the church. Two of his children died there, and anxious to get away from a house of painful associations he moved in 1813 to **Rydal Mount** (VI, B2), only two miles away, off the old road between Grasmere and Ambleside, and above Rydal Water. There he remained for the rest of his life, writing poetry, supplementing his meagre income by becoming distributor of stamps for Westmorland, and receiving many visitors. From overseas came Emerson and Hawthorne; Matthew Arnold, a fervent disciple; Edward Fitzgerald, who used to refer to him as 'Daddy' and said that he was somewhat stingy. Coleridge's son told Fitzgerald that, for a joke, two friends of Wordsworth once stole a leg of mutton from his larder.

Wordsworth resigned from the stamp office in 1842, secured a civil list pension and became poet laureate in 1843. He died on April 23, 1850, and is buried in the churchyard at Grasmere. His sister Dorothy, who had always lived with him, survived another five years, and is buried in the same churchyard. Her journals, besides being a valuable source for his life, show her as a woman of deep perception who greatly influenced her brother's development.

It is impossible in a short book to mention more than a few of the topographical features that inspired Wordsworth's poetry. There are few features round Grasmere itself that he left uncelebrated. Helm Crag, just north of Grasmere, was to him 'that ancient woman seated on Helm Crag', which occurs in one of the 'Poems on the Naming of Places', which mention many of the features in or near the Vale of Grasmere. Outside the Grasmere area, there are in the Sty Head Pass (south of Derwentwater) the famous Borrowdale Yews, or rather three decayed trunks of Wordsworth's 'fraternal four'. A few miles farther east is Blea Tarn, and there the Blea Tarn Farm remains 'the one abode, no more', as mentioned in 'The Excursion'. A series of thirty-three sonnets is devoted to the River Duddon, which rises in the Wrynose Pass near Grasmere—'Still glides the Stream, and shall for ever glide'. North of the lower section of Ullswater there is Gowbarrow Park, where Wordsworth saw 'a host of golden daffodils'. Ardent Wordsworthians need no advice, but those coming to the Lakes for the first time would find it rewarding to steep themselves in Wordsworth's poetry. He wrote also a *Topographical Description* of the Lake District which has been well rifled by writers on the district.

The Lake School label has stuck to Coleridge, but his poetry—the best of which was written before he settled here—draws hardly any inspiration from the district. He is mainly connected with **Keswick** (VI, B2) on the River Greta, about fifteen miles north of Grasmere. In 1800 he took Greta Hall (now a school) on a small hill on the west side of the town. Here he wrote the second part of 'Christabel' and the 'Ode to Dejection', and indulged more heavily in opium than before. The Lake District has the curious distinction of being associated with the two great opium addicts of English literature—Coleridge and De Quincey. It was the latter's opinion that opium killed Coleridge as a poet, whereas in De Quincey's case opium dreams provided material for some of the most magnificently sustained flights of impassioned expression to be found in English prose.

Lamb and his sister visited Coleridge for three weeks in 1802: 'such an impression I never received from objects of sight before', said Lamb in a letter to a friend. 'We have seen Keswick, Grasmere, Ambleside . . . we have clambered up to the top of Skiddaw'—he missed seeing Wordsworth, who had gone to Calais, but stayed a couple of days at Dove Cottage. In the following year Hazlitt paid a visit, and painted portraits of Wordsworth and Coleridge. In the same year Coleridge's brother-in-law Southey came to reside at Greta Hall. Each occupied a different floor of the house; then Coleridge departed for Malta in search of health, did not return to Keswick until 1806, and thereafter appears only as a visitor to the Lake District, his last visit being in 1812.

Southey lived the remainder of his life at Greta Hall,* and the whole house became his possession in 1809. He worked very hard indeed, but managed to get a government pension of £160 a year in 1807, increased to £300 in 1835. 'To think', he said, 'how many mouths I must feed out of one inkstand.' There was not only his family, but he had continually to help Coleridge. Shelley and his first wife stayed with Southey during the winter of 1811-12. Shelley was disappointed in

* Not open to the public, but the Fitz Park Museum in Station Street, Keswick, contains manuscripts of Southey, Wordsworth and Sir Hugh Walpole. Open weekdays 10 a.m. to 8 p.m.

Southey, whose revolutionary ardour of early years was spent, and Shelley adds further that 'his wife is very stupid—Mrs Coleridge is worse'. Shelley came to Keswick again in 1813, and stayed at Chestnut Hill, but did not call on Southey. That year brought another distinguished visitor, Sir Walter Scott, who had recently and magnanimously refused the poet laureateship so that it might be bestowed on Southey; and many years later Landor called on Southey too.

Southey's last years were marked by tragedy: his wife's mind failed and she died in 1837; he married again two years later, but on returning from honeymoon was overcome by mental exhaustion, and the last year of his life for him was a virtual trance. He died on March 21, 1843, and is buried in the churchyard at **Crosthwaite**, less than a mile from Keswick. The statue of him inside the church carries an inscription by Wordsworth.

As we have already mentioned, De Quincey took over Dove Cottage from Wordsworth. He had already stayed there with Wordsworth, and settled in it in 1809 after the furnishing had been done by Dorothy Wordsworth. Five thousand books went into the little cottage with him, and Coleridge took full advantage of them when on an extended stay with Wordsworth at Allan Bank, borrowing as many as five hundred volumes at a time. De Quincey lived 'with a single female servant (*honi soit qui mal y pense*)'—he says in his *Confessions*, and this girl was the Barbara Lewthwaite of Wordsworth's poem. His life, in his own phrase, was much 'insulated in reverie', and he tried with varying success to eke out his scanty paternal inheritance, but there was a period of two years when the effects of opium rendered him incapable of work. Here occurred that extraordinary incident of the Malay (described in the *Confessions*) who took enough opium 'to kill some half-dozen dragoons, together with their horses'.

De Quincey became acquainted with Margaret Simpson, daughter of a farmer who lived in Nab Cottage (between Rydal and Grasmere—it is still there) and sometimes stayed with the family. He had thoughts of marriage, tried to conquer the opium habit, succeeding for a time after his marriage in 1816, and then slipped back again. His first children were born here, and he was particularly fond of children throughout his life. When Wordsworth's daughter Kate, of whom De

Quincey was passionately fond, died in 1813 he was prostrate with grief, and in a passage of great pathos describes how every night for two months running he stretched himself upon her grave in Grasmere churchyard. For about a year, when editor of the *Westmorland Gazette*, De Quincey lived in Kendall, and in 1821 decided to seek work in London, leaving his wife and family at Dove Cottage. He reappeared in the Lake District for a short time in 1825, and then left it for ever. Many years later he wrote the *Recollections of the English Lake Poets*, and its indiscreet revelations offended the families concerned. Wordsworth was very angry.

There are certain minor figures of the Lake Poets' circle who are of some interest. A great admirer of Wordsworth and a close friend of De Quincey was John Wilson, better known as 'Christopher North' of the *Noctes Ambrosianae*. He lived in a cottage called Elleray, still there a short distance north of Windermere, for forty years. To the local population he was well known in his time as an angler, athlete and climber. At Storr's Hall in **Bowness** (now an hotel) he, Wordsworth, Southey and others gathered in 1825 to attend the regatta at Storr's Point in honour of Scott's fifty-fourth birthday. The view from Elleray is particularly fine, and De Quincey said that it was what one might expect 'on Athos seen from Samothrace'; but Emerson was disappointed, and declared that he had seen better in some parts of Massachusetts.

Harriet Martineau came to the Lakes in 1845 for the sake of her health. She built a house called The Knoll, on the slopes of Wansfell, just by **Ambleside** (VI, B3), which is still there. She came to know Wordsworth, who was friendly and helpful with advice. He suggested that when she entertained her friends she should give them just tea, and if they wanted more must pay for it! Some neighbours were suspicious of her because of her advanced opinions. Like Wordsworth, she also wrote a guide to the Lake District. She died at The Knoll on June 27, 1876, and was buried at Birmingham. Mrs Hemans lived during the years 1829-31 at Dove Nest, at the foot of Wansfell, but farther south than Harriet Martineau's home. She also came to know Wordsworth, who commemorated her in his 'Epitaphs'.

Going outside the Lake Poets and their associates, there is Keats, who toured the Lakes ecstatically with his friend Charles Brown in June 1818. Keats's first sight of Windermere astonished him. 'I cannot describe them,' he says, 'they surpass my expectation—beautiful water —shores and islands green to the marge—mountains all round up to the clouds.' At Bowness he asked a waiter about Wordsworth, and was disgusted to hear that he was electioneering in the Tory interest. He called at Rydal Mount to find Wordsworth out, and left a note. Then on to Grasmere, where he recognized 'the ancient woman seated on Helm Crag' he had read about in Wordsworth's poem. He stayed a couple of nights in Keswick, climbed Skiddaw and then went on to Scotland.

Tennyson, who was influenced by Keats more than by any other English poet, was first acquainted with the Lakes when his friend of Cambridge days, James Spedding, invited him in 1835 to stay at Mirehouse in Cumberland to meet Edward Fitzgerald, whom Tennyson had known slightly at Cambridge. He came again in 1850, calling at Mirehouse during his honeymoon on his way to Tent Lodge (which has survived) at the head of Coniston Water. He stayed there some months, and among his visitors was Carlyle. Whilst here Tennyson was offered and accepted the poet laureateship. He was again at Tent Lodge in 1857, and Matthew Arnold and Lewis Carroll were among his visitors.

Dr Arnold, the great headmaster of Rugby, settled in 1832 in a house called Fox House, which is on a little road beside the River Rothay, and about a mile north-west of Ambleside. Here the young Matthew Arnold lived, and as a young man was a frequent visitor in the Lake District. Emerson and Carlyle, also visitors at Rydal Mount, did not admire Wordsworth: the former thought the poet's mind narrow and very English; the latter considered that his speech was prolix and thin, and altogether a small man.

The last of the great names closely connected with the Lakes is that of Ruskin. As a boy he was often there with his parents, and in 1871 bought a house called Brantwood* at **Coniston** (VI, B3), overlooking Coniston Water and the mountain called Coniston Old Man. Frequently

* Open Monday to Friday 9 a.m. to 4 p.m., Saturday 9 a.m. to 12 noon. Also in Coniston is the Ruskin Museum, open daily 10 a.m. to 6 p.m., with drawings, manuscripts and other relics.

away at first on professorial duties at Oxford, he retired to seclusion at Coniston in 1884. His brain decayed in his final years, and he would sometimes sit for hours looking at the view across the lake. He died on January 20, 1900, and was buried in the churchyard at Coniston.

Coming to our own century, Sir Hugh Walpole wrote a 'Lakeland saga' collectively entitled *The Herries Chronicles*, the main scenes of which are set in Borrowdale. Walpole lived latterly at the estate called Brackenburn in Borrowdale, where he died on June 1, 1941, and is buried in the churchyard of St John's, Keswick. Beatrix Potter, creator of Peter Rabbit, and so many other delightful children's stories, paid a visit to the hamlets of Sawrey in 1896. She decided to buy Hill Top Farm* in **Near Sawrey** (VI, B3), a short distance from the mid-point of the western shore of Lake Windermere, and settled there until her death on December 22, 1943.

AREAS ROUND THE LAKE DISTRICT

In the south, on the A65, is **Kirkby Lonsdale** (VI, C3) which is the 'Lowton' of *Jane Eyre*. Two and a half miles south-east of the town there is **Cowan Bridge**, where there survives part of the building that was once the first Clergy Daughters' School founded in England. It is now part of Brontë Cottages, and is marked by a tablet. Here Charlotte and Emily Brontë were educated in 1824-5. Their two eldest sisters had preceded them at the school and both died of typhus contracted there, but Charlotte and Emily escaped the fever. Charlotte Brontë describes conditions at the school (called 'Lowood' in *Jane Eyre*) in severe terms, considered by some to be somewhat unfair, but she claimed that the description was accurate. 'An exposed and hilly road' leads from Cowan Bridge to **Tunstall**, just over three miles south of Kirkby Lonsdale, and it is the 'Brocklebridge' of *Jane Eyre*. Charlotte and Emily often worshipped in the old church there.

It was in the Lake District, at the house of Sir James Kay Shuttleworth on the shores of Lake Windermere, that Mrs Gaskell and Charlotte Brontë first met. Mrs Gaskell often stayed in the village of **Silverdale** (VI, B3) in Morecambe Bay, in a square building known as

* Open from Easter to September, weekdays 10.30 a.m. to 6 p.m., Sunday 2 to 6 p.m. Contains illustrations of her books, and personal relics.

Lindeth (or Gibraltar) Tower, which has survived. Here she found a very pleasant retreat from the smoke of Manchester, and her books were mostly planned and largely written in that tower. She stayed on some occasions at the near-by Wolf House. Silverdale is almost certainly the 'Abermouth' of *Ruth*.

Beyond the north-east corner of the Lake District there existed for five hundred years, until its demolition in 1935, the mansion of the Musgrave family at **Edenhall**, on an unclassified road three miles north-east of Penrith. The famous glass goblet of the family (the 'luck') was celebrated in Uhland's poem 'The Luck of Eden Hall', which is familiar in Longfellow's translation. Sir Walter Scott first visited the Lake District in 1797, and then went on to **Gilsland** (VI, C1), twelve miles or so north-east of Carlisle and near the 'waste of Cumberland' he described in *Guy Mannering*. He saw a beautiful girl on horseback, found out that she was Charlotte Mary Charpentier, the daughter of a French refugee, and secured an introduction. A few months later they were married in the cathedral at **Carlisle** (VI, B1). The house in which Miss Charpentier stayed before marriage still exists at 81 Castle Street, Carlisle.

Leaving the mainland, we must go to the Isle of Man to note the birth of the Manx poet Thomas Edward Brown at **Douglas** (VI, A5) in 1830. Educated at King William's College and Christ Church, Oxford, he became a master and then Vice-Principal of King William's College, Castletown. After 1861 he was a schoolmaster first in Bristol and then for nearly thirty years at Clifton College, but often spent holidays in the Isle of Man, and loved especially to talk to old sailors. His Manx poems are nowadays unduly depreciated; there is much good poetry in his *Fo'c'sle Yarns* and *Manx Witch and Other Poems*. There are relics of Brown in the Manx Museum,* Crellin's Hill, Douglas. Another Manxman was Sir Hall Caine (though born in Runcorn, Cheshire), the son of a ship's smith of Ballaugh. Some of his childhood was lived in the Isle of Man. His better work is to be found in the novels, such as *The Manxman*, which depict the life and character of the Manx people. The last years of his life were spent at **Greeba Castle** (VI ,A5), on the slopes of Greeba Mountain four miles north-west of Douglas. He died there on August 31, 1931.

* Open weekdays 10 a.m. to 5 p.m.

Scotland

South-east
Edinburgh
South-west
North-east
North-west

SOUTH-EAST

The 'Scott country' is nearly the whole of Scotland, as well as parts of England, Wales, the Continent of Europe and the Near East, but Scott's greatest work is laid in the Scottish Border, which falls largely within our present area.

At **Coldingham**, about ten miles north-west of Berwick-upon-Tweed, a woman's skeleton was discovered early in the nineteenth century immured upright in the walls of the Benedictine priory, an incident of which Scott made use in *Marmion*. About three miles north-west of Coldingham, past St Abb's Head, there are the ruins of **Fast Castle** (VII, G3), generally regarded as the 'Wolf's Crag' of *The Bride of Lammermoor*, which is laid mainly on the coasts of East Lothian and Berwickshire. A few miles to the west of Fast Castle (on the A1 between Grants House and Cockburnspath) is an old tower supposed to be the original of Lucy Ashton's home in that novel.

Scott was at school at **Kelso** (VII, G4), about eight miles north-east of Jedburgh, in 1783, and the grammar school he attended used to be held in the nave of the abbey church. East of the Abbey there is Garden Cottage, now called Waverley Lodge, where he used to stay with a kindly aunt; and at a small house called Rosebank, on the left bank of the Tweed just a little south of Kelso, he spent some happy holidays with an uncle. The house called the Butts was the residence of his great-grandfather, a gentleman who refused to shave until the Stuarts were restored and not unnaturally was referred to as 'Beardie'.

About two miles north of Kelso, in the village of **Ednam** (VII, G4, James Thomson was born in the former manse on or about September 7, 1700. He is commemorated by an obelisk on Ferney Hill close by. When he was an infant his father moved to **Southdean** (VII, F5 on the A6088, about seven miles south of Jedburgh). His father's old church, in which there used to be a memorial to the poet, is now a ruin. He was first educated at the parish school, and later at the grammar school, at that time held in an aisle of the old abbey at **Jedburgh** (VII, F4 on the A68). Burns was a visitor to Jedburgh in 1787, when he stayed at 27 Canongate, but the house has been demolished. Wordsworth lodged at 5 Abbey Close (which has survived) during his first tour of Scotland in 1803, and was visited by Scott. Above **Ancrum** (on B6400 and off the A68 about four miles north-west of Jedburgh), there are several caves on the banks of the river, and in one of them James Thomson carved his name.

Thorlieshope, in Liddesdale, between Canonbie and Hawick, was where Dandie Dinmont (in *Guy Mannering*) lived with his famous terriers. At **Selkirk** (VII, F4 on the A7), Andrew Lang was born on March 31, 1844, at a house now called Viewfield, and was educated at the grammar school there. Lang was one of Scott's greatest admirers, and his paternal grandfather was a friend of Scott. In the West Port at Selkirk a tablet marks the site of the Forest Inn where Burns lodged in 1787. **Ashiestiel** (VII, F4, on the Tweed, about four miles west of Abbotsford) is the house occupied by Scott when he was sheriff-deputy* of Selkirkshire during 1804-12. During this period he wrote *The Lady of the Lake*, *Marmion* and *The Lay of the Last Minstrel*.

In 1811 Scott bought a property of about a hundred acres called Clarty or Cartley Hole; he enlarged the house, then rebuilt it in

---

* The Court Room used by Scott at Selkirk Town Hall is now a museum partly devoted to a collection relating to Scott. Open May 16 to September 15, daily 3 to 6 p.m.

baronial style, and finally the mansion, named **Abbotsford** (VII, F4),* was surrounded by about a thousand acres. It is situated on the Tweed, two miles west of Melrose, and by the A7. Many distinguished visitors called upon Scott here, among them Wordsworth, Washington Irving and Maria Edgeworth. He died in the dining-room on September 21, 1832, and was buried in the east aisle of the north transept of **Dryburgh Abbey** (VII, F4, situated on a loop of the Tweed, off the A68 and about six miles north of Jedburgh).

Scott advised that to 'view fair Melrose aright' one must 'visit it by the pale moonlight', but apparently he himself never saw the beautiful ruins of Melrose Abbey by moonlight. The town of Melrose is the 'Kennaquhair' of *The Monastery* and *The Abbot*. South of it rise the Eildon Hills, so much loved by Scott, and where Thomas the Rhymer is supposed to have spent three years after his capture by the Queen of the Fairies. This poet and seer, known also as True Thomas and Thomas of Ercildoune, now called Earlston, lived in that town most of his life. A stone on the wall of the church states that 'Auld Rymer's race lies in this place'. A little north of Abbotsford there is Allan Water, and the glen there is the 'Glendearg' of *The Monastery*.

A few miles west of this area so richly associated with Scott's life lies the heart of Selkirkshire, formerly known and sometimes still referred to as Ettrick Forest, the country of James Hogg the 'Ettrick Shepherd'.† He was born towards the end of 1770 at **Ettrick** (VII, E5), and the site of his birthplace, between the church and the school, is marked by his monument. He received very little education, became a shepherd, and began to write songs. In 1802 he met Scott, and supplied him with some ballads for *The Scottish Ministrelsy* collection. After a farming venture in Dumfriesshire he returned bankrupt, and shortly afterwards farmed unsuccessfully at Mount Benger, which is about twelve miles from Selkirk (on the A708) and near the Gordon Arms Inn. Then he spent some years in Edinburgh, and on his return farmed

---

* Open March 31 to mid-October on weekdays 10 a.m. to 5 p.m., and on Sunday (including Easter and Whit Sunday) 2 to 5 p.m. from June to September. Contains personal relics, Scott's library and many historical and other relics collected by him.

† The Selkirk Museum, open weekdays 9 a.m. to 6 p.m., has relics of Hogg.

at Eltrive (or Altrive) Lake, a little to the south of the last farm. There he died on November 21, 1835, and was buried in Ettrick churchyard. Among his many distinguished friends were Wordsworth and John Wilson, and the latter has depicted him in *Noctes Ambrosianae*.

Tibbie Shiels' Inn, which is at the south-western end of St Mary's Loch and a few miles west of Altrive Lake, was made famous by Hogg, Wordsworth and others, and there is a monument to Hogg on the slope behind the inn. The beautiful valley of the Yarrow in Selkirkshire evoked from Wordsworth a series of poems: 'Yarrow Unvisited'; 'Yarrow Visited' (1814), when he met Hogg; and 'Yarrow Revisited' (1831), when he saw Scott for the last time.

Innerleithen (VII, F4, in the neighbouring county of Peeblesshire, about five miles south-east of Peebles) claims that its well is the original of Scott's *St Ronan's Well*. About a mile to its south, there is Traquair House on Quair Water, which probably suggested the 'Tully-Veolan' of *Waverley*. **Broughton** (VII, E4, on the A701 about eight miles south-west of Peebles) has a house called The Green where John Buchan when a boy used to stay with his grandparents. The scene of his first novel, *John Burnet of Barns*, is an old mansion whose ivy-clad tower survives at Barns, three miles south-west of Peebles. At **Peebles** (VII, E4) the seventeenth-century Cross Keys Inn, near Northgate, claims to be the original of the 'Cleikum Inn' of *St Ronan's Well*.

Just over three miles south-west of Peebles, near Manor church, is the house called Hallyards where Scott stayed with Professor Adam Ferguson in 1797. On that occasion he visited David Ritchie, the original Black Dwarf, a deformed and uncanny person who inspired something akin to terror in Scott. The hut in which Ritchie lived, which has been rebuilt, is a mile away. Before quitting Peeblesshire we must mention that it is the country of Allan Ramsay's *The Gentle Shepherd*, some of Hogg's poems, Scott's *St Ronan's Well* (set in upper Tweeddale), and part of *Old Mortality* centres round St Mary's Loch.

Going northwards into Midlothian, there is in the Esk Valley the mansion of **Hawthornden** (VII, E3), built by William Drummond of Hawthornden in 1638. Drummond was born in the former mansion on December 13, 1585, and the old tower of that building is incorporated in the present one. This scholar, recluse and poet, known as the

Scottish Petrarch, was visited by Ben Jonson in 1618, and took careful notes of the latter's conversation, providing us with a useful source of information on Jonson's life. Drummond died on December 4, 1649, and was buried in the churchyard at **Lasswade** (VII, E3), about two miles to the north. From 1798 until 1804 Scott spent his summers at Lasswade Cottage, which since his time has been enlarged, and the village is possibly the 'Gandercleugh' of his *Tales of My Landlord*.

A mile south of Lasswade, and near Polton Station, De Quincey settled at Mavisbush (now called De Quincey Cottage) in 1840, and lived there except for intervals at Glasgow and Edinburgh for the rest of his life. A complete child in the affairs of the world, the widowed De Quincey was lovingly looked after by his eldest daughter. Recklessly charitable, his cottage was often besieged by beggars, genuine and fraudulent.

Only a short distance to the south is the Stevenson country. Swanston Cottage, in the village of **Swanston** (VII, E3), five miles south-west of Edinburgh and on the edge of the Pentland Hills, was the holiday home of the Stevenson family during 1867-81. The cottage contains relics of Stevenson, but is not open to the public. The village figures in *St Ives*. Two miles north-west of **Colinton** (VII, E3, off the A70 and on the Water of Leith) there is the manse where Stevenson spent boyhood holidays with his grandfather, a period he described as his 'golden age'. The church where he used to worship, now in ruins, is at **Glencorse**, three miles or so south of Swanston.

Penetrating farther into the Pentland Hills, the area around Newhall House (about twelve miles south-west of Edinburgh) provided part of the setting of Ramsay's *The Gentle Shepherd*; and the 'Habbie's Howe' of the drama is disputably identified as in a dell beyond the gates of Newhall. At **Auchendinny** (VII, E3, off the A701 and about eight miles south of Edinburgh) there is the house of Henry Mackenzie, author of *The Man of Feeling* and a friend of Scott.

The town and district of **North Berwick** (VII, F3) in East Lothian have been delineated by Stevenson with characteristic charm in the essay 'The Lantern Bearers'. Tantallon Castle, about three miles east of the town, figures in *Marmion*. It was from the shore at **Gullane**, eighteen miles north-east of Edinburgh, that Allan Breck (in *Catriona*) made his final escape; and the trees of Archerfield here appear as the 'Graden sea-wood' in the story of 'The Pavilion on the Links'. The mansion of **Biel** (VII, F3) on Biel Water (off the A1), about five miles south-west of **Dunbar**, is generally regarded as the birthplace of William Dunbar, the greatest of the old Scottish poets. He was born about 1460; very little is known of his life, but he was probably employed by James IV on courtly and political business. Some authorities think that he perished on the battlefield of Flodden, but his death is generally placed about the year 1520. He may have been educated at the school (the John Knox Memorial Institute is the successor of the old school) at **Haddington** (VII, F3, on the A1 and about fifteen miles east of Edinburgh). Carlyle's wife was born at Haddington, and is buried in the east end of the abbey ruins near the river.

Three miles south-west of Haddington, at **Bolton** (VII, F3, the parents and brother of Robert Burns are buried in the churchyard. They lived in a lane off the Haddington-Bolton road, and a stone tablet by the roadside marks the site of the house. On the outskirts of **South Queensferry**, which is nine miles north-west of Edinburgh, and near the viaduct approach to the Forth Bridge, is the old Hawes Inn. It figures in the first chapter of *The Antiquary*, and here, in Stevenson's *Kidnapped*, the abduction of David Balfour was plotted.

EDINBURGH

The' Athens of the North', a name for **Edinburgh** (VII, E3) to which Scott and others objected, has a very distinguished connexion with literature. Drummond of Hawthornden was educated at the Old High School (now the Royal High School) when it used to be in Infirmary Street, and the exterior of the old building is still there. The University of Edinburgh possesses Drummond's library.

Allan Ramsay came to Edinburgh in 1701 as apprentice to a wig-maker. Later he opened business on his own account, and had a shop in the High Street. After a successful career as wig-maker, bookseller (he opened the first circulating library in Scotland) and poet, he retired about 1755 to an octagonally shaped house of his own design (XI, B5, called by his friends the 'Goose-pie') on the north side of Castle Rock. It survives incorporated in a group of turreted and gabled buildings in

Ramsay Lane. He died there on January 17, 1758, and is buried in the Greyfriars churchyard (XI, C6), where there is a monument to him. In the same churchyard are also buried Duncan Ban MacIntyre (the 'Burns of the Highlands'), who died in Edinburgh in October 1812, and Henry Mackenzie, author of *The Man of Feeling*.

John Gay made the acquaintance of Ramsay when on a visit to Edinburgh with his patroness the Duchess of Queensberry, and stayed in Queensberry House (now a home for aged folk) in the Canongate. On the other side of the street there used to be an alehouse where he tippled claret. James Thomson, destined for the ministry, entered Edinburgh University in 1715, but disliked the curriculum and preferred reading English poetry. He joined a literary club, and three of his poems appeared in the *Edinburgh Miscellany* in 1720. He gave up the idea of the ministry and made his way to London in 1725.

John Home, author of *Douglas*, was also destined for the ministry. Born at 29 Quality Street, Port of Leith, on September 21, 1722, he was educated at the grammar school there and passed on to Edinburgh University. He became a probationer of the kirk, then after a varied career elsewhere settled in Edinburgh in 1779. He died at Merchiston on September 5, 1808, and is buried in the churchyard at Leith. Yet another aspirant for the ministry was Mark Akenside, who entered Edinburgh University in 1739, but after a few months decided to take up medicine. A brilliant student, he was elected a member of the Medical Society when only nineteen. Already a poet before he came to Edinburgh, he published privately two poems before he left in 1741. Oliver Goldsmith began studying medicine at the University in 1752, and between lectures characteristically indulged in a great deal of conviviality. He joined a students' association called the Medical Society, sang Irish songs to them and often lost his money at play. After a year he decided to complete his medical studies on the Continent.

Goldsmith's friend of later days, James Boswell, was born in Edinburgh on October 18, 1740, but exactly whereabouts is unknown. After his first schooling he attended the Old High School in Infirmary Street, and then proceeded to the University. Then he studied civil law at Glasgow, was taken to London by his father, and returned to law studies at Edinburgh. He chafed, and longed for the gaieties of London without neglecting the gaieties of Edinburgh; published some worthless pieces of prose and verse, and having a keen desire to meet Samuel Johnson, persuaded his father to allow him to return to London in 1762. Thereafter for many years his life was divided between London, the Continent and Edinburgh. In 1772 he took over the flat off Lawnmarket (XI, C5), in James's Court—it is still there, in the east corner—vacated by David Hume. Here, in the following year, Boswell and his wife entertained Johnson at the beginning of their tour to the Hebrides. Johnson at first put up at Boyd's Inn (no longer there) in the Canongate, and then stayed some days with the Boswells. The brilliant men of Edinburgh came to see Johnson, and some of the intellectual exchanges are preserved in Boswell's *Tour to the Hebrides*. Mrs Boswell, though polite to Johnson, did not care for him, and when Boswell and Johnson set out on their tour she said that though she had often seen 'a bear led by a man, she had never before seen a man led by a bear'. Boswell gave up his flat probably in 1782, when on his father's death he inherited the property of Auchinleck.

Smollett, whose cousin (as we shall mention in due course) was visited by Johnson, was in Edinburgh in 1766, a famous man courted by the brilliant men of the city. Later, in *Humphry Clinker*, he characterized Edinburgh as a hotbed of genius. He stayed with his sister in a house over the archway leading to St John Street off Canongate. Its façade has survived.

The brief life of Robert Fergusson was mostly spent in Edinburgh. The son of a clerk to a haberdasher, he was born on September 15, 1750, in a lane that long ago was covered over by North Bridge Street. He went from a local school to St Andrews University with the object of studying for the church, but turned instead to medicine, and became known as a poet. On returning to his native city he became a copying clerk in the commissary clerk's office. He wrote poems for a magazine, became famous and was hailed as the successor to Allan Ramsay. A fall down stairs brought on an illness that resulted in insanity, and he was confined in an asylum where he died on October 16, 1774. He was buried in the Canongate churchyard (XI, D4).

Burns, on his first visit to Edinburgh in 1786 (to arrange for a second edition of his poems) placed a gravestone, with a poetical epitaph, over

Fergusson's remains. He lodged in Lady Stair's Close and over the Lawnmarket entrance to the Close a tablet commemorates the fact, but the house has disappeared. Lady Stair's House★ here has manuscripts and other relics of Burns, as well as Scott's dining-table. After the publication of his poems, and especially after Henry Mackenzie in a review had called him a 'heaven-taught ploughman', Burns was lionized by Edinburgh society. Burns twice again visited Edinburgh during 1787-8, on the later visit staying in St James's Square. Scott, then a lad of fifteen, met him at Sciennes Hill House, No. 7 Braid Place (off Causewayside, and marked with a tablet), and it was their only meeting. Scott, alone of the company present, identified a quotation on a print that particularly interested Burns. The print is preserved at the Chambers Institution in Peebles.

In Edinburgh Burns met and became enamoured of a certain Mrs McLehose: both were married, but Burns wished to marry the lady, whom he called Clarinda; an extraordinary correspondence followed, and the affair did not end until Burns's final visit to Edinburgh in 1791, after which he sent her his lyric 'Ae fond kiss'. She survived until 1841, and is buried in Canongate churchyard. There is a monument to Burns, modelled on the temple of Lysicrates at Athens, below Calton Hill, and Flaxman's statue of him is in the National Portrait Gallery (XI, C3) in Queen Street. One of his haunts, the White Hart Inn in Grassmarket (later patronized also by Wordsworth) has survived.

The literary golden age of Edinburgh, which opened with Burns, closes with Scott. The son of a writer to the signet or solicitor (portrayed as the elder Fairford in *Redgauntlet*), Scott was born on August 15, 1771, in College Wynd, now covered over by Guthrie Street. He was educated at the Old High School at Kelso and Edinburgh University. He was apprenticed to his father, but turned to the study of civil law, and was called to the bar in 1792. Scott's home from infancy until 1797 was at 25 George Square (XI, C6); then soon after marriage he moved to 108 George Street (XI, A4) for two years, followed by three years at 10 south Castle Street (XI, A4). During 1802-26 he lived at 39 Castle Street

★ Open daily 10 a.m. to 4 p.m. (10 a.m. to 5 p.m. during the Festival), Saturday 10 a.m. to 1 p.m., closed on Sunday. The house also exhibits relics of Stevenson.

(XI, A4), where many of the Waverley Novels were written. All these houses have survived. It was at the Assembly Rooms in George Street that Scott publicly announced in 1827—what had for long been an open secret—that he was the author of the Waverley Novels.

Only one of his novels, *The Heart of Midlothian*, has much of its scene laid in Edinburgh. Near the statue of the fifth Duke of Buccleugh in High Street there is a heart-shaped design and a line of white 'setts' that mark the site of the Old Tolbooth or prison which was 'The Heart of Midlothian'. The doorways and keys of the Old Tolbooth are preserved at Abbotsford. Another Edinburgh connexion with the novels is that of Heriot's Hospital in Lauriston Place, which was founded by George Heriot, the jeweller depicted as Jingling Geordie in *The Fortunes of Nigel*. The Scott Monument* in Princes Street (XI, C4) depicts him with his dog Maida, and in the niches are characters from his works.

Scott, when he was a principal clerk of the session, had as one of his colleagues James Ferrier, father of the novelist Susan Ferrier, who was born in Edinburgh on September 7, 1782. She lived for many years with her parents at 25 George Street, a house that has survived. She came to know Scott quite well, and visited him at Ashestiel and at Abbotsford. She died in Edinburgh on November 5, 1854, and is buried in the churchyard of St Cuthbert (XI, A5, known also as the West Kirk) behind St John's Church off Princes Street.

Also buried in the same churchyard is Thomas De Quincey, whose first acquaintance with Edinburgh was in the company of his friend John Wilson (Christopher North). In 1819 Wilson took a house at 29 Ann Street (it has survived) and lived there until he moved to 6 Gloucester Place (XI, A3, marked by a tablet), dying there on April 3, 1854, and is buried in Dean cemetery on the west side of the city. De Quincey took up lodgings at Wilson's Ann Street house in 1828, and spent most of his life there until he moved to Lasswade in 1840. At

---

* Open weekdays 10 a.m. to 7 p.m. in summer, 10 a.m. to 3 p.m. in winter. A staircase leading to the top passes a chamber containing relics of Scott. Huntly House in Canongate (open weekdays 10 a.m. to 5 p.m., and from June to September 6 a.m. to 9 p.m. on Wednesday) has Scott manuscripts and a large collection of newspaper and periodical articles on him.

Lasswade he found his younger children too disturbing, so he took lodgings at 42 Lothian Street (marked by a tablet), where he died on December 8, 1859. Charming company and a brilliant conversationalist (only a little of his conversation is recorded), De Quincey received many invitations to dinner, but because of extreme shyness he rarely honoured them.

Wilson's *Noctes Ambrosianae* appeared in the great Tory review, *Blackwood's Magazine*. The other great magazine of the period, *The Edinburgh Review*, was founded by Sydney Smith, who in 1802 suggested it during meetings at the house of Lord Jeffrey (18 Buccleugh Place, marked by a tablet). Smith had earlier connexions with Edinburgh, occasionally preaching there, and one of his residences, 46 George Street, has survived.

Shelley made a disastrous mistake when he married the unfortunate Harriet Westbrook in Edinburgh in 1811, and they lived for several weeks at 60 George Street. They returned in 1813, not long before their separation, and stayed at 36 Frederick Street. Both houses are still there, though considerably altered since their time.

At about this time the family of the young George Borrow took up quarters in the Castle—Borrow's father was a recruiting officer. Borrow was sent to the Old High School, and he has described vividly in *Lavengro* the fights between the boys of the Old Town and the New Town. From the vague chronology of the book one gathers that the Borrow family were in Edinburgh during about 1813-15.

Carlyle walked the hundred miles from his home when he entered Edinburgh University in 1809 to study for the ministry. When he left the University, Carlyle became schoolmaster, gave up the idea of the ministry, and returned to Edinburgh in 1819 and took pupils. 'Three most miserable years' followed, during which he began to suffer from the dyspepsia that troubled him throughout life. During part of this period he was lodging near Leith Walk in the Pilrig quarter. When Jane Welsh, whom he first met at her home in Haddington, visited Edinburgh, Carlyle called on her at 22 George Square. They were married in 1826, and spent the first eighteen months of marriage at 21 Comely Bank (marked by a tablet). Dickens seems an unlikely figure in Edinburgh; nevertheless he paid two visits, the first in 1834 and the second in 1841, when he received the freedom of the city and stayed at the Royal Hotel in Princes Street.

One of Edinburgh's greatest literary natives, Robert Louis Stevenson, was born at 8 Howard Place (XI, B1), now the Stevenson Memorial House,* on November 13, 1850. In 1853 his family moved to 1 Inverleith Terrace, which has not survived, and in 1857 to 17 Heriot Row (XI, A3, marked by a tablet) which remained Stevenson's home until 1879. He was first educated at a preparatory school in India Street, continuing schooling at the Edinburgh Academy in Henderson Row and at a private school in Frederick Street. In 1867 he entered Edinburgh University with the object of becoming a civil engineer—both his father and grandfather were distinguished engineers. A few years later he shocked his family by announcing that he wished to become a writer—he had been writing since childhood—but his father objected though realizing that because of frail health the lad was ill-suited for engineering. He insisted on Stevenson's taking up a regular profession, so the latter studied law, was called to the Bar but never practised. Meanwhile his first essay had been published, in the *Cornhill*, when he was twenty-two; other essays followed, but he was not making a living and was supported by his father. When he was twenty-five he met Fanny Van de Grift Osbourne in France, was determined to marry her, went to the United States a few years later with no money and few prospects, and married Mrs Osbourne after she had secured a divorce. Stevenson wandered much in search of health until finally settling in Samoa, where he died after four years on December 3, 1894.

Two literary natives of Edinburgh, Kenneth Grahame and Conan Doyle, were born in the same year. Grahame, a descendant of Robert Bruce and the son of an advocate, was born at 30 Castle Street (opposite the house so long occupied by Scott) on March 8, 1859. Early in life he passed out of Edinburgh and spent the rest of his days in England. Arthur Conan Doyle was born at 11 Picardy Place (the house has survived), between York Place and Leith Walk, on May 22, 1859. His grandfather was John Doyle the portrait painter and caricaturist,

* Open weekdays 10 a.m. to 5 p.m. (10 a.m. to 4 p.m. in winter), Saturday 10 a.m. to 1 p.m. Contains letters, manuscripts and personal relics.

and John Doyle the *Punch* artist was his uncle. He was educated at Stonyhurst College and then qualified as a doctor at Edinburgh University. Dr Joseph Bell, under whom he studied, was the prototype for Sherlock Holmes.

James Barrie entered Edinburgh University in 1878, graduated M.A. in 1882, and was a contemporary of Doyle. When a student he lodged at 3 Great King Street, and his landlady is supposed to be the prototype for *The Old Lady Shows her Medals*. He spent about three years in journalism in Edinburgh, then in 1885 decided to settle in London. The University has a Memorial Hall to him in Marshall Street. One of the greatest of English critics, George Saintsbury, was Professor of Rhetoric and English Literature at Edinburgh University from 1895 until 1915. He resided first at Murrayfield House, and from 1900 until retirement, at 2 Eton Terrace.

Before leaving Edinburgh we must mention the National Library of Scotland* (near Parliament House, but in George IV Bridge), which has letters of Burns, Boswell, Scott, Carlyle and Stevenson, and manuscripts of Scott and Carlyle.

SOUTH-WEST

This area includes the Burns country, which comprises much of Ayrshire and Dumfriesshire. In June 1789 Burns took a farm at **Ellisland** (VII, D5) on the south bank of the Nith, six miles north of Dumfries, and did not prosper. He then became an exciseman, leaving the running of the farm to his wife and sisters. The farm and farmhouse (the latter has been enlarged since Burns's time) were presented to Dumfries as a national possession. Burns's room is shown to visitors at reasonable times, and the stackyard where 'Mary in Heaven' was composed and the so-called 'Tam o' Shanter' walk (that great poem was written during this period) may be viewed.

In 1791 Burns gave up Ellisland, obtained the office of exciseman in **Dumfries** (VII, D6), and settled in Wee Vennel (now Bank Street), but his house has disappeared. Later he moved to Mill Vennel (now Burns

* Open weekdays 9.30 a.m. to 4.30 p.m., Saturday 9.30 a.m. to 12.30 p.m.; additional hours on Thursday 5.30 to 8.30 p.m.; closed last week of July and first week of August.

Street) and his home there is preserved as Burns's House.* He died of rheumatic fever in the upper room of this house in July 21, 1796, and was buried in the churchyard of St Michael, but in 1815 his remains were transferred to the mausoleum called Burns's Tomb,† where his wife and several of his children are also buried. Wordsworth, during his first Scottish tour of 1803, visited the tomb in the churchyard, and in his poem 'At the Grave of Burns' refers to its being 'grass-grown'. When Keats was in Dumfries in 1818 the mausoleum had been erected—'not very much to my taste' he said. Whilst here, Keats wrote the delightful 'Meg Merrilees', about the old gypsy who figures also in Scott's *Guy Mannering*, and a sonnet 'On Visiting the Tomb of Burns'.

Two old taverns in Dumfries which were haunts of Burns, the Globe in High Street and the Hole in the Wa' in Queensferry Square, exhibit personal relics of the poet. In the church of St Michael a tablet on a pillar near the entrance marks his pew. The Dumfries Burgh Museum‡ (The Observatory, Corberry Hill) on the Maxwelltown side, has some Burns manuscripts and relics as well as manuscripts of Barrie, whose family settled here in 1873. Barrie was at school at Dumfries Academy, off Academy Street and overlooking the river, though the present buildings were erected after his time.

One of the most notable appreciations of Burns was written by Carlyle, a native of **Ecclefechan** (VII, E6) in Annandale (on the A74 about ten miles east of Dumfries). The son of a mason, Thomas Carlyle was born on December 4, 1795, in a house built by his father, now called the Arched House.§ After receiving the first rudiments of learning from his parents, he was sent in 1805 to the grammar school at Annan (the Public Library there preserves some relics of

---

* Open weekdays 10 a.m. to 5 or 9 p.m. according to the season, and 2 to 4.30 p.m. on Sunday. Contains manuscripts, personal relics, and manuscripts and books presented by Barrie.

† Open daily in summer.

‡ Open April to September on weekdays (except Tuesday) 10 a.m. to 1 p.m., 2 to 7 p.m., Sunday 2 to 6 p.m.; October to March on weekdays only 10 a.m. to 1 p.m., 2 to 5 p.m.

§ Open weekdays 10 a.m. to 8 p.m. or sunset. Contains letters and personal relics.

Carlyle). From Annan he proceeded to Edinburgh University, and returned to Annan with a mathematical tutorship in 1814. He left in 1816. Some of his experiences at the grammar school are related in *Sartor Resartus*, in which work Ecclefechan appears as 'Entephfuhl'. Carlyle is buried beside his parents in the churchyard at Ecclefechan. Not far away, at **Craigenputtock** (VII, D5), about twelve miles north-west of Dumfries, is the farm situated in moorland where *Sartor Resartus* was written. The farm was inherited by Jane Welsh Carlyle; there she and her husband lived during the years 1828-34, and Emerson was among their visitors. Carlyle bequeathed the property to Edinburgh University to found scholarships.

Moffat (VII, E5 on the A701 about twenty miles north-east of Dumfries) was in the eighteenth century to Scotland what Bath was to England, and among its literary visitors were Boswell and Burns. In its High Street is Moffat House, now an hotel and formerly the mansion where James Macpherson was a tutor in 1759. Three miles north-east of Moffat (on the A708) is Burns's Cottage, not itself connected with the poet, but standing on the site of an inn where he wrote 'O Willie brewed a peck o' maut'. A mile nearer Moffat and on the same road is Craigieburn House (it cannot be seen from the road), the birthplace of Jean Lorimer, a farmer's daughter celebrated by Burns as 'Chloris'. Seven miles north-east of Moffat there is the great waterfall known as the Grey Mare's Tail, to which Scott refers in *Marmion* as 'white as the snowy charger's tail'.

There are other associations with Scott in this area. At **Irongray** (VII, D6, on the B729 five miles north-west of Dumfries) there is a stone erected by Scott in the churchyard to the memory of Helen Walker, on whom he based the character of Jeanie Deans in *The Heart of Midlothian*. Another five miles or so farther north-west, just over a mile north of **Dunscore**, is the ruined tower of Lag, all that remains of the mansion of Sir Robert Grierson, the persecutor of Covenanters whom Scott depicted as Sir Robert Redgauntlet. A very different character, and one who honoured the memory of Covenanters, was Robert Paterson, whose remains lie in the churchyard at **Caerlaverock** (VII, E6), about six miles south-east of Dumfries. He was the 'Old Mortality' whom Scott met once and whom he depicted in the novel of that name. A humble stonecutter, 'Old Mortality' travelled through Scotland repairing the graves of Covenanters.

Another two miles southwards there are the ruins of Caerlaverock Castle, the 'Ellangowan' of *Guy Mannering*. The novel is set in the district of Galloway, which covers both Kirkcudbrightshire and Wigtownshire. Creetown, at the head of Wigtown Bay, is claimed as the 'Portanferry' of the novel, but Glencaple (near Dumfries) also makes the same claim. Another novelist, S. R. Crockett, used the mountainous part of Galloway for the setting of *The Raiders*, and Hestan Island in Auchencairn Bay is the 'Isle Rathan' of the novel. Crockett was born at **Little Duchrae**, about twelve miles north-west of Kirkcudbright, on September 24, 1860. He became a minister of the Free Church, wrote successful novels and resigned from the ministry so as to devote himself to writing. He died at Avignon on April 21, 1914, and is buried at **Balmaghie**, about ten miles north of Kirkcudbright.

Borgue (VII, C6), about five miles south-west of Kirkcudbright, is the birthplace of William Nicholson, the Galloway Poet. Born in August 1782 or 1783, he was by turns pedlar, piper and drover, and peddled his own poetry. His best work, the ballad 'Brownie of Blednoch', is so good that it is difficult to understand why it has been almost completely forgotten except in Galloway. Nicholson died at Borgue on May 16, 1849, and is buried in the churchyard of Kirkandrews near by. There is a memorial to him in Borgue. The village is the scene of Stevenson's *The Master of Ballantrae*, and not Ballantrae on the Ayrshire coast, as is often assumed. Stevenson did visit Ballantrae in 1876, and tells us that he was stoned by some of the inhabitants because of the eccentricity of his dress.

Proceeding westwards, about two miles south of **Wigtown** (VII, C6) there are the ruins of Baldoon Castle, the home of David Dunbar, original of the bridegroom (Frank Hayston) in *The Bride of Lammermoor* whose life was attempted by his wife on the bridal night. Farther west, and about three miles north-west of **Glenluce** (VII, B6), are the ruins of Carscreugh Castle, the seat of the Lord Stair whose daughter was the original of *The Bride of Lammermoor*.

After leaving Dumfries, Keats and his friend Charles Brown proceeded to Ireland, but whilst there abandoned their original idea of a trip to the Giant's Causeway and returned to Ayrshire to explore further the Burns country. Keats had seen Ailsa Craig off the Ayrshire coast, and the 'craggy ocean pyramid' inspired a sonnet in which that phrase occurs. He also wrote a sonnet in Burns's birthplace, which is at **Alloway** (VII, C4, a mile and a half south-west of Ayr, and off the A77). The son of a farmer, Burns was born on January 25, 1759, in a small cottage built by his father and which has been preserved as Burns's Cottage.* He was baptized in the Auld Kirk, beside the river, in **Ayr** (VII, C4).

We have to jump chronology to mention two interesting connexions of Burns's poems with Ayr. Beyond the Aulk Kirk and a little lower down the river is the Auld Brig, which in the poem 'The Brigs of Ayr' prophesies that the New Bridge which stood another hundred yards lower down would not survive long, and the prophecy came true in 1877 when the present structure was built to replace it. The Tam o' Shanter Inn† (now a museum) in High Street is generally considered the starting-point of Tam's terrifying ride; and it was through the east window of the Auld Kirk at Alloway that Tam witnessed the 'warlocks and witches in a dance'. Tam fled over the Auld Brig o' Don, the single-arched bridge near the Burns Monument at Alloway, and ended his ride at Kirkoswald (see p. 285).

When Burns was about six his family moved to a farm called Mount Oliphant, just over a mile to the south-east of Alloway; by the time he was fifteen he was his father's chief labourer, and at sixteen wrote his first poem. In 1777 there was another move, to the farm of **Lochlea** (VII, C4), which is still in existence, near **Tarbolton** (VII, C4, west of the A75). At Tarbolton Burns helped to found in 1780 the Bachelors' Club,‡ which has been preserved under that name by the National

---

* Open daily 9 a.m. to 7 p.m. (9 a.m. to 5 p.m. November to March) and from 2 p.m. on Sunday. The same hours apply to the adjoining Burns Museum, which contains many manuscript poems and letters, the family Bible and other relics. Half a mile south of Alloway is the ruined old Alloway Kirk, and Burns's parents are buried in its churchyard. A little further on is the Burns Monument, open daily, Sunday opening at 2 p.m.

† Open daily at reasonable hours. Contains personal relics.

‡ A notice on the house gives directions for obtaining entry. Contains facsimiles of letters and poems.

Trust. In the following year he became a freemason, and the Masonic Club at Tarbolton has memorials of him in their Hall. A little to the east of the village is a mill generally regarded as the 'Willie's Mill' of 'Death and Dr Hornbook'.

Montgomerie Castle (known in Burns's day as Coilsfield House), stands half a mile south-west of Tarbolton, and is the 'Castle o' Montgomery' where Burns's Mary Campbell ('Highland Mary') was a servant. She died six months after betrothal to Burns. A monument (on the A758) near the junction of the Fail and Ayr rivers and a short distance south of Tarbolton, marks their last parting. However, some authorities think that the parting occurred higher up the Ayr, where it is joined by the Mauchline Burn.

Irvine (VII, C4), about twelve miles north of Ayr, was where Burns went to learn flax-dressing during the years 1781-3, but New Year festivities resulted in a fire that destroyed the shop and his prospects in that direction. The house in which he lodged in Glasgow Vennel has survived and is marked with a tablet. Irvine was the birthplace of James Montgomery, born on November 4, 1771, the son of the pastor of the Moravian congregation there, and remembered now for his hymns. John Galt the novelist was also born in Irvine, on May 2, 1779, the son of a commander of a West Indiaman.

After his father's death in 1784 Burns and his brother gathered what assets they could from the unsuccessful farm at Lochlea and started a farm at **Mossgiel** (VII, C4) near Mauchline and about a mile south of Lochlea. The farm has survived, but the farmhouse has been almost entirely rebuilt. Most of the poetry of Burns's first publication was written here, and it was here that he ploughed up the mouse and the mountain daisy, incidents that evoked two of his greatest poems. At **Mauchline** (VII, C4, on the A76), he fell in love with Jean Armour, and after many troubles married her in his friend Gavin Hamilton's house, which is situated between the churchyard and the tower called the Castle. A plan inside the churchyard gate gives the positions of the graves of four of Burns's children and of his contemporaries, some of whom figure in the poem 'The Holy Fair', which has its setting in the churchyard. In the old church here (the present building dates from 1829) Burns and Jean Armour proclaimed their marriage two days after the ceremony in Gavin Hamilton's house, and were reprimanded for their past behaviour. In Loudoun Street, and opposite the churchyard gate, a certain 'Poosie Nansie' (whose real name was Ann Gibson) had her cottage, and there Burns set the scene of 'The Jolly Beggars'.

About half a mile north of Mauchline there is the Burns Memorial,* a red tower that houses a Burns museum. At the village of **Catrine**, about two miles east of Mauchline, Catrine House still stands where Burns 'dinner'd wi' a Lord', just before he set out for his first visit to Edinburgh, as he records in the 'Lines on Meeting with Lord Daer'.

As already mentioned, Tam o' Shanter's ride began at Ayr and ended at **Kirkoswald** (VII, B5, on the A77 about ten miles south-west of Ayr). Tam was modelled on Douglas Graham, and Tam's 'ancient, drouthy cronie', on John Davidson. Both are buried in the churchyard at Kirkoswald, and Souter Johnnie's House† there has been preserved.

Our final association with Burns in Ayrshire is at **Kilmarnock** (VII, C4, on the A77 and about twelve miles north-east of Ayr). The first edition of his poems was printed at Kilmarnock in 1786 after Jean Armour's father had refused to recognize her union with Burns and the latter was thinking of emigrating. The Angel Hotel (disguised as 'Begbie's') and the Laigh Kirk in Kilmarnock are introduced into the satiric poem 'The Ordination'; and in the churchyard of the Kirk is Burns's epitaph on Tam Samson. There is a Burns Monument and Museum‡ in Kay Park in the form of a temple with a tall tower. Kilmarnock claims one literary native of note, Alexander Smith, who was born on December 31, 1830. Poet and essayist, he is remembered—unhappily by only a few—for the charming volume of essays entitled *Dreamthorp*. His veneration for Burns resulted in a notable edition of the latter's poetry.

Burns is the dominating literary figure in Ayrshire, but the county has important connexions with other men of letters. George Douglas Brown, the son of a farmer, was born at **Ochiltree** (VII, C4, on the A70, ten miles east of Ayr) on January 26, 1869. Disgusted by the novelists

* Open daily at reasonable hours.
† Open April 1 to September 30, daily 2.30 p.m. to dusk.
‡ Open daily mid-April to mid-September 12.30 to 4 p.m., 5 to 9 p.m.; mid-September to mid-April 10 a.m. to 12 noon, 1 to 5 p.m. Contains books, manuscripts, relics and the McKie collection of Burnsiana.

(collectively known as the Kailyard School) who idealized Scottish rural life, he wrote a powerful counterblast in *The House with the Green Shutters*, in which Ochiltree appears as 'Barbie'. Brown died in London in 1902, and is buried in his mother's grave in the cemetery at Ayr.

Auchinleck House, three miles west of the village of **Auchinleck** (VII, C4, on the A76) brings us back to Boswell and Johnson. They called here in 1773 near the end of their tour, and Boswell's father, Lord Auchinleck, and Johnson were soon engaged in heated argument, but unfortunately Boswell declined to exhibit them as 'intellectual gladiators for the entertainment of the public'. Johnson was 'less delighted with the elegance of the modern mansion than with the sullen dignity of the old castle' beside it. Boswell lived at Auchinleck House in early life and inherited it on his father's death in 1782, and occupied it for several years of his married life until his wife's death. He is buried in the village church.

On their way down from Glasgow to Auchinleck, Boswell and Johnson had called at Loudon and Eglinton Castles and visited the ruins of Dundonald Castle. The last had been a residence of Scottish kings, among them Robert II, and Johnson was 'very jocular on the homely accommodation of "King *Bob*", and roared and laughed till the ruins echoed'. Our last locality in Ayrshire is the little town of **Beith** (VII, C3, off the A737 and about twelve miles south-west of Glasgow). Two miles east of it lies the old mansion of Hessilhead, where Alexander Montgomerie, author of 'The Cherrie and the Slae', was probably born about 1556.

Leadhills (VII, D5), about twenty miles south of Lanark, in the neighbouring county of Lanarkshire, was where Allan Ramsay was born on October 15, 1686. His father was manager of Lord Hopetoun's lead-mines in Crawford Moor, and died when his son was an infant. Ramsay was educated at Crawford near by, and in 1701 was sent to Edinburgh to learn wig-making. At **Biggar**, about eight miles south-east of Lanark, Dr John Brown, the son of a noted biblical scholar, was born on September 22, 1810.

A mile or so to the south of Lanark are the famous Falls of Clyde, visited by William and Dorothy Wordsworth and Coleridge in 1803. Coleridge was searching for the appropriate epithet for the falls, and decided on 'majestic'. Two other tourists, a lady and a gentleman, were present, and the latter said to Coleridge: 'It is a majestic fall, sir.' Coleridge agreed. 'Majestic, sublime and beautiful,' continued the gentleman. 'Very pretty indeed,' said the lady—and Coleridge was rendered explosively speechless. The ruins of Cora Castle, standing on the cliff edge nearest the finest of the falls, are mentioned as the 'time-cemented tower' in Wordsworth's poem on the falls.

From **Lesmahagow**, about five miles south-west of Lanark, Smollett derived the name of that extraordinary character Captain Lismahago in *Humphry Clinker*. On the north side of **New Lanark** (VII, D4) there is the mansion of Lord Braxfield, the 'hanging judge' depicted by Stevenson in his finest, though unfortunately unfinished novel *Weir of Hermiston*. Craignethan Castle, near **Crossford** (on the A72 and about four miles north-west of Lanark) is generally regarded as the 'Tillietudlem Castle' of *Old Mortality*. About eight miles north-west of Lanark, at **Cambusnethan**, J. G. Lockhart, who became the son-in-law and biographer of Scott, was born at the manse on July 14, 1794.

And so on to **Glasgow** (VII, C3) and places near it. Pepys, who spent a week touring Scotland when he accompanied the Duke of York (later James II) on a visit in 1682, described Glasgow as 'a very extraordinary town indeed for beauty and trade, much superior to any in Scotland'.

In the High Street (on the east side of the city, with which we deal first) is the site, now covered by a goods station, of Glasgow University, which stood there for four hundred years before moving to new buildings in 1870 on Gilmorehill. There have been some notable men of letters at the University. The first, Robert Henryson, became a member in 1462, very soon after its foundation. Smollett was sent there in 1736 to study medicine, displayed youthful high spirits and a taste for literature, which found expression in satire upon Glasgow writers and the composition of a very bad tragedy called *The Regicide*. After three years he decided to seek his fortune in London. He revisited Glasgow in 1766, and he and his mother stayed with a Dr Moore, and saw the doctor's little son who forty years later became the hero of Corunna.

In 1759 Boswell became a student and attended Adam Smith's

lectures. He was converted to Roman Catholicism and thought of entering the priesthood, which so upset his father that he gave up the idea on condition that he be allowed to give up law to enter the Army. Boswell studied for only a few months, but revisited Glasgow when on tour with Johnson. They stayed at the Saracen's Head, the site of which is now covered by 203 Gallowgate. They met the professors of the University, who, said Boswell, 'did not venture to expose themselves much to the battery of cannon which they knew might play upon them'.

Thomas Campbell, who was born in High Street (at its junction with Balmanno Street—the house has long since disappeared) on July 27, 1777, was educated at Glasgow Grammar School and the University, which he entered in 1791 to prepare for the Church. In his fourth year his father, a trader with Virginia, lost much money, and Campbell took up tutoring, but returned later to his studies. He took up law and migrated to Edinburgh University in 1796. John Wilson (Christopher North) who entered in 1797, distinguished himself as a student and even more as an athlete. 'I consider Glasgow as my mother,' he said. In 1803 he proceeded to Oxford.

William Motherwell, a lyric poet little read now, was born on October 13, 1797, at 117 High Street. After schooling at Edinburgh and Paisley, he studied classics for a year at Glasgow University, and then found employment at Paisley. He returned to Glasgow in 1830 when he became editor of the Glasgow Courier, and died in the city on November 1, 1835. John Buchan, who was educated at Hutcheson's Boys' Grammar School, attended lectures at the University and in 1895 was awarded a scholarship at Brasenose College, Oxford.

Scott laid some of the scene of Rob Roy in Glasgow. At the southern end of High Street is 'the Cross', a relic of the Old Tolbooth (prison) described in the novel. In the crypt of the cathedral is 'Rob Roy's Pillar', behind which the outlaw stood when whispering his warning to Francis Osbaldistone; and the duel between Francis and Rashleigh Osbaldistone took place in the grounds behind where the University used to stand. At 34 Ken Street (marked by a tablet), off Gallowgate, Edward Irving lived, and there he was visited by his friend Carlyle.

No. 79 Renfield Street, off St Vincent Street, on the west side of

Glasgow, has a tablet recording the fact that De Quincey lodged there during his visit of 1846-7. He had previously stayed for two years in the city with friends. Bret Harte, who was American consul in Glasgow during 1880-5, lived at 35 Burnbank Gardens, which lies off Western Street. Sir James Barrie, when a small boy, attended Glasgow Academy, which stands beside the River Kelvin and off Western Road, and lived at 5 Burnbank Terrace near by. On the south side of Glasgow, in the Gorbals district, there is a rose-garden covering the site of a cemetery in which John Wilson, Burns's 'Dr Hornbook', was buried. Wilson, a notorious apothecary who was obliged to leave Ayrshire, is satirized in 'Death and Dr Hornbook'.

At **Barrhead**, about six miles south-west of Glasgow, the poet John Davidson, son of a minister of the Evangelical Union, was born on April 11, 1857. At **Paisley** (VII, C3), about six miles west of Glasgow, Robert Tannahill was born on June 3, 1774, at 8 Castle Street, and his birthplace has survived. After schooling he was apprenticed to his father, a weaver, and after apprenticeship found employment elsewhere, but returned to Paisley on his father's death. Most of his poems were written in a thatched cottage still to be seen in Queen Street. Latterly given to melancholia, he drowned himself at Paisley on May 17, 1810. A monument marks his grave in the West Relief Cemetery, and there is another monument in the grounds of the Abbey. The Museum* in High Street has relics of the poet. Another native of Paisley is John Wilson (Christopher North), born at 63 High Street—the house has been rebuilt—on May 18, 1785, the son of a manufacturer of gauze. He was educated at the local grammar school and the manse of Mearns before proceeding to Glasgow University.

At **Greenock** (VII, B3) on the Clyde, some fifteen miles north-west of Glasgow, the grave of Burns's 'Highland Mary' is to be found in the cemetery at the top of Nicolson Street, transferred thither from the graveyard of the Old West Kirk, which in 1920 was re-erected on the Esplanade. And in Greenock, John Galt—whose best novels, *The Ayrshire Legatees* and *The Entail*, deserve a far wider public—died on April 11, 1839, in West Burn Street, where he had lived with his sister for

* Open weekdays 10 a.m. to 5 p.m., Tuesday and Saturday 10 a.m. to 8 p.m.

five years. The house is marked with a tablet. He is buried in the old cemetery in Inverkip Street, which continues on from West Burn Street.

The island of Arran, in the Firth of Clyde, provides some of the scene of Scott's *Lord of the Isles*; and Goatfell, on its western side, is depicted as 'Ben Ghoil, the Mountain of the Wind'. On Castle Hill at **Cardross**, three miles west of Dumbarton, there is a cairn with a medallion portrait of R. B. Cunninghame Graham, who for some time lived at **Ardoch** near by.

On the A812 and situated three miles north of Dumbarton, there is the town of **Renton** (VII, C3) in the valley of the Leven. Half a mile south of it there once existed the old grange of Dalquharn, in which Tobias George Smollett was born in March 1721. He was educated in Dumbarton before being sent to Glasgow University. When famous he revisited the scenes of his childhood, and stayed with his cousin James Smollett at **Bonhill**, the ancestral home of the family, just a few miles from Renton on the other side of the river. Two years after Smollett's death Johnson and Boswell called on James Smollett, who was preparing to erect at Renton a Tuscan column to commemorate his cousin. A long Latin inscription, already composed, was being discussed. Someone suggested that it should be in English, but Johnson said that 'an English inscription would be a disgrace to Dr Smollett'—he made a similar remark later in connexion with Goldsmith's epitaph. So the Latin inscription stands, and includes Johnson's revisions.

Knockderry Castle, near **Cove** (VII, B3) and on the tongue of land between Loch Long and Gareloch, takes us back to Scott, who uses it as 'Knock Dunder' at the end of *The Heart of Midlothian*. Not far away, at **Dunoon** on the Firth of Clyde, there is a statue of Burns's 'Highland Mary', who was born at the farm of Auchnamore, a mile from the town.

Loch Lomond (VII, C2) has been visited and praised by many men of letters: Smollett, uttering his opinion through a character in *Humphry Clinker*, preferred it to anything in Italy; Johnson and Boswell went boating on it; Scott in *Rob Roy* considered it one of the most 'sublime spectacles in Nature'; Keats found the northern end 'grand in excess'; and there is much other praise, but Wordsworth raised a dissentient voice, finding that 'the proportion of diffused water is too great'—*this* from the poet of Nature. We are now encroaching on the *Rob Roy* country, reserved for our section on the north-west of Scotland.

NORTH-EAST

At **Falkirk** (VII, D3, on the A9 about ten miles south-east of Stirling) there is the Cross Keys Inn where Burns stayed when on his tour of the eastern Highlands in 1787. On that tour he stayed too at what is now the Golden Lion Hotel in **Stirling** (VII, D2). The magnificent Argyll's Lodging here in Castle Wynd was built in 1632 by the poet Sir William Alexander, Earl of Stirling. After a busy life of royal and political service, including administration in Nova Scotia and Canada, he died insolvent in London on September 12, 1640, and was buried in Stirling in a church which has disappeared. **Dunfermline** (VII, E2), about twenty miles east of Stirling, is considered by some authorities to be the native town of Robert Henryson (or Henderson), the first genuine lyrist among the poets of Scotland. He was born not later than 1430, and was probably a clerical schoolmaster at Dunfermline Abbey.

At **Kirkcaldy** (VII, E2) on the Firth of Forth and about ten miles east of Dunfermline, Adam Smith was born on June 5, 1723, in the High Street, and the house is marked with a tablet. He retired to his native town in 1767, and there wrote *The Wealth of Nations* and thus founded what Carlyle called 'the dismal science' of political economy. Carlyle himself was a schoolmaster at the burgh school here during 1816-19, and formed a lasting friendship with Edward Irving, who had preceded him at the school. But Carlyle was ill-fitted for and disliked teaching: 'it were better to perish than continue schoolmastering', he said. His lodging in Kirk Wynd is marked with a tablet. That charming child prodigy Margaret Fleming, known as Pet Marjorie, whom Scott knew and played with, was born in the High Street, and is buried in Abbotshall cemetery. Dr John Brown wrote a charming essay on her which is included in his *Horae Subsecivae*.

Farther north-eastwards on the Firth of Forth we find the town of **Largo** (VII, F2), where was born Alexander Selkirk (1676-1721), the shoemaker's son who ran away to sea and is famous as the prototype of

Robinson Crusoe. There is no evidence, however, that Defoe knew him personally. A statue of Selkirk stands near the harbour.

About eight miles north-east of Dunfermline (off the A909) there is the house called Blairadam which was visited by Scott, who describes its grounds in *The Abbot*. That novel takes us to Lochleven Castle near by, on an island in **Loch Leven**, where Mary Queen of Scots was imprisoned, and the episode forms a large part of *The Abbot*. The poet and prelate Gavin Douglas was imprisoned in the now ruined Castle at **St Andrews** (VII, F2) on the Fife coast during 1515-16 for receiving bulls from the pope. He is remarkable as being the first translator of a classical work (Virgil's *Aeneid*) into English. Andrew Lang is buried in the East Cemetery of St Andrews.

The hero of *Waverley* was imprisoned at Doune Castle (on the A84 about six miles north-west of Stirling); so in actuality was John Home, author of *Douglas*, who was captured at the battle of Falkirk by the Young Pretender's forces, but managed to escape by twisting bed-clothes into a rope. At Cambusmore, a house beside the River Teith between **Doune** and **Callander**, Scott stayed on some occasions when seeking local colour for *The Lady of the Lake*.

Perth (VII, E1), at the head of the Firth of Tay, is of course associated with *The Fair Maid of Perth*. The great judicial combat described with Scott's characteristic gusto took place in the North Inch, the park beyond Perth Bridge; the ordeal of 'bier-right' was laid in St John's Church, which is near the river between High Street and South Street; and in Curfew Road stands the Fair Maid's House.* Falkland Palace, which is not far away (it is about ten miles north of Kirkcaldy) also figures in the novel, but it is the earlier palace on this site that belongs to the period of the story.

Ruskin spent a little of his early boyhood, during one of the annual tours with his parents, in **Bridgend**, on the east bank of the Tay opposite Perth Bridge. The house, in Main Street, is marked by a tablet. About half a mile away (on the Bowerswell Road) is the large house called Bowerswell, now an old people's home, in which Ruskin was married to Effie Gray, whose parents lived at Perth and were old friends of his family. John Buchan, the son of a minister of

* The upper rooms are open to the public daily, 9 a.m. till dusk.

the Free Church of Scotland, was born in Perth on August 26, 1875. William Soutar, a vernacular poet of our day, was born in Perth on April 28, 1898, and died there in Wilson Street (the house has a tablet) on October 15, 1943.

Crieff (VII, D1), eighteen miles west of Perth, was the birthplace, about 1705, of the minor poet and critic David Mallet, whose real name was Malloch. Most of his adult life was spent in London, and he is remembered now for his base ingratitude to his friend and patron Pope. Dr Johnson said of him that 'he was the only Scot whom Scotchmen did not commend'. On the A822 between **Crieff** and **Amulree** there is the Sma' Glen, and near its northern end a large flat stone indicates the traditional resting-place of the remains of Ossian, the semi-legendary bard who is claimed both by Scotland and Ireland.

> *In this still place, remote from men*
> *Sleeps Ossian, in the Narrow Glen,*

wrote Wordsworth after his visit of 1803. James Macpherson published what he claimed were translations of Ossian's poems, and in the famous Ossianic controversy that ensued, Dr Johnson stated forcibly that Macpherson was an impostor. Macpherson issued a challenge; Johnson bought a stout oak stick, and in a famous letter said that he would not desist from detecting what he thought was a cheat through any fear of the menaces of a ruffian. Macpherson never produced the originals that Johnson and other enemies claimed should have been produced—if they existed.

North-eastwards from the Sma' Glen there is **Dunkeld**, where Gavin Douglas was appointed bishop in 1516, but he lived in very troubled times and was soon deprived. His last years were spent in London, where he died. The A9 from Dunkeld leads to **Blair Atholl** (VIII, E6), about three miles west of which are the Falls of Bruar visited by Burns in 1787. His poem 'The Humble Petition of Bruar Water', addressed to the fourth Duke of Atholl, resulted in the planting of the fir plantations we see there. At **Dundee** (VII, F1) can be seen the grave and monument, in the Western Cemetery, of William Thom the weaver poet. His life was chiefly one of poverty, and he lived in many places, settling finally in Dundee, where he died on February 29, 1848.

At **Dunsinane**, about ten miles north-east of Perth, there are the remains of an ancient fort which may be the relic of the castle of the historical Macbeth. **Glamis Castle★** (VII, F1) is situated a mile north of the village of **Glamis** (which lies on the A94). Macbeth, who lived in the eleventh century, was Thane of Glamis, and Glamis Castle is one of three places claimed by tradition as the scene of Duncan's murder. What survives of the medieval castle within the striking cluster of seventeenth-century turrets, battlements and roofs is, however, later than Macbeth's time. Thomas Gray stayed at the castle in 1765 as the guest of the Earl of Strathmore, whom he had known at Cambridge, and gives a description of the grounds in one of his letters. The poet Beattie, who was Professor of Moral Philosophy at Marischal College, Aberdeen, called on Gray, and after his visit the college offered Gray the honorary degree of Doctor of Laws, but he declined the honour.

About ten miles to the west, and near **Blairgowrie**, is the spectacular and beautiful Gorge of the Ericht. Situated high up on its red sandstone cliffs is the mansion of Craighall Rattray, which is one of the claimants as the original of 'Tullyveolan' in *Waverley*. Another claimant, Grandtully Castle, is not far away, situated near the River Tay about three miles north-east of **Aberfeldy**. A few miles farther north-eastwards, and less than a mile north of Pitlochry, is the village of **Moulin** (VII, E1), a mile beyond which there is Kinnaird Cottage, where Stevenson stayed for two months in 1881. Whilst here he wrote, among other stories, 'Thrawn Janet' and 'The Merry Men'.

'I should scarcely have regretted my journey,' said Dr Johnson, 'had it afforded nothing more than the sight of Abarbrothick,' as **Arbroath** (on the Angus coast) was then called. The town is the 'Fairport' of Scott's *Antiquary*. **Kirriemuir** (VII, F1, on the A926, and six miles north-west of Forfar) is the birthplace of Sir James Barrie. The son of a weaver, he was born on May 9, 1860, at 9 The Tenements, Brechin Road.★ He died in London, and was buried in Kirriemuir Cemetery. Near **Laurencekirk** (VIII, H6), eight miles north of Montrose, James Beattie was born on October 25, 1735. His first employment was as school-

---

★ Open May to September on Wednesday and Thursday 2 to 6 p.m.; on Sunday also, at same time, from July to September.

† Open daily, admission on application. Contains Barrie mementoes.

master and parish clerk in the parish of **Fardoun** near by. The scenery of the area is reflected in his finest poem, 'The Minstrel'. Dr Johnson, who had known Beattie in London, passed through Laurencekirk on his tour.

In 1930 some letters of Johnson and Boswell, and the latter's journals, were discovered at Fettercairn House (the home of Boswell's executor Sir William Forbes) in the village of **Fettercairn**, about ten miles north-west of Montrose and five miles from Laurencekirk. At **Monboddo** (VIII, H6, off the A94 and about fifteen miles north of Montrose) Boswell and Johnson called on the eccentric Lord Monboddo who, like Johnson, kept a negro servant. Boswell considered his lordship's dwelling 'a wretched place' and 'a poor old home', but it has been enlarged and improved since then. About six miles farther north-eastwards, and just over a mile south-west of Stonehaven, is the churchyard at **Dunnottar**, where Scott in 1793 met Robert Paterson ('Old Mortality', whom we mentioned earlier) busy at his self-appointed task of restoring the graves of Covenanters.

The ancient royal burgh of **Aberdeen** (VIII, H5) has some interesting connexions with men of letters. James Beattie entered Marischal College there in 1749, graduated M.A. in 1753, returned in 1758 to become a master at the grammar school, and two years later was appointed Professor of Moral Philosophy at his old college. He died in Crown Court, on the north side of Upper Kirkgate, on August 18, 1803, and was buried in the churchyard of St Nicholas. Beattie was absent when his friends Boswell and Johnson visited Aberdeen in 1773. They stayed at the New Inn (no longer there), where Johnson had 'several platefuls of Scotch broth'. Boswell: 'You never ate it before.' Johnson: 'No, sir; but I don't care how soon I eat it again.' Johnson received the freedom of Aberdeen at an impressive ceremony at the town hall.

Byron when a boy lived for eight years in the burgh. His mother had parted from her debt-harassed husband, and in 1790 she set up house first in Queen Street and later at 64 Bond Street, but neither dwelling has survived. During 1794-8 Byron attended the grammar school, which was then in Schoolhill and is now situated in Skene Street. He was idle and pugnacious, but generous-hearted. A statue of him stands in front of the school. In a footnote in the tenth canto of *Don Juan* he says that he used to peer fearfully over the black wall of the old Bridge of

Balgownie (a little to the north of Aberdeen), for an old rhyme predicted that the bridge would fall with 'a wife's ae son and a mare's ae foal'—and he was an only son. Byron and his mother used to make excursions to the surrounding countryside. Some summer holidays were spent at a farmhouse at **Ballaterach**, about thirty-five miles west of Aberdeen, and there Byron learned to swim in 'the billows of Dee's rushing tide'. On an excursion to the Linn of Dee, about twenty miles farther west, Byron tripped on heather and an attendant saved him from falling into the torrent. Many years later, in 'The Island', he recalled 'the Highlands' swelling blue', and in a footnote adds that from this period dated his love of mountainous countries.

Half a mile north-west of **Lumphanan** (VIII, G5, on the A980 and about twenty miles west of Aberdeen) Macbeth's Cairn marks the alleged spot where Macbeth was killed by Macduff, after his last stand at the Peel Bog, which is a mile away to the south-west. However, the cairn was built long after Macbeth's time. Penetrating more deeply into the Highlands, we find at **Braemar** (VIII, F5, on the A93) the cottage in Castleton Terrace (marked with a tablet), where Stevenson stayed for some months in 1881. There one day he saw the map of an island drawn by his stepson; he filled in some imaginary names and wrote 'Treasure Island' across the top, and from these beginnings the first part of the story was written at Braemar. It was completed at Davos in Switzerland. William Thom the weaver poet, already mentioned in connexion with Dundee, lived from about 1840 until 1844 at **Inverurie** (VIII, H5, on the A96 and about fifteen miles north-west of Aberdeen). His house in North Street is marked with a tablet.

On the Aberdeenshire coast and about seven miles south of **Peterhead** stands the unoccupied **Slains Castle** (VIII, H4) where Boswell and Johnson stayed at the invitation of the Earl of Erroll, and the latter said that its situation was the noblest he had ever seen. Whilst here Johnson insisted on being rowed to the Bullers of Buchan (a little to the north of the castle), a great natural hollow in the rock popularly called 'the Pot' and by Boswell a 'monstrous cauldron'. Their next call was at **Banff** (VIII, G3), on the coast and thirty miles or so away to the north-west. They found in Low Street 'an indifferent inn' (the Black Bull, no longer in existence) where Johnson was angry because the windows had no pulleys, and he concluded that it was a defect general in Scotland. Also in Low Street there used to be a house where Byron and his mother occasionally stayed.

At **Cullen** (VIII, G3) on the Banffshire coast and about ten miles west of Banff, Johnson was disgusted at breakfast by the sight of dried haddocks broiled, and they had to be removed. In Grant Street there is a house (now a tea-room) where George Macdonald lived. Macdonald, born at Huntly in Aberdeenshire on December 10, 1824, depicted the life of the fisher-folk at **Lossiemouth** (about fifteen miles farther west) in *Malcolm* and other novels.

To return to Dr Johnson. He was impressed by the cathedral ruins at **Elgin** (VIII, F3, on the A96), but he and Boswell fared ill at the Red Lion (it is still there) in High Street, and for the first time he 'had seen a dinner in Scotland he could not eat'. On the way to Nairn they passed at **Hardmuir** (VIII, E3) the 'blasted heath' (now cultivated land) where Macbeth and Banquo are supposed to have met the witches. After **Forres** and **Nairn** (VIII, E4)—the latter place said Johnson was 'in a state of miserable decay', but he would alter his opinion now—they visited Cawdor Castle, five miles south-west of Nairn. The castle, another place assigned by tradition as the scene of Duncan's murder, is a building of the fifteenth to seventeenth centuries on the site of an older structure.

After inspecting the fortifications of **Fort George**, eight miles west of Nairn, Boswell and Johnson proceeded to **Inverness** (VIII, E4), staying at Mackenzie's Inn, which is no longer there. They thought they saw the ruins of Macbeth's castle (where Shakespeare places the murder of Duncan), but what they actually saw were the ruins of the successor of that castle, which was replaced in 1834 by yet another building. Macbeth's original castle was situated about a quarter of a mile east of where the railway station now stands. Here we will leave the travellers and pick up their trail later.

NORTH-WEST

In **Cromarty** (VIII, E3), at the end of Cromarty Firth, Sir Thomas Urquhart, who translated Rabelais so racily, was born in 1611. Cromartie House, in the south-east of the town, stands on the site of his birthplace. Educated at King's College, Aberdeen, he became an ardent Royalist and fought for Charles I and Charles II. He died abroad about 1660, but exactly where is unknown, and is commemorated by a memorial in the old parish church in Cromarty.

Going to the far north, there is in the valley of the Strath Hope, at **Allt-na-Cailliach** (VIII, D1) in Sutherland, a great waterfall, and at its foot a dwelling once existed in which the Gaelic poet Robert Mackay was born in 1714. Known as Rob Donn, he never learned to read or write, and composed in the Sutherland dialect. He was by turns a herd, gamekeeper, boman (principal herd) to Lord Reay, soldier, and again boman. He died in 1778, and is buried in the churchyard at **Balnakill**, a little to the north-west of Durness, not far from Cape Wrath. Over in Harris, which is the southern part of the island of Lewis, there is **Amhuinnsuidhe Castle** (VIII, A1), about eight miles north-west of **Tarbert**, on the coastal road. Here Barrie stayed, and part of *Mary Rose* was written in the castle.

We left Boswell and Johnson at Inverness, after which they made for Loch Ness, stopped at **Fort Augustus**, and then reached Glen Moriston. Now they were on the 'Road to the Isles'. Here Johnson sat down by the stream, and the idea first occurred to him of writing a description of his journey. They pushed on to **Glenelg** (VIII, B5), where they had to sleep on hay at a wretched inn, and next day crossed to Skye, landing at **Armadale**. They were met by Sir Alexander MacDonald, whom Johnson had known in London, and were made welcome in his house (no longer there) on the shore. Then they crossed to the island of Raasay (VIII, A4), where at Raasay House (now an hotel) they were entertained by the Macleod of Raasay. Returning to Skye, they called on the famous Flora Macdonald at **Kingsburgh** (VIII, A3), and Johnson slept in the Young Pretender's bed. It is unfortunate that this house of such rich associations has disappeared; the present Kingsburgh House occupies the same site. Flora Macdonald is buried in the graveyard at **Kilmuir** (VIII, A3), and Johnson's tribute to her is on the gravestone.

Boswell and Johnson stayed for ten days with the Macleod of Macleod at **Dunvegan Castle★** (VIII, A4). After a few more calls in Skye

★ Open in summer from Monday to Friday 2 to 5 p.m. Among the possessions at the castle are letters from Johnson and Scott—the latter paid a visit in 1815.

they visited some of the neighbouring islands. They were entertained by MacQuarrie of Ulva, whose family had owned the island for nine hundred years. Their host's 'mean house', as Boswell called it, was destroyed by fire in 1954. Of Iona, off the west coast of Mull, where St Columba built a monastery and where he died and is buried, Johnson said that 'that man is little to be envied, whose patriotism would not gain force upon the plain of Marathon, or whose piety would not grow warmer among the ruins of Iona'. Keats and his friend Charles Brown also visited Iona, as well as Mull and Staffa, during their tour of 1818. The island contains, in St Oran's Chapel, the tomb of Scott's *Lord of the Isles*.

Opposite the eastern side of Mull, and grandly situated on a chain of rocks overhanging the sea at the mouth of Loch Aline, are the ruins of Ardtornish Castle, the former headquarters of the 'Lords of the Isles', but in the period covered by Scott's poem their main residence was in Islay.

At **Sunipol**, in the northern part of Mull and about eight miles west of Tobermory (which was visited by Boswell and Johnson) Thomas Campbell was a tutor in 1795. Here he wrote 'The Exile of Erin' and formed the idea of writing—or possibly began writing—'The Pleasures of Imagination'. Loch-na-Keal, midway on the Atlantic side of Mull, is the 'Loch Gyle' of Campbell's ballad 'Lord Ullin's Daughter'. Off the great southern promontory of the island, known as the Ross of Mull, lies an archipelago of rocks called the Torrans, where the 'Covenant' in Stevenson's *Kidnapped* was wrecked, and David Balfour was cast up on the islet of Erraid. On Duart Point, in the south-east of the island, there is a lighthouse erected in honour of William Black, some of whose novels are set in the islands and Western Highlands.

After visiting the islands Keats and his friend climbed Ben Nevis, and on its summit Keats wrote a sonnet, but not a good one. Their six hundred miles of walking and four hundred of riding through the Lake District were exhausting Keats, who moreoever caught a cold when in Mull. At Inverness he consulted a doctor, and was sent to Cromarty to take ship for London.

Near Ben Nevis, and just over a mile north-east of Fort William, is Inverlochy Castle, below whose walls Montrose defeated the

Covenanters in 1645. The battle is described in Scott's *Legend of Montrose* and Neil Munro's *John Splendid*. Another historical event, the Appin Murder in 1752, took place at **Appin** (on the A828), about ten miles north-east of Oban, and it is the principal theme of Stevenson's *Kidnapped* and its sequel *Catriona*. A monument on the hill above the ferry at **Ballachulish** (VIII, C6), which is about ten miles farther north-eastwards, marks the place where James of the Glens was wrongly hanged for the murder. It was to **Glen Coe**, only a few miles away, that Allan Breck and David Balfour escaped after the murder. Many of their adventures are set on Rannoch Moor, which stretches away to the east beyond Glen Coe. (Incidentally, Ossian is supposed to have been born beside Loch Triochatan in Glen Coe.)

North-eastward of this area, and lying off the A9 just over two miles beyond **Kingussie**, is the mansion of **Balavil** (VIII, E5), formerly called Belleville, built by James Macpherson, whom we have mentioned in connexion with the Ossianic controversy. He was born at **Ruthven** near by on October 27, 1736. South of Rannoch Moor lies Loch Tulla, and at its south-western end is **Inveroran**, near which village Duncan Ban MacIntyre, the 'Burns of the Highlands', was born of humble parentage on March 20, 1724. He never learned to speak or write in English, but is a prized Gaelic poet. Not far away, and nearly two miles south-west of **Dalmally**, there is a monument to him on a hill on the old road to Inveraray.

Four miles north-east of **Oban** (VII, A1) there are the ruins of Dun-staffnage Castle, built on a rock in a commanding position at the entrance to Loch Etrive. It figures in Scott's *Lord of the Isles* and as 'Ardenvohr' in his *Legend of Montrose*. Boswell and Johnson returned to the mainland at Oban after their visit to the Western Isles; and Scott visited the town in 1814, after a cruise of the Orkney and Shetland Islands and the Hebrides, which provided material for *The Pirate* and *The Lord of the Isles*. Soroba Lodge, a mile south of Oban, was occupied during 1866-1874 by Robert Buchanan, remembered less for his poetry than for his attack on Swinburne and others in a review in which he coined the phrase 'The Fleshly School of Poetry'.

After leaving Oban Boswell and Johnson proceeded to **Inveraray** (VII, B2, on the A83), near the north-western shore of Loch Fyne. They found an 'excellent inn' and Johnson was in high spirits. 'Come', he said when calling for a gill of whisky, 'let me know what it is that makes a Scotchman happy', and it was his first taste of liquor on the tour. They called at Inveraray Castle,* the seat of the fifth Duke of Argyll. Boswell was cold-shouldered by the duchess, whom he had previously offended, but the duke invited him and Johnson to dinner. Johnson mentioned that his horse was but a poor creature; the duke supplied him with a fresh animal, and the travellers proceeded to Loch Lomond.

Burns was in Inveraray in 1787, and being ignored by the duke, scratched some satirical verses on the window of his inn. The Bard of the Lowlands complained that 'there's naething here but Highland pride'. The graphic closing scenes of *Catriona* take place in the town at the time of the third Duke of Argyll. Neil Munro, who was born here on June 3, 1864, laid some of the scene of *John Splendid* and *The New Road* in his native town. About seven miles north-west of Inveraray there are the ruins of the so-called Rob Roy's House on the farm of Ben Buie, and it is alleged that he lived there for some time.

We now enter a Highland area that Scott made very much his own. At the eastern end of Glen Vorlich in Perthshire, on the southern side of Loch Earn, is Ardvorlich House, depicted as 'Darlinvarach' in *A Legend of Montrose*. A few miles away to the south-west, at the eastern end of Loch Voil, is **Balquhidder** (VII, C1). The famous freebooter Rob Roy, whose surname was MacGregor, is buried in the cemetery of the ruined Old Church there. In front of the church there are three uninscribed tombstones enclosed by a railing, and the central one is alleged to be Rob Roy's, but they are much older than his time. However, there is no doubt that his remains lie somewhere in the churchyard. The tombstone on the left is supposed to be that of his wife; on the right, that of his sons, one of whom ('Robin Oig') is depicted by Stevenson in *Kidnapped* as engaging in a piping contest with Alan Breck in a cottage in the village.

Some fifteen miles south-westwards we enter the wildly beautiful country of the Trossachs and Loch Katrine, amidst which is set *The*

* Open May to September daily (except Friday and Sunday mornings) 10.30 a.m. to 12 noon, 2 to 6 p.m.

Lady of the Lake and some of the scenes of *Rob Roy*. Glengyle, at the head of Loch Katrine, was where Rob Roy MacGregor was born in 1671. Wordsworth and his sister were among the first English visitors to this area, and the latter has recorded her impressions in her *Journals*. Wordsworth has a magnificent sonnet on the Trossachs, and a poem on 'Rob Roy's Grave', in which he wrongly supposes it to be at the head of Loch Katrine. The waterfall which Scott describes in *Waverley*, and beside which the heroine of the story sang to her harp, is on the north side of Loch Ard, which lies about four miles south of the Trossachs.

We close our description of the associations of Scotland with a reference to the most picturesque of her modern sons. On the largest of the three islands in the **Lake of Menteith** (VII, C2), lying about three miles to the west of Aberfoyle, R. B. Cunninghame Graham is buried amidst the ruins of the priory of Inchmahone. He died at Buenos Aires on March 20, 1936, and lies beside his wife, whose grave he had dug with his own hands thirty years earlier.

Ireland

Dublin and its environs
South-east
South-west
Central and west
North

Dublin and its Environs

The literary associations of **Dublin** (IX, H1) go back to Edmund Spenser, who arrived in the city in November 1580 as the secretary of Lord Grey de Wilton, recently appointed Lord-Deputy of Ireland. Spenser was a busy man, well paid, and managed to secure landed property in other parts of the country. In 1581 he was appointed Clerk of the Irish Court of Chancery, and about this time leased for six years the Dublin house of Lord Baltinglas, who had led a Catholic rising and escaped to Spain. In 1588 Spenser resigned his clerkship and pursued his career elsewhere in Ireland. The dramatist James Shirley came over from London in 1636, under the patronage of the sixteenth Earl of Kildare, just about the time that the first public theatre was opened in Ireland. His play, *The Royal Master*, was acted both at this theatre (in Werburgh Street, Dublin) and in Dublin Castle. Shirley returned to London about 1640.

The greatest literary figure connected with Dublin is Jonathan Swift, the posthumous child of a Dublin lawyer who was descended from a Yorkshire family; and through his mother (a native of Leicester) he was a cousin of Dryden. He was born on November 30, 1667, at 7 Hoey's Court, Dublin. The house has long disappeared—very little remains of the Dublin of Swift's day—but in Werburgh Street, by the entrance to Hoey's Court, there is a bust of Swift in a niche on the wall of a public house. Leaving her infant son in charge of a nurse, Swift's mother returned to her native Leicester, and the nurse took the child to her native Cumberland. At the age of six, and now under the care of his uncle, Godwin Swift, he was sent to School in Kilkenny and in 1782 entered Trinity College, Dublin. According to his own account, he did not benefit greatly from his university education, studying what pleased him, and he had an especial distaste for philosophy and theology. He graduated B.A. in 1686, not through merit but by 'special grace'. He continued residence at Trinity College, and now began to break loose, though formerly well-behaved. When James II was in Ireland after losing his throne and there were troubles in Dublin, Swift decided to join his mother in Leicester. He returned for a short stay in 1691, and again in 1694, when he was ordained.

Though frequently in Dublin during the following twenty years, it was not until 1713 that he became Dean of St Patrick's Cathedral, Dublin. His beloved Stella as usual followed him. So, a year later, did Esther Vanhomrigh, who was passionately in love with him, and whom he had met in London. His Vanessa, as he called her, went to live at **Celbridge Abbey** (X, G6) on the Liffey, about twelve miles west of Dublin. There Swift sometimes visited her, and according to tradition a seat below the rocks by the river bank was their usual retreat. In 1723 Vanessa wrote either to Swift or to Stella (it is not clear which) inquiring if they were married. Swift rode in fury to Celbridge, threw down the letter in her presence, and departed without a word. Deeply shocked, she revoked the will that she had drawn up in Swift's favour, and left instructions for the publication of his correspondence with her and for the poem 'Cadenus and Vanessa' which describes their courtship. Within a few months she was dead, and Swift retired to the south of Ireland. Stella was pained by the tragedy, and when someone remarked that Vanessa must have been a remarkable woman to inspire such poetry, she replied that the Dean could write well upon a broomstick.

Dividing his time between London and Dublin, Swift continued to pour out his scathing satires, and the greatest of them, *Gulliver's Travels*, appeared in 1726. He was in England when Stella was reported as dying, and returned to Dublin in 1727, never again to leave Ireland. Stella Johnson died on January 28, 1728: Swift was given the news at eight in the evening, and late at night began to write the 'Character of Mrs Johnson'. Whether they were ever married cannot be decided on the evidence available. She was buried in St Patrick's Cathedral, but Swift was too ill to be present. His own faculties were beginning to decline; he gave way to ever deeper pessimism, and hoped for death. In 1738 mental decay became very pronounced, and his final years were very distressing to his friends. He died on October 19, 1745, and was buried near Stella in the south aisle of St Patrick's. A Latin epitaph he wrote for himself is inscribed over the door of the vestry, in which he states that 'he lies where furious indignation can no longer rend his heart'—a not surprising sentiment from the greatest misanthrope among men of letters and the greatest of English satirists.

Swift's deanery has been rebuilt, but the cellars may date from his time. The deanery possesses a few relics, and Marsh's Library* adjoining St Patrick's has Swift's copy of Clarendon's *History* scored in Swift's hand. St Patrick's Hospital in James's Street, which possesses a fine collection of Swiftiana, was founded through a bequest by Swift.

Congreve, who had been at school with Swift, followed him to Trinity College in 1685, and had the same tutor, but hardly anything is known of his college life, not even if he took a degree. Richard Steele, who came to know Swift in London, was born in Dublin in March 1672, but where precisely is not known. He was baptized in the church of St Bridget, or St Bride, which used to be outside the wall on the south of the city. Steele's father, an attorney, died when the boy was five, and his mother soon afterwards. Placed under the care of an uncle, he was sent to school in London, and never returned to his native land.

One of Congreve's contemporaries in the drama, George Farquhar, entered Trinity College in 1694, and is said to have been expelled soon afterwards for perpetrating a profane joke. He became an actor in Dublin, and in a performance of Dryden's *Indian Emperor* accidentally

---

* Open Monday, Tuesday, Wednesday, Friday 11 a.m. to 2 p.m., 3 to 4.30 p.m.; Thursday and Saturday 10.30 a.m. to 12.30 p.m.

L

stabbed a fellow-actor, who recovered after hovering between life and death. Farquhar, unnerved, gave up acting; fortunately he met an actor who advised him to take up play-writing and gave him ten guineas, and he went to London. Returning to Dublin in 1703, he appeared in the title part of his own comedy *Sir Harry Wildair*. His performance was poor, but yielded him a much-needed £100.

Trinity College claims great names among its alumni, and two of the greatest, Goldsmith and Burke, were contemporaries, but apparently did not come to know each other until much later. Goldsmith had to enter the college as a sizar (a free student expected to perform menial tasks) in 1744. He made no progress in mathematics or logic; his tutor was severe and brutal; and when his father died in 1747 he was in great difficulties, but with the help of relatives and by pawning books and writing street ballads he was able to continue his studies. Once he was publicly admonished for taking part in an organized attack on bailiffs. He was unsuccessful in trying to obtain a scholarship, but obtained an exhibition worth about thirty shillings annually. Ignoring college rules, he celebrated with a dance and supper, and during festivities his tutor entered the room. Goldsmith received corporal punishment and his guests were forcibly ejected. The humiliation made him decide to leave the country, but poverty forced him to join his elder brother at Cork. The brother effected a reconciliation; Goldsmith returned to college, and took his B.A. degree in 1749. The pane of glass in his room on which he scratched his name is preserved in the college library, and his statue stands on College Green.

Burke, whose statue is near Goldsmith's, was born at 12 Arran Quay (the house was demolished in 1950) on or about January 12, 1729. His father was an attorney of Protestant faith, and his mother a catholic. His early days are obscure, but after schooling in Co. Kildare he entered Trinity College in 1743. A somewhat desultory student who took up one subject after another, he had an especial interest in the classics, particularly Cicero, on whom he tried to model himself. He secured a scholarship, graduated B.A. in 1748, and in 1750 went to London to study law. He returned to Ireland for a short time in 1766, when he stayed in Loughrea, Co. Galway, and received the freedom of Galway. Burke and Goldsmith belonged to the circle of Dr Johnson's friends, and figure prominently in Boswell's *Life of Johnson*. Boswell himself once visited Ireland to seek a young lady known as 'la belle Irlandaise', who merely laughed at him. Not many years ago a most important discovery was made of a large collection of his manuscripts at Malahide Castle (ten miles north-east of Dublin), the seat of his descendant Lord Talbot de Malahide.

Burke's great political opponent, Richard Brinsley Sheridan, was also a native of Dublin. He was born on October 30, 1751, at 12 Dorset Street Upper; the house is marked by a tablet. His father, an actor, was Swift's godson, and his grandfather a friend of Swift. Educated first by his father and then at a school in Dublin, his family took him in 1762 to London.

Sheridan's Dublin schoolmaster had for another pupil many years later Thomas Moore, who was born at 12 Aungier Street on May 28, 1779, and the house has survived, refronted and marked with a bust. The son of a grocer and wine merchant, Moore began writing poetry before he entered Trinity College in 1794. Whilst at college he made a translation, which the provost thought of submitting for a special prize, but eventually decided that it was too amatory and convivial to present to his staid colleagues. At college and in Dublin society Moore was noted for his singing and playing. After graduating in 1779 he proceeded to London to study law. A statue of him stands on College Green.

A very different kind of person, C. R. Maturin, author of the once-popular *Melmoth the Wanderer*, was born somewhere in the city some time during 1782, and was a distant relative of Lady Wilde, mother of Oscar Wilde. He distinguished himself at Trinity College, and then entered the Church, becoming curate of St Peter's in Aungier Street. He lived at 37 York Street (the house survives) and was a noted eccentric in his later years. He died at his home on October 30, 1824. Scott, who admired his macabre stories, did not know of his death when he came to Dublin and had hoped to call on Maturin. 'Dublin is splendid beyond my expectations,' he wrote to Miss Edgeworth, whom he was due to visit, and the enthusiastic visitor was enthusiastically received by Dubliners. Trinity College conferred an honorary degree on him, and the biographer of Swift visited St Patrick's and the deanery.

Thomas De Quincey was a visitor to Dublin, at the age of fourteen, when he came with his friend Lord Westport, heir of the Earl of Altamont, and stayed at the earl's town house, no longer there, in Sackville (now O'Connell) Street. He witnessed the brilliant scene, which he describes in his *Autobiographic Sketches*, of the last sitting of the Irish House of Lords. Another visitor from England was Mrs Hemans (she had an Irish grandfather), who settled in 1831 in Dublin, where a brother of hers was commissioner of police. She lived first at 36 Merrion Row, later at 21 Dawson Street, and both houses have survived. Before long her health declined; she died on May 16, 1835, and is buried in St Ann's Church, Dawson Street.

We return to native Dubliners with George Darley, born somewhere in the city in 1795. He entered Trinity College in 1815, graduating in 1820, and wished to take up literature, but was opposed by his family, whose interests were in brewing and building. Totally estranged from them, he left for London soon after leaving college. The novelist Samuel Lover was born in Dublin on February 24, 1797. Educated privately, he entered his stockbroking father's office, disliked it, quarrelled with his father, and took up painting. A gifted song-writer and reciter, he produced a eulogy at a banquet to Thomas Moore which secured him the gratitude of Moore and the entrée to social circles. He migrated to London in 1835, pursued painting and song-writing successfully and began to write novels, and then resumed residence in Dublin. He died on July 6, 1868, whilst on a health visit to St Helier, Jersey, and is buried in Kensal Green Cemetery, London.

A better novelist, Charles Lever, was a younger contemporary of Lover and also a native of Dublin. He was born, of English parentage, on August 31, 1806. Graduating at Trinity College after an undistinguished career, he studied medicine at Göttingen and Stevens's Hospital in Dublin, failed the examination but obtained the degree of Bachelor of Medicine at Trinity College. He practised as a doctor, married, gambled and lost heavily at cards and turned to literature for another source of income. *Harry Lorrequer* and other novels from his pen made the *Dublin University Magazine* (he was one of its founders) in which they appeared famous. Lever was much abroad, and was British consul first at Spezia and later at Trieste, but was often back in Dublin frequenting literary circles and collecting material for his novels. He died at Trieste on June 1, 1872.

Thackeray, during his Irish tour of 1842, came to know Lever, and stayed with him at the latter's house called Templeogue (no longer extant) near Dublin. Thackeray's impressions of Dublin must be read in his *Irish Sketch Book* (partly written at Templeogue, and dedicated to Lever), one of his most delightful works, but little read. Thackeray's great admirer, Trollope, was in Ireland during the former's travels there, but they did not come to know each other until after Trollope had finally left Ireland in 1859. His last residence in Ireland was at **Donnybrook**, now a southern suburb of Dublin, where he settled in 1854.

One of the more significant Anglo-Irish poets, James Clarence Mangan, was born on May 1, 1803, at 3 Fishamble Street (the house has disappeared). He was brilliant at school, managing to learn four languages, but the bankruptcy of his father, a grocer, obliged him to seek employment early to support the family. First at a scrivener's and then at an attorney's office he toiled for ten years, and being somewhat eccentric was persecuted by fellow-clerks. He took to opium, and never fully realized the genius he undoubtedly possessed. His habits hastened his end, which came as a result of cholera on June 20, 1849.

Another native of Dublin with brilliant gifts, but more fully realized, was J. Sheridan Le Fanu, born on August 28, 1814, the son of a churchman who was a nephew of Sheridan. At first educated privately, he entered Trinity College in 1833 and there was noted for his brilliance. He had begun writing verses as a child, and before he left college was contributing to the *Dublin University Magazine*. Later he took to journalism and writing stories, but it was not until after his wife's death in 1858 that he produced the brilliant stories of the supernatural, particularly *Uncle Silas*, by which he is best known. He settled latterly at 18 Merrion Square South (the house is still there, but is now 70 Merrion Square) dreaming very strange dreams, and writing in bed on mere scraps of paper. He died there on February 7, 1873, and is buried in Mount Jerome Cemetery.

Sir Samuel Ferguson the poet and antiquary came to Trinity College from Belfast, graduating B.A. in 1826 and M.A. in 1832. He took up study of the law, eventually becoming Deputy-Keeper of Public Records. He contributed poetry to the *Dublin University Magazine* from its foundation. His house in Dublin, 20 North Great George's Street, where for many years he dispensed delightful hospitality for those who cared for the arts, has survived. He died at Strand Lodge in **Howth,** nine miles north-east of Dublin, on August 9, 1886.

The historian W. E. H. Lecky was born at Newtown Park, near Dublin, on March 26, 1838, the son of a man of means. After schooling at Armagh and Cheltenham he entered Trinity College in 1856, graduating B.A. in 1859. He was brilliantly successful with his *History of Rationalism* by the time he was twenty-seven. From now on he lived much in London, where he died. His cremated remains were interred in Mount Jerome Cemetery.

Oscar Wilde was born at 21 Westland Row, Dublin (the house has survived), on October 16, 1854. His father, Sir William Wilde, was an antiquarian, writer and surgeon. Oscar entered Trinity College in 1871. A lazy student, nevertheless his bent for classical studies secured him a foundation scholarship and many prizes, including the Berkeley gold medal for Greek. He kept apart from his contemporaries, who thought him effeminate, but when one of them laughed at a poem of his own that Wilde was reading aloud he fought and defeated the ill-mannered fellow, and from that moment his stock rose. Wilde's unkempt rooms were on the north side of a little square called Botany Bay. As well as 21 Westland Row, there is another house standing in which he lived, and that is 1 Merrion Square.

Ireland has produced several writers who have contributed brilliantly to English dramatic literature, and three of them—Sheridan, Wilde and Shaw—were natives of Dublin. George Bernard Shaw was born on July 26, 1856, at 3 Upper Synge Street, which has become 33 Synge Street, and the house has survived. His father was an ineffectual and impoverished corn miller who drank a great deal in secret, and his mother a professional singer. Bernard Shaw received some education privately and then entered the Wesley Connexional School (later Wesley College). Meanwhile the family had moved into better quarters in Hatch Street. In 1871 he became a clerk in an estate agency; a few months later his mother and two sisters left for London, and in 1876

Shaw followed them. He did not see Ireland again for nearly thirty years. A house called Torca Cottage (marked by a tablet) stands on the hill at **Dalkey** (IX, H1), nine miles south-east of Dublin, where the Shaw family used to spend their summers from 1866 until 1874.

The chief figure of the Irish literary revival that began in the 'nineties is William Butler Yeats, born on June 13, 1865, in **Sandymouth**, a suburb of Dublin. Two years later his father, a painter, decided to move to London, but the family returned in 1881 to live in Howth, and Yeats was sent to the Dublin High School. After leaving school he studied art, but meanwhile had begun to write poetry, and when his parents moved again to London he joined them later and decided to pursue literature. Yeats was intermittently in Dublin thereafter until 1922, when he became a senator of the Irish Free State and bought 82 Merrion Square, Dublin, a house that survives. He lived there until 1929, when he took a flat at 42 Fitzwilliam Square.

Meanwhile, through the efforts of Lady Gregory, George Moore and Edward Martyn, Yeats's play *The Countess Kathleen* was produced in Dublin in 1899, an event which marked the foundation of the modern Irish theatre and which culminated in the building of the Abbey Theatre in 1901. The Abbey produced some of the finest acting in the world, and for it were written some magnificent plays. The most famous was Synge's *Playboy of the Western World*, which on its production in 1907 met a hostile reception, and Yeats, an ardent admirer of Synge's genius, defended the author. The Abbey Theatre, which stood at the corner of Abbey Street and Marlborough Street, was burned down in 1951, and has been rebuilt in Pearse Street.

When he was studying at the Metropolitan School of Art Yeats became acquainted with George William Russell, better known as AE. AE's family had moved to Dublin when he was about ten, and he was sent to Rathmines School. His first employment was at the Phoenix brewery, and then he became a clerk in a drapery business. His first book of poems, *Homeward*, gained wide attention. He lived in Dublin until 1932, and thereafter in London.

Synge, who was to become one of the three literary advisers of the Abbey Theatre, was born on April 16, 1871, at **Newtown Little**, near Rathfarnham (now a suburb of Dublin). After education at private schools and with a tutor, he entered Trinity College in 1888, distinguished himself in Hebrew and Irish studies, and graduated B.A. in 1892. He went to Germany to study music, but decided to turn to literature and during the next few years divided his time mainly between France and Ireland, reading much and writing prose and verse. In Paris he met Yeats, who advised him to visit the Aran Islands (Synge had been there once) and other wild areas of Ireland and to depict ways of life not hitherto attempted in literature. The advice was turned to brilliant account. In the last six years of his life Synge lived much in or near Dublin, but his health was declining, and he died in a Dublin nursing home on March 24, 1909. He is buried in Mount Jerome Cemetery.

Among others that Yeats knew in Dublin was Patrick Pearse, who was born in Dublin on November 10, 1879. A schoolmaster, gifted poet, fervent patriot and brilliant orator, he commanded the Irish Republican Army in the Easter Rising of 1916, and was executed on May 3, 1916. George Moore, who at the turn of the century felt that artistically he was in the doldrums, under the influence of Yeats and Edward Martyn moved to Dublin in 1901, eager to become a leader in the Irish literary revival. He settled first in Ely Place, and later at 4 Upper Merrion Street. At the latter house, which is still there, he wrote much of *Hail and Farewell*, a valuable and fascinating record of some aspects of the literary revival. By the time he left Dublin in 1911 he was somewhat disillusioned.

James Joyce was born on February 2, 1882, at 41 Brighton Square (the house survives) in the suburb of **Rathgar**. His father, a hearty, witty man of means, figures in *Ulysses*. He was educated at Clongowes Wood College in **Sallins**, Co. Kildare, at Belvedere College in Great Denmark Street, Dublin, and at University College in Dublin, where he graduated in modern languages. Gerard Manley Hopkins had been professor of classics at University College during 1884-9 (he died in Dublin on June 8, 1889) and it is noteworthy that the two modern writers who experimented in daring word-coinage were connected with the same college. After graduating, Joyce left Dublin and spent the rest of his life chiefly in Paris, Trieste and Zürich. When his mother died in 1904 he returned to Dublin, and also paid later visits, the last in

1912, when he tried unsuccessfully to secure publication for *Dubliners*. In that book he presents a series of stark vignettes of the city; in *Ulysses*, a work that has exercised a great influence on writers, he depicts one day in the lives of three Dubliners. At **Sandycove** (IX, HI), about eight miles south-east of Dublin, is the Martello Tower, now a Joyce museum,* where *Ulysses* begins and in which Joyce lived for a short time. He died at Zürich on January 13, 1941, and is buried there.

Oliver St John Gogarty, born in Dublin on August 17, 1878, was a fellow-student with Joyce at Trinity College, and was depicted as Malachy Mulligan in *Ulysses*. A surgeon, poet and brilliant writer of memoirs, he knew most of the writers of the Irish literary renaissance, and depicted them in the autobiographical volumes which began with *As I Was Going Down Sackville Street*. He died in 1957. James Stephens claimed that he was born on the same day and in the same year as Joyce, but was born in Dublin probably in 1880. When he was two his father died, and on his mother's remarriage he was placed in an orphanage, from which he eventually ran away, and was largely self-educated. Most of his life was spent in London, but during 1919-24 he was Registrar of the National Portrait Gallery in Dublin. *The Crock of Gold*, his best book, was written in Dublin. The Dublin playwright Sean O'Casey was born in a slum in the city on March 31, 1884. His early plays, produced at the Abbey Theatre, depicted the humours and tragedies of slum life.

SOUTH-EAST

At **Annamoe** (IX, H2), in the Wicklow Mountains, about ten miles north-west of Wicklow, Laurence Sterne when a child was taken by his mother to visit a relative. He tells the story of 'a wonderful escape in falling through the mill-race whilst the mill was going, and of being taken up unhurt'. The Wicklow Mountains were a favourite resort of Synge, who wrote delightfully of the area in his *In Wicklow and West Kerry*.

* Open during summer, 3 to 6 p.m. daily. (It is probable that further extension of opening times, extending to winter-time, will be made in due course.)

The vale of **Avoca** (IX, H2), lying about fifteen miles south-west of Wicklow, has been made famous by Thomas Moore—

> *There is not in the wide world a valley so sweet,*
> *As that vale in whose bosom the bright waters meet*

—though most people would consider that there are many places more beautiful in a land endowed with so much beauty. The Meeting of the Waters to which Moore refers is that of the Great Avon (or Avonmore) with the Little Avon (or Avonbeg), and there is another meeting of waters near by. There are several places in the area mentioned by Moore. Near the Meeting of the Waters is the stump of Moore's tree, beneath which he is supposed to have often rested, but souvenir hunters long ago robbed the tree of any chance of survival.

To the east of the Wicklow Mountains, and about six miles east of Athy, is **Ballitore** (IX, G2), once inhabited by Quakers and where Edmund Burke was at school during 1741-3. Another school with famous names is not far away, at **Kilkenny** (IX, F3), twenty miles north of Waterford. Kilkenny College stands on the site of St John's College, where Swift, Congreve and Farquhar were educated.

Enniscorthy Castle (IX, G3), fifteen miles north of Waterford, was a residence of Spenser for one or more short periods, and it has survived virtually unaltered since his time. At **Wexford** (IX, H4) there is a house (marked by a tablet) in the Cornmarket that used to be the home of Thomas Moore's mother; and in South Main Street is the house, formerly the rectory, where Oscar Wilde's mother was born.

Clonmel (IX, E4), thirty miles north-west of Waterford, was where Laurence Sterne was born on November 24, 1713. His father was an army officer, and the boy's first ten years were spent wherever his father happened to be quartered. Another army officer's son, George Borrow, was educated at Clonmel Grammar School (near the West Gate) when his father's regiment was quartered in the town in 1815. In *Lavengro* Borrow says that his education would not have been what it was, 'perfect', had he 'never had the honour of being *alumnus* in an Irish seminary'. Another resident of Clonmel was Anthony Trollope, who had lodgings here during 1844-5.

During his stay in Ireland Borrow learned something of the Irish language, but he probably knew nothing of the Gaelic poets celebrated in his time and connected particularly with Co. Waterford. These poets, Donnchadh Rua Mac Conmara (died 1814) and Tadhg Gaelach Ó Suilleabháin (died 1800) lived part of their lives at **Kilmacthomas** (IX, F4), about fifteen miles south-west of Waterford. Mac Conmara is buried at **Newtown**, two miles to the north-west, and Ó Suilleabháin at **Ballylaneen**, three miles to the south.

Mullinahone (IX, F3), sixteen miles south-west of Kilkenny, was where Charles Joseph Kickham, poet, novelist and Fenian leader, lived most of his life. He was born either there or near **Cashel** about 1828. His novel *Knocknagow* is based on the life of this part of Co. Tipperary. He died at **Blackrock** near Dublin on August 21, 1882, and is buried beside the Catholic Church at Mullinahone. His house in Felthard Street is marked by a tablet.

SOUTH-WEST

Kickham has a monument in **Tipperary** (IX, E3), where a contemporary poet and another active participant in the Fenian movement, Ellen O'Leary, was born in 1831. 'Darby' Ryan (Diarmaid O Riain), who wrote in English and Irish, was born in the village of **Bansha,** five miles south-east of Tipperary, and is buried there.

This southern part of the province of Munster is very much connected with Spenser and Ralegh. Spenser spent eighteen years in Ireland, ten of them in Munster. When he resigned his position in Dublin in 1588 the plantation of Munster with English colonists was in progress. He purchased the Clerkship of Munster, and was granted over 3,000 acres of land in Co. Cork on the understanding that he provided twenty-four English families with homes. Within his lands was the old castle of **Kilcolman** (IX, D4), three miles from **Doneraile** and near the Awbeg river, and in this castle or in a house near by he lived for ten years. The Awbeg appears in *The Faerie Queene* as the 'Mulla', and the Blackwater into which it flows is disguised as the 'Awniduff'.

Spenser was unhappy in Ireland: the Irish were hostile, much of his land was desolate and wild, and wolves lurked in a countryside more thickly wooded than now. His famous *View of the Present State of Ireland* is typical of the Elizabethan official outlook. He took solace in writing poetry, continuing and completing *The Faerie Queene*. In 1589 Ralegh called on him, and the event is described in the poem 'Colin Clouts Come Home Again', in which Ralegh is characterized as the 'Shepherd of the Ocean'. Spenser showed Ralegh the manuscript of *The Faerie Queene*: Ralegh was enchanted, and persuaded Spenser to accompany him to London, where part of the poem was read to the queen. A year later Spenser returned to Kilcolman. About 1593 he met and fell in love with Elizabeth Boyle (related to Richard Boyle, later first Earl of Cork), and his courtship is curiously recorded in the sonnet-series 'Amoretti'. He was married to her in June 1594 either in the church of St Mary (which survives) at **Youghal** (IX, E5), or in St Finnbarr's Cathedral in Cork—the present cathedral is a later building on the same site. His happiness was celebrated in *Epithalamion*.

After a quarrel over land with a neighbour, Lord Roche, when the decision in the courts went against Spenser, he resigned the Clerkship of Munster, and was later appointed Sheriff of Cork. Before long a great rebellion broke out: first Co. Cork was overrun, and then the entire province of Munster. Kilcolman Castle was burned; Spenser and his wife with their four children fled to Cork, and then to London. Spenser's eldest son succeeded to Kilcolman, and descendants of the poet survived in Ireland into the nineteenth century.

Ralegh first came to Ireland as captain in command of a hundred soldiers in June 1580. Military duties took him to **Smerwick**, where he took part in the slaughter of the Spanish and Italian garrison with typical Elizabethan ruthlessness, and there he met Spenser for the first time. Later he went to Cork, and was enrolled in the government of Munster. In 1586 he received from the queen, as his part in the plantation of Munster, 40,000 acres of land in Cos. Waterford, Tipperary and Cork. He had various residences, among them the castle at Cork, the castle at Lismore and the manor house at Youghal. Cork Castle has gone; Lismore Castle (IX, E4), nearly twenty miles north of Youghal and situated on a great cliff above the Blackwater, he began to rebuild and repair, but the task was completed after his time. Ralegh was Mayor of Youghal during 1588-9, and his residence there, since called Myrtle Grove, is a charming Elizabethan building which has survived with little alteration since his time. Under the yew-tree in front of the house he is supposed to have smoked his pipe, and here he is supposed to have planted potatoes. He certainly introduced potatoes into Ireland, though exactly where is of no particular consequence, and certainly did not foresee the fatality that lay in that root. He was out of Ireland before the great rebellion of 1589, after which he sold his estates at a loss.

Congreve also is connected with Youghal and Lismore. Soon after his birth his father, an army officer, was stationed at Youghal, where he obtained the position of land steward to the Earl of Cork, and moved to Lismore. The Old Church Cemetery at **Cobh** (IX, E5, known as Queenstown between 1849 and 1922), fifteen miles east of Cork, is the burial-place of Charles Wolfe, author of 'The Burial of Sir John Moore'. Owing to consumption he had resigned his church living and spent the last two years of his life in Cobh, where he died in 1831. The only poem by which he is remembered was published in 1817, and then forgotten until Byron's praise drew attention to it.

The old castle at **Cork** (IX, D5) was not Ralegh's only residence there, for Tivoli House in the suburb of **Tivoli** is on the site of his residence, and it is said that the trees he planted there have survived.

At **Shandon** on the north side of the city is the church of St Ann, so charmingly sung by the Rev. Francis Mahony (better known by his pseudonym of Father Prout) in the poem 'The Bells of Shandon'. Father Prout is buried in the graveyard of St Ann's. Much of the setting of William Black's novel *Shandon Bells* is in Cork and **Glengariff**.

Probably somewhere in **Kinsale** (IX, D6), eighteen miles south of Cork, lie the mortal remains of Cyril Tourneur the dramatist. He had been secretary to Sir Edward Cecil on the miserably unsuccessful English expedition to Cadiz in 1625. The flagship of the expedition put in at Kinsale to land the sick, Tourneur among them. He died there on February 28, 1626, but there appears to be no record of his burial. Farther westwards, and about forty miles south-west of Kinsale, there is the village of **Union Hall** on the west side of Glandore Harbour. At Rock Cottage (no longer there) Swift stayed after the death of his beloved Vanessa in 1723, and composed his Latin poem 'Carberiae Rupes' whilst sheltering from a storm.

About seven miles farther westwards is **Skibbereen** (IX, C6), and situated south of it there is Drishane House, the home for most of her life of Edith Somerville. She was born in Corfu on May 2, 1858. She collaborated with her cousin Violet Martin (1862-1915) under the pseudonym of Somerville and Ross. Best known are their *Some Experiences of an Irish R.M.* and *Further Experiences*, but less well known is the more solid achievement of *The Real Charlotte*, all excellent portrayals of Anglo-Irish life. Edith Somerville died at Drishane House on October 8, 1949.

Some twenty miles to the north-west, in and around Glengariff Bay, is one of the most beautiful areas of Ireland. Thackeray said that 'were such a bay lying upon English shores it would be a world's wonder'. On **Garnish Island** (IX, B6, also known as Ilnacullin) Bernard Shaw stayed at the Eccles Hotel and there wrote the greater part of *Saint Joan*.

Many men and women of letters have visited the Lakes of Killarney. Wordsworth, contrary to one's expectation, considered that 'this is the finest portion of the British Isles', and Scott went farther—'the grandest sight I have ever seen'. Moore has some well-known lines on Innisfallen Island (on Lough Leane), which Macaulay considered 'the gem of Killarney, not a reflex of heaven, but a bit of heaven itself'. Thackeray, who devoted two chapters of his *Irish Sketch Book* to the town and the lakes, watched a stag hunt on Innisfallen. Shelley and his wife and her sister lived in **Killarney** (IX, B5) for a few months in 1813 after they had left Wales. When the birth of a child was imminent, Shelley decided to move his wife to London, leaving the hapless sister-in-law to fend for herself 'with plenty of books and no money'. Tennyson was for a short time in Killarney, and whilst there wrote the splendid lyric 'Blow, bugle, blow'. In College Street in the town can be seen the memorial to the Four Kerry Poets.

To the north-west of Killarney, and at the base of a peninsula between Brandon Bay and Tralee Bay, there used to be a castle at **Castlegregory** whose owner entertained Ralegh and Spenser in 1580. Ralegh was on his way to attack the Spaniards who had landed at Smerwick. Well inland from here is **Mallow**, twenty-two miles north-west of Cork, and the birthplace of Thomas Osborne Davis, the poet and leader of the Young Ireland movement. Trollope resided at Mallow during 1845-51, and whilst here witnessed the potato famine which spread such misery throughout Ireland. At **Rath Luirc** (Charleville, IX, D4), about twenty miles north of Mallow, there is the grave of the Gaelic poet Seán Clárach Mac Domhnaill; and another Gaelic poet, Aindrias MacCraith, known as 'the Merry Pedlar', is buried in the churchyard at **Kilmallock**, six miles north-east of Rath Luirc.

Croom, twelve miles north-west of Rath Luirc, used to be the meeting-place of the Maigue Poets—Maigue being the name of the river here. Two of them, Mac Domhnaill and MacCraith, have been mentioned above; the other, Sean Ó Tuama, was born here and is buried in the local cemetery. Not far away, five miles west of Adare and about fifteen miles south-west of Limerick, is the demesne of Curragh Chase. In a house there (destroyed by fire in 1941) the poet Aubrey De Vere was born on January 10, 1814. He was educated privately and at Trinity College, Dublin. Often in England, he came to know intimately many English writers. Tennyson spent a month at Curragh Chase in 1848, and De Vere paid many visits to Tennyson's homes at Farringford and Aldworth. He died at Curragh Chase on January 21, 1902, and is buried beside the ruined St Mary's Church at **Askeaton** (IX, C3), about five miles away to the north-west.

CENTRAL AND WEST

At **Cloughjordan** (IX, E2), ten miles north-east of Nenagh and thirty-five miles north-east of Limerick, the poet Thomas MacDonagh was born in Main Street (the house survives) in 1878. He was a friend of Patrick Pearse, took part in the Easter Rising of 1916, and was executed on May 3, 1916. **Banagher** (IX, E1), on the east bank of the Shannon and about twenty miles south of Athlone, was where Anthony Trollope was first stationed when he came to Ireland in 1841 as a post office surveyor. There he possibly wrote part of his first novel, *The Macdermots of Ballycloran*. His years in Ireland formed the first happy period of his life—'a very jolly life', he says—and developed the taste for hunting which finds expression in several of his novels.

In the area of **Lough Ree** (X, D6) we reach the 'Goldsmith country'. There has been much dispute about Goldsmith's actual birthplace. For long it was supposed to be **Pallas**, about three miles east of Ballymahon and about eighteen miles north-east of Athlone. The more recent claim is for **Smith Hill,** a mile to the north of Elphin and about eighteen miles north of Roscommon. Whichever the locality, he was born in 1728, when his father was curate of **Kilkenny West.** Two years later his father moved to **Lissoy** (X, E6), about ten miles north-east of Athlone. The boy's first instruction was from a dame teacher, who thought him stupid, long outlived him and was proud of being his first teacher. At six he went to the village school, kept by an old soldier who is depicted in 'The Deserted Village'. Lissoy is the 'Auburn' of the poem, in which he recalls the scenes of his childhood, but disconcerts by introducing the nightingale, which is not found in Ireland. Possibly Goldsmith recollected the incidents of childhood in an English setting. After Lissoy he was educated at Athlone and then at Edgeworthstown.

On his last homeward journey from school, on horseback, he decided to stop for the night at **Ardagh** (X, E6), five miles south-east of Longford, and inquired for the inn. He happened to speak to the local wag, who directed him to a private house. Goldsmith, only sixteen, decided to act the experienced man of the world, and invited the owner and his wife and daughter (who all kept up the joke) to supper. In the morning he was undeceived. The incident was used many years later for *She Stoops to Conquer, or the mistakes of a night.* Some people have tried to spoil a good story, which is probably true, by saying that it is derived from the play. Ardagh House, where the incident occurred, is still there, and is now the Convent of the Sisters of Mercy.

Goldsmith proceeded to Trinity College, Dublin, and after graduating led a desultory existence, sometimes helping with the school at Pallas run by his brother. He declined to take holy orders, as suggested; his uncle secured him a tutorship, but he soon gave that up, and decided to go to America. He was given a horse and £30 and went to Cork, sold the horse to pay for his passage but missed his ship, and arrived home penniless and with an animal that could only by courtesy be called a horse. Then his uncle gave him £50 so that he could study law in London, but the money was spent in gambling in Dublin. Finally, with the persuasion and help of the family, it was decided that he should study medicine in Edinburgh, and in 1753 he left his native land for ever.

Edgeworthstown (X, E5), eight miles south-east of Longford, takes its name from a family settled there from Elizabethan times. The most famous member is Maria Edgeworth, who came here in 1773 after her father's second marriage. She was employed by her father in keeping accounts and in dealings with tenants. Her literary career began with books for children, and then in 1800 her first novel, *Castle Rackrent*, was published with considerable success. In 1825 Scott and his son-in-law Lockhart spent a week with her, and in 1829 Wordsworth called on her. She died here on May 22, 1849, and is buried in the family vault in St John's churchyard at Edgeworthstown. Her home, Edgeworthstown House, is at the eastern end of the town.

Well away to the east of this area there is **Laracor** (X, F6), two miles south of Trim, where Swift was rector from 1700 to 1710, though with frequent absences in Dublin and London. In 1701 his Stella accompanied him from London and settled here, but the so-called Stella's House here was built after her time, though on the same site as her old home. A modern church occupies the site of Swift's church, and preserves his communion plate. Swift wrote part of *Gulliver's Travels* at Cuilcagh (or Quilca) House, which no longer exists, and which stood three miles north-east of **Virginia** on Lough Ramor, some twenty-five miles north-west of Laracor. **Slane** in the Boyne valley, and nine miles west of Drogheda, was the birthplace of Francis Ledwidge, son of a farm labourer and a poet of brilliant promise who was killed in the First World War.

And now for the west of Ireland. On the north side of **Gort** (IX, D2), about twenty-five miles south-east of Galway, there stood until recent years Coole Park, the residence for many years of Lady Gregory. Born at **Roxborough**, Co. Galway, she became a brilliant playwright, and it was through her influence that Synge, Yeats and other dramatists found a centre in Dublin for the production of their plays. Her house was a meeting-place that drew many famous literary figures. The Autograph Tree in the grounds, inscribed with the initials of Yeats, Shaw and others, is the only reminder of a famous literary circle. Lady Gregory died at Coole Park on May 22, 1932. Ballylea Castle near by, now a ruin, was bought by Yeats in 1917 for £35 and converted into a home where he lived for several years.

At the entrance to Galway Bay are the **Aran Islands** (IX, B2), first visited by J. M. Synge in 1898, and he stayed there every autumn, living as one of the inhabitants, from 1899 to 1902. He wrote a book on the islands, but more significant, stories he heard there were used for his plays *The Shadow of the Glen* and *Riders to the Sea*. From the speech of Irish folk he wrought a nervous prose style to depict, in his own words, 'the rich joy found only in what is superb and wild in reality'.

On a promontory in Lough Carra, and just over two miles north of **Ballinrobe**, is **Moor Halle** (X, B6), where George Moore was born on February 24, 1852. His family claimed descent from Sir Thomas More. Educated at Oscott, near Birmingham, his life was spent mainly at Moore Hall until he became of age, when he went to Paris to study art. He died in London, and his ashes were scattered on an island in Lough Carra.

Westport House at **Westport** (X, B5), the seat of the Marquess of Sligo, was where De Quincey stayed in 1800 with his friend Lord Westport after a visit to Dublin. De Quincey travelled over various parts of Ireland, but unfortunately he tells us little about them in his *Autobiographic Sketches*. Canon J. O. Hannay, better known as George A. Birmingham, was rector of Westport for over twenty years. The setting of his novels is in the mainland and islands of Co. Mayo. The rectory at **Frenchpark**, about ten miles south-west of Boyle, was the birthplace of Douglas Hyde, remarkable as poet, Gaelic revivalist and first president of Eire. He did much to preserve the Irish language, and was first president of the Gaelic League.

NORTH

W. B. Yeats was descended on both sides from Protestant stock long established in **Sligo**(X, C4) . As a boy he spent many a happy holiday with his maternal grandparents there. The first poetry he read was from a songbook he found in his grandfather's stables, and he drew much inspiration from the district. Much of his finest earlier poetry recalls the names of Sligo, Drumahair, Dooney; and the Lake Isle of Innisfree lies in Lough Gill to the west of Sligo. He died at Roquebrune in the south of France on January 28, 1939, and was buried there; but in accordance with his dying wish his remains were transferred in 1948 to the churchyard at **Drumcliff** (X, C4), five miles north-west of Sligo, where his great-grandfather had been rector. Another poet of the Irish literary revival, Eva Gore-Booth, was born in 1870 at the demesne of Lissadell near **Carney,** on the north side of Drumcliff Bay.

To the east lies **Enniskillen** (X, E4), situated on the river joining the upper and lower portions of Lough Erne, and there Oscar Wilde was educated at the Portora Royal School from 1864 to 1871. He disliked games and exercise, and was not notable as a scholar except in Greek. An earlier student at the same school was Henry Francis Lyte, the hymn-writer best remembered for 'Abide with me'. William Allingham, a minor poet who influenced the early work of Yeats, was born at **Ballyshannon** (X, D3), some twenty-five miles north of Sligo, on March 19, 1824. His birthplace in The Mall is marked by a tablet. He worked in his father's bank, then in the customs office, and after transference to England lived there for the rest of his life. **Mountcharles,** four miles west of Donegal, is the birthplace of Seumas MacManus, born on December 31, 1869. This area of Co. Donegal is the setting of his novels.

The dramatist George Farquhar was born at **Londonderry** (or Derry, X, E2), probably in 1677, and said by some to have been the son of a dean of Armagh, by others the son of a prebendary of Raphoe, Co. Donegal. **Limavady** (X, F1), nearly twenty miles north-east of Londonderry, was where Thackeray was served at an inn by a maid with whom he was 'eternally in love during the ten minutes' of his stay, and whom he has immortalized as 'Peg of Limavady' in a chapter, mostly in verse, of *The Irish Sketch Book.* Peg lived in Ballyclose Street. Thackeray's friend Charles Lever practised as a doctor at **Portstewart** (X, F1), four miles north-west of Coleraine, in the 1830's, and there found some of the material for his novels.

About three miles east of Antrim, at **Donegore,** is the grave of Sir Samuel Ferguson, who was interred in the family burying-place. He was born at **Belfast** (X, H3) on March 10, 1810, and educated at the Academical Institution there before proceeding to Trinity College, Dublin. An earlier poet who was also a native of Belfast was William Drennan, born in 1754, the first to use the name of Emerald Isle for Ireland in a poem. Trollope lived in Belfast during 1853-4, and there completed *The Warden*, the first novel of the Barsetshire series and his first success.

Swift's first church living, in 1694, was at **Kilroot** (X, H2), a little to the south-west of Whitehead on Belfast Lough. Whilst here he became enamoured of a Belfast lady to whom he promised marriage if she would be patient whilst he secured advancement. He left for England in 1696, returned three years later with a living at Laracor, was reminded of his promise and was prepared to marry the lady, but on terms so humiliating that she refused. Swift's old church here is now a ruin, but there survives near the railway line the curious little house with semi-circular gables in which he lived.

On the south side of the main Belfast-Bangor road, and a mile south of **Crawfordsburn**, there is **Clandeboye*** (X, H3), the seat of the Marquess of Dufferin and Ava. At the southern end of the estate there is the well-known Helen's Tower, erected by the first Marquess in memory of his mother, Helen Lady Dufferin, the poet and a grand-daughter of Richard Brinsley Sheridan. On the top storey of the tower, inscribed in gold, are the verses addressed by Lady Dufferin to her son on his coming of age, and lower down there are tablets with verses composed by Tennyson, Browning and Kipling. Lady Dufferin is best remembered by her poem 'The Irish Emigrant', and the stile referred to in the poem is at the entrance to the graveyard at **Killyleagh**, situated on Strangford Lough and some twenty miles to the south.

Dromore (X, G3), about sixteen miles south-west of Belfast, is associated with Jeremy Taylor, whose sermons and other writings are among the finest monuments of seventeenth-century prose. Appointed Bishop of Down and Connor in 1660, he became also administrator of the See of Dromore, and was somewhat unhappy in his episcopate because his high church views were acceptable neither to his clergy nor his congregations. He lived at first near Dromore and later in Castle Street, **Lisburn** (X, G3), eight miles south-west of Belfast, where he died on August 13, 1667, and the cathedral there has a monument to him. He is buried in Dromore Cathedral, which he had rebuilt on the ruins of the former building. The little church at **Ballinderry** (X, G3), a

* For admission apply to the steward.

village on the east shore of Lough Neagh, was partly built by Jeremy Taylor.

Thomas Percy of the *Reliques* became Bishop of Dromore in 1782, died there in September 30, 1811, and is buried in the transept he added to the cathedral. George William Russell (AE) was born in William Street in **Lurgan**, just over twenty miles south-west of Belfast, on April 10, 1867, and lived there until his family moved to Dublin about ten years later. Farther westwards, at **Donaghmore** three miles north-west of Dungannon, Charles Wolfe was rector during 1818-21. His health declined following rejection by a lady for whom he had given up an academic career, and he resigned his living.

In the lands of Gosford Castle, adjoining the town of **Markethill** (seven miles south-east of Armagh), can be seen the ruins of the castle visited by Swift during 1728-9. We are apt to think of Swift as an Irishman, whereas he was an Englishman, but the Brontë sisters, all born in England, were of pure Celtic descent. Their father, Patrick Brontë, was born at **Ballynaskeagh**, five miles north-west of Rathfriland. Before leaving Ireland he changed his paternal name, which was Prunty. Three miles north-east of Rathfriland, at **Ballyroney**, the novelist Mayne Reid was born in 1818. The son of the Presbyterian minister there, and educated for the ministry, he found the idea distasteful and emigrated to the United States.

We close the account of the literary associations of Ireland with another of her Gaelic poets, Peter O'Doirnin, who for many years ran a school near **Forkhill**, about six miles north of Dundalk. Born in Co. Tipperary, he migrated because of political troubles there. He died at **Friarstown**, near Forkhill, on April 5, 1768, and is buried in the churchyard at **Urney**, three miles north of Dundalk.

Appendix

Museums and Literary Houses

Museums and Libraries with Manuscripts, etc.

CAMBRIDGE

University Library, Burrell's Walk. Weekdays 9.30 a.m. to 6.30 p.m. Saturday 9 a.m. to 1 p.m. (visitors must be accompanied by a graduate or undergraduate in academic dress).
Trinity College Library. Weekdays 1 to 4 p.m.
Fitzwilliam Museum, Trumpington Street. Weekdays 10 a.m. to 5 p.m.; April to September 10 a.m. to 4 p.m.; on Sunday (2 to 5 p.m.; April to September 2 to 4 p.m.) the picture galleries only are open.

DUBLIN

Trinity College Library. Weekdays 10 a.m. to 3 or 4 p.m., Saturday 10 a.m. to 1 p.m.

EDINBURGH

National Library of Scotland. Weekdays 9.30 a.m. to 4.30 p.m., Saturday 9.30 a.m. to 12.30 p.m.; additional hours on Thursday 5.30 to 8.30 p.m.; closed last week of July and first week of August.

ETON COLLEGE

Open daily. School Yard and Cloisters 10 a.m. to 5 p.m. (10 a.m. to 8 p.m. during summer); College Chapel, Lower School and certain other buildings, with a guide (apply at School Office) 11.30 a.m. to 12.30 p.m., 2.30 to 5 or 6 p.m. (from 10.30 a.m. during holidays).

KESWICK

Fitz Park Museum, Station Street. Weekdays 10 a.m. to 8 p.m.

LLANGOLLEN (Denbighshire)

Plas Newydd. Daily, except Sunday during winter, 11 a.m. to 4 p.m.

LONDON

British Museum, Bloomsbury. Weekdays 10 a.m. to 5 p.m., Sunday 2.30 to 6 p.m.

Public Record Office Museum, Chancery Lane, E.C.4. Monday to Friday 1 to 4 p.m.; closed on Bank Holidays.

Victoria and Albert Museum, South Kensington, S.W. Weekdays 10 a.m. to 6 p.m., Sunday 2.30 to 6 p.m.

National Portrait Gallery, St Martin's Place, Trafalgar Square. Monday to Friday 10 a.m. to 5 p.m., Saturday 10 a.m. to 6 p.m., Sunday 2 to 6 p.m.

OXFORD

Bodleian Library. Weekdays 9.30 a.m. to 6.30 p.m., Saturday 9.30 a.m. to 12.30 p.m. (except holidays and the week beginning the first Monday in August).

Bodleian Library Extension, Parks Road. Weekdays 10 a.m. to 12.30 p.m., 2.30 to 5 p.m. (Saturday 10 a.m. to 12.30 p.m.).

Literary Houses, Museums and other buildings connected with specific Writers

AUSTEN, Jane

CHAWTON, *near* ALTON, Hampshire
Chawton Cottage. Daily, including Bank Holidays, 11 a.m. to 4.30 p.m. Other times can be arranged by applying to resident caretaker.

STONELEIGH ABBEY, *near* LEAMINGTON SPA, Warwickshire
Daily, from Good Friday to mid-October including Bank Holidays, 2.30 to 5.30 p.m.

BACON, Sir Francis

GORHAMBURY HOUSE, *near* ST ALBANS, Hertfordshire
Thursday only from May 1 to September 25, 2 to 6 p.m.; weekdays during August, 2 to 6 p.m.

BARRIE, Sir James

DUMFRIES BURGH MUSEUM. See under BURNS
KIRRIEMUIR, Angus
9 Brechin Road. Open daily on application.

BENNETT, Arnold

STOKE-UPON-TRENT, Staffordshire
Bennett Museum, 205 Waterloo Road, Burslem. Monday, Wednesday and Saturday 2 to 5 p.m.; Thursday 2 to 7 p.m.

BORROW, George

NORWICH
Borrow House, Willow Lane. In private occupation; apply *in advance* to the tenant, Mrs Baker.
Central Public Library.

BRONTË SISTERS

HAWORTH, *near* KEIGHLEY, Yorkshire
Brontë Parsonage Museum. Weekdays 11 a.m. to 6 p.m. (11 a.m. to 5 p.m. in winter); Sunday 2 to 5 p.m.

333

BROWN, Thomas Edward

DOUGLAS, Isle of Man
Manx Museum, Crellin's Hill. Weekdays 10 a.m. to 5 p.m.

BUNYAN, John

BEDFORD
The Bunyan Meeting Library and Museum, Mill Street. Tuesday
to Friday 10 a.m. to 12 noon, 2.30 to 4.30 p.m.; other times by
special arrangement.
The Bunyan Collection, Public Library, Harpur Street. Weekdays
10 a.m. to 8 p.m. (Thursday 10 a.m. to 1 p.m.).

ELSTOW, *near* BEDFORD
The Moot Hall. Tuesday to Saturday 11 a.m. to 5 p.m., Sunday
2.30 to 5.30 p.m., and on summer Bank Holidays.

BURNS, Robert

ALLOWAY, Ayrshire
Burns's Cottage and Museum. Daily 9 a.m. to 7 p.m. (November
to March, 9 a.m. to 5 p.m.), Sunday opening at 2 p.m.
Burns Monument. Daily at reasonable hours, Sunday opening at
2 p.m.

AYR
Tam o' Shanter Inn. Daily at reasonable hours.

DUMFRIES
Burns's House, Burns Street. Weekdays 10 a.m. to 5 or 9 p.m.,
according to the season, Sunday 2 to 4.30 p.m.
Burns's Tomb. Daily, at reasonable hours, in summer.
Dumfries Burgh Museum, The Observatory, Corberry Hill.
April to September weekdays (except Tuesday) 10 a.m. to 1 p.m.,
2 to 7 p.m., Sunday 2 to 6 p.m.; October to March, weekdays
only, 10 a.m. to 1 p.m., 2 to 5 p.m.

EDINBURGH
Lady Stair's House, Lady Stair's Close, Lawnmarket. Weekdays
10 a.m. to 4 p.m. (10 a.m. to 5 p.m. during the Festival), Saturday
10 a.m. to 1 p.m.

KILMARNOCK, Ayrshire
Burns Monument and Museum, Kay Park. Daily, mid-April to
mid-September 12.30 a.m. to 4 p.m., 5 to 9 p.m.; mid-September
to mid-April 10 a.m. to 12 noon., 1 to 5 p.m.

KIRKOSWALD, Ayrshire
Souter Johnnie's House. April 1 to September 30, daily 2.30 p.m.
to dusk.

MAUCHLINE, Ayrshire
Burns Memorial. Daily at reasonable hours.
TARBOLTON, Ayrshire
Bachelors Club. A notice on the house gives directions for obtaining entry.

BYRON, Lord

NEWSTEAD ABBEY, *near* NOTTINGHAM
Easter to September 30, daily 2 to 5 p.m.; conducted tours at each hour weekdays and half-hourly Sunday. For admission between October 1 and Easter apply to the Corporation of Nottingham. The gardens are open throughout the year, summer weekdays 10 a.m. to 8 p.m. (or dusk if earlier); winter 10.30 a.m. to dusk, Sunday 2 to 8 p.m. or dusk.

CARLYLE, Thomas

ECCLEFECHAN, Dumfriesshire
The Arched House. Weekdays 10 a.m. to 8 p.m. or sunset.
LONDON
Carlyle's House, 24 Cheyne Row, Chelsea, S.W.3. Weekdays (except Tuesday) 10 a.m. to 1 p.m., 2 to 6 p.m., Sunday 2 to 6 p.m., or dusk, if earlier.

CHATTERTON, Thomas

BRISTOL
Chatterton House, Redcliffe Way. Wednesday and Saturday 3 to 5 p.m.; other times can be arranged by writing to the caretakers, Mr and Mrs Hambling.

CHURCHILL, Sir Winston

BLENHEIM PALACE, WOODSTOCK, Oxfordshire
March 24 to July 31, Monday to Thursday, and on Easter Saturday, Sunday and Monday, but closed at Whitsun week-end; from August 2 to September 18 daily except Friday, but including August Bank Holiday week-end; from September 22 to October 30, Monday to Thursday. Hours of opening 1 to 6 p.m. November 7 to March 20, Thursday only, 1.30 to 4.30 p.m.

COLERIDGE, S. T.

NETHER STOWEY, Somersetshire
Coleridge's Cottage Museum. Daily (except Saturday), 11 a.m. to 1 p.m., 2 to 5 p.m.

COWPER, William

OLNEY, Buckinghamshire
Cowper Memorial Museum. Weekdays 10 a.m. to 5 p.m.

CRANE, Stephen

BREDE, Sussex
Brede Place, Stubbs Lane. March 15 to October 15 on Wednesday
and Bank Holidays 3 to 6 p.m.

DANIEL, Samuel

SKIPTON CASTLE, Yorkshire
Daily (except Good Friday and Christmas Day) 10 a.m. to sunset
weekdays and 2 p.m. to sunset Sunday.

DICKENS, Charles

BROADSTAIRS, Kent
Bleak House. Open every day from Good Friday until the last
Sunday in September, 2–5 p.m.; with additional hours (7–9 p.m.)
from mid-June to mid-September, and 10.30 a.m. to 12.30 p.m.
on Sunday from Easter to the end of September.

LONDON
Dickens House, 48 Doughty Street, W.C. 1. Weekdays 10 a.m.
to 12.30 p.m., 2 to 5 p.m.; closed on Bank Holidays.

PORTSMOUTH
Charles Dickens Birthplace Museum, 393 Commercial Road,
Mile End. Weekdays: summer 10 a.m. to 7 p.m., winter 10 a.m.
to 5 p.m.

ROCHESTER
Public Museum, Eastgate House, High Street. Daily (except
Friday) 2 to 5.30 p.m. Conducted parties can be arranged by
appointment.
Restoration House, Maidstone Road. Admission on application
at reasonable hours.
Watts's Charity, 97 High Street. Weekdays 2 to 5 p.m.

DISRAELI, Benjamin

HIGH WYCOMBE, Buckinghamshire
Disraeli Museum, Hughenden Manor. February to December,
Tuesday to Friday 2 to 6 p.m., Saturday and Sunday 10 to 1 p.m.,
2 to 6 p.m.; also on Bank Holiday Monday; closed on Tuesday
after Bank Holidays.

DORSET, Earl of. See SACKVILLE

DRYDEN, John

CROXALL HALL, *near* LICHFIELD, Staffordshire
Admission at reasonable hours on application.

DUFFERIN, Lady

CLANDEBOYE (HELEN'S TOWER), *near* BELFAST, Co. Down
For permission to view apply to the steward of the estate.

ELIOT, George

ARBURY HALL, *near* NUNEATON, Warwickshire
April 5 to October 5, Thursday, Saturday, Sunday, Bank Holidays
and the Tuesday following, 2.30 to 6 p.m.

EVELYN, John

ALBURY PARK HOUSE, *near* GUILDFORD, Surrey
Daily 1.30 to 5 p.m.

FITZGERALD, Edward

IPSWICH
Christchurch Mansion, Christchurch Park. Weekdays 10 a.m. to
6 p.m. (10 a.m. to 4.30 or 5 p.m. in winter), Sunday 3 to 5 p.m.
(2.30 to 4.30 p.m. in winter).

GIBBON, Edward

SHEFFIELD PARK, FLETCHING, *near* LEWES, Sussex
The Gardens only are open to the public. April to October
Wednesday, Saturday, Sunday and Bank Holidays 2 to 7 p.m.
(in October 12 noon to 5 p.m.).

GRAY, Thomas

GLAMIS CASTLE, Angus
May to September, Wednesday and Thursday 2 to 6 p.m.; also on
Sunday 2 to 6 p.m., from July to September.

HARDY, Thomas

HIGHER BOCKHAMPTON, *near* DORCHESTER, Dorsetshire
Thomas Hardy's Birthplace. Thursday, Saturday, Sunday 2 to
6 p.m. (closed from November to end of January).
DORCHESTER
Dorset County Museum, High Street. Weekdays 10 a.m. to
1 p.m., 2 to 6 p.m. (closed Boxing Day and Good Friday).

HAZLITT, William

MAIDSTONE
Museum and Art Gallery, Chillington Manor, St Faith's Street. Weekdays, summer 10 a.m. to 6.30 p.m.; winter 10 a.m. to dusk (closed on Bank Holidays).

HOBBES, Thomas

CHATSWORTH, *near* BAKEWELL, Derbyshire
March 30 to October 12, Wednesday and Thursday 11.30 a.m. to 4 p.m., Saturday and Sunday 2 to 5.30 p.m., Bank Holidays and Good Friday 11.30 a.m. to 5.30 p.m.

HARDWICK HALL, *near* CHESTERFIELD, Derbyshire
April 2 to October 5, Wednesday, Thursday, Saturday, Sunday and Bank Holidays 2 to 5 p.m.

HOGG, James

SELKIRK
Selkirk Museum, Ettrick Terrace. Weekdays 9 a.m. to 6 p.m.

HUGO, Victor

GUERNSEY, Channel Islands
Hauteville House, Hauteville Street, St Peter Port. Weekdays (except Thursday afternoon) 10 a.m. to 12.30 p.m., 2 to 4.30 p.m.

JAMES, Henry

RYE, Sussex
Lamb House, West Street. Tuesday 2.15 to 6 p.m.

JEFFERIES, Richard

SWINDON, Wiltshire
Richard Jefferies Museum, Coate Farm. Wednesday and Saturday 2 to 5 p.m.

JOHNSON, Samuel

BIRMINGHAM
Aston Hall, Trinity Road, Aston. On summer weekdays 10 a.m. to 5 p.m., Sunday 2 to 5 p.m.; winter, weekdays only, 10 a.m. to dusk.

INVERARAY CASTLE, Argyllshire
May to September daily (except Friday and Sunday morning) 10.30 a.m. to 12 noon, 2 to 6 p.m.

LICHFIELD
Dr Johnson's Birthplace, Bread Market Street. Daily April to September 10 a.m. to 6 p.m., October to March 10 a.m. to 4 p.m. (Monday 10 a.m. to 1 p.m.).

LONDON
    Dr Johnson's House, 17 Gough Square, E.C.4. Weekdays
    10.30 a.m. to 5 p.m. (October to April 10.30 a.m. to 4.30 p.m.).
SKYE
    Dunvegan Castle. Monday to Friday in summer only, 2 to 5 p.m.

JOYCE, James

SANDYCOVE, *near* Dun Laoghaire, Co. Dublin
    Joyce Museum. During summer 3 to 6 p.m. daily. It is probable
    that a further extension of opening times, extending to winter-
    time, will be made in due course.

KEATS, John

LONDON
    Keats House and Museum, Keats Grove, Hampstead, N.W.3.
    Weekdays 10 a.m. to 6 p.m. (closed on Boxing Day).

KIPLING, Rudyard

BURWASH, Sussex
    Bateman's. Wednesday, Saturday, Sunday 2 to 5 p.m., Bank
    Holidays 11 a.m. to 6 p.m., Good Friday 2 to 6 p.m. (but from
    November to February by appointment only). Parties can view by
    arrangement with the tenant on days when the house is normally
    closed.
ROTTINGDEAN, BRIGHTON, Sussex
    The Grange Art Gallery and Museum. Weekdays 10 a.m. to
    7 p.m., Sunday 2 to 6 p.m.

LAWRENCE, T. E.

CLOUDS HILL, *near* BERE REGIS, Dorsetshire
    Sunday, Wednesday, Thursday 2 to 6 p.m. in summer, 12 noon to
    dusk in winter.

LYTTON, Lord

KNEBWORTH HOUSE, KNEBWORTH, Hertfordshire
    May 1 to September 28, Wednesday to Sunday inclusive, 2 to
    5 p.m.; same hours on Whit Monday and August Bank Holiday.

MILTON, John

CHALFONT ST. GILES, Buckinghamshire
    Milton's Cottage. Weekdays (except Tuesday) 10 a.m. to 1 p.m.,
    2.15 to 6 p.m., Sunday 2.15 to 6 p.m.; closes at dusk from October
    to March.

MORRIS, William

WALTHAMSTOW, Essex
William Morris Gallery, Lloyd Park, Forest Road. Weekdays,
10 a.m. to 5 p.m. (in summer Tuesday and Thursday times are
10 a.m. to 8 p.m.), and the first Sunday in each month 10 a.m. to
12 noon, 2 to 5 p.m.; closed on Bank Holidays.

PEPYS, Samuel

CAMBRIDGE
Pepysian Library, Magdalene College. Monday to Saturday
during term 2.30 to 3.30 p.m.

POPE, Alexander

STANTON HARCOURT, *near* OXFORD
Open daily.
STOURHEAD, *near* MERE, Wiltshire
The house is open Wednesday, Thursday, Saturday, Sunday and
Bank Holidays (except Boxing Day) 2.30 to 6 p.m. or dusk; the
pleasure grounds are open April to September 2 to 7 p.m. on
Friday and Sunday, on other days and on Bank Holidays 11 a.m.
to 7 p.m.; October to March, Sunday 2 to 7 p.m. or dusk,
Monday, Wednesday, Thursday, Saturday and Bank Holidays
11 a.m. to 7 p.m. or dusk.

POTTER, Beatrix

NEAR SAWREY, *near* HAWKSHEAD, Lancashire
Hill Top Farm. Easter to September, weekdays 10.30 a.m. to
6 p.m., Sunday 2 to 6 p.m.

RALEGH, Sir Walter

EAST BUDLEIGH, *near* EXMOUTH, Devonshire
Hayes Barton. June to September, weekdays 10.30 a.m. to 1 p.m.,
2 to 6.30 p.m.

RUSKIN, John

BEMBRIDGE, Isle of Wight
Ruskin Gallery, Bembridge School. By appointment only.
CONISTON, Lancashire
Brantwood. Monday to Friday 9 a.m. to 4 p.m., Saturday 9 a.m.
to 12 noon.
Ruskin Museum. Daily 10 a.m. to 6 p.m.

SACKVILLE, Charles, Sixth Earl of Dorset

SEVENOAKS, Kent
> Knole. April to October, Wednesday, Thursday, Friday, Saturday and Bank Holidays including Good Friday 10 a.m. to 12 noon, 2 to 4.30 p.m.; November, December and March, Wednesday, Thursday, Friday, Saturday and Bank Holidays (except Boxing Day) 10 a.m. to 12 noon, 2 to 3.30 p.m.
CROXALL HALL. See under DRYDEN

SCOTT, Sir Walter

ABBOTSFORD, Roxburghshire
> March 31 to mid-October, weekdays 10 a.m. to 5 p.m.; Sunday opening, 2 to 5 p.m., from June to September only, including Easter and Whit Sunday.
EDINBURGH
> Huntly House, Canongate. Weekdays 10 a.m. to 5 p.m.; from June to September additional hours on Wednesday evening 6 to 9 p.m.
> Scott Monument, Princes Street. Weekdays in summer 10 a.m. to 7 p.m.; in winter 10 a.m. to 3 p.m.
> Lady Stair's House. See under BURNS.
KENILWORTH, *near* WARWICK
> Kenilworth Castle. Weekdays 9 a.m. to 6 or 8 p.m. (closes at 4 p.m. in winter), Sunday 2 to 6 or 8 p.m. (2 to 4 p.m. in winter).
PERTH
> Fair Maid's House, Curfew Road. Daily 9 a.m. to dusk.
GRETA BRIDGE, *near* BARNARD CASTLE, Yorkshire
> Rokeby Hall. Permission to view the grounds may be obtained by writing to the owner, Major H. E. Morritt.
SELKIRK
> Sir Walter Scott's Court Room, Town Hall. May 16 to September 15, daily 3 to 6 p.m.
SKYE. See under JOHNSON

SHAKESPEARE, William

LONDON
> Middle Temple Hall, off Fleet Street. Open during law terms 10 a.m. to 12.30 p.m., 3 to 5 p.m.; during vacations 10 a.m. to 5 p.m.
OXFORD
> Crown Inn (Painted Chamber), 3 Cornmarket Street. Monday to Friday 9.30 a.m. to 12.30 p.m., 2.30 to 4.30 p.m. (subject to slight variation).

341

STRATFORD-ON-AVON, Warwickshire
Birthplace, Henley Street. April to October, weekdays 9 a.m. to 12.45 p.m., 2 to 6 p.m., Wednesday and Saturday 9 a.m. to 6 p.m. (9 a.m. to 7 p.m. in summer), Sunday 2 to 6 p.m.; November to March, weekdays only 9 a.m. to 12.45 p.m., 2 to 4 p.m.
Anne Hathaway's Cottage, Shottery. Same as Birthplace.
Holy Trinity Church. Open always except during services.
Grammar School, Church Street. Weekdays during the Easter and summar holidays only, 10 a.m. to 12 noon, 2 to 4 p.m.; closed during special summer courses.
New Place Museum, Chapel Street. April to October, Monday, Tuesday, Thursday, Friday 9 a.m. to 12.45 p.m., 2 to 6 p.m. (2 to 7 p.m. during August), Wednesday and Saturday 9 a.m. to 6 p.m., Sunday 2 to 6 p.m.; November to March 9 a.m. to 12.45 p.m., Sunday 2 to 4 p.m.
New Place Garden. Summer, weekdays 9 a.m. to 9 p.m., Sunday 12 noon to 9 p.m.; in winter closes at 4 p.m.

WILMCOTE, *near* STRATFORD
Mary Arden's Cottage. April to October, Monday, Tuesday, Thursday, Friday 9 a.m. to 12.45 p.m., 2 to 6 p.m., Wednesday, Saturday 9 a.m. to 6 p.m. (9 a.m. to 7 p.m. in August), Sunday 2 to 6 p.m.; November to March, weekdays only, 9 a.m. to 12.45 p.m., 2 to 4 p.m.

SHAW, Bernard

AYOT ST LAWRENCE, *near* WELWYN GARDEN CITY, Hertfordshire
Shaw's Corner. Summer, Wednesday to Saturday and Bank Holidays 2 to 6 p.m., Sunday 11 a.m. to 1 p.m.; winter, Saturday and Sunday only, 2 to 4 p.m.

SIDNEY, Sir Philip

PENSHURST PLACE, *near* TUNBRIDGE WELLS, Kent
April 5 to October 11, Wednesday, Thursday, Saturday and Easter, Whitsun and August Bank Holidays 2 to 5 p.m.; also on the first, third and fifth Sundays in the month and Whit Sunday.

WILTON HOUSE, *near* SALISBURY, Wiltshire
April 1 to October 15 daily 10 a.m. to 6 p.m.; October 16 to March 31, Wednesday, Saturday and Sunday only 10 a.m. to 4 p.m. (but sometimes open on additional days). The gardens are open all the year, daily 9 a.m. to sunset.

STEVENSON, R. L.

EDINBURGH
Stevenson Memorial House, 8 Howard Place. Weekdays 10 a.m. to 5 p.m. (10 a.m. to 4 p.m. in winter), Saturday 10 a.m. to 1 p.m. Lady Stair's House. See under BURNS.

SWIFT, Jonathan

DUBLIN
Marsh's Library, adjoining St Patrick's Cathedral. Monday, Tuesday, Wednesday, Friday 11 a.m. to 2 p.m., 3 to 4.30 p.m., Thursday and Saturday 10.30 a.m. to 12.30 p.m.

TANNAHILL, Robert

PAISLEY, Renfrewshire
Museum and Art Gallaries, High Street. Weekdays 10 a.m. to 5 p.m., Tuesday and Saturday 10 a.m. to 8 p.m.

THACKERAY, W. M.

CLEVEDON COURT, CLEVEDON, near BRISTOL, Somerset
Thursday 11 a.m. to 1 p.m.

TROLLOPE, Anthony

WINCHESTER, Hampshire
Hospital of St Cross. Admission on application at reasonable hours.

VANBRUGH, Sir John

AUDLEY END, near SAFFRON WALDEN, Essex.
April 20 to October 5, Thursday, Saturday, Sunday and Bank Holidays 9.30 a.m. to 5.30 p.m.
BLENHEIM PALACE. See under CHURCHILL
CASTLE HOWARD, near YORK
April 6 to September 28, Wednesday, Thursday, Sunday 1.45 to 5.15 p.m., Bank Holiday Mondays 11.30 a.m. to 5.30 p.m., Bank Holiday Tuesdays 1.45 to 5.15 p.m.

WALTON, Izaak

SHALLOWFORD, near STAFFORD
Izaak Walton Cottage and Museum. Daily except Tuesday 10 a.m. to 4 p.m.

WELLS, H. G.

UPPARK, near PETERSFIELD, Sussex
April 6 to September 28, Wednesday, Thursday, Sunday and Bank Holidays 2.30 to 6 p.m.

WHITE, Gilbert

SELBORNE, Hampshire
Oates Memorial Library and Museum (incorporates the Gilbert White Museum). April to October, weekdays (except Friday) 11 a.m. to 1 p.m., 2.30 to 5.30 p.m., Sunday 2.30 to 5.30 p.m.

WORDSWORTH, William

COCKERMOUTH, Cumberland
Wordsworth House, Main Street. Monday and Saturday 2 to 5 p.m.; admission on other days on application.

GRASMERE, Westmorland
Dove Cottage. April to October, weekdays 10 a.m. to 6 p.m.; October to April, weekdays (except Thursday) 10 a.m. to 4.30 p.m. Wordsworth Museum. April to October only, weekdays (except Friday morning) 10 a.m. to 6 p.m.

HAWKSHEAD, Lancashire
Grammar School. Admission on application. No longer a school.

WYATT, Sir Thomas

MAIDSTONE, Kent
Allington Castle. April 1 to October 31, Monday to Friday, conducted visits at 3 p.m., 4 p.m. and 5 p.m.

Maps and Plans

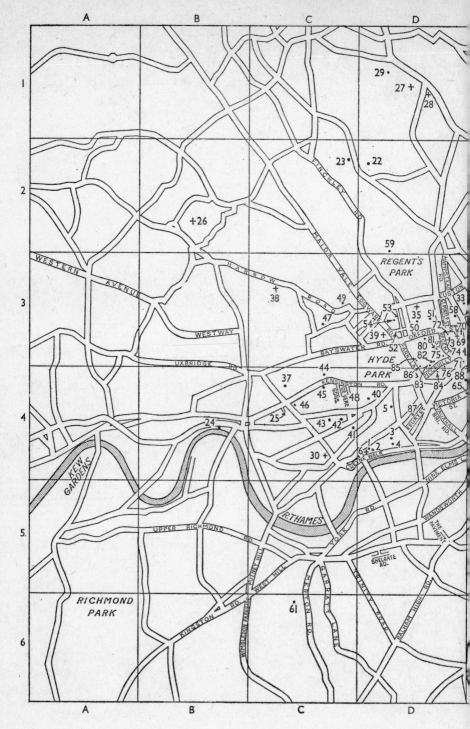

MAP I

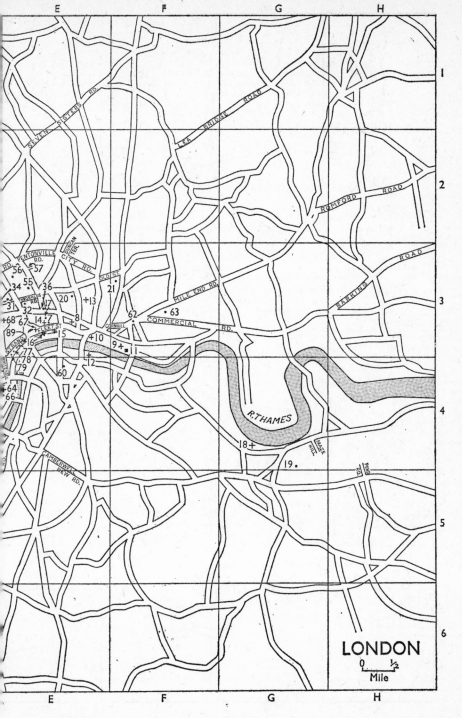

LONDON

0   ½
Mile

MAP I

M★

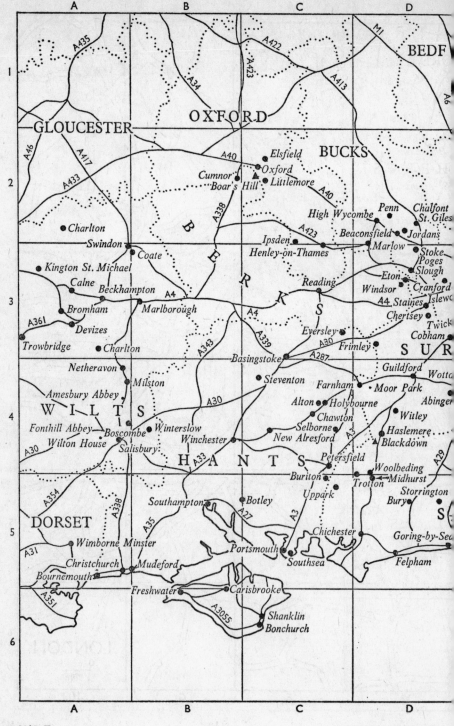

MAP II

SOUTH-EAST ENGLAND

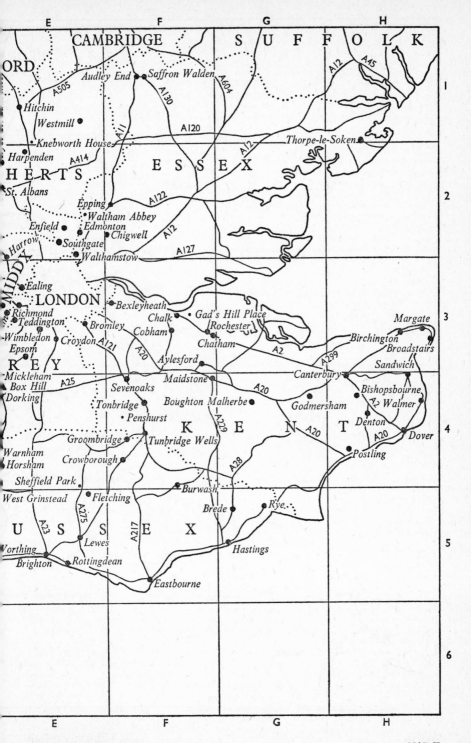

SOUTH-EAST ENGLAND

MAP II

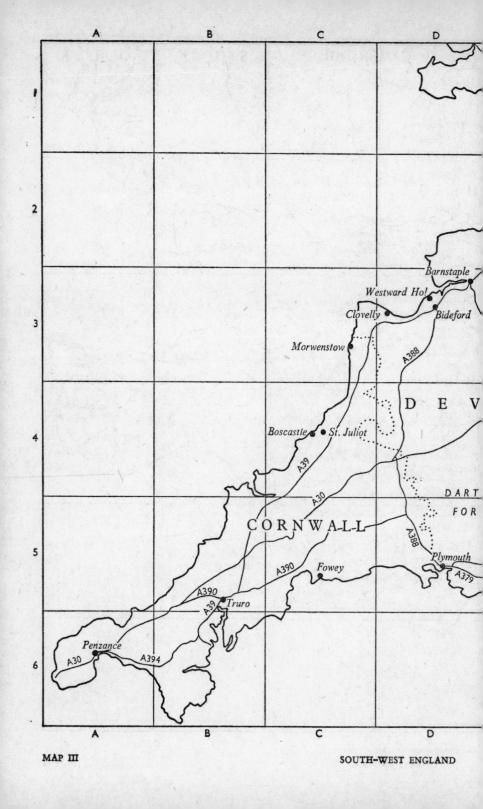

MAP III

SOUTH-WEST ENGLAND

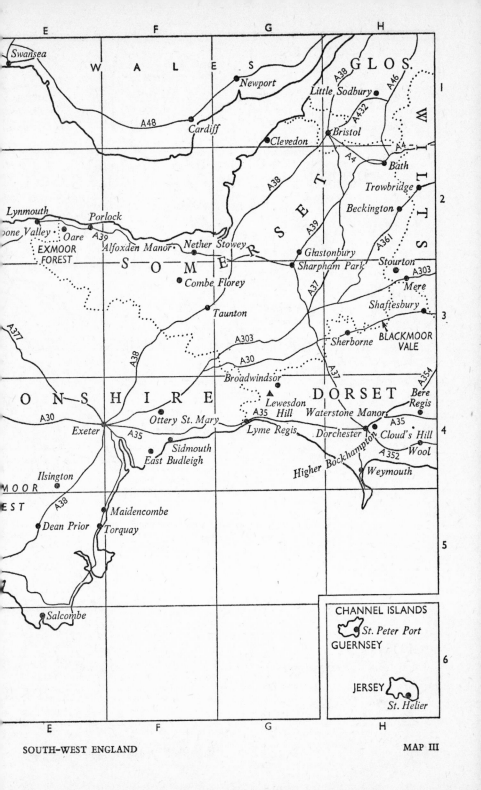

SOUTH-WEST ENGLAND

MAP III

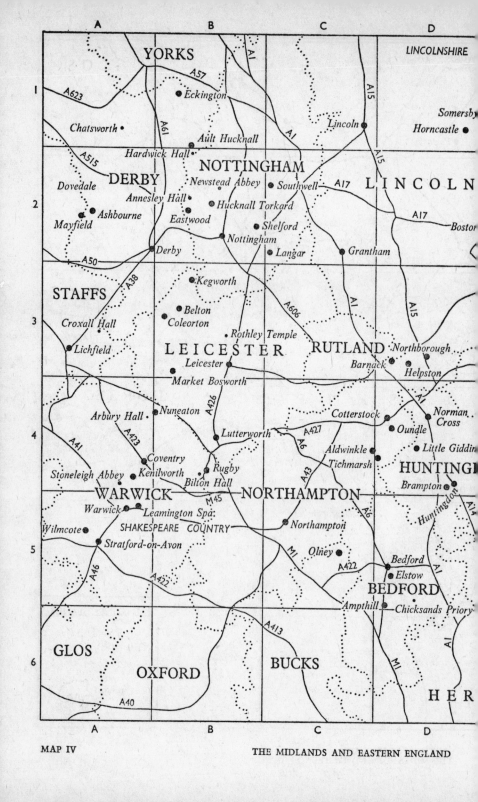

MAP IV   THE MIDLANDS AND EASTERN ENGLAND

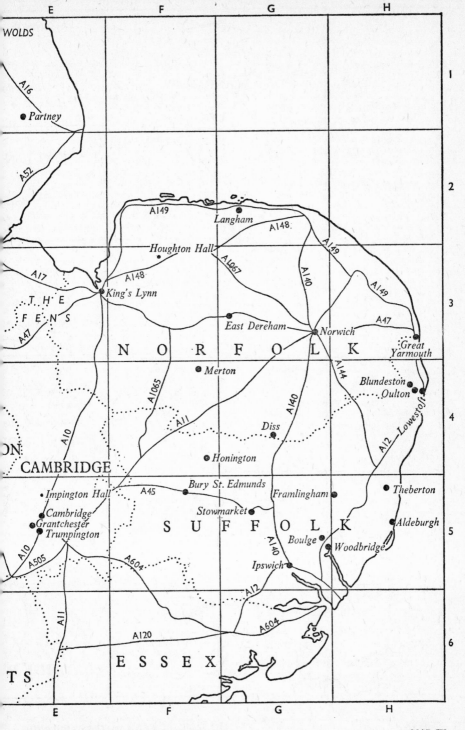

THE MIDLANDS AND EASTERN ENGLAND   MAP IV

MAP V

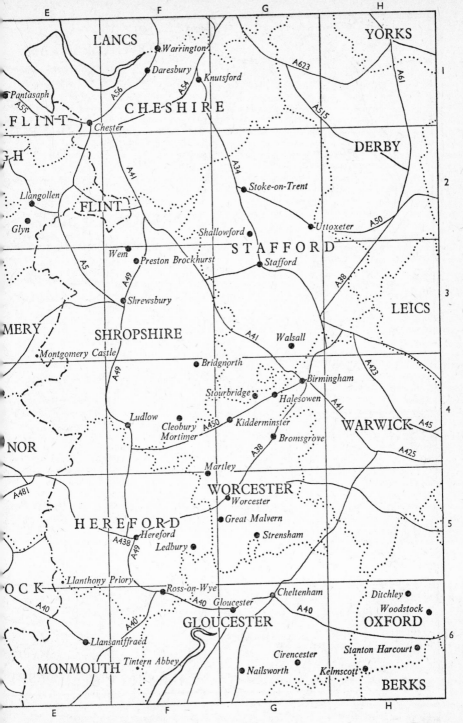

THE MIDLANDS AND WALES

MAP V

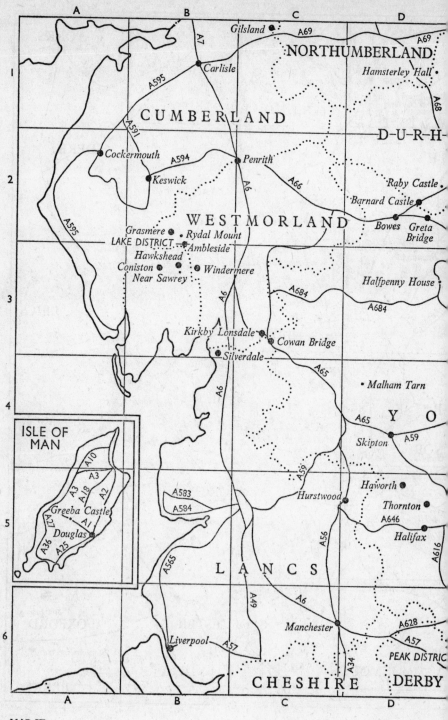

MAP VI

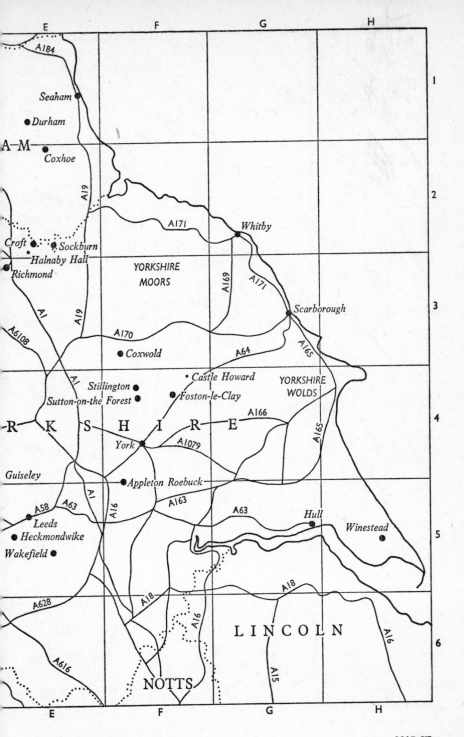

NORTHERN ENGLAND

MAP VI

MAP VII

SOUTHERN SCOTLAND

SOUTHERN SCOTLAND

MAP VII

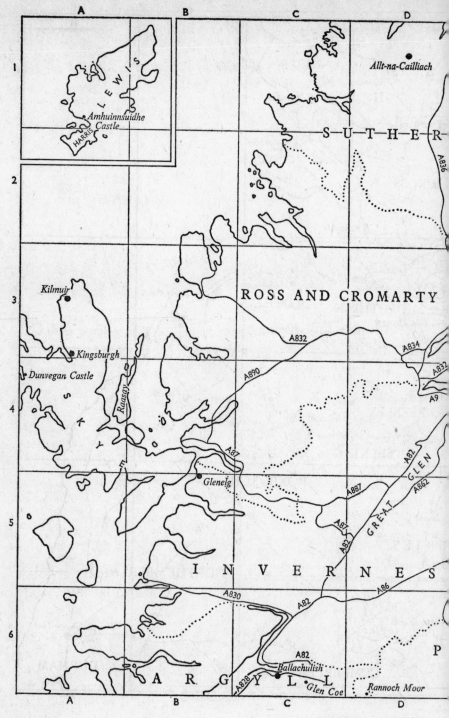

Allt-na-Cailliach

S-U-T-H-E-R

A836

ROSS AND CROMARTY

Kilmuir

A832

A834

A890

A832

A9

Kingsburgh

Dunvegan Castle

S
K
Y
E

Raasay

A87

GLEN

A82

Glenelg

A887

A862

A87

GREAT

A82

I   N   V   E   R   N   E   S

A830

A82

A86

A82

Ballachulish

A82

A   R   G   Y   L   L

A828

Glen Coe

Rannoch Moor

P

MAP VIII   **NORTHERN SCOTLAND**

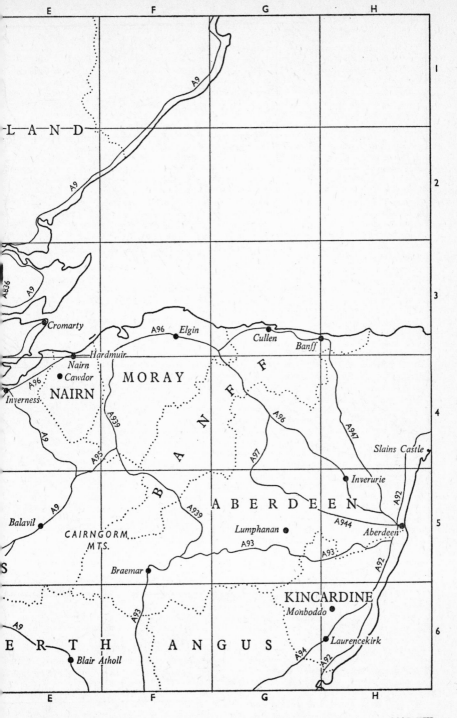

NORTHERN SCOTLAND

MAP VIII

MAP IX

IRELAND: SOUTH

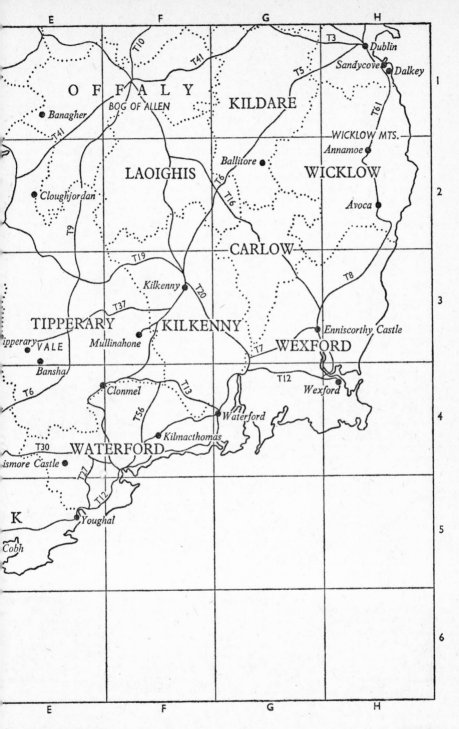

IRELAND: SOUTH

MAP IX

MAP X

IRELAND: NORTH

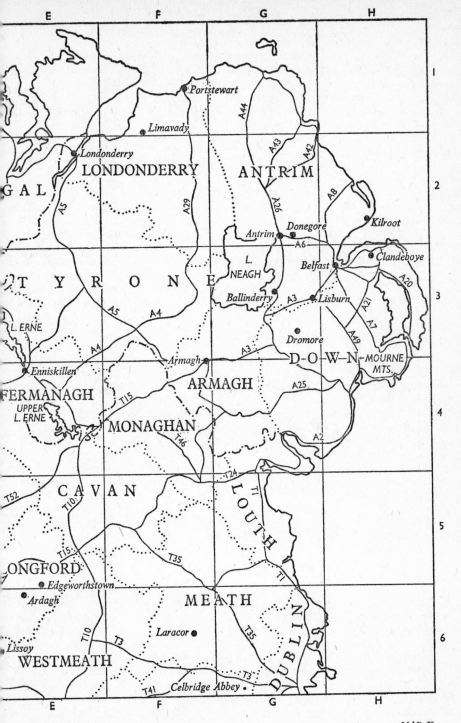

IRELAND: NORTH

MAP X

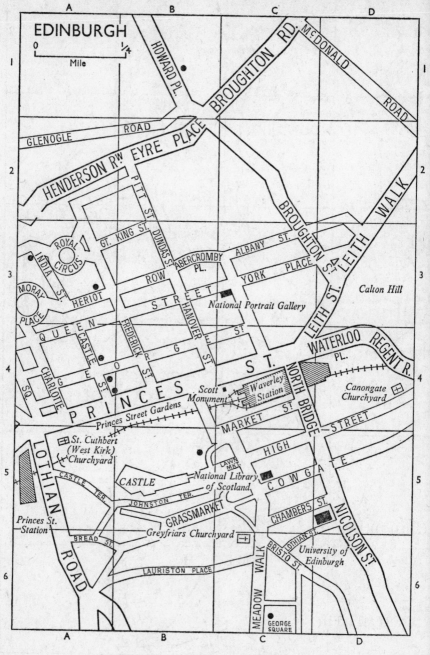

MAP XI

Index

Index

N*

GREENOCK (Renfrew): Galt, 'Highland Mary', 289-90
Gregory, Lady (1852-1932), 313; Coole Park, 323
GRETA BRIDGE (Yorks): Scott, 250
GRONGAR HILL (Carmarthen): John Dyer, 228
GROOMBRIDGE (Kent): Mark Rutherford, 77
Grote, George (1794-1871): London, 46
GUISELEY (Yorks): Brontë sisters, Longfellow, 248
GULLANE (East Lothian): *Catriona*, 271-2
GWAENYNOG (Denbigh): Johnson, 236

HADDINGTON (East Lothian): Carlyle, 272
HAFOD HOUSE (Cardigan): Peacock, 235
Hakluyt, Richard (1553?-1616): Oxford, 210-11
HALESOWEN (Worcs): Shenstone, 182-3
HALIFAX (Yorks): Emily Brontë, Defoe, Sterne, 247-8
HALLYARDS (Peebles): Scott, 270
HALNABY HALL (Yorks): Byron, 249
HAMPTON COURT (Middx): Pope, 59
HAMSTERLEY HALL (Durham): Surtees, 251
HARDWICK HALL (Derby): Hobbes, 195-6
Hardy, Thomas (1840-1928): Higher Bockhampton, 104; Dorchester, 105-6; London, 26, 42-3; St Juliot, 133-4; Sturminster Newton, 104; Wimborne, 103; *Dynasts*, 106; *Far from the Madding Crowd*, 105, 107;

Group of Nobles Dames, 107; *Jude the Obscure*, 103, 106, 109, 205; *Mayor of Casterbridge*, 106; *Pair of Blue Eyes*, 133; *Return of the Native*, 105; *Tess of the D'Urbervilles*, 92, 98, 104-7, 109; *Trumpet Major*, 106; *Two on a Tower*, 103; *Under the Greenwood Tree*, 104; *Woodlanders*, 106, 107
HARLOW (Essex): Prior, 141
HARPENDEN. *See* MACKERY END
HARROW-ON-THE-HILL (Middx): Arnold, 56
HARROW SCHOOL (Middx): Byron, Calverley, Sir Winston Churchill, Galsworthy, Sheridan, J. A. Symonds, Trevelyan, Trollope, 54-6
HARROW WEALD (Middx): W. S. Gilbert, Trollope, 55-6
HARROWDEN. *See* ELSTOW
Harte, Bret (1839-1902): Glasgow, 289; London, 41; Frimley, 86
HARTSHILL (Warwicks): Drayton, 188
HASLEMERE. *See* BLACKDOWN; SHOTTERMILL
HASTINGS (Sussex): Lamb, Patmore, D. G. Rossetti, 78
Hawker, R. S. (1803-73): Stoke Damerel, 132; Oxford, 214; Morwenstow, 133
HAWKSHEAD (Lancs): Wordsworth, 256
HAWORTH (Yorks): Brontë sisters, 246
HAWTHORNDEN (Midlothian): Wm Drummond, Ben Jonson, 270-1
Hawthorne, Nathaniel (1804-64), 121, 205, 257; Liverpool, 243; Leamington Spa, 186; London, 41; Uttoxeter, 198
HAYES BARTON. *See* EAST BUDLEIGH

Strachey, G. Lytton (1880-1932): Cambridge, 173

STRATFORD-ON-AVON (Warwicks): Shakespeare, 183-5; Dickens, Washington Irving, Mrs Gaskell, 185-6; Marie Corelli, Trevelyan, 186

STRENSHAM (Worcs): Butler (1612-1680), 182

STURMINSTER NEWTON (Dorset): Hardy, 104

Suckling, Sir John (1609-42): Whitton, 58; Cambridge, 171

SUNIPOL (Mull): Thos Campbell, 299

Surrey, Henry Howard, Earl of (1517?-47): London, 6-7; Windsor, 60; Framlingham, 144

Surtees, R. S. (1803-64): Durham, Hamsterley Hall & Ebchester, 251; Brighton, 80

SUTTON-ON-THE-FOREST (Yorks): Sterne, 244, 245

Swain, Charles (1801-74): Manchester, 242

SWALLOWFIELD (Berks): Mary Russell Mitford, 88-9

SWANSEA (Glamorgan): Dylan Thomas, 229

SWANSTON (Midlothian): Stevenson, 271

Swift, Jonathan (1667-1745), 97, 113; Dublin, 305-7; Kilkenny, 316; Leicester, 191; Moor Park, 85-6; Kilroot, 326; London, 19-20; Laracor, 323; Chester, 234; Cirencester, 181; Celbridge, 306; Markethill, 327; *Battle of the Books*, 85; *Journal to Stella*, 234; *Tale of a Tub*, 85

Swinburne, A. C. (1837-1909); London, 40-1; Bonchurch, 99; Eton, 62; Oxford, 208

Symonds, J. A. (1840-93); Bristol, 125; Harrow, 55; Oxford, 209, 216-17

Synge, J. M. (1871-1909): Rathfarnham & Dublin, 313-14; Aran Islands, 323-4; *In Wicklow and West Kerry*, 315

Tannahill, Robert (1774-1810): Paisley, 289

TANTALLON CASTLE (East Lothian): *Marmion*, 271

TAN-YR-ALLT (Caernarvon): Shelley, 237

TAPPINGTON-EVERARD (Kent): *Ingoldsby Legends*, 72

TARBOLTON (Ayr): Burns, 283-4

TAUNTON (Somerset): Daniel, Kinglake, 126

TAVISTOCK (Devon): Wm Browne, 132

Taylor, John (1580-1653): Gloucester, 181; York, 244

Taylor, Jeremy (1613-67): Cambridge, 161, 165; Golden Grove, 228; Dromore & Lisburn, 326

TEDDINGTON (Middx): R. D. Blackmore, Traherne, 59

TEMPLE GRAFTON (Warwicks): Shakespeare, 184

Tennyson, Lord (1809-92), 143, 146, 326; Somersby, 156; Louth, 156; Cambridge, 172; London, 36; Lake District, 261; High Beech, 54; Tunbridge Wells & Boxley, 77; Cheltenham, 181-2; Killarney, 320; Shawell, 190; Morwenstow, 133; Shiplake-on-Thames, 177; Clevedon, 125; Twickenham, 59; Farringford, 99; Lyme Regis, 108; Blackdown, 95; *In Memoriam*, 54, 125, 156, 182, 190